A Documentary History of Russian Thought

From the Enlightenment to Marxism

Translated and Edited by

W. J. Leatherbarrow and D. C. Offord

Ardis, Ann Arbor
1987

Copyright © 1987 by Ardis Publishers
All rights reserved under International and Pan-American
Copyright Conventions.
Printed in the United States of America

Translated from the original Russian

Ardis Publishers
2901 Heatherway
Ann Arbor, Michigan 48104

Library of Congress Cataloging in Publication Data

Main entry under title:

A Documentary history of Russian thought.

Bibliography: p.
1. Political science—Soviet Union—History—19th
century—Addresses, essays, lectures.   2. Slavophilism—
Addresses, essays, lectures.   3. Populism—Soviet Union—
History—19th century—Addresses, essays, lectures.
4. Philosophy, Russian—Addresses, essays, lectures.
I. Leatherbarrow, William J.   II. Offord, Derek.
JA84.S65D63 1985   320.5'0947   85-18639
ISBN 0-87501-018-0 (alk. paper)

CONTENTS

PART VI.   REVOLUTIONARY POPULISM

Preface

We have approached the preparation of this volume with two broad aims in mind. Firstly, we have tried to provide a comprehensive anthology of Russian social and political thought which might serve as a textbook to encourage the further study of this subject among students of literature, politics and history in universities and colleges. The understandable emphasis given in the West to Russian and Soviet marxist thought has, we feel, obscured the achievements of those thinkers who articulated the earlier preoccupations of the Russian intelligentsia in the nineteenth century. Their work deserves a wider audience.

We have tried to avoid competing with previous anthologies of Russian thought: Marc Raeff's *Russian Intellectual History* and the three-volume set *Russian Philosophy* edited by J.M. Edie, J.P. Scanlan and M.B. Zeldin (see Bibliography for details). Of these the latter, as its title indicates, addresses itself to a range of Russian philosophical activity, whereas the present volume is concerned almost entirely with Russian historical thought; Raeff's work is deliberately selective, whereas we have tried to provide a more complete picture of the evolution of the Russian intelligentsia. To this end we have included selections not only from the better-known Russian thinkers but also from comparatively neglected figures among, for example, the liberal westernizers, the conservative tradition and the Populist movement.

Our second aim is related to this attempt to provide a broadly-based selection: we would hope that this volume might also serve as an illustrated history of Russian social thought in the nineteenth century. Our selections were not made at random, but were chosen with a view to exploring some persistently recurring themes. Some of these are obvious and have been fully examined in the scholarly literature (for example, Russia and the West, the individual and society, etc.); others are less familiar and deserve further analysis (for example, Russian views of law, the notion of obligation amongst the Russian intelligentsia, etc). We hope that the analytical essays and selections which make up this volume will encourage discussion of these and other matters.

During our work we have drawn freely upon the expertise of others, and we would particularly like to thank our colleagues in the Universities of Sheffield and Bristol for the patience and skill they have shown in helping to unravel linguistic difficulties and trace obscure references. Our typist, Mrs Iris Anderson, has given unstintingly of her time to produce the final manuscript, and our gratitude to her is immense.

Finally, this project was greatly encouraged in its draft stages by the enthusiasm of the late Carl Proffer. He had hoped to suggest further items for inclusion, and the fact that he was unable to do so has in our view diminished this volume. Nevertheless, it is to his memory that our work is respectfully dedicated.

W. J. L.
D. C. O.

Part I

Gentry Revolutionaries and Conservatives

Introduction

The penetration of progressive ideas into Russia, as a consequence of Catherine the Great's enthusiasm for European Enlightenment philosophy in the early period of her reign, produced effects which were more muted than those produced by the same ideas in Western Europe. The collapse of the Ancien Régime in France and the execution of Louis XVI appalled and frightened Catherine, and, in an effort to close the Pandora's box which she herself had helped to open in Russia, she finished her reign with intemperate attacks on any symptoms of the "French madness" among her subjects. But the France of Louis XVI and the Russia of Catherine were essentially poles apart. The grip of tradition and autocracy in Russia was too firm to be pried open overnight and the forces of reaction soon calmed any potentially revolutionary situation. But the comparatively undramatic nature of the Russian Enlightenment should not obscure its long-term consequences for the development of political thought in that country. The process of conscious technical westernization undertaken by Peter the Great brought inevitably in its wake changing perceptions among the Russian upper classes and, eventually, the moral and cultural westernization of Catherine's reign. The results of this were, firstly, the creation of an intellectually westernized and enlightened elite among the Russian nobility, some of whom had been sent by Catherine to study in the West, and secondly the questioning by these noblemen of inherited native traditions. Such questioning was bound to have far-reaching implications for a social and political order based solely on tradition, so that the progressive nobility of Catherine's Russia became the seed from which the nineteenth-century radical intelligentsia was to grow.

The ideas espoused by these progressive noblemen were as diverse as the European thinkers whose works they read: Voltaire, Montesquieu, Beccaria, Rousseau, Mably, Priestly, Locke and the French Encyclopedists stand out among many others. Yet Enlightenment thought shared a common belief that the laws of nature, upon which the physical world is erected, were ultimately knowable, and that man's increasing enlightenment would allow him first to understand and then to control the world in which he lived. This faith in the power of reason and in the perfectibility of man also colored Enlightenment views on man's relationship to society, and it fostered the belief that societies were perfectible if based on rational social relations and an enlightened code of law. The potentially revolutionary implications of such ideas for societies based on "irrational" social and political structures are all too clear.

Catherine the Great's mistake was to believe that such enlightened ideas could be appropriated by an existing autocratic authority to form a kind of "enlightened despotism" which would impose the fruits of learning and the advantages of progress upon society without the risk of creating popular unrest or raising questions about the very nature of monarchical power. But Catherine was not alone in misreading the meaning of progressive thought for Russian society: both the autocrat and the enlightened nobility were guilty of failing to perceive the gulf that existed between European Enlightenment ideals and Russian reality. Catherine may have deceived herself initially into thinking that the forces unleashed by these ideas could be controlled and contained within a framework of autocratic power, but equally the progressive intelligentsia failed to see that the tension between libertarian principles and deep-rooted Russian social and political traditions would not easily be resolved. Ultimately the fate of the first Russian "radical," Alexander Radishchev, and the outcome of the Decembrist movement were to testify eloquently to these tragic failures of perception.

The Enlightenment supplied both a framework and a sound philosophical basis for political disaffection in Russia. This disaffection found particular expression in the questioning of two of Russia's most ancient political and social structures: autocracy and serfdom. The Western spirit of legalism, enshrined in the concepts of personal rights and natural law, provided a yardstick for assessing the appropriateness of such institutions in an age of reason. Alexander Radishchev (1749-1802) has been described as the first Russian radical for his questioning of the legality of Russian institutions and his desire to see society based on a rational code of law. Both a product and a victim of Catherine's reign, he served as a page in Catherine's court for four years and was one of several young noblemen sent abroad in 1766 to study law at the University of Leipzig. He returned to Russia in 1771 steeped in Enlightenment philosophy, and entered the civil service. At the same time he began his literary career, producing an annotated translation of Mably's *Observations sur l'histoire de la Grèce* in 1773, which contained the comments on autocracy reproduced in this volume. This was followed by poems, essays, the ode "Freedom" (1783), *A Journey from Petersburg to Moscow* (1790) and a treatise on immortality completed in 1796.

A Journey from Petersburg to Moscow is regarded as Radishchev's masterpiece, although it makes tedious reading today. It is a sentimental and overblown travelog exposing the excesses and injustices of serfdom. Published anonymously, it aroused the anger of the reactionary Catherine. Its author was identified and sentenced to death. This sentence was commuted to ten years in exile. On Catherine's death in 1796 Radishchev was allowed to return to European Russia and was finally amnestied in 1801 on the accession of Alexander I. Broken, dispirited and still treated with suspicion, he committed suicide in 1802.

At the root of Radishchev's critique of autocracy and serfdom is the concept of natural law, so widely discussed in the age of Enlightenment. Following Locke and Rousseau, Radishchev argues that man has entered a social state because he perceives in it advantage. But the civil law to which he subjects himself upon entering the social state must guarantee him that equality and those rights which he might enjoy in a state of nature. This forms the basis of a social contract. The individual undertakes to accept a limit, defined by law, on the unlimited freedom possessed under natural law, in order that he might enjoy his remaining freedom in security. Society undertakes to provide this security in exchange for obedience to the law. But, just as all men are created equal in nature, so they should remain equal in the eyes of the law. If the individual breaks the law, or if society fails to provide security or observe the equality of citizens before the law, then the contract is broken. Radishchev clearly argues that the unlimited autocracy, widespread serfdom and lack of a rational code of law in Catherine's Russia constitute a violation of the social contract which relieves citizens of the duty of obedience and gives them the right to rebel. The extract from *A Journey from Petersburg to Moscow* in this volume shows Radishchev warning his sovereign and fellow citizens of the dire consequences of society's failure to observe the social contract.

Revolutionary or reformer? Opinion is divided over Radishchev's intentions. Some commentators have emphasized the radical strand in his thought and have read *A Journey from Petersburg to Moscow* as a revolutionary clarion call inviting the oppressed to rise up against the tyrant and justifying tyrannicide. Certainly Radishchev's thought is libertarian and subversive, but to claim him uncritically as the first Russian revolutionary is to overlook at the very least the ambiguity in his writings. Although natural law might sanction rebellion against social relations which cannot demonstrate their justice and rationality, Radishchev still seems anxious to avert the threat by timely action on the part of the authorities. He might have *expected* revolution from below, but, in the extracts given in this volume at least, he *advocates* reform from above.

Moreover, Radishchev, like the other gentry thinkers represented in this chapter, was hidebound by inherited notions characteristic of his social class. Paramount among these was the tradition of the nobility's obligation to serve. This obligation is clearly described in the extracts from Karamzin in this volume, but it may also be detected in Radishchev's quaint *Discourse on what it means to be a Son of the Fatherland,* which we have translated in its entirety. One suspects that the specter of widespread popular revolution was as unappealing to Radishchev as it was to Karamzin. The nobleman serves the fatherland not by invoking insurrection, but by seeking to establish the rule of truth and justice in its institutions and among its foremost citizens.

The tradition of gentry service, the conception of society as a balance of obligations and rights, and the desire to introduce legality into social relations without wishing to unleash the elemental forces of popular revolt are all implicit in the writings and activities of the Decembrists. These young noblemen and army officers were in some respects Radishchev's heirs: they inherited the same European spirit of legalism and rationalism and reinforced it through experiences peculiar to their generation. In the wake of Napoleon's retreat from Russia after 1812 Russian armies entered Paris. This allowed many young officers and noblemen to experience conditions in Western Europe at first hand and to compare them with conditions in the Russia of Alexander I. Alexander's accession in 1801 had aroused hopes of reform among the progressive nobility, hopes that were kept alive by Mikhail Speransky's scheme for governmental reform. But Alexander's early liberalism evaporated, Speransky's reforms were not completed, and by the end of the Napoleonic campaign Alexander was securely in the grip of a kind of mystical conservatism, whereby he perceived himself as a quasi-divine defender of the European status quo. Their hopes disappointed, their awareness of Russia's backwardness sharpened, these army officers and progressive noblemen resorted to underground activity, the formation of secret societies and the discussion of projects for political change. The outcome of this activity was the abortive revolt of December 1825 at the accession of Alexander's successor, Nicholas I. Lack of adequate preparation and an unsure sense of revolutionary tactics (for this was indeed an attempted revolution and not merely another of the palace coups used so often in the past to unseat unpopular Russian monarchs) allowed the revolt to be easily suppressed. Five of the ringleaders, including Pavel Pestel, whose thought is represented in this volume, were hanged, and over a hundred others were sentenced to exile or service as common soldiers.

The organizational history of the Decembrist movement is beyond the scope of this brief introduction, and the interested reader is referred to the Selected Bibliography. However, the two main wings of the movement in the period immediately preceding the revolt were the Northern Society and the Southern Society. The aims of these societies are represented by extracts from draft constitutions drawn up by two of their leading members: Nikita Muravev (1796-1843) of the Northern Society, and Pavel Pestel (1793-1826) of the Southern Society. Both of these documents advocate a constitutional Russia based upon the rule of law, but the important differences between them suggest the diversity of Decembrist opinion. Muravev clearly favors a federal form of government, while the more authoritarian Pestel advocates a centralized power and emphasizes the importance of obedience. Both demand the emancipation of the serfs, yet both stop short of accepting the need for either the nationalization of the land or its complete redistribution. Muravev avoids the issue altogether by insisting that the land must remain the property of the landowner, and Pestel devises a two-tier system whereby some of the land is communally owned for the bare sustenance of all citizens while the rest is acquired by and for the profit of those citizens capable of maximizing its resources. Muravev's project owes an unmistakable debt to the American Constitution, but Pestel's more radical and dictatorial scheme clearly derives from the Jacobins and the French Revolution.

It would be wrong to conclude that the Russian Enlightenment bore only radical and reformist fruit. The tendency in both Soviet Russia and the West to emphasize the achievements of Russian radicalism and liberalism should not blind us to the fact, neatly pointed out by Richard Pipes,[1] that there was enough of intellectual repute in the conservative tradition to engage some of the finest minds of the age. Nikolai Karamzin (1766-1826) is a compelling example of a conservative political thinker whose thought is neither obscurantist nor irrational. Author, leader of Russian Sentimentalism, reformer of the Russian language and official historian of the Russian state, Karamzin occupies an honorable place in the history of Russian culture. He had traveled abroad in 1789-90 and subsequently described his impressions in the sentimental and introspective *Letters of a Russian Traveler,* the publication of which began in 1791. Karamzin's observations in this work are personal rather than political, but he did observe the revolution in France and was horrified by its later excesses. He came to feel that the tyranny of the left might be more to be feared than any tyranny of the right, and that personal freedom might be safer in a traditional autocracy than under the rule of the masses. Moreover, the destruction of tradition in revolutionary France persuaded Karamzin of the virtues of a settled political order such as existed in Russia. Needless to say, Karamzin's admiration for the Russian status quo as a framework within which individual freedom and individual talent might flourish is founded upon an unwillingness to concede that the privileges of the nobility might be shared by the lower social orders.

Karamzin's advocacy of autocracy in his *Memoir on Ancient and Modern Russia* (1811) is not a blueprint for despotism. The work was intended to urge Alexander not to impose constitutional restrictions upon his sovereign power, yet, as Andrzej Walicki has pointed out,[2] Karamzin envisaged autocracy as undivided, not unlimited, power. Only tradition and historical continuity can impart stability and wellbeing to a nation, so that if Russia is to avoid the chaos of revolutionary France there should be no unnecessary interference with existing institutions of the kind proposed by Speransky.

The gentry thinkers of this period formed an isolated group, estranged from the Russian people by their Europeanism and excluded from authority by autocratic insistence upon the indivisibility of monarchical power. With the rise of Sentimentalism and Romanticism this intellectual class was to discover the Russian people, firstly as a remote ideal and only much later as a political reality. As Marc Raeff observes,[3] the Russian people was gradually to displace the state as the object of the gentry's sense of an obligation to serve. As this process advanced, Russian thought gradually acquired that populist quality which was to distinguish it in the nineteenth century.

Alexander Nikolaevich Radishchev
[ON AUTOCRACY]⁴

Autocracy is the condition most contrary to human nature. Not only can we not grant unlimited power over ourselves, but neither does the law, that expression of the popular will, have any right to punish criminals other than the right of ensuring that its precepts are not violated. If we live under the authority of the law, then this is not because we must do so out of necessity, but because we derive some advantage from it. If we surrender to the law some of the rights and freedoms to which we are entitled by nature, then we do so in order that they should be used for our benefit. In this respect we enter into an unspoken agreement with society. If this agreement is broken then we are freed from our obligations. An injustice perpetrated by a sovereign ruler gives the people the same or greater right to judge that ruler as he has under the law to judge criminals. The sovereign is the first citizen of the people's society.

1773

Alexander Nikolaevich Radishchev
A DISCOURSE ON WHAT IT MEANS TO BE A SON OF THE FATHERLAND [5]

Not all who are born in the fatherland are worthy of the majestic title of son of the fatherland (patriot). Those under the yoke of slavery are not fit to be adorned with this name. Wait, those of you with sensitive souls! Don't pronounce judgement on my arguments while you still stand on their threshold.

Step up and see for yourselves! Who is not aware that the name of son of the fatherland is only applicable to men, and not to beasts, cattle or other dumb animals. It is well known that man is a free creature in that he is endowed with intelligence, reason and free will; that his freedom consists in the choice of what is best; that he recognizes and chooses what is best by means of reason, attains it with the help of intelligence and always strives towards the beautiful, the sublime and the exalted. All this he finds in sole accordance with natural and revealed laws, otherwise known as divine laws, and with civic and social laws derived [from them].

But is he in whom these faculties, these human sensations, are deadened worthy of being adorned with the majestic name of son of the fatherland?

He is not a man, but what? He is lower than cattle, for cattle too follow their own laws and are not observed to step outside them. But here we are not concerned with those unfortunates who have been deprived by perfidy or force of that supreme human advantage, and who because of this have reached such a state that without compulsion and fear they make nothing of such sensations. They are like beasts of burden who do no more than their prescribed work, from which they cannot free themselves. They are like horses condemned to pull a cart their whole life long, with no hope of liberation from their yoke, receiving the same recompense as horses and suffering the same blows. We are not discussing those who can see no end to their yoke but death, when their labors and sufferings will cease, although it does occasionally happen that cruel grief envelops their spirit in meditation, ignites the faint light of their reason, and forces them to curse their miserable state and seek an end to it. Here we are not speaking of those who feel nothing apart from their humiliation, who move and crawl about in a mortal sleep (lethargy), who approximate to human beings only in appearance, who are burdened with the weight of their fetters, deprived of all blessings, excluded from the whole heritage of mankind, oppressed, humiliated and despised. They are little more than corpses buried alongside each other, doing man's necessary labor out of fear, and desiring nothing but death. For them in fact the smallest desire is forbidden and the slightest initiative punished. They are allowed only to grow and die; they are not asked what they have done worthy of humanity, what praiseworthy accomplishments they have left behind to testify to their existence, or what good or value has been brought to the state by this great legion of hands.

No, we are not concerned with them here. They are not members of the state. They cannot be men if they are nothing but machines driven by a tormentor, dead bodies, beasts of burden!

The title "son of the fatherland" demands to be borne by a man, a man! But where is he? Where is this son worthy of carrying a great name?

Is he in the embraces of languor and voluptuousness? Enveloped in the flames of pride, ambition and brute force? Buried in unsavory profiteering, envy, evil desires, enmity and dissension with everyone, even with those who feel the same and strive after the same things? Or is he wallowing in the mire of indolence, gluttony and drunkenness? A featherbrain who spends the day from noon onwards (for only then does his day begin) flying about the whole town, through streets and houses, for the sake of the most senseless chatter, for the seduction of virtue, the corruption of good behavior and the ensnaring of the innocent and open-hearted. With his head made up like a flour shop, his brows like bags of soot, his cheeks like cartons of white lead and rouge—or, rather, like a painter's palette—his skin taut like the skin of a drum, so that in all his finery he is more like a monster than a man. And his dissolute life, proclaimed by the stench emanating from his mouth and whole body, has to be camouflaged by a whole chemist-shop of sweet-smelling sprays. In a word, a man of fashion discharging to the letter all the laws of high society foppishness. He eats, sleeps, stupefies himself with drink and voluptuousness beyond the point where his strength is exhausted, then changes his clothes, talks all kinds of nonsense, shouts, and runs from place to place. In brief, a dandy.

Is this man a son of the fatherland? Or is it that man over there, majestically raising his gaze to the heavenly vault while trampling underfoot all before him and torturing those close to him with his violence, persecution and oppression; locking them up, depriving them of their rank and property, and by means of torture, temptation, deceit, even murder—in fact, by all the means at his disposal—tearing apart all those who dare pronounce the words: mankind, freedom, peace, honesty, sanctity, the right to property, and so on? Streams of tears and rivers of blood not only fail to touch him, but even gladden his heart. Nobody who opposes his words, his opinions, his deeds, or his intentions has the right to exist! Is this man a son of the fatherland?

Or he who stretches out his hands to seize all the wealth and property in the fatherland, or, were it possible, in the whole world; who is prepared cold-bloodedly to take away from his unfortunate fellow-countrymen the last crumbs sustaining their lives of despondency and exhaustion, to steal and plunder their specks of property; who is transported by joy if a new opportunity for acquisition presents itself, even if this is to be purchased with whole rivers of the blood of his brethren, or if it deprives his fellow-men of their last refuge or daily bread, so that they die in hunger, cold or heat. Let them sob, let them kill their offspring in despair, let them risk their lives a thousand times over—none of this touches his heart or means anything to him. He has increased his possessions and that is all that counts. Is this the man worthy of the title, son of the fatherland?

Or is it the man who sits at a table overflowing with the produce of all four elements and whose gratification demands the sacrifice of several servants who could be serving the state? This sacrifice is necessary so that when he is sated he can be carried off to bed, there peacefully to engage in the consumption of whatever further produce takes his fancy, until sleep finally deprives him of the strength to move his jaws. Is he the son of the fatherland, or is it one of the other four types described earlier? (For we rarely encounter the fifth example as such a distinct type.) We can see a mixture of these types everywhere, but unless the son of the fatherland is among them we cannot yet see him!

The voice of reason, the laws inscribed in nature and in the hearts of men, will not allow the types described above to be called sons of the fatherland! Even those who are just like these types will pass judgment (oh, not on themselves, for they do not regard themselves as such, but on others exactly like themselves) and exclude them from the ranks of the sons of the fatherland; for there is no man, no matter how depraved and blinded with self-esteem, who does not at least to some extent sense the truth and beauty of things.

There is no man who would not feel sorrow if he found himself humiliated, abused, forcibly enslaved, deprived of all means and all capacity for peace and pleasure, and nowhere finding consolation. Does this not prove that man loves honor, and that without it he is soulless. There is no need to explain here that I mean by this true honor, for false honor offers the human heart not deliverance, but only subjugation to those evils listed above, and will never bring it peace.

The sense of true honor is innate in every man, but it illuminates his thoughts and deeds only to the extent that he draws near to it, by following the torch of reason which accompanies him through the darkness of passion, vice and prejudice towards the calm light of honor. There is no mortal, however alienated from nature, who does not possess that impulse which is locked in the heart of every man and which steers him to the love of honor. Everyone would rather be respected than reviled. Everyone strives towards further self-improvement, fame and glory, no matter how assiduously Aristotle, that flatterer of Alexander of Macedonia,[6] tried to prove the contrary by asserting that nature herself had so arranged the human species that one part—moreover, by far the bigger part—must inevitably be in a state of servitude and consequently unable to know what honor is, while the smaller part dominates since not many possess noble and sublime emotions.

It is beyond argument that by far the most significant proportion of the human species is indeed sunk in the darkness of barbarism, bestiality and servitude. But this in no way proves that man is not born with an instinctive striving towards the exalted and towards self-perfection, that is to say with an instinctive love of true glory and honor. The cause of this decline is either the kind of life led, the circumstances in which one is condemned to live, or inexperience, or the coercion of those who oppose the just and legitimate ennobling of human nature and who by force and perfidy condemn it to blindness and servitude, which weakens the human heart and human reason by inflicting the heavy yoke of scorn and oppression, thus stifling the force of the eternal spirit.

Do not try to justify yourselves at this point, oppressors and enemies of mankind, by claiming that these terrible bonds are part of a natural order which demands subordination! Oh, if only you were to penetrate the chain of nature as far as you are capable (which is very far!) you would think differently; you would discover that love, not force, maintains the order and hierarchy of the world. The whole of the natural order is subject to it, and wherever it is found there are none of those infamous spectacles which evoke tears of compassion in the sensitive heart and shake the true friend of humanity.

What would the natural world be without this driving force but a disordered confusion (chaos)? It would have lost the supreme capacity to survive and perfect itself. In each human heart everywhere there is born that ardent desire to gain honor and win the praise of others. This derives from man's innate sense of his own limitations and dependence. This sense is so strong that it always drives man to acquire for himself those qualities and abilities which will earn the love of both God and his fellow-men and satisfy his conscience. And having earned the regard and respect of others a man can be trusted to preserve and perfect his own qualities.

If this is so, then who can doubt that this powerful love of honor and desire to gratify one's conscience with the respect and praise of others is the supreme and truest means of attaining human happiness and perfection. For what other means does man have of overcoming those difficulties which inevitably lie along the path to blissful tranquility, and of refuting those attacks of faintheartedness which fill men with trepidation at the sight of their own shortcomings? What hope is there of deliverance from the fear of falling forever beneath the terrible weight of our shortcomings if we are deprived of the sweet hope of finding refuge firstly in a supreme being who is not an avenger but the source of all blessings, and then in people like ourselves, with whom nature has united us for mutual help, and who are inwardly willing to offer this help, since no matter how muffled that inner voice, they feel that they ought not to commit the kind of sacrilege which hinders man's legitimate striving after self-perfection.

Who has sown in man's soul this instinct to seek a refuge, this innate sense of dependence which so clearly reveals to us that twofold way to salvation and happiness? What is it finally that inspires man to embark on this path, drives him after these two means of attaining human bliss and causes him to worry about reaching them? The answer is, in fact, nothing less than an inborn ardent urge to attain those qualities and that moral beauty which deserve God's favor and the love of one's fellow-men, the urge to make oneself worthy of their goodwill and protection.

Anyone who looks at human activity will see that this is one of the main driving forces behind the world's most sublime creations. It is the source of those honorable motives which inspire men at the onset of creativity. It is the reason for that sweet sensation of tranquility and a quiet conscience which as a rule always attends the heart of man whenever he is filled with the grace of God and has attained the love of others, which generally takes the form of joy at the sight of him, along with praise and exclamations. It is the object of the true man's aspirations, where he finds his real satisfaction. It is now clear that the true man and the son of the fatherland are one and the same; therefore it is a genuine distinguishing sign of a son of the fatherland to be *aspiring* in this way.

By this means a man begins to give dignity to the majestic title of son of the fatherland and of the monarchy. To achieve this he must honor his conscience and love his neighbors, for only through love can one find love. He must carry out his calling as wisdom and integrity dictate, with no concern for winning honors, praise or glory, for these are companions, or rather shadows, which will attend virtue naturally whenever it is illumined by the ever-burning sun of truth. Those who chase after fame and praise will not only never win them from others, but may even forfeit them.

The true man is the man who faithfully observes all the laws laid down for his happiness, and obeys them religiously. A noble modesty, untouched by superficiality and hypocrisy, accompanies all his feelings, words and deeds. He submits with due reverence to all the demands of order, organization and the general good. Not for him a small role in the service of the fatherland: he knows that in serving it he is assisting, as it were, in the healthy functioning of the body of state. He would sooner agree to die and disappear than set others a bad example and thus deprive the fatherland of their service, which might well have adorned and strengthened it. He is afraid of polluting the wellbeing of his fellow-citizens; he burns with the tenderest desire for the peace and security of his fellow-countrymen; there is nothing he wishes more than to see them loving one another. He tries to light that salutary flame in all hearts without fear of the difficulties that confront him in this noble feat. He overcomes all obstacles, is constantly vigilant in the defense of honesty, gives good advice and directions, helps the unfortunate, and delivers others from the dangers of going astray and falling into vice. If he were convinced that his death would bring strength and glory to the fatherland, then he would not hesitate to sacrifice himself; if, however, his life is needed by the fatherland then he will dedicate it to the observance wherever possible of the laws of nature and the fatherland. He tries with all his might to avert everything that could stain the purity and weaken the good intentions of these laws, which would be tantamount to destroying the happiness and perfectibility of his fellow-countrymen. In a word, he is *moral,* and that is the second mark of a true son of the fatherland!

The third, and it would seem final, distinguishing characteristic of the son of the fatherland is the fact that he is *noble.* A man is noble when he is renowned for his wise and philanthropic qualities and behavior, when his reason and virtue distinguish him among his fellows, and when, inflamed by truly wise aspirations and obedient to the law and its custodians, the powers that be, he devotes all his strength and effort to regarding not only himself, but also all he possesses, as belonging to the fatherland and merely pledged for his use as a sign of the goodwill of his compatriots and his sovereign, that father of his people who spares nothing for the good of the fatherland. A man is really noble when his heart cannot help but tremble with tender joy at the very name of his fatherland, and who cannot feel otherwise whenever he thinks of his fatherland (which is all the time), as though someone had mentioned the part of it dearer to him than anything else in the world. He will not sacrifice the good of the fatherland for the sake of any prejudice, no matter how resplendent, that might dance before his eyes. Instead he puts the good of the fatherland before everything. His greatest reward is to be found in virtue, that is to say in that inner harmony of all inclinations and desires with which the most wise Creator infuses the innocent heart and which nothing in the world can match for the peace and joy it brings. For true nobility consists of virtuous deeds animated by true honor, and this is to be found only in ceaseless work for the benefit of the human race, and particularly one's fellow-countrymen, rendering unto each in accordance with his deserts and the established laws of nature and democracy. Today, as in enlightened antiquity, only those adorned with these qualities are truly respected and praised. That is the third characteristic of the son of the fatherland!

But no matter how splendid, glorious and exquisite these qualities might be to the sensible heart, and despite the fact that every man is capable of possessing them, they cannot help but become adulterated, confused, obscure and muddled without the appropriate upbringing and enlightenment through science and knowledge. For without these man's finest faculties are soon transformed, as ever, into the most harmful impulses and desires, flooding whole nations with dishonor, unrest, discord and disruption. For then human understanding becomes obscure, confused and completely fanciful. Consequently, before a person can hope to possess those qualities of a true man mentioned earlier, he must first accustom his spirit to hard work, diligence, obedience, modesty and intelligent compassion; to the desire to do good to all men, to love for his fatherland, and to the wish to emulate those who have set good examples of all this. Also he must learn to love knowledge and the arts insofar as his position in social life permits. He must apply to himself the systematic study of history, philosophy and thought, not in an academic manner, merely for the sake of learned argument, but in a real way which teaches man his true obligations. And to refine his tastes he must learn to love music, sculpture, architecture and the works of great painters.

Those who consider this discourse to be merely a platonist system of social education which we shall never see realized are completely wrong, for before our very eyes just such a form of education, based on identical principles, is being introduced by monarchs inspired with divine wisdom; and enlightened Europe watches in amazement as these successes make giant strides towards the intended goal.

1789

Alexander Nikolaevich Radishchev
A JOURNEY FROM PETERSBURG TO MOSCOW (Extracts)[7]

Introduction

...I looked about me—and my heart was stung by the sufferings of humanity. Then I looked inside myself—and I saw that man's woes derive from man, and often simply because he does not know how to look at the world about him. Is it really so, I asked myself, that nature is so miserly towards her children that she has concealed the truth forever from him who errs innocently? Is it possible that this stern stepmother has created us so that we may experience only woe and never happiness? My reason trembled at this thought, and my heart thrust it aside. I found that man is his own comforter. "Lift the veil from the eyes and senses nature has bestowed—and you will be happy." Nature's voice spoke loudly in the depths of my being. I cast off the despondency into which I had been plunged by sensitivity and compassion; I sensed within myself the strength to overcome the error of my ways; and—unspeakable joy!—I felt that it was possible for every man to play a part in working for the benefit of his fellow men. It was this thought which prompted me to sketch out what you are about to read...

Khotilov: A Project for the Future

We have gradually brought our beloved fatherland to the flourishing state in which it now stands. We can see knowledge, art and industry raised to the highest standards of perfection attainable by man. We can see that throughout our realm human reason, freely spreading its wings, aspires unerringly and without hindrance to greatness, and has nowadays become a reliable guardian of social legislation. Under its powerful protection our heart too can say freely and with inexpressible joy, in prayers offered up to the almighty Creator, that our fatherland is an abode pleasing to the Deity. For its constitution is based not on prejudices and superstitions, but on our inner sense of the gifts bestowed by the Father of All. Unknown to us is the enmity which has so often come between people of different creeds. Unknown to us also is compulsion in our beliefs. Born in such freedom, we truly consider each other as brothers belonging to a single family and having a common father in God.

The torch of learning, held aloft over our legislation, now distinguishes it from the legislation of many other countries. A balanced separation of power, equality of property, these have destroyed the very roots of civil discord. Moderation in punishment, which makes men respect the laws of the supreme authority as if they were the commands of tender parents to their offspring, has forestalled even ingenuous misdeeds. Clarity in the statutes concerning the acquisition and disposal of property prevents family disputes from arising. The boundaries separating one citizen and his property from the next are deep, plainly visible, and sacredly respected by all. Personal offenses are rare among us and are settled amicably. Popular education has concerned itself with making us gentle, peace-loving citizens, but above all with making us men.

Enjoying tranquility at home, having no external enemies, and having brought society to the highest bliss of civic concord, shall we be so devoid of a sense of humanity, so insensitive to feelings of pity, so devoid of noblehearted tenderness and brotherly love, that we endure before our very eyes an eternal reproach to us—for, to the shame of our most distant descendants, a whole third of our fellow-men, our equal compatriots, our beloved brothers in nature, wear the heavy fetters of slavery and bondage. The bestial custom of enslaving men like oneself, which originated in the hot latitudes of Asia, a custom befitting only savages, a custom signifying a heart of stone and a complete lack of soul, quickly spread far and wide over the face of the earth. And we Slavs, the sons of glory,[8] we who are renowned in name and deed among the peoples of the world, we have been infected with the darkness of ignorance and have adopted this custom. And to our shame, to the shame of our past, to the shame of this age of reason, we have preserved it intact to this very day.

It is known to you from the deeds of your fathers, it is known to all from our chronicles, that the wise rulers of our people, motivated by true philanthropy and having come to understand the natural bond on which social agreement is based, did try to put an end to this hundred-headed evil. But their sovereign deeds came to nothing because of that estate, then renowned for its proud preeminence in our land, but now decayed and fallen into contempt, the hereditary nobility. Our royal ancestors, for all their scepter's might, were powerless to break the shackles of civil bondage. Not only were they unable to carry out their good intentions, but through the various tricks of that aforementioned estate they were moved to enact laws contrary to their judgment and desires. Our fathers beheld, perhaps with heartfelt tears, these destroyers tightening the bonds and strengthening the fetters of the most useful members of our society. The agricultural workers are slaves among us even to this day. We do not acknowledge them as fellow-citizens equal to ourselves, and we have forgotten that they are men. O beloved fellow-citizens! O true sons of the fatherland! Look about you and acknowledge your error. The servants of the everlasting God, moved by the same desire as ours for the good of society and the happiness of man, have explained to you in their teachings in the name of the all-bountiful God whom they profess how contrary it is to His wisdom and His love to rule arbitrarily over those next to you. They have tried with arguments drawn from nature and our own hearts to reveal to you your cruelty, injustice and sinfulness. Their voice still rings out loudly and solemnly in the temples of the living God: "Come to your senses, ye who have strayed; relent, ye who are hard of heart; break the fetters of your brethren; throw open the dungeons of bondage and allow those who are the same as you to taste the sweetness of life in society, for which they too were destined by the Almighty, just as you were. They can enjoy the beneficial rays of the sun just as much as you; they have the same limbs and senses as you, and they should have an equal right to use them."

But if the servants of the Divinity have set before your gaze the injustice of slavery on a human level, we consider it our duty to show you the harm it does to society and its injustice at a civic level. It would appear to be superfluous, now that the spirit of philosophical inquiry is so well established, to seek out and renew the arguments in favor of the essential equality of men and therefore of citizens. For him who has grown up under the protection of liberty and is filled with noble sentiments rather than prejudices, the feelings normally in his heart are proof enough of this all-important equality. But it is the misfortune of mortals in this world to lose their way even in the light of day and not see what is right before their eyes.

When you were young you were taught in school the principles of natural law and civil law. Natural law showed you men hypothetically outside society, who had acquired from nature the same constitution and therefore possessed the same rights. Consequently they were equal in all respects and no man was subject to any other. Civil law showed you men who had exchanged this unlimited freedom for the right to enjoy freedom in peace. Yet, though all had set a limit to their freedom and submitted their actions to the law, the fact that they would have been equal from birth in a natural and free state meant that they should be equal also within the limitations they had set to their freedom. Consequently, here too no man should be subject to another. The prime authority in society is the law, for it is the same for all men. But what was it that impelled men to enter a social state and willingly set limits to their actions? Reason tells us: for their own good; our hearts tell us: for their own good; and uncorrupted civil law says: for their own good. We live in a society which has already passed through many stages of development, and therefore we have forgotten its original principles. But take a look at all new nations and at all societies in a state of nature, if we can put it like that. First, they consider enslavement a crime; second, only the criminal or the enemy is subject to the burden of bondage. When we consider these points we can see how far we have deviated from the aim of society, and how far removed we still are from the ideal of social happiness. All that we have said is familiar to you; you imbibed such principles with your mother's milk. Only momentary prejudice, only selfishness (do not take offense at my words!) blind us and make us like men raging in the darkness.

But who among us wears the fetters, who feels the burden of slavery? The agricultural worker! The man who feeds us in our leanness and satisfies our hunger, who gives us health and prolongs our life, yet who has no right himself to dispose of what he cultivates and produces. Who has the most right to a cornfield if not the man who works it? Let us imagine that men have come into a wilderness in order to establish a society. With a mind to feeding themselves they divide up the land, which is overgrown with grass. Who should have a share in this division? Should it not be he who knows how to plough it, and has sufficient strength and determination to undertake the task? A share would be useless to the very young, the very old, the weak, the infirm or the negligent. The land would remain desolate and the wind blowing over it would never stir an ear of corn. If it is useless to the man who works it, then it is also useless to society, for the worker cannot render up his surplus to society if he does not even produce enough for himself. Consequently, in primitive society he who could work a field had a proprietary right to it, and in working it had the exclusive benefit of it. But how far we have departed from primitive social principles governing ownership. With us he who has a natural right to it is not only excluded from it completely, but while working another's field he sees his livelihood dependent on another's power! Your enlightened minds cannot fail to have understood these truths, but, as I have already said, any actions you may take in consequence of these truths are punctuated by prejudice and selfishness. Do your hearts, filled as they are with love for humanity, really prefer selfish feelings instead of those which can sweeten the heart? Where is the self-interest in this? Can a state in which two-thirds of the citizens are deprived of civil rights and are to a degree dead to the law, be called happy? Only the insatiable bloodsucker will say that the peasant must be happy in that he has never known anything better.

We shall now try to refute these savage laws drawn up for the benefit of the powerful, just as our predecessors once unsuccessfully tried to do by their actions.

Civic happiness can take many forms. They say that a country is happy if it enjoys peace and order. It appears to be happy when its fields do not lie fallow and when proud buildings arise in its towns. It can be said to be happy when the force of its arms extends far and wide and it rules beyond its frontiers not just by might, but through the impact of its ideas upon the minds of others. But all these forms of happiness may be said to be external, fleeting, transient, partial and abstract.

Let us look at the valley lying before our gaze. What do we see? A vast military camp. Silence reigns everywhere in it. All the soldiers stand in their places. In their ranks we see the most precise order. At a single command, at one wave of the commander's hand, the whole camp stirs and moves in perfect order. But can we say that these soldiers are happy? They have been transformed into puppets by the precision of military discipline and are deprived of even that freedom of movement which distinguishes animate matter. They know only the commander's orders, think only what he wants them to think, and go where he commands. Such is the power of discipline over the strongest force in the country. United they can achieve anything, but divided and individually they graze like sheep wherever the shepherd wishes. Order at the expense of freedom is as inimical to our happiness as are fetters themselves. A hundred slaves, chained to the benches of a ship propelled by their oars, live quiet and ordered lives; but if you look into their hearts and souls you will see agony, grief and despair. Often they must wish to put an end to their lives, but even this is denied them. To end their suffering would bring them happiness, but slavery and happiness are incompatible, and so they must live. Therefore, let us not be blinded by the outward peace and order of the country, and let us not consider it happy on those grounds alone. You must always look into the hearts of the citizens. If there you find peace and tranquility then you may truly say that these people are happy...

But let us return to the more immediate point about the condition of the agricultural worker, which we find so injurious to society. It is detrimental to the growth of both agricultural production and population. It is harmful in the example it sets and in the unrest it creates. Man, impelled by motives of self-interest, undertakes that which brings him short-term or long-term advantage and he forsakes that in which he perceives no advantage either now or for the future. As a result of this natural instinct everything we undertake for our own sakes and without compulsion we do diligently, assiduously and well. On the other hand, all that we do not do freely, all that is not for our own benefit, we do negligently, lazily and in any old fashion. This is the case with the agricultural workers in our country. The fields are not their own and the harvest does not belong to them. For this reason they cultivate the land lazily and do not worry about whether it goes to seed while they are working on it. Compare this field with the one the arrogant landowner allots to the worker for his own bare sustenance. The worker is unstinting in the labor he devotes to this one. Nothing distracts him from his work. He boldly overcomes the ravages of the season; he devotes his leisure time to work; he shuns days set apart for holidays—and all because he is looking after himself, working for himself and producing for himself. And so his field yields him an abundant harvest, whereas the fruits of his labor on another's field will die, or rather bear no future harvest. These fields would thrive and soon sustain the citizens if the cultivation of the land were done zealously, if it were free.

But if forced labor yields smaller harvests, then it follows that agricultural production which fails to reach its quota impedes population growth. Wherever there is nothing to eat those who must eat to survive will disappear: they will die of starvation. Thus, by yielding an inadequate harvest, the field where there is enslavement will bring death to those citizens whom nature intended to enjoy her abundance. But is this the only way in which slavery hampers potential abundance? In addition to lack of food and clothing, it also means work to the point of exhaustion. Add to this the outrages perpetrated through arrogance and the pernicious abuses of authority, which can lurk behind the finest human sentiments, and you will see with horror just how destructive slavery is. It differs from battle and conquest only in that whereas these cut men down, slavery does not allow them even to be born. But it causes even greater harm. Anyone can see that conquest destroys incidentally and momentarily, but slavery destroys continuously and over a long period of time. Conquest ceases its ferocity when its course is run, but slavery begins where conquest leaves off and cannot be changed except by internal upheavals, which are always dangerous.

But there is nothing more harmful than always having to witness the effects of slavery on those it involves: master and slave. On the one side there grows arrogance, and on the other servility. There can be no bond here other than brute force. And that, once it has established itself in a small way, soon painfully spreads its despotic and imperious effects everywhere. But the champions of slavery, those with the power and the sword in their hands, are still its most fanatical advocates, despite being themselves locked in its shackles. It would appear that the spirit of freedom has so dried up in the slaves that not only do they not wish to end their own suffering, but they also find it distressing to see others free. They come to love their fetters, if it is possible for a man to love his own ruination. I sometimes think I see in them the serpent that brought about the fall of the first man. Examples of tyrannical power are infectious. It must be admitted that we ourselves, we who have taken up arms in the name of courage and natural law with the aim of destroying this hundred-headed monster that devours society's food, intended for the sustenance of the citizens—we too have perhaps crept into acts of despotism, and although our intentions have always been good and intended to promote general wellbeing, our autocratic act cannot be justified by its usefulness. And so we now beg your forgiveness for our inadvertent arrogance.

Do you not know, dear fellow citizens, how great is the destruction that awaits us and what peril we face! All the hardened feelings of the slaves, which have not been released by a fine gesture of freedom, are becoming stronger and intensify their innermost instincts. A stream whose course is blocked becomes stronger the more resistance it meets. Once it has breached the dam nothing can stop its flow. Such is the case with our brothers who are kept in fetters. They are awaiting the right time and the right opportunity. The alarm bell is ringing. And the destructive force of savagery will overflow with great speed. We shall find ourselves surrounded with swords and venom. Death and burning will be the promised reward for our harshness and inhumanity. And the more dilatory and stubborn we are in freeing them from their shackles, the swifter will be their revenge. Bear in mind events of the past. Even a deception managed to arouse the slaves to such rage that they set about destroying their masters! Tempted by a crude pretender they streamed after him, wishing only to be free from the yoke of their masters.[9] And in their ignorance they could think of no other way to achieve this than by doing away with them. They spared neither sex nor age. They sought the pleasure of revenge rather than the benefit of losing their shackles.

This is what lies before us; this is what we must expect. The threat of destruction is steadily mounting, and danger already hangs over our heads. Time has already raised its scythe and awaits the right moment. The first flatterer or friend of humanity who comes along to awaken the unfortunates will precipitate the scythe's sweep. Beware!

But if the fear of destruction and the danger of upsetting all that has been achieved can move the weak among you a little, shall we not be courageous enough to overcome our prejudices, scorn selfishness, free our brethren from the fetters of slavery and re-establish the natural equality of all? Knowing how your hearts are disposed, I feel that you would rather be convinced by arguments drawn from the human heart than by prudent, calculating self-interest or, even worse, fear of danger. Go forth, my dear people, go to the dwellings of your brothers and proclaim to them the change in their lot. Proclaim with sincere feeling: "Moved to pity by your fate, out of sympathy for our fellow-men, recognizing your equality with us and convinced that this is in the general interest, we have come to kiss you as our brothers. We have left behind the proud discrimination which has for so long kept us apart. We have forgotten the inequality that once existed between us. We rejoice today in our victory. Let this day, when the shackles of our dear fellow citizens are smashed, become the most illustrious page in our history. Forget the harm we have done you in the past, and let us truly love one another."

Let these be your words; you can already hear them in the depths of your hearts. Do not delay, my beloved friends. Time is short; our days pass and we do nothing. Let us not end our lives filled with good intentions which we have been unable to translate into practice. Let us not leave it for posterity to take advantage of this opportunity, seize our crown of glory, and say of us: "They had their day."

1790

Nikolai Mikhailovich Karamzin
A MEMOIR ON ANCIENT AND MODERN RUSSIA
[Some Observations on the Reign of Alexander I][10]

So far I have spoken of past reigns; now with my conscience and my sovereign before me I shall speak of the present reign, to the best of my understanding. What gives me the right to do this? Love for the fatherland and for the monarch, a certain amount of ability given me perhaps by God, and some knowledge gained from world chronicles and from conversations with great men, that is, through their works. What do I want? To test with the best of intentions Alexander's magnanimity and to say what I consider to be true and what history will some day confirm.

Two schools of thought predominated when Alexander came to the throne: some wished him, to his eternal glory, to take measures to curb the unlimited autocracy which had proved so harmful in the reign of his father. Others, doubtful of the chances of success of such an undertaking, wanted him only to restore Catherine's system which had fallen into ruin, but which had been so happy and so wise in comparison with Paul's.[11] In actual fact, can one limit autocracy in Russia in any way without weakening the tsar's authority, so salutary for the country? Superficial minds will find no difficulty in answering: "Yes, one can. One only has to establish a law that is higher even than the sovereign!" But whom shall we entrust with the task of ensuring that such a law is not violated? The Senate? The Council? Who will make up the membership of these institutions? Will they be appointed by the sovereign or by the state? If the former they will be the tsar's sycophants, if the latter they will want to argue with the tsar over authority—in which case I foresee an aristocracy instead of a monarchy. Moreover, what will the senators do if the monarch breaks the law? Make representations to His Majesty? What if he merely laughs at them? Will they incite the people against him? Every good Russian heart will shudder at the thought of this. Two political authorities in the one state are like two fierce lions in one cage, ready to tear each other apart; law without the power to implement it amounts to nothing. Autocracy founded and has resurrected Russia.[12] Any change in her political constitution has led in the past and must lead in the future to her ruin, for she consists of so many very different parts, each of which has its own particular civic value. What apart from unlimited autocracy can produce unity of action in such a machine? If Alexander, inspired by magnanimous hatred for the abuses of autocracy, were to take his pen and prescribe for himself laws other than those of God and conscience, then the true and virtuous Russian citizen would presume to stay his hand and say:

"Sire! You exceed the limits of your authority. Taught by a long history of disasters, Russia before the holy altar entrusted the power of autocracy to your ancestor and demanded that he rule over her supremely and indivisibly. This precept is the foundation of your authority, you have no other. You may do anything, but you may not limit your authority by law!" But let us imagine that Alexander actually prescribes for monarchical power some kind of statute based on principles of public good and ratifies it by a sacred oath. Would this oath be binding on Alexander's successors unless it were backed up by other means, means which would be either infeasible or dangerous for Russia? No, let us leave such schoolboy philosophizing and affirm that our sovereign has only one sure way of ensuring that his successors do not abuse their power: he must reign virtuously and accustom his subjects to goodness. Then he will give rise to salutary customs, principles and popular opinions which will keep future sovereigns within the limits of legal authority far more effectively than any transient forms. How? By the fear of arousing public hatred by a contrary system of rule. A tyrant may occasionally follow a tyrant safely, but he may never follow a wise ruler! "The sweet repels us from the bitter," as Vladimir's legates said after experiencing European faiths...

Let us now look at domestic policies, past and present. Instead of quickly reverting to the order established in the reign of Catherine, an order affirmed by the experience of 34 years and vindicated, so to speak, by the disorders of Paul's reign; instead of abolishing only the superfluous and introducing only the necessary; in a word, instead of basing their reforms on an initial investigation, Alexander's advisors wanted to see innovations in the main organs of monarchical power, ignoring the wise old precept that all novelty in the political order is an evil to which we should resort only when necessary; for time alone gives statutes due weight, since we respect more that which we have long respected and do everything better from habit...

"In a monarchy," writes Montesquieu, "there must be a repository of law." "Le Conseil du Prince n'est pas un dépôt convenable. Il est, par sa nature, le dépôt de la volonté momentanée du Prince qui exécute, et non pas le dépôt des lois fondamentales. De plus, le Conseil du Monarque change sans cesse; il n'est point permanent: il ne saurait être nombreux; il n'a point à un assez haut degré la confiance du peuple; il n'est donc pas en état de l'éclairer dans les temps difficiles, ni de le ramener à l'obéissance."[13] Whatever changes come about will not materially alter the points we have raised: the Council will either become the Senate, or a section of it, a Department. But this is merely playing with names and forms, giving them an importance which only the things they describe should possess. I congratulate the inventor of the new form or preface to the laws, which reads: "Having considered the opinion of Council..."—but the Russian sovereign will only heed wisdom where he finds it: in his own mind, in books, or in the minds of his most outstanding subjects. In an autocracy laws need no approval other than the sovereign's signature: he has total power. The Council, the Senate, committees and ministers are only executive organs or the sovereign's proxies: they need not be consulted when he himself acts...[14]

Only those laws are salutary which have long been desired by the best minds in the state and which have, as it were, been anticipated by the people as the most immediate remedy for a given evil. The establishment of the ministries and Council struck everybody by its suddenness. At the very least the authors of these new reforms should have explained their advantages: I read them and see nothing but dry forms. They draw lines for my eyes, but leave my mind untouched. They tell Russians: "So far things have been like that, but now they will be like this." Why? They don't say. When Peter the Great introduced his important state reforms he gave account to the people: just look at the Church Statute, where the Emperor reveals to you his whole heart, all the motives, causes and aims behind this statute. In general Russia's new legislators are more notable for their clerical abilities than their statesmanship...

This is the way good Russians regard the new political institutions; on seeing how unripe they are they pine for the old order. Throughout the brilliant reign of Catherine II, with some help from the Senate, the Colleges and the Procurator-General. Things went well. Prudent legislators when required to make changes to the political statutes have always tried to depart as little as possible from the old forms. "If you must introduce changes in the number of officials and their powers," says the perceptive Machiavelli, "then at least keep their titles unchanged for the people." We are doing quite the opposite: we leave the thing itself unchanged and chase after new names, thinking up new methods of achieving the same result! We feel an evil we have grown accustomed to much less than we do a new one, while we don't always trust new benefits. The reforms effected so far do not reassure us of the value of future ones: they are awaited more with dread than with hope, for it is dangerous to tamper with ancient political structures. Russia has been in existence for about a thousand years, and not in the form of a savage horde, but as a great state. Yet we are constantly being told of new structures and new statutes, as though we had only recently emerged from the dark American forests! We need more prudence in the preservation, rather than the creation, of political structures. History quite rightly condemns Peter the Great's excessive passion for imitating foreign powers, but are things not even worse in our age? Where, in which European country, do the people prosper, where does justice flourish, where does good order prevail? Where are hearts content and minds at peace? In France? Certainly they have a Conseil d'État, a Secretaire d'État, a Sénat conservateur, Ministres de l'Intérieur, de la Justice, des Finances, de l'Instruction publique, de la Police, des Cultes—

and it is true that Catherine II had neither these institutions nor these officials. But where do we find a civil society fulfilling its true aim—in the Russia of Catherine II or in Napoleon's France? Where is there more tyranny and autocratic will? Where are state affairs conducted with greater legality and consistency? We see in Alexander's fine soul a strong desire to affirm in Russia the rule of law. By leaving existing institutions intact but promoting them, so to speak, with a constant spirit of zeal for the common good he could have attained this end more easily and made it difficult for his successors to depart from the lawful order. It is much easier to do away with the new than with the old. Alexander is much more likely to impress his successors by affirming the power of Senate than by attributing power to the present Council. Innovations only lead to further innovations and favor rampant tyranny.

Let us say and say again that one of the prime causes of the dissatisfaction which Russians have shown with the present government is its excessive taste for political reforms which shake the foundations of the Empire and the advantages of which are still open to doubt...

The act I wish to turn to now has offended many and pleased no one, even though in conceiving it the Sovereign was inspired by the most sacred humanitarianism. We have heard of monstrous landowners who inhumanly traded in people. On purchasing a village they would pick out those peasants fit for military service and sell them off separately. Let us assume that such beasts still exist today: trade of this kind should be outlawed by strict decree and the estates of these unworthy landowners held in trust. Governors could ensure that this law is enforced. But instead of this, the sale and purchase of recruits has been banned. Up to now the better farmers have willingly toiled for ten or twenty years to amass seven or eight hundred rubles in order to buy a recruit and thus keep their own families intact.[15] Now such farmers have been deprived of their greatest incentive to engage in useful hard work, to produce and lead a sober life. What do riches mean to a father if he cannot use them to save a beloved son? True, the wine-producers rejoice, but fathers of families weep. The state needs recruits, but it is better to draw them from among unhappy people, rather than happy ones, for the latter fare far worse in the army. Let me ask whether the peasants of a tyrannical landowner—one whose greed is such that he is quite capable of selling them as recruits—have found themselves in clover following the prohibition of such sales? Perhaps they would have been better off in the regiment! Meanwhile the landowners of lesser means have lost a way of getting rid of bad peasants or household serfs, to the benefit of themselves and society. The lazy intemperate peasant used to have to mend his ways in the army's harsh school, while the diligent, sober one remained behind at the plough. This example used to have a salutary effect: other peasants would give up their drinking knowing that their master might sell them as recruits. These days how can the small landowner put the fear of God into his dissolute peasants, now that he no longer has the recruiting office? With the stick? With hard labor? Wouldn't it be better to frighten them with the regiment's cane? People say that we have better soldiers nowadays, but is this true? I have asked a few generals, and they have not noticed any improvement. At any rate it is true that the peasants in the villages have become worse. The father of three, or perhaps two, sons prepares one of them well in advance to enter the army and does not marry him off. This son is aware of his fate and so takes to drink, for he knows that good behavior will not save him from military service. The legislator must look at things from all angles, not just one; otherwise in attempting to eradicate one evil he might occasion a greater one.

Thus, so they say, the present government had the intention of giving proprietary serfs their freedom... What would the emancipation of the serfs in Russia mean? That they be free to live wherever they wished, that their masters be relieved of all authority over them, and that they be subject only to the authority of the government. Very well, but these agricultural workers will have no land, for the land—and this is incontrovertible—belongs to the gentry class. They will either stay on with their previous masters, paying them quitrent, working their masters' fields, delivering up their grain where necessary—in other words, working for them as before—or else, dissatisfied with the conditions, they will move to another, less demanding landlord. In the first case will not the masters, relying on a man's natural love for his native area, impose the most onerous terms upon the peasants? Hitherto they have spared the peasants, considering them their own property, but now self-interested landowners will want to extract from the peasants all that is physically possible. They will draw up contracts and the peasants will break them—and there will be lawsuits, endless lawsuits! In the second case, with the peasant here one day and somewhere else tomorrow, will not the treasury suffer losses in the collection of soul-tax and other revenues?[16] Will not agriculture also suffer? Will not many fields lie fallow and many granaries remain empty? For it is largely the gentry and not the free farmer who supplies our markets with grain. Another thing: without seignorial justice, which is free of charge and decisive, will not the peasants start fighting among themselves and seeking justice in the towns? What ruin! Without the surveillance of their masters who have their own district police, the *Zemskaia Isprava,* which is much more effective than all the District Courts, the peasants will take to drinking and making mischief. What a rich harvest for the inns and for corrupt officials, but what a setback for morals and state security! In brief, at present the gentry, spread throughout the realm, assist the monarch in the preservation of peace and order. If you take away from them this supervisory power then the monarch is left like Atlas with the whole of Russia on his shoulders. Could he bear it? A collapse would be terrifying. The first duty of the monarch is to watch over the internal and external security of the state; looking after particular estates and individuals comes second. He wishes to make the peasants happier by granting them freedom; but what if this freedom proves harmful to the state? And would the peasants be happier freed from their master's authority, but left at the mercy of their own vices, of tax-farmers and of unscrupulous judges? There is no doubt that peasants belonging to a reasonable landowner, who is content with a modest quitrent or labor on two or three acres of land,[17] are happier than state peasants, for they have in him a vigilant guardian and protector. Would it not be better to take measures to restrain harsh landowners? These men are known to the regional authorities. If the latter do their job properly, the former will soon disappear. For until Russia has wise and honest regional governors even free settlers will not prosper. I do not know whether Godunov did well or not to deprive the peasants of their freedom (for the conditions prevailing at that time are not fully known),[18] but I do know that now is not the time to restore it to them. Then they had the habits of free men—today they have the habits of slaves. It seems to me that from the point of view of political stability it is safer to enslave men than to give them freedom at the wrong time. Men must be prepared for such freedom through moral reforms, but does our system of wine concessions and the terrible spread of drunkenness serve as a salutary preparation? In conclusion we would say this to our dear Monarch: "Sire, history will not reproach you for an evil which you have inherited (let us assume for a moment that serfdom is an unequivocal evil)—but you will answer to God, your conscience and posterity for every harmful consequence of your own statutes."...

* * *

There are few angels in this world and few outright villains. Most people are a mixture of the two, good and bad together. A prudent government finds means to encourage the good tendencies and restrain the evil ones in its officials. It achieves the former by means of rewards and distinctions and the latter by the fear of punishment. No one who knows the human heart and the structure and mechanism of civil societies can doubt the truth of Machiavelli's dictum that fear is the commonest and most effective of all human motives. If on your travels you come across a land where all is quiet and well-ordered, where the people are content, the weak are not oppressed and the innocent are safe, then you can say with confidence that this is a land where crime does not go unpunished. How many lambs would become tigers if it were not for fear! The love of virtue for its own sake is the act of a highly moral nature—a rare phenomenon in the world, otherwise people would not dedicate altars to virtue. Ordinary men observe the principles of honesty not so much in the hope of thereby gaining certain advantages, but out of fear of the penalty incurred by open violation of these principles. One of the most significant political evils of our age is the absence of fear... No doubt the sensitive heart is averse to severity, but where severity is necessary for the sake of public order such scruples are out of place. How is the monarch traditionally depicted by painters? As a warrior with a sword in his hand, not as a shepherd with flowers! There will be no justice in Russia if the sovereign, having entrusted it to the courts, does not watch over the judges. This is not England: over many centuries we have come to regard the monarch as the judge and to accept his benign will as the supreme law. The sirens might chant around the throne: "Alexander, establish in Russia the rule of law..." etc. I would interpret this chorus as meaning: "Alexander, let us rule Russia in the name of the law while you have a quiet time on the throne: all you have to do is lavish favors and award us ranks, ribbons and money!" In Russia the sovereign is the living law: he favors the good and punishes the bad, and the love of the former is attained through the fear of the latter. Not to fear the sovereign is not to fear the law. All power is concentrated in the Russian monarch; our government is paternal and patriarchal. The father of a family judges and punishes without protocol: the monarch, in different circumstances, must act in the same way, solely according to his conscience. What is Alexander not capable of perceiving if he wishes to? Let him punish the criminal! Let him also punish those who promote criminals to important positions! Let the ministers at least be answerable for the choice of top officials! A salutary fear must spread its branches throughout the land... The tyrant is despised, but softheartedness in a ruler is a virtue only when he knows that he has a duty to temper it with reasonable severity. Forgiveness in the sovereign is praiseworthy only when he applies it to personal and private offenses; it must not extend to social offenses. If forgiveness is often harmful, tolerance is even more so. The former is seen as weakness, the latter as careless indifference or lack of perception. We have just referred to personal offenses against the monarch. These rarely occur without involving harm to the state as well. So no one in Russia should be allowed, for example, to display open disaffection or show disrespect for the monarch, whose sacred person stands as a symbol of the fatherland. Give people freedom and they will kick dirt in your face, but say a firm word in their ear and they will lie at your feet!

Having spoken of the need for fear to preserve us from evil, let us say something about rewards. Rewards are beneficial in moderation—otherwise they are useless or harmful... Honor, honor should be the principal reward! The Romans conquered the world with oakleaf wreaths. In the most important respects people have not changed: attach to any decoration the notion of supreme virtue, that is to say bestow it only upon people of supreme qualities, and you will see it become an object desired by all, despite its insignificant monetary value. Thank God, we still have aspirations and tears still flow from our eyes at the thought of Russia's misfortunes. In the very chorus of discontent, in the most flagrant complaints against the government, you can often hear the voice of grateful love for the fatherland. The people are there, you only have to know how to check their capacity for evil and encourage their inclinations to goodness by means of a sensible system of punishments and rewards. But, I repeat, the former is the more important...

* * *

Autocracy is the Palladium of Russia; its integrity is vital for Russia's happiness. It does not, however, follow from this that the sovereign, who is the sole source of power, should have cause to degrade the gentry, who are as ancient as Russia herself. The gentry have always been a brotherhood of illustrious men serving the grand princes or the tsars, and nothing else. It is bad if a servant gains mastery over a weak lord, but a wise lord respects his chosen servants and is adorned by their honor. The rights of the nobility are not a division of monarchical authority, but the latter's main and indispensable weapon, which keeps the wheels of state in motion. Montesquieu has said: "Point de Monarque—point de noblesse; point de noblesse—point de Monarque!" The gentry are an hereditary estate; order demands that certain people be trained for the fulfilment of certain obligations, and that the monarch should know where to turn for servants who will act for the fatherland's benefit. The ordinary people work, the merchants trade, and the gentry serve, for which they are rewarded with distinctions and benefits, respect and material comfort. Personal, changeable ranks cannot take the place of the hereditary, permanent nobility, and, necessary as they are to mark grades in the state service, they should not in a sound monarchy weaken rights of birth or acquire their privileges. Noble status should not be conditional upon rank, but rank upon noble status; that is to say, the attainment of certain ranks should be necessarily conditional on the candidate being of the nobility, which has not been the case in Russia since the time of Peter the Great, an officer being ex-officio a nobleman. [19] The path to high rank should not be closed to exceptional talent, which may be found in any social class, but let the sovereign in such cases bestow nobility before bestowing rank, and let him do this with full pomp and ceremony, on the whole infrequently and with the utmost discrimination. The advantages of such a practice are tangible: 1) The frequent promotion of commoners to the rank of minister, lord or general is a drain on the treasury, for the award of such ranks must be

accompanied by the award of wealth commensurate with their eminence.
The gentry, on the other hand, having inherited wealth, can manage even in
the highest positions without financial assistance from the treasury; 2) The
gentry are offended when they are presented with men of low birth on the
steps of the throne, where they have become accustomed since days of old
to seeing stately boyars. There is no objection if these are people of rare and
sublime talents, but if they are men of ordinary ability it would be better if
their high positions were occupied by noblemen; 3) Nature furnishes man
with mind and heart, but it is upbringing which forms them. The nobleman,
favored by fortune, is accustomed from the cradle to respect himself, to
love the fatherland and the sovereign for the advantages he has gained at
birth, and to be drawn towards distinction, which was the lot of his
ancestors and which will be the reward for his own future services. This way
of thinking and feeling bestows upon him that nobility of spirit which
above all else was the reason for the creation of an hereditary nobility. It is
an important advantage which the natural gifts of a commoner can rarely
match, for, even when he has attained distinction, the commoner still fears
scorn, usually dislikes the gentry, and hopes that through personal
arrogance he will make people forget his lowly origins. Virtue is rare. You
will find in this world more ordinary souls than superior ones. It is not only
my opinion, but also that of all right-thinking politicians, that a monarchy
is best supported by a nobility with firmly established rights. Thus I would
wish Alexander to make it a rule to enhance the dignity of the gentry, whose
luster may be seen as a reflection of the tsar's brilliance, and to do this not
merely by state charters, but also by means of those, so to speak, innocent
and effortless signs of consideration which are so effective in an autocracy.
For example, why should the Emperor not appear occasionally at solemn
assemblies of the nobility, in his role as head of the nobility, dressed not in
the uniform of a guards officer, but in that of a nobleman? This would have
much more effect than eloquent letters and wordy assurances of
monarchical consideration for the society of the nobility. But the most
palpable way for Alexander to elevate the gentry would be by a law to
admit every nobleman into military service as an officer, conditional only
upon his knowing well the principles of mathematics and the Russian
language. Pay a salary only to recruits and then all the nobles, in
accordance with the good of a monarchy founded on conquests, would
take up the sword instead of the pen with which nowadays rich and poor
alike, to the undoubted detriment of the state, arm their children in
chanceries, archives and courts. For such gentry feel a revulsion for
military barracks where their young men, through sharing menial work
and menial amusements with common soldiers, might suffer physically and
morally. Indeed, what is necessary for service that cannot be learned in the
rank of officer? It is far pleasanter for a noble to learn at this rank than as a
non-commissioned officer. Our army would be enriched by young, well-

bred noblemen who are today languishing in government offices. The guards would remain an exception—only there would we still begin service as non-commissioned officers. But even in the guards a sergeant of noble birth should be distinguished from the son of a soldier. The severity of military service can and should be relaxed where it does not serve to promote victory. Severity in unimportant matters lessens a man's zeal for work. Keep soldiers occupied with games and guard parades by all means, but do not wear them out in the process. Work on a man's soul rather than his body. The heroes of guard parades turn out to be cowards on the field of battle: how many times have we seen this! Officers in Catherine's time often went about in frock-coats, but they also went bravely into the attack...

* * *

States, like people, have their allotted lifespan. Thus philosophy has discovered and history has dictated. Just as a sensible mode of life prolongs a man's span, so does a sensible political system prolong the duration of states. Who can estimate the years Russia has before her? I can hear the prophets of impending doom, but thank God I do not believe them in my heart. I can see danger, but I don't yet see doom!

Russia still has 40 million inhabitants, and the autocracy is blessed with a sovereign who zealously guards the public good. If, being human, he makes mistakes, then without doubt he does so with good intentions, which serves to reassure us that he will correct them in the future.

If Alexander were in general to be more cautious in the introduction of new political institutions, striving above all to strengthen the existing ones and paying more attention to people than to forms, if through judicious severity he were to induce the lords and officials to the zealous discharge of their responsibilities... then Russia would bless Alexander, all reservations would evaporate, disaffection would disappear, habits beneficial to the state would develop, and the progress of affairs would become more regular and established. The new and the old would fuse into one, the past would be recalled less and less frequently, and malicious gossip, although it would not die down completely, would lose its sting! The fate of Europe does not now depend on us. Who knows whether France will change her terrible system, or whether God will change France; but storms do not last forever! The day when we again see clear skies over Europe and Alexander enthroned over a unified Russia, we shall extol Alexander's good fortune which he merits by virtue of his rare goodness!

Out of love for the fatherland and for the Monarch I have spoken frankly. I shall now revert to the silence of a true subject with a pure heart, praying that God will watch over the Tsar and the Russian Empire!

1811

Nikita Mikhailovich Muravev
A PROJECT FOR A CONSTITUTION (Extracts)[20]

First draft
Introduction

The experience of all nations and all epochs has shown that autocratic power is equally ruinous for both rulers and society; it accords with neither the principles of our holy faith nor those of sound reason. One cannot allow the arbitrary rule of one man to become a principle of government. One cannot accept that all rights belong to one side and all duties to the other. Blind obedience can be based only on fear and is worthy of neither a reasonable ruler nor reasonable ministers. By putting themselves above the law sovereigns have forgotten that they are thereby outside the law, outside humanity! They cannot have recourse to the law in matters concerning others and not acknowledge the law's existence when the matter concerns themselves. There are two possibilities: either the laws are just—in which case why do they not wish to submit to them themselves—or they are unjust—in which case why do they subject others to them? All European nations are securing laws and freedom. More than any other, the Russian people deserves both.

But what form of government is appropriate for the Russian people? Small nations usually fall prey to their neighbors and do not enjoy independence. Larger nations enjoy outward independence, but usually suffer from internal oppression, and in the hands of a despot they are used as a means for oppressing and destroying neighboring nations. Vast territory and a large army prevent some nations from being free; yet those nations which do not possess these inconveniences suffer because of their weakness. Only a *Federal* or *Union* government has resolved this contradiction, satisfied all conditions and reconciled a nation's greatness with the freedom of its citizens.

Under the supervision of the sovereign there is one Legislative Assembly located in the capital and responsible for the general administration of the state as a whole. Particular decisions affecting the regions are left to local legislative assemblies organized along the lines of that in the capital, and in this way the welfare of the whole and the parts can be attained...

Second Draft
Chapter I
On the Russian People and Government

1) The Russian people, free and independent, is not and cannot be the property of any single person or family.

2) The source of *supreme power* is the people, to whom belongs the exclusive right to make fundamental resolutions for itself.

Chapter II
On Citizens

3) Citizenship is defined in the procedures of this Constitution as the right to participate in the government of society, either *indirectly,* i.e., by choosing officials or electors—or *directly,* by standing oneself for election to public office in the *legislature, executive* or *judiciary* ...

5) Citizenship is dependent on meeting the following conditions: (i) being not less than 21 years old; (ii) being of known and fixed abode; (iii) being of sound mind; (iv) being personally independent; (v) being punctilious in the payment of public dues; (vi) being innocent in the eyes of the law.

6) A foreigner not born in Russia but having lived there for seven consecutive years has the right to request Russian citizenship through the courts, so long as he renounces in advance on oath all allegiance to the government to which he was previously subject.

7) No foreigner who has not acquired citizenship may carry out any civil or military duty in Russia. He does not have the right to serve in the Russian armed forces or to acquire land.

8) Twenty years from the promulgation of this Constitution of the Russian Empire no one who has not become literate in the Russian language may be recognized as a citizen.

9) A citizen loses rights of citizenship *temporarily:* (i) if he is legally declared not of sound mind; (ii) if he is on trial; (iii) if a court rules that he should temporarily sustain loss of rights; (iv) if he is declared bankrupt; (v) if he defaults on payment of public dues; (vi) if he is in the service of another individual; (vii) if is he without known abode, occupation and means of support.

Rights of citizenship are lost *permanently:* (i) if he acquires citizenship of another country; (ii) if he accepts service or a post in another country; (iii) if he is sentenced by a court to legal punishment involving loss of civil rights; (iv) if without the permission of the People's Assembly he accepts an award, pension, decoration, honorary title or paid rank from a foreign government, state or nation.

Chapter III
On the Status, Personal Rights and Duties of Russians

10) All Russians are equal before the law.

11) Considered to be Russians are all native inhabitants of Russia and the children of foreigners born in Russia who come of age, unless they declare that they do not wish to enjoy this privilege.

12) Everyone is obliged to carry out his social duties, obey the laws and authorities of the fatherland, and come to the defense of their country when the law so demands.

13) Serfdom and slavery are abolished. The slave who touches Russian soil becomes free. The distinction between well-born and commonfolk is not recognized in that it is contrary to our faith, whereby all men are *brothers,* all are *well-born* in that they are born by the will of God, all are born *for the good* and are *simply men;* for we are all weak and imperfect.

14) Everyone has the right to express his ideas and feelings without hindrance and to communicate them in print to his compatriots. Books, like all other acts, are subject to prosecution in civil court and will be tried by jury.

15) Existing merchant and trade guilds and corporations are abolished.

16) Everyone has the right to engage in whatever trade seems to him the most profitable: agriculture, cattle, hunting, fishing, craftwork, factory work, trade, etc.

17) Every litigation involving value in excess of 25 silver rubles must go before a jury.

18) Every criminal case must be tried by jury.

19) Anyone suspected of malicious intent may be taken into custody by the duly constituted authorities in accordance with recognized procedure, but within 24 hours of being in the custody of those who detained him he must be informed in writing of the reason for his detention, otherwise he must be released immediately.

20) Unless accused of a criminal offense, a detainee must be released immediately if bail is put up for him.

21) No one may be punished except in accordance with a law promulgated *before the commission of the crime* and duly and legally enacted.

22) This Constitution defines to which officials and under what circumstances will be granted the right to issue written orders for the *detention* of a citizen, for *searching his home, seizing his papers* and *opening his mail.* In the same way it assigns responsibility for such acts.

23) The right to property, referring *only to things,* is sacred and inviolable.

24) Land owned by landowners will remain their property. Peasants' homes and their gardens will be acknowledged as their property, along with all agricultural implements and cattle thereon.

25) Economic and appanage peasants will be known as *common owners,* as at present are the free farmers,[21] insofar as the land on which they live is granted to them in common ownership and is recognized as their property. The appanage administration is abolished.[22]

26) Subsequent legislation will define the process whereby these lands pass from common ownership to private ownership by individual peasants, and on what principles this division of common land between individuals will be based.

27) Peasants living on leased estates are also freed, but the land remains with those to whom it is leased for the duration of the lease...

29) The division of men into fourteen grades is abolished. Civil ranks adopted from the Germans and in no way differing from one another are abolished in accordance with ancient resolutions of the Russian people. The titles and classes of smallholder (*odnodvorets*), petit bourgeois (*meshchanin*), nobleman (*dvorianin*) and distinguished citizen (*imenityi grazhdanin*) are all replaced by the titles *Citizen* or *Russian*...

32) Citizens have the right to organize themselves into societies and associations without the need to obtain permission or assent, provided only that their actions do not contravene the law.

33) Every such society has the right to formulate its own regulations provided that they do not conflict with this Constitution or public law...

35) No violation of the law may be justified on the grounds that orders were received from superiors. First the violator will be punished and then he who has authorized the violation.

36) Citizens have the right to address their complaints and petitions to the People's Assembly, the Emperor, and the ruling bodies of the state.

37) Underground cells, fortified casemates and all so-called state dungeons in general are abolished. No one may be confined anywhere except in public prisons designated for this purpose.

38) Those remanded in custody awaiting trial should not be confined in the same place as convicted prisoners; neither should those convicted of debt or petty crime be confined with real criminals and villains.

39) Prison officers must be elected by the people from the ranks of honest citizens and must be answerable for all illegal or inhuman treatment of prisoners.

40) Present police officials are dismissed and will be replaced by public election.

41) Any citizen who by force or bribery interferes with the free election of public representatives will be brought to trial.

42) No one may be disturbed in the exercise of his religious beliefs in accordance with his conscience and feelings, provided only that these do not contravene the laws of nature or morality...

Chapter VI
On the People's Assembly

59) The People's Assembly, consisting of the *Supreme Duma* and the *Chamber of People's Representatives,* is invested with all legislative authority...

Chapter IX
On the Powers and Privileges of the People's Assembly and the Drafting of Laws

78) The People's Assembly will meet at least once a year...

79) Each Chamber itself decides on the rights and election of its members. In both a majority is sufficient for a decision...

80) Each Chamber has the right to institute procedures for the punishment of its members for unseemly behavior and criminal offenses, *but under no circumstances for their opinions...*

81) The sessions of both Chambers are public. However, at the Emperor's suggestion both Chambers may deliberate in closed session and exclude unauthorized persons in advance... Women and minors under the age of 17 are not allowed to attend sessions in either Chamber.

82) Each Chamber will keep daily minutes of its proceedings, and these will be published from time to time except when certain matters have been ruled as secret...

84) Under no circumstances, other than treason, criminal behavior, or the violation of public order, may a member of the People's Assembly be arrested during a sitting or while on his way to or from a sitting. He may not be troubled anywhere on account of what he may have said in his Chamber, and no one has the right to demand explanation of opinions he may have expressed...

85) No official in public service may serve as a member of either Chamber while he retains his official position.

86) No Representative or member of the Duma may be appointed during the period for which he is elected to any newly-created public office or to one for which the rewards are increased or improved...

88) Each bill must undergo three readings in each Chamber. A minimum of three days must elapse between readings. Each reading is followed by debate. After the first reading the bill is printed and distributed to all members present.

89) In order to acquire the force of law each bill must be submitted to the Emperor after it has been approved by the Duma and Chamber of Representatives. If the Emperor approves the bill he signs it. If not he returns it with his comments to the Chamber where it was introduced; the

Chamber enters all the Emperor's comments in its minutes and re-opens the debate. If after this second debate two-thirds of the members remain in favor of the bill, then it is transmitted to the other Chamber along with all the Emperor's comments. Here too it is debated again and if approved by a majority it becomes *law* at that point...

90) If the Emperor fails to return a bill submitted to him within a period of ten days (excluding Sundays) then the bill becomes law...

91) A bill which is thrown out by one Chamber may not be reintroduced before the next session of the People's Assembly.

92) The People's Assembly is empowered to make and abrogate judicial and executive legislation as follows: (i) Promulgate a civil, criminal, commercial and military code for Russia; establish institutions for public order, principles of legal procedure and the internal running of administrative bureaux. (ii) Legislate in cases of invasion or rebellion for a particular region to be put on a military footing or under martial law. (iii) Publish laws on amnesty. (iv) Dissolve regional government assemblies if they exceed their authority and order the electorate to proceed to new elections. (v) Declare war. (vi) Draw up statutes for the organization, maintenance, control, disposition and mobilization of land and sea forces, for the fortification of frontiers, shorelines and docks, for the recruitment and reinforcement of armed forces, and for internal security. (vii)... Legislate for all financial matters. (viii) Undertake all government measures concerning industry, the national budget, post-stations, the post-office, the maintenance of land and waterway communications and the introduction of new ones, the establishment of banks. (ix) Sponsor the sciences and the useful arts, and grant authors and inventors exclusive rights to benefits derived from their works and inventions for a given length of time. (x) Set principles for the reward of public officials, define conditions of service in all branches of the administration, and take responsibility for statistical accounts in all areas of government. (xi) Receive ministerial reports in cases of the physical or mental indisposition of the Emperor, or his death or abdication, and appoint a regent or proclaim a new Emperor. (xii) Elect regional governments.

93) The People's Assembly is not empowered to institute new constitutional laws or repeal existing ones. In other words, it cannot legislate on any matter not mentioned in this description of its powers.

94) The People's Assembly, consisting of men chosen by the Russian people and representing it, will assume the title of *Majesty*...

96) Until the People's Assembly decrees otherwise all taxes will remain as they are, with the following exceptions: (i) Those presently known as petit bourgeois (*meshchane*) are no longer required to pay more in soul-tax than economic and other peasants, and their payments will be brought into line. (ii) Minors under the age of 17, as well as people reaching the age of 60, are exempted from soul-tax. (iii) This tax is to be spread

equally among remaining citizens, insofar as all are equal before the law and must bear the same responsibilities.

97) The People's Assembly will from time to time make public a detailed account of all public income and expenditure.

98) The People's Assembly has no right either to impose or prohibit any particular religious denomination or sect. A citizen's faith, conscience and opinions are not subject to the authority of the People's Assembly, as long as they do not assume the form of illegal activities. But any sect based on depravity or unnatural practices will be prosecuted by the authorities on the basis of general decrees. The People's Assembly has no right to violate freedom of speech or of the press.

99) The People's Assembly will neither debate nor vote in the presence of the Emperor. In response to any speech by the Emperor the leaders of both Chambers must reply that the People's Assembly will take his proposals into account...

Chapter X
The Supreme Executive Power

101) The Emperor is the supreme official of the Russian Government. His rights and privileges are as follows: (i) His authority is hereditary in a direct line from father to son, but from father-in-law it passes to son-in-law. (ii) He combines in his person all executive power. (iii) He has the right to stop the processes of the legislative authorities and compel them to reconsider a law. (iv) He is supreme commander of land and sea forces. (v) He is supreme commander of any unit of the land forces on active service for the Empire. (vi) He may demand the written opinion of the head of any executive department on any matter concerned with his duties. (vii) He conducts negotiations with foreign powers and concludes peace treaties on the advice and consent of the Supreme Duma, on the basis of a two-thirds majority of members present. A treaty thus concluded becomes the law of the land. (viii) He appoints ambassadors, ministers and consuls and represents Russia in all her relations with foreign powers. He appoints all officials not specifically mentioned in this Constitution. (ix) He may not, however, include in treaties any article which violates the rights and condition of citizens within the fatherland. Likewise, he cannot without the consent of the People's Assembly stipulate conditions for attacking another country nor concede any territory belonging to Russia. (x) He appoints judges to supreme courts on the advice and consent of the Supreme Duma. (xi) He fills all posts which fall vacant when the People's Assembly is in recess. The appointed temporary officials hold office on his authorization, which remains in force until the end of the next sitting of the Duma. (xii) He appoints heads to each branch of government or each

department, that is: The Head of the Treasury (Minister of Finance), the Head of the Department of Land Forces (Minister of War), the Head of the Admiralty (Naval Minister), and the Head of the Foreign Office. (xiii) He is obliged at each session of both Chambers of the People's Assembly to report on the state of affairs in Russia and recommend those measures which he deems necessary or appropriate. (xiv) He has the right to convoke both Chambers, but the Supreme Duma only on matters concerning negotiations or state trials. (xv) He has no right to employ the military forces within Russia to deal with rebellion without approaching the People's Assembly, which must immediately satisfy itself as to the necessity of martial law. (xvi) On his insistence both Chambers will debate his proposal in secret session if he regards this as necessary. (xvii) If the Chambers cannot agree on a date of adjournment, then he may adjourn them for a period not exceeding three months. (xviii) He receives the envoys and representatives of foreign governments. (xix) He supervises the strict implementation of public laws. (xx) He authorizes the appointment of all officials of the Empire. (xxi) He is granted the title of *His Imperial Majesty*—none other is permitted... (xxii) The People's Assembly determines the formal ceremony with which this title is conferred upon a new Emperor. (xxiii) On his accession the Emperor swears the following oath in the People's Assembly: "I solemnly swear that I will faithfully carry out the duties of Russian Emperor and will with all my might preserve and defend this Constitution of Russia."

102) The Cabinet is abolished; tribute payable to the Emperor by the peoples of Siberia, as well as all other Imperial tribute, will go into the State Treasury, but the Emperor will receive the sum of two million silver rubles per annum for his own and his family's expenses. He need not render account for this sum.

103) Members of the Emperor's family are not distinguished from ordinary persons and are subject to the same institutions and governmental authority as all others. They enjoy no special rights or privileges.

104) The existence of a so-called Court cannot be legally acknowledged in a well-ordered country. Therefore although the Emperor has the power to maintain [Court officials], [the latter] cannot be considered to serve the public if they have devoted themselves to the service of a single individual, and for this reason they will receive no remuneration or salary from the public purse, although the Emperor has the right to pay them a salary from his allowance. Furthermore, they relinquish rights of citizenship, i.e., the right to elect or be elected to public office, while they remain in private service.

105) The ruler of the Empire may not leave the Empire without creating serious difficulties: (i) It would impede government affairs. (ii) The balance of power would be disturbed. (iii) It would be unbecoming for the leading public servant not to be among his public. (iv) The nation, in

the person of the ruler, might suffer gross insult from foreigners. (v) Such a journey would entail the sort of expenses prohibited by this Constitution. (vi) Moreover, when out of the country the Emperor would be more likely to be influenced by envious foreigners and become an instrument of their evil designs. For these reasons under no circumstances may the Emperor travel beyond the frontiers of the fatherland, not even to Russia's overseas colonies.[23]

106) The Emperor's departure from Russia will be understood as tantamount to his having abandoned it and having abdicated his Imperial calling. In such circumstances the People's Assembly will immediately proclaim a successor as Emperor.

107) The age of majority for an Emperor is 18 years.

108) If the successor to the throne has not reached the age of 18 then his place as Emperor is taken by the Chairman of the Supreme Duma... Every four years a new Regent is chosen in turn, first by the Duma from among members of the Chamber of Representatives, then by the Chamber of Representatives from among members of the Duma, and so on until the heir reaches the age of majority.

109) ...The Temporary Regent enjoys all the rights granted by this Constitution to the Emperor...

111) Women may not succeed to Imperial power and acquire no right to it through marriage. A country of free people is not an heirloom, nor can it be a wedding present. The title of Emperor is hereditary for the sake of convenience, and not so that it should in reality become the property of a given family. And so, when the male line is severed, the people will establish a form of rule or will proceed to the election of another royal family...

112) Apart from peace treaties, reports on the state of Russia presented to the People's Assembly, suggested measures or promulgation of laws, commissions for envoys and officials of the Empire, and laws ratified by the People's Assembly, the Emperor signs no papers. All other papers... are signed by the Heads of Departments...

114) ...The Emperor is not subject to the judicial processes. If the Emperor himself personally commits a crime, for which no other person is responsible, then this will be ascribed to his being of unsound mind, and the People's Assembly will at once institute a regency...

1821-22

Pavel Ivanovich Pestel
RUSSIAN LAW (Extracts)[24]

Introduction: Fundamental Concepts

Every association of several persons for the attainment of a given aim is called a society. The stimulus for such an association, or its aim, is the gratification of common needs, which, as they arise from common and identical properties in human nature, are the same for all men. It follows from this that members of any society are able to agree unanimously on the aim. But when it comes to the actions or means to be employed to attain this aim, then violent argument and endless disagreement must arise among them, since the selection of means derives not so much from common properties in human nature as from the particular character and personal qualities of each separate individual. The character and personal qualities of people are so diverse that if everyone were to be inflexible in his opinions and not heed those of others, then there would be no possibility of choosing means for the attainment of a given aim, let alone of marshaling them and putting them into effect. In such cases nothing would remain to be done other than destroy society before each action. But if the members do not wish to see their society destroyed then each of them must be prepared to modify some of his own opinions and personal ideas in order to create a single consensus, on the basis of which means which lead to action may be chosen.

But who will propose such a definitive opinion? Who will select the means? Who will determine the methods? Who will arrange the action? All these difficulties may be resolved in two ways. In the first, the moral superiority of one or more members of society reconciles all the various difficulties and carries other people with it by the force of its superiority, sometimes with the assistance of other, external factors. In the second case, the members of society entrust one or more among them with the responsibility of selecting the means and grant them the right to take charge of the common effort. In each of these cases members of society are divided into those who command and those who obey. This division is inevitable because it derives from human nature, and so it exists, and must exist, everywhere. On this natural division is based the difference in the duties and rights of both categories of person... When a civil society acquires the name of state, then those who command are known as the Government and those who obey are known as the People. From this it follows that the main and primary components of every state are the government and the people.

The government is responsible for taking charge of common activity and for choosing the best means to secure the happiness of each and every person in the state. Therefore it has the right to demand obedience from the people. The people have a duty to obey the government, but in return they may demand that the government should work unfailingly towards the attainment of social and personal happiness and should command only that which leads truly to this goal and is necessary for the attainment of the goal. Only on this balance of mutual obligations and mutual rights can the existence of any state be based, and therefore when it loses this balance a state shifts from a natural and salutary condition to one which is coercive and sick. The main aim of this "Russian Law," and the basic duty of any legislator, is to establish this balance on a firm foundation...

In a state, therefore, the main point is the concept of obligations entailing corresponding rights. Obligations in a state derive from the aim of the state. The aim of a state system ought to be the greatest possible happiness of each and every member. Therefore everything that leads to such happiness is an obligation. But insofar as concepts of happiness are many and varied, there is a need to establish some basic or fundamental rules. The primary and most essential obligations are those God imposes on man through faith. They link the spiritual world with the natural, this transient life with life eternal, and for this reason all state regulations should be linked to, and be in accordance with, man's obligations in respect of faith and the Almighty Creator. This first sort of obligation concerns the spiritual world, and is known to us from the Holy Scriptures. The second sort concerns the natural world. These are known to us from the laws of nature and natural needs. God, as the Creator of the universe, also created the laws of nature and natural needs. These laws are deeply inscribed in our hearts. Every man is subject to them and no one is capable of subverting them. Accordingly, state regulations should correspond just as much to the immutable laws of nature as to the sacred precepts of faith. Finally, a third category of obligations arises out of the formation of civil societies or states. The first rule in this case is that all the state's efforts in the pursuit of happiness must accord with spiritual and natural laws. The second rule is that all state statutes must be directed solely towards the wellbeing of civil society, and therefore any act contrary to this wellbeing, or injurious to it, must be considered criminal. The third rule is that the wellbeing of society must be regarded as more important than individual happiness, and if the two conflict then the former should take priority. The fourth rule is that the wellbeing of society should be defined as the happiness of the totality of the people, from which it follows that the real aim of a state system must necessarily be the greatest possible good of the greatest number of people in the state. This is why the benefit of the individual part must always yield to the benefit of the whole, the whole being the totality or mass of the people. The fifth and final rule is that the individual, in the pursuit of personal happiness, must not step outside his own area of action and encroach upon the activities of others—in other words, the happiness of one should not bring harm, still less ruin, to another. As soon as all the actions of government and private individuals are based on these rules the state will enjoy the greatest possible wellbeing. All laws and government statutes must necessarily and fully accord with these rules.

...The government exists for the good of the people, and has no other grounds for its existence... whereas the people exists for its own sake and to carry out the will of God, Who has called upon men in this world to glorify His name and be virtuous and happy... Therefore the Russian people is not the possession or property of any individual or family. On the contrary, the government belongs to the people—it is established for the good of the people, and it is not the people which exists for the good of the government.

...Applying these immutable and indisputable basic principles to Russia it is clear to see that these very principles necessarily demand a change in the existing political order in Russia and its replacement by a structure based solely on precise and just laws and statutes, which will leave nothing to personal and arbitrary will and which will assure the Russian people with complete exactness that it is indeed an organized civil society and not someone's property or possession, which it never can be. From this emerge two main requirements for Russia: first, the complete transformation of the political order and its organization; and second, the publication of a complete new code of laws which will preserve what is of value and eradicate what is harmful.

This double goal cannot successfully be attained other than through the establishment of a Provisional Supreme Administration and the publication of a Russian Law for all to see.

Chapter I
[Russia is a Single and Indivisible State]

States may be either *unitary* or *federal.*

Unitary states are those in which all the parts or regions which make up the state possess and recognize the same supreme authority, the same form of rule and the same laws, and where no single region has the right individually to issue its own laws and statutes.

Federal states are those in which the regions, although recognizing the same supreme authority and being committed to act jointly in all foreign affairs, nonetheless reserve the right to make their own laws and issue their own statutes on their own internal civil and political matters, and to organize their government in the way they each see fit...

At first glance the federal state system might seem convenient and pleasant, for each region is granted the possibility of acting according to its own will and discretion. But on close examination one is soon convinced of the decisive advantage which the unitary state structure has over the federal, particularly as far as Russia is concerned, with its vast territory and the large number of different races and peoples inhabiting it.

The general disadvantages of the federal state system include the following among many others:

1) The supreme authority in a federal system in effect issues not laws, but merely advice, since it can effect its laws only through the local authorities and has no other means of enforcement of its own. If a region does not wish to follow this advice, then it can only be compelled to do so through internecine war. It follows from this that the seed of destruction is planted at the very root of the system.

2) Individual laws, individual forms of rule, as well as the individual concepts and patterns of thinking which emerge from these, further weaken the link between the various regions. They will come to regard the supreme authority as a tiresome and unpleasant thing, and each regional government will argue that it could have arranged state affairs regarding its own region better without the interference of the supreme authority. Another seed of destruction.

3) Each region, forming so to speak a small separate state within the federal state, will be only tenuously connected to the whole, and even in war-time it might act without enthusiasm for the overall state structure, particularly if a cunning enemy were clever enough to woo it with promises of regional advantages and privileges. The particular wellbeing of the region might in the short term have a more decisive influence on the imagination of its rulers and people than the general wellbeing of the whole state, the benefits of which for the region may not be readily apparent at a given time.

4) The word "state" will in such a system be an empty word, since nowhere will people be aware of the state, only of their region. Thus love of the fatherland will be reduced to love of one of its regions...

As far as Russia in particular is concerned, we need only remember just how heterogeneous are the components which make up this large state in order to be fully convinced of how ruinous the federal state system would be. Not only are its regions governed by various institutions and judged by various civil laws, but they also speak different tongues and profess different faiths. Their inhabitants are of different origins and at one time belonged to different powers. So if this heterogeneity were to be reinforced through a federal system, it is easy to predict just how quickly these diverse regions would secede from the Russian core, which would lose in the process not only its power, greatness and strength, but also perhaps its very existence as one of the principal great states. Russia would once again experience all the woes and unutterable harm inflicted in ancient times by the appanage system, which was nothing more than a kind of federal state structure.[25] Thus, if other states can still doubt the harm caused by the federal system, Russia cannot afford to share such doubts. She has paid dearly in bitter experience and long years of disaster for this mistake in her past political structure. And so, taking all these factors into account, the fundamental law of the Russian state will decree that all thoughts of adopting a federal structure be rejected out of hand as utterly ruinous and wholly evil.

Consequent upon what has been said here, the Russian state... is declared to be single and indivisible, and all federal principles in the structure, organization and existence of the state are totally rejected...

Chapter III
[All Must be Equal before the Law]

...Civil societies, and consequently states too, are created for the greatest possible good of each and every citizen, and not for the good of the few at the expense of the majority. All people in a state have an equal right to the benefits afforded by that state, and all are equally obliged to bear the burdens associated with state organization. It follows from this that all people in the state must necessarily be completely equal before the law and that any statute which violates this equality is an intolerable abuse which must be eradicated...

[The Nobility]

The nobility is an estate, quite separate from the masses of the people, which has its own special privileges, detailed in the following five points: 1) The nobility owns other people, regarding them as its own property and calling them serfs... 2) The nobility pays no capitation tax and makes no contribution to the general welfare. 3) The nobility may not be sentenced to corporal punishment like other Russians, not even for the most heinous offenses. 4) The nobility is not subject to conscription, and it occupies all offices and posts in the government to the exclusion of other Russians. 5) The nobility is known as the class of the wellborn, having coats of arms in addition to various titles.

These five privileges constitute nobility. The word "privilege" is used here, rather than "right," because the advantages mentioned and enjoyed by the nobility are not based on any prior obligations, nor are they necessary for the discharge of any obligation. Therefore they cannot be regarded as rights. Moreover, not only are these advantages not based on prior obligations, but on the contrary they even serve to excuse those who enjoy them from all obligations; and so they must be recognized as privileges rather than rights. We must now consider whether, in a well-ordered state, such privileges should be granted to a particular class.

1) To own other men like property, to sell them, mortgage them, give them away or inherit them like objects, to use them according to one's whims without their prior consent and solely for one's own profit, gain, even at times caprice, is shameful, contrary to humanity, contrary to natural laws, contrary to the Holy Christian faith, and contrary, finally, to the commandments of the Almighty, Who has declared through the Holy Scriptures that all men are equal in His sight and that only their deeds and their virtues create differences between them. Therefore, no longer in Russia can one man be permitted to own another and call him his serf.

2) A civil society is created for the greatest possible good of each and every citizen. This is achieved by various means and processes, among which is the need to collect revenues. Since all citizens have an equal right to enjoy society's benefits, they have an equal obligation to contribute to the creation of these benefits. Moreover, only a corrupt authority would heap all the burdens on some and all the advantages on others... Therefore the nobility cannot be exempted from the payment of taxes.

3) The nature of punishment should correspond to the nature of the crime, and not to the social class of the criminal; for crime is the product of a person's evil qualities and not a mark of his belonging to a particular class... Therefore the nobility should be in the same position as other Russians and be subject to the same punishments for similar crimes. If corporal punishment is deemed necessary, then it should be applied to the nobility just as it is to others.

4) The recruitment of conscripts into the army is an institution essential for the security of the state and its very existence, and so it must necessarily exist. But since the benefits derived from military power are felt equally by all members of society, then all social classes should play an equal part in making up this power. The nobility, therefore, cannot be relieved of this personal obligation, and its present privileged position in this respect should be abolished... As far as the nobility's exclusive right to occupy all public offices is concerned, then this right must be distributed among all Russians in general and should cease to be the exclusive privilege of the nobility alone. Whoever earns the right to a public office by virtue of his knowledge, capabilities and qualities should be entitled to exercise this right on principle, without regard to his background or class.

5) People are all born for the good in the sense that they are all created by the Almighty, and therefore it is unjust to reserve the term "wellborn" just for the nobility. Consequently, the nobility's privileged use of this term should be abolished. The titles of Prince, Duke, Count, Baron, etc. all derive from the time when such titles indicated various positions or levels

in the power structure. But since nowadays they signify neither one nor the other, then they are merely empty sounds which serve only to gratify inflated vanity and proud conceit. So such titles cannot exist in a state... based on real justice, true morality, good sense and reason...

[Serfs of the Nobility]

The achievements of widespread enlightenment, which are spreading ever further and wider, the better understanding of the relationship between the various members and parts of the state, the spirit of the age which strives towards freedom based on law—all of these compel us to desire the complete abolition of serfdom in Russia and not to forget the value of the peasant class, particularly at a time when Russia is aiming to establish a sound legal order and to improve the condition and status of all its other social classes... But since such an important undertaking demands mature reflection and will bring about an extremely important change in the state, it cannot be brought to a satisfactory conclusion unless it is introduced gradually. The Supreme Administration should invite projects for dealing with this matter from competent assemblies of the nobility, and then take measures on the basis of these projects, always being guided by the following three main principles: 1) The emancipation of the serfs should not deprive members of the nobility of the income which they receive from their estates. 2) The emancipation must not lead to unrest and disorder in the state, and the Supreme Administration must undertake to treat all who breach the peace with merciless severity. 3) The emancipation must lead to an improvement of the peasant's present condition, and not merely grant him the illusion of freedom.

[Domestic Serfs]

Domestic serfs are the most pitiful estate in the whole of Russia. A soldier conscripted for 25 years at least gains his freedom at the end of his term and may then take up the occupation of his choice. The domestic serf serves his master his whole life long and has no right to hope; the will of his lord alone is his lot until the end of his days. Such a state of affairs can be allowed to continue no longer, and all that has been said in the preceding paragraph about the peasants applies also to domestic serfs. The Supreme Administration should ask competent assemblies of the nobility to submit projects for dealing with these too, with a view to devising means for the gradual emancipation of domestic serfs.

In this respect two possible methods could profitably be employed. The first would be to specify a number of years within which the domestic serf must gain his freedom from his master. The second would be to fix a sum of money which would allow the domestic serf to buy his freedom... The fixing of the redemption sum would take into account particular circumstances and the various skills which masters might have taught their domestics. Even with these arrangements there will still be domestics who remain serfs, and for these cases in particular the projects mentioned earlier... will be needed...

[The Land]

Man can live only on the land and can derive his living only from the land; therefore, the land is the property of the whole human race, and no one should be excluded from the use of it, either directly or indirectly. First, thought must be given to producing enough for every man to be able to survive, then to producing a surplus. To the first every man has an indisputable right, simply because he is a man. But only he who knows how to acquire it has a right to the second. Having created the opportunity for every man to acquire life's basic essentials, without in the process subjugating him to others, it will be necessary to safeguard a man's complete freedom to acquire and retain any surplus... The means to this lie in dividing the land in every district (*volost'*) into two halves... One half will be designated common land, the other private land. The common land will be jointly owned by all inhabitants of the district and will become their inalienable property; it may be neither sold nor mortgaged. It will be set aside for the purpose of providing all citizens without exception with their basic needs, and may be used by each and every one of them. Private land will belong either to the state or to private individuals who will have complete freedom of possession and the right to do with it what they wish. These lands, intended for the creation of private wealth, will serve to produce surplus... In this way every citizen is assured of his basic needs and those who are in a position to take advantage of it are granted the full freedom to acquire surplus. If at first sight the introduction of such a system seems fraught with major difficulties one only has to remember... that such a decision would be likely to encounter far greater difficulties in countries other than Russia, for in Russia popular understanding has always inclined towards it and has been accustomed from ancient times to seeing the land thus divided into two parts.

1814-23

Part II

Early Russian Idealism;
From the Wisdom-Lovers to the Slavophiles

Introduction

The failure of the Decembrist revolt had important consequences for Russian political and intellectual life. The most immediately apparent of these was the period of reaction ushered in by Nicholas I, whose attempts to contain revolutionary activity through the imposition of intellectual conformity culminated in the theory of Official Nationality introduced by his Minister of Education, Sergei Uvarov, in the early 1830s. But the failure of Decembrism was also seen by some Russian intellectuals as a final confirmation of the bankruptcy of such Enlightenment values as rationalism, legalism and empiricism. There had been a pronounced anti-Enlightenment trend in Russian thought since the Napoleonic wars and this had taken the form of increasing disaffection with rationalism and growing interest in metaphysical and mystical modes of thought. The mysticism of Alexander I and the rise of Freemasonry during his reign serve to illustrate this trend, as does the Romantic nationalism which followed Napoleon's defeat in 1812.

The shift away from Enlightenment ideals was matched by a developing interest in German Romanticism. In the 1820s great enthusiasm was shown for Schelling's philosophy of nature and philosophy of art by a group of young men who called themselves "Wisdom-Lovers" (*Liubomudry*) and who formed a secret society in 1823. The founders of this society were V.F. Odoevsky, N.M. Rozhalin, D.V. Venevitinov, A.I. Koshelev and I.V. Kireevsky. Their choice of the term "liubomudrie" to denote speculation, in place of the more Western "filosofiia," suggests their desire to break with eighteenth-century rationalism. The Wisdom-Lovers published an almanac *Mnemosyne* in 1824-25 and although their society was hurriedly disbanded in the aftermath of the Decembrist revolt their influence continued to be felt throughout the 1820s and into the 1830s.

Taking their lead from their German mentor the Wisdom-Lovers and their followers developed an organic and intuitive philosophy of nature in opposition to the mechanistic and rationalistic view conceived by Enlightenment thinkers. Nature was seen not as an objective, mechanical and material entity, separated from consciousness and subject to rational comprehension, but rather as the outward physical manifestation of the spirit which informs and unifies all being. All creation, including consciousness, thus forms an organic whole comprehensible only through intuitive and supra-rational modes of cognition. Art was a vital tool in the perception of the metaphysical, rather than physical, nature of reality, in that inspiration afforded a means of transcending the material world.

Such a view of nature encouraged a similarly Romantic philosophy of history. These Russian idealists in their flight from materialism spurned the view that history was the outcome of physical laws as these were understood by man and subsequently applied to the natural world. Instead history was considered to obey metaphysical laws; it was, to borrow Belinsky's later, Hegelian phrase, "thought thinking itself."[1] The events of history were outward symptoms of the growth of a unitary universal purpose. True enlightenment consisted not in the rational analysis of, and mechanical interference in, the growth of this organism, but in the intuitive grasp of the process and one's role in it, whether as individual or nation. The "virtues" of enlightened, civilized nations—scepticism, rationalism, analysis and materialism—served if anything to conceal the patterns of history from those who practiced them. Conversely, relatively primitive nations in which instinct had not been overlaid by analysis were more closely attuned to the rhythms of progress. The same ideas were applied to social and political structures; attempts to understand and even construct societies on the basis of mechanical, rational and contractual principles ran counter to nature. Nations too were organisms instinctively obeying collective principles, not structures held together by agreements. True law was moral, not juridical.

As Isaiah Berlin observes, ideas such as these, particularly when they were reinforced by the remarkable spread of Hegelianism in Russia, drew educated Russians in both a reactionary and a progressive direction.[2] Some discovered in the specter of history obeying the requirements of organic growth only the cul-de-sac of historical passivity and fatalism. Others sensed that if history were a process of constant change it would be irrational not to act in a way which would further the cause of revolution. In each case such ideas fostered among Russians an unprecedented interest in the nature of history and speculation about the historical role prescribed for Russia, a nation which many felt had to a greater degree than others preserved its national instincts. After all only a tiny minority of Russians had been touched by the alien trappings of Enlightenment thought.

Yet there was a darker side to this Romantic nationalism: Nicholas I exploited such interest in Russian national characteristics and the reaction against European rationalism to promote the most reactionary chauvinism and bolster his oppressive regime. The theory of Official Nationality was an attempt to intellectualize reaction, and its central tenets were delineated by Uvarov in 1833:

Our common obligation consists in this: that the education of the people be conducted in the joint spirit of Orthodoxy, Autocracy and Nationality...
In the midst of the rapid collapse in Europe of religious and civil institutions, at the time of a general spread of destructive ideas, at the

sight of grievous phenomena surrounding us on all sides, it is necessary to establish our fatherland on firm foundations upon which is based the wellbeing, strength and life of a people. It is necessary to find the principles which form the distinctive character of Russia, and which belong only to Russia; it is necessary to gather into one whole the sacred remnants of Russian nationality and to fasten to them the anchor of our salvation.[3]

The "theory" became jingoism and its three central tenets a slogan aimed at promoting among Russians submission in place of questioning, admiration for traditional institutions such as "paternal" autocracy, and a belief in the superiority of all things Russian to their Western equivalents.

It was against this background that Pyotr Chaadaev (1793-1856) published his first *Philosophical Letter* in the journal *Telescope (Teleskop)* in 1836. Chaadaev, a man of brilliant intellect who had served in the Napoleonic campaigns but had resigned his commission in 1821, had completed his *Letter* in 1829 after a period devoted to the study of the philosophy of history. This study had been prompted by a time spent in Western Europe between 1823 and 1826, during which Chaadaev came to recognize Russia's cultural isolation and backwardness. In this period he also met Schelling and came under the sway of German metaphysical idealism. The *Letter* was the first in a series of eight and the only one to be published in Chaadaev's lifetime. Its appearance produced a sensational reaction: Chaadaev was officially pronounced insane and kept under house arrest until 1838; the editor and censor of *Telescope* were discharged and the journal itself suppressed. Alexander Herzen likened the appearance of the *Letter* to a pistol shot ringing out in the dark night of Nicholaevan Russia.[4]

In fact Chaadaev's *Letter* presented a devastating critique of Russia and her history which challenged the basic assumptions of Official Nationality. Russia's isolation from other cultures and lack of historical continuity were seen by Chaadaev as the inevitable concomitants of an "inorganic" culture based wholly upon borrowing. Cut off from European cultural growth by the adoption of Byzantine Christianity, Russia had contented herself with the wholesale appropriation of the superficial products of other cultures. She had contributed nothing distinctive to the universal history of mankind. If Russia was to play a positive role in the history of the world she must rejoin the European cultural organism and repeat, if need be, the whole history of that world.

Chaadaev's critique of Russia is rooted in a philosophy of history which affirms the centrality of the principle of unity. History is unified in its articulation of the designs of a single divine Idea, which Chaadaev calls Providence and which is represented on earth in the unity of the Roman Church. The history of Catholic Europe is thus the history of the elaboration of a single idea and a single purpose. Russia, sunk in its Orthodox separatism, is guilty of historical egoism which disrupts the unity of history. Nations, like individuals, must learn to submit and play out their role in the historical drama.

Chaadaev's relegation of Russia to the historical dustbin and his affirmation of the superiority of Western cultures created widespread resentment among his countrymen. Possibly as a consequence of this he went on in a later work, the *Apologia of a Madman* (1837), to draw less austere conclusions about Russian history from the same philosophical premises. He now argued that perhaps Russia's very isolation and non-participation in universal culture expressed the historical role determined for her by Providence. Fresh and untainted by the culture of the West, she was able to be the bearer of some wholly new idea or principle which would set universal history on a further stage in its growth.

The questions implicit in Chaadaev's paradoxical views on Russia were to dominate Russian intellectual history for decades to come: what were the principles of Russian culture, if any, and how did they differ from those of Europe? Was Russian culture superior or inferior to European culture? Did Russia's future lay in emulation of the West or in the pursuit of native tradition? The discussion of such questions in private and often secret "philosophical circles" (for the universities had been tamed under Nicholas's repression) fuelled the great debate between *Westernizers* and *Slavophiles* during the 1830s and 1840s. The Westernizers were a loosely knit group of often diverse thinkers who shared a common belief that Russia was a backward European nation which should benefit from European rationalism and progress and adopt the fruits of European civilization, in order to discover its own ultimately distinctive historical aim. The Westernizers were sceptical of the value of "distinctively Russian" traditions and institutions, such as serfdom, autocracy and Orthodoxy, in which they saw nothing but reactionary darkness.

The early Slavophiles were more clearly a definite "group" and they shared a common core of convictions which extended the Westernizer-Slavophile disagreement beyond the immediate question of Russia's relationship to Western Europe and induced profound debate on such fundamental issues as the value of religion, whether material or spiritual values should form the basis of a society, and how the concepts of freedom and authority should be understood. The Slavophiles advocated a specifically spiritual, as opposed to materialist, culture and they considered that the principles of such a culture, now hopelessly deformed in the West, had survived in pre-Petrine Russia and could still be discerned beneath the thin European veneer of the Petrine state.

Central to Slavophile ideology were the historical and theological writings of Alexei Khomyakov (1804-60), a nobleman of singular breadth of learning, whose profound knowledge of Orthodox theology was matched by an informed respect for German Romantic thought and who corresponded widely with many leading churchmen and intellectuals of his time. The roots of Khomyakov's world-view may be found in his fragmentary *Notes on Universal History*. Here he contends that "freedom and necessity constitute the hidden principle around which all human thought is in various ways concentrated."[5] Human history illustrates the opposition of these principles: some nations are founded on the principle of Necessity, which Khomyakov terms "Kushite" (from the Biblical land of Kush -Ethiopia); others on the principle of Freedom, which he describes as "Iranian." The Western nations embody the principle of Necessity, for their societies are based upon rigid laws which are external to man—the laws of nature, reason, science and society, all demanding obedience. Russia, however, is an Iranian nation; its social relations are based not on necessity but on the sense of free organic unity, not on an extraneous law, but on an inner moral law, shared by all men. This sensed inner moral law defines Russia as a religious culture, quite distinct from the essentially secular and contractual societies of Western Europe. Khomyakov used the term *sobornost'* (conciliarism) to describe this sense of communality and unity freely acknowledged rather than externally imposed, and he defended it as a feature of Orthodox nations. *Sobornost'* reconciles those human aspirations towards unity and freedom which are mutually exclusive in Catholic and Protestant Europe. As he insists in the extracts given here, Catholicism offers unity at the expense of freedom and Protestantism freedom at the expense of unity. In Russia, however, the Orthodox Church and social institutions such as the peasant commune testify to the nation's instinct for communality without the sacrifice of personal freedom.

Ivan Kireevsky (1806-56), erstwhile Wisdom-Lover and during the early 1830s of Westernizer outlook, became one of the foremost ideologists of Slavophilism. For much of his life he was personally close to Khomyakov and he used the latter's historical views to construct a coherent critique of Western European culture. Kireevsky sensed in the West a purposelessness, lack of conviction and moral apathy which he attributed to the "painful inadequacy" of European abstract thought and the "one-sided, deceptive, corrupting and treacherous" rationalism visited upon Western civilization by the three influences of Roman Catholicism, the primitive barbarian world which destroyed the Roman Empire, and the ancient, pagan, classical world. These led to the triumph of formal reason over all other modes of cognition. Without rejecting the value of reason, Kireevsky argued that it must be supplemented by other forms of perception to achieve the ideal of "integral knowledge." Alone it could yield only disillusion and despair. Russia's role was to afford a new religious culture combining the fruits of knowledge and faith.

In a memorandum submitted to Alexander II on his accession in 1855

Konstantin Aksakov (1817-60) attempted to draw from Slavophile ideology conclusions about Russia's social and political structures. His work serves above all else to explain the political failure of Slavophilism, for the theological and epistemological roots of the movement could translate only into the most naive and childlike political philosophy. Aksakov's memorandum provides a political utopia, an idealized vision of pre-Petrine Muscovy as a never-never land where the people do not aspire to political power but enjoy unlimited moral freedom, where the monarch rules not despotically but as a benign, paternalistic custodian, and where the relationship between ruler and people is based on the principle of non-interference. Such a mythical vision, as Raeff observes,[6] ill-befitted an emerging modern nation which had survived the reaction of Nicholas I, albeit with lasting scars, and which was now poised on the brink of political and social reforms which were, in the eyes of many, to make political revolution inevitable. The Slavophiles had even less to offer the new, radicalized generation of intellectuals than they had had to offer their fathers. By the 1860s, and with the deaths of its leading exponents, classical Slavophilism had departed the political arena. Despite the survival of Slavophile-related ideas such as *pochvennichestvo* (the cult of the Soil) and Panslavism, and the clear debt owed by the Populists to certain Slavophile tenets, Russian political thought was henceforth to be dominated by the doctrines of those who had emerged from under the wing of Westernism.

Pyotr Yakovlevich Chaadaev
LETTERS ON THE PHILOSOPHY OF HISTORY

Letter I

Madame,[7]

...With regard to external matters, it is enough for now for you to know that only the doctrine founded on the supreme principle of *unity* and the direct transmission of truth through an uninterrupted succession of its ministers is the one which most conforms with the true spirit of religion, for it is epitomized in the idea of the fusion of all the moral forces in the world into a single thought, a single feeling, and in the gradual establishment of a social system or *Church,* which will make truth reign among men. Any other doctrine, by the mere fact of its separation from the original teaching, rejects the effect of the sublime invocation of Our Saviour: "Holy Father, keep them in Thy name which Thou has given me, that they may be one, as we also are,"[8] and does not desire the reign of God on earth...

I believe I once told you that the best way to preserve religious feeling is to observe all the customs prescribed by the Church. This exercise in submission, which involves more than is commonly realized and which the greatest minds have consciously imposed upon themselves after due reflection, is true worship rendered unto God. Nothing so fortifies the spirit in its beliefs as the strict observance of all obligations attached to them. Moreover, most of the rites in the Christian religion, inspired by Supreme Reason, are of real efficacy for those who know how to experience the truths they express...

There is a certain aspect of life which pertains not to physical being, but to intelligence. It must not be neglected. There is a regime for the soul as there is for the body. One must know how to submit to it. This an old truth, I know, but it seems to me that in our country it still very often has all the force of novelty. One of the most deplorable features of our peculiar civilization is that we are still only beginning to discover truths which have long been truisms elsewhere, even among nations less advanced in certain respects than we are. This is the result of our never having marched in step with other nations; we belong to none of the great families of mankind; we are neither of the West nor of the East, and we possess the traditions of neither. Standing, as it were, outside time, we have not been touched by the universal education of mankind.

That wonderful intermingling of human ideas through the succession of the centuries, that history of the human spirit which has led man to the heights he has reached today in the rest of the world, has had no effect on us. That which in other lands has long constituted the very basis of social life is still only theory and speculation for us. Let me ask you, Madame, by way of illustration: you, who are in so fortunate a position to benefit from all that is true and good in the world and neglect nothing which will bring the sweetest and purest joys to the soul, where are you, I ask, with all these advantages? You are still wondering how to fill your day, let alone your life. You lack completely those things which elsewhere constitute the necessary framework for life, within which daily events are arranged naturally, and which are as indispensable for a healthy moral life as fresh air is for a healthy physical existence. You understand I am not speaking here of moral principles or philosophical maxims, but simply of a well-ordered life and those habits and intellectual routines which ease the spirit and regulate the soul.

Look around you. Don't we all have one foot in the air? We all look as though we are traveling. No one has a definite sphere of existence; no one has proper habits; there are no rules for anything; there is no home base; everything passes, leaving no trace either outside or within us. In our home we are like visitors, among our families we are like strangers, in our cities we are like nomads, more nomadic than those whose animals graze on our steppes, for they are more attached to their deserts than we are to our cities. And you must not think that this is not important. Poor souls that we are, let us not add ignorance of ourselves to our other afflictions; let us not pretend to a life of pure intelligence; let us learn to live reasonably within our given reality. But first let us talk a bit more about our country; it will not deflect us from our theme. Without this preamble you will not grasp what I have to say to you.

Every nation has a period of violent agitation, of passionate unrest, of activity without conscious aim. During these periods men become wanderers over the world, in both body and spirit. This is an age of grand emotions, of great undertakings and great national passion. At such times nations toss about vigorously, without apparent object, but not without benefit for generations to come. All societies have passed through such periods. They provide societies with their most vivid memories, their heroic legends, their poetry, with all their strongest and most fertile ideas. These represent the necessary basis for a society. Otherwise it would have nothing in its memory to cling to or to cherish; it would have only the dust of its earth. This interesting epoch in a nation's history represents its adolescence, the moment when its faculties develop most forcefully, and the memory of which provides joy and edification in its age of maturity. We Russians have none of this. At first brutal barbarism, then crude superstition, then cruel and degrading foreign domination,[9] the spirit of which was later inherited by our national rulers—such is the sad history of our youth. We had nothing like that period of exuberant activity, the exalted play of a nation's moral forces. The period in our social life which corresponds to this moment was filled with a dull and somber existence, lacking vigor and energy, when nothing animated us but crime and nothing pacified us but servitude. There are no charming recollections or gracious images in our national memory, nor forceful lessons in our national tradition. Cast a glance over all the centuries through which we have lived and over all the land we inhabit—you will find no endearing memory, no venerable monument to speak to you forcefully of the past or allow you to relive it in a vivid and picturesque manner. We live only in the narrowest of presents, without a past and without a future, in the midst of a flat calm. And if we manage to stir ourselves from time to time it is not in the hope or desire for some common good, but with the puerile frivolity of a child who raises himself and stretches out his hands towards the rattle which his nurse offers him.

The true development of mankind in society does not begin for any nation until life has become more ordered, easier and sweeter than it was amidst the uncertainties of its earlier epoch. As long as societies are poised without convictions and without rules even for day-to-day affairs, as long as life has no purpose, how can you expect the seeds of good to germinate in them? This is the chaotic fermentation of things in the moral world, similar to the upheavals in the earth which preceded the present state of the planet. We are still at this stage.

Our first years, spent in immobile brutishness, have left no trace on our minds, and we have nothing of our own on which to base our thinking. Moreover, cut off by a strange destiny from the universal movement of humanity, we have not even assimilated any of mankind's traditional ideas. Yet it is on these ideas that the lives of nations are founded; it is from these ideas that their future grows and their moral development unfolds. If we wish to acquire an outlook similar to that of other civilized nations we have somehow or other to repeat the whole education of mankind. To help us in this we have before us the history of other nations and the results of the passing of centuries. Without doubt this is a difficult task, and possibly it is not given to one man to exhaust this vast subject, but before anything else we must understand what we are dealing with, what is this education of mankind, and what is the place we occupy in the general order.

Nations live by the mighty impressions which past centuries have left upon their minds and by contact with other nations. In this way each individual is aware of his link with humanity as a whole.

What is the life of man, asked Cicero, if the memory of past events does not serve to bind the present with the past. But we Russians, entering the world like illegitimate children, without a heritage, without a link with those who lived on earth before us, we have in our hearts none of those lessons learned before we came into being. Each one of us must seek to renew the bond that has been broken in the family. What is a matter of habit and instinct among other nations we must drive into our heads with hammer blows. Our memories do not go back beyond yesterday; we are in a certain sense strangers to ourselves. We march through time so singularly that as we advance the past escapes us irrevocably. This is the natural consequence of a culture based wholly on borrowing and imitation. With us there is no inner development, no natural progression; new ideas sweep away the old ones because they don't derive from them, but come to us from who knows where. Since we accept only ready-made ideas, those indelible traces left in men's minds by a progressive development of ideas, giving them strength, have no effect on our intelligence. We grow, but we do not mature; we advance, but obliquely, that is in a way which leads nowhere. We are like children who have not learned to think for themselves; when they become adults they have nothing of their own; all their knowledge is on the surface of their being; their whole soul is outside them. This is precisely our situation.

Nations are just as much moral beings as individuals are. They are educated over the centuries, whereas individuals are educated over years. In a way you can say that we are an exceptional people. We are one of those nations which does not seem to form an integral part of humanity, but which exists only to serve as a great lesson to the world. The lesson we are destined to provide will certainly not go unnoticed, but who knows when we shall again take our place in the midst of humanity, and what miseries we shall have to endure before we reach our destiny?

The peoples of Europe have a common physiognomy, a family resemblance. Despite the broad division of these people into Latin and Teutonic branches, into southern and northern, there is a common bond which unites them in one whole and which is clear to anyone who has studied in depth their common history. You know that it was not very long ago when all Europe was called Christendom, and this word had its place in public law. As well as this general character, each of these peoples has a particular character, which is, however, simply a part of its history and tradition. It is the hereditary patrimony of ideas of these peoples. Every individual in these nations enjoys his share of this heritage, and during his lifetime he amasses without strain or effort the notions which permeate his society, and profits by them. You can draw the comparison yourself and see how much we can gain in this way from the simple commerce of elementary ideas, to be used for better or worse in directing our lives. And bear in mind that this is not a matter of study or reading, or anything literary or scientific, but is simply the contact of intelligences, the kind of ideas which the infant acquires in his cradle, which surround him in his play, which he gets from his mother's caresses, and which in the form of a variety of sensations penetrate the very marrow of his bones, along with the air he breathes, forming his moral being even before he is delivered into the world and society. Do you want to know what these ideas are? They are the ideas of duty, justice, law and order. They derive from the very events which form societies over in Europe; they are integral elements in the social life of these nations.

Such is the atmosphere of the West. This is more than history, more than psychology; it is the physiology of European man. What have we got in our country to put in its place? I don't know if we can deduce from what I have just said anything perfectly absolute, or derive from it some firm principle, but we can see that the strange situation of a people whose thought cannot be linked to any set of ideas progressively developing in society, one slowly giving rise to another, and a people which has taken no part in the general development of the human spirit, apart from the blind, superficial and, more often than not, clumsy imitation of other nations, must have a powerful effect on the spirit of every individual in it.

As a result you will find that we all lack a certain confidence, a certain method in our thinking, and a certain logic. The western syllogism is unknown to us. It is something more than frivolity which afflicts our best minds. The finest ideas, lacking relationship or context, are paralyzed like sterile visions in our heads. It is in the nature of man to lose himself when he can find no way to relate to what has come before him and what will follow. He then loses all consistency, all certitude. No longer guided by a sense of continuity, he becomes lost in the world. There are lost souls of this sort in all countries, but with us it is a general characteristic. I am not talking about that lightness of spirit with which we used to reproach the French, and which is in effect the ability to treat matters lightly but without sacrificing either depth or breadth of mind, a characteristic which brought infinite grace and charm to their affairs. No, I have in mind the carelessness of a life lacking experience and foresight, which is unconcerned with anything except the ephemeral existence of the individual in isolation from the species; a life which values neither honor nor the progress of any system of ideas or interests, not even family heritage or that fund of prescriptions and perspectives which, in an order founded upon memory of the past and anticipation of things to come, constitutes public and private life. We have in our heads nothing common to us all; everything is individual, everything is drifting and incomplete. I even fancy that in our look there is something strangely vague, cold and uncertain, rather like the features of people on the lowest rung of the social ladder. In foreign lands, especially in the south where people's features are so lively and expressive, I often compared the faces of my compatriots with those of the natives and was struck by this mute quality in ours.

Some foreigners have credited us with a sort of careless temerity, encountered most often in the lower classes of a nation. But, observing only certain isolated features of our national character, they could not assess the whole. They did not see that the same principle which makes us so audacious at times makes us permanently incapable of profundity and perseverance. They did not see that what makes us indifferent to the hazards of life also makes us indifferent to all good, all evil, all truth, all deceit, and that it is precisely this which deprives us of all those incentives which lead man along the path to perfection. They did not see that it is precisely this slothful audacity which is responsible for the fact that in our country even the upper classes are not, sad to say, exempt from the vices which elsewhere exist only among the lowest orders. They did not see, finally, that, although we have some of the virtues of a young and backward people, we have none of the virtues of mature and highly cultured nations.

I am certainly not trying to claim that we have all the vices while the peoples of Europe have all the virtues. God forbid! But I do say that, in order to judge nations properly, one must study the general spirit which constitutes their existence, for it is only this spirit, rather than such and such a trait of character, which can lead them along the path of moral perfection and unending progress.

The masses are subject to certain forces located at the summit of society. They do not think for themselves; there is among them a certain number of thinkers who do the thinking for them, who provide an impetus for the collective intelligence of the nation and set it in motion. While this minority meditates the rest feel, and the general movement occurs. Except for certain brutish nations which preserve only the outer appearance of human nature, this is true of all the peoples of the earth. The primitive peoples of Europe, the Celts, the Scandinavians, the early Germans, had their druids, their skalds, their bards, who were in their way forceful thinkers. Look at the North American people, who are being destroyed by the materialistic civilization of the United States: among them too there are men of admirable profundity.

Now I ask you, where are our sages, our thinkers? Who has ever done the thinking for us? Who thinks for us today? And yet, situated between the two great divisions of the world, between East and West, with one elbow resting on China and the other on Germany, we ought to have united in us the two principles of intellectual life, imagination and reason, and brought together in our civilization the history of the entire globe. But this was not the part Providence assigned to us. Far from it; she seems to have taken no interest in our destiny. Suspending in our case her beneficial action on the human spirit, she has left us totally to ourselves, has refused to have anything to do with us, and has wished to teach us nothing. Historical experience does not exist for us; centuries and generations have passed without bearing us fruit. You would think, looking at us, that the general law of humanity has been revoked in our case. Alone in the world, we have given nothing to the world, taught the world nothing; we have not added a single idea to the fund of human ideas; we have contributed nothing to the progress of the human spirit, and we have disfigured everything we have taken of that progress. From the first instant of our social existence nothing has emanated from us for the common good of humanity; no useful idea has sprouted on the sterile soil of our fatherland; not a single great truth has sprung from our midst. We have never taken the trouble to invent anything ourselves, while from the inventions of others we have adopted only the deceptive appearances and useless luxuries.

It's a strange thing! Even in the world of science, which embraces all, our history has no link with anything; it explains nothing, demonstrates nothing. If the barbarian hordes which threw the world into confusion had not passed through the land where we now live before falling on the West, we would hardly have merited a chapter in the history of the world. For people to notice us we have had to stretch from the Bering Straits to the Oder. At one time a great man wanted to civilize us, and in order to give us a taste for enlightenment he threw us the mantle of civilization.[10] We took up the mantle, but left the civilization. On another occasion, another great prince, associating us with his glorious mission, led us victorious from one end of Europe to the other.[11] On our return from this triumphal march across the most civilized countries in the world we brought back only ideas and aspirations which gave rise to an immense calamity, which set us back half a century.[12] We have something in our blood which drives off all true progress. In short, we have existed, and still exist today, merely to serve as some great lesson for future generations capable of understanding it. Today, whatever anyone says, we represent a lacuna in the intellectual order. I cannot help but be struck by this void and by the astonishing solitude of our social existence. It is certainly due in part to some inconceivable destiny, but also partly due to man, as is always the case in the moral world. Let us consult history once more, for it is history which explains nations.

What were we doing while the edifice of modern civilization was arising out of the struggle between the energetic barbarism of the Northern peoples and the high idea of Christianity? Obedient to our fatal destiny, we turned to miserable Byzantium, the object of profound contempt among these peoples, for a moral code on which to base our education.[13] A moment earlier an ambitious spirit[14] had excluded this family from the universal fraternity, so that we adopted an idea already disfigured by human passion. In Europe at that time everything was animated by the vivifying principle of unity. Everything emanated from it, and everything came together in it. The whole intellectual movement of those times worked towards the unity of human thought, and all purpose arose from this powerful need to arrive at a universal idea, which is the spirit of modern times. Strangers to this marvelous principle, we became a prey for conquest; and when, freed from the foreign yoke, we might have profited from the ideas which had developed during this period among our Western brothers had we not been separated from the common family, we fell into an even harsher servitude, sanctified moreover by the fact of our deliverance.[15]

What vivid light was then emerging in Europe out of the apparent darkness which had covered it! Most of the knowledge which the human spirit is today so proud of had already been perceived by individual minds. Society had already assumed a definite character, and, by going back to pagan antiquity, the Christian world had discovered the forms of beauty which it had lacked. Isolated in our religious separatism we felt nothing of what was happening in Europe. We had nothing to do with the great things that were going on in the world. The great qualities with which religion had endowed modern man, and which from the point of view of sane reason had elevated him as high above the ancient peoples as they in turn had stood above the Hottentots and the Lapps, the new forces with which it had enriched human intelligence, the customs which submission to an unarmed authority had rendered as sweet as they had previously been brutal—none of this had occurred among us. We did not budge, despite calling ourselves Christians, while Christianity advanced majestically along the road marked out for it by its divine founder, carrying generations along after it. While the world was being completely rebuilt, we were building nothing. We carried on huddling in our hovels of logs and straw. In a word, the new destinies of the human race were not fulfilled in our land. Though we were Christians, the fruits of Christianity did not ripen for us.

I ask you, is it not absurd to suppose, as is generally done in our country, that we can appropriate at a stroke, without even bothering to find out how it developed, all of this progress so slowly made by the peoples of Europe under the direct and evident influence of a unique moral force?

Nothing is understood of Christianity if it is not seen that it has a purely historical aspect which is so essentially a part of the dogma that it contains in a certain way all of the Christian philosophy, in that it reveals what Christianity has done for man and what it can do for him in the future. Thus the Christian religion may be seen not only as a moral system conceived in the perishable forms of the human mind, but as a divine, eternal power acting universally in the intellectual world, whose visible action should be a perpetual lesson to us. This is the proper meaning of the dogma expressed symbolically in the belief in a single universal Church. In the Christian world everything must necessarily converge towards the establishment of a perfect order on earth, and everything does indeed do so, otherwise the word of the Lord would be given the lie by fact. He would not be with his Church to the end of time. The new order, the reign of God, which redemption was to bring about, would be no different from the old order, the reign of evil, which it was supposed to supplant. There would still be only that imaginary perfectibility of which philosophy dreams and which is refuted by history's every page: that vain activity of the mind which satisfies only our material needs and which always elevates man to some height or other only to precipitate him into an ever deeper abyss.

But, you will say, are we not Christians then? And can one be civilized only in the European manner? Certainly we are Christians, but then aren't the Abyssinians too? Certainly man can be civilized in a way other than the European; is not Japan civilized, and more so than Russia if we are to believe one of our compatriots? And yet, do you believe that Abyssinian Christianity and Japanese civilization will bring about that order of things which I have described and which is the ultimate destiny of the human race? Do you believe that it is these absurd aberrations of divine and human truth which will bring about heaven on earth?

There are two quite distinct things in Christianity. One is its action on the individual, the other is its effect on universal intelligence. These come together naturally in the Supreme Reason and lead necessarily to the same end. But the timespan within which the eternal designs of Divine Wisdom are realized is beyond our limited point of view. We must distinguish the divine action which is manifested at a given time in the life of man from that which occurs only in the infinite. On the day of the final completion of the work of redemption all hearts and minds will form but one sentiment and one idea, and all walls separating peoples and their beliefs will fall. But today each must realize his place in the order of the general vocation of Christians; that is to say, the means he can find in and around him for working towards the goal set for the whole of human society.

Thus there necessarily arises a certain circle of ideas, within which move the minds of the society where this end is to be accomplished, that is, where the revealed idea is to mature and reach its full plenitude. This circle of ideas, this moral sphere, produces naturally a certain mode of existence and a point of view which, although not precisely the same for each person, nevertheless—and this refers to us just as it refers to European peoples—gives rise to a certain way of life, the result of that immense intellectual work over a period of eighteen centuries, in which all passions, all interests, all sufferings, all dreams and all the efforts of reason have participated.

All the nations of Europe held hands as they advanced through the ages. Today, whatever they might do to go their separate ways, they always come back to the same path. In order to understand the development of this family of peoples we do not need to study history. Just read Tasso and you will see them all prostrate at the foot of Jerusalem's walls.[16] Remember that for fifteen centuries they had but a single language in which to speak to God, a single moral authority, a single religious conviction. Just think that for fifteen centuries, every year on the same day, at the same hour, in the same words, they all as one raised their voices to the Supreme Being in order to celebrate His glory in the greatest of His blessings. A marvelous symphony, a thousand times more sublime than all the harmonies of the physical world! But since this sphere wherein the men of Europe live, and which is the sole means for mankind to reach his ultimate destiny, is the result of the influence which religion has exercised among them, and if the weakness of our beliefs or the insufficiency of our dogma has until now kept us outside the universal movement in which the social idea of Christianity was developed and formulated and has relegated us to the category of peoples who must profit only indirectly and very late from the full effect of Christianity, then it is clear that we must seek to revive our beliefs by all means possible, and try to give ourselves a truly Christian impulse, for it is Christianity which has accomplished everything in Europe. This is what I meant when I said that we must repeat in our country the education of mankind from the very beginning.

The whole history of modern society occurs on the level of beliefs. It is thus a veritable education. Founded initially on this basis, history has always been advanced by thought. Interests have always followed ideas, never have they preceded them. Interests have always been provoked by beliefs, never the other way around. All political revolutions were in essence moral revolutions. Man sought truth and found liberty and well-being. This is how the phenomenon of modern society and its civilization must be understood, otherwise it is not understood at all.

Religious persecution, martyrdom, the spread of Christianity, heresies, Church councils—these are the events which filled the first centuries. The movement of this age as a whole, including the barbarian invasion, is linked with these efforts of the modern spirit in its infancy. The second epoch was taken up with the establishment of hierarchy, the centralization of spiritual power, and the continued propagation of religion in northern lands. Then there followed the exaltation of religious sentiment to the highest degree and the consolidation of religious authority. The philosophical and literary development of the mind and moral improvement under the sway of religion complete this history, which can be called sacred just as much as that of the chosen people of old. Finally, it was another religious reaction, a new blossoming of the human mind stimulated by religion, which determined the present shape of society. Thus the great—one might say, the sole—interest of modern peoples has always centered on beliefs. All material, positive and personal interests were absorbed in that.

I know that instead of admiring this prodigious striving of human nature towards possible perfection, people have called it fanaticism and superstition. But, whatever is said, judge for yourself what a profound mark must have been made on the character of these peoples, for better or worse, by a social development produced entirely by a single sentiment. Let a superficial philosophy make as much fuss as it likes about religious wars or stakes set alight by intolerance;[17] as far as we are concerned, we can only envy the lot of those peoples who, out of the clash of convictions and bloody conflicts in the name of truth, have created for themselves a world of ideas which we cannot even imagine, let alone enter into body and soul, as we claim we can.

Again, all is certainly not reason, virtue and religion in the countries of Europe—far from it. But everything there is in some mysterious way dominated by a force which has reigned supreme there for centuries on end. Everything there is the result of that long sequence of events and ideas which has produced the present state of society...

The effect of Christianity is in no way limited to its immediate and direct influence on the spirit of men. The immense result it is destined to produce must be the outcome of a multitude of moral, intellectual and social combinations, in which the complete freedom of the human spirit must necessarily be allowed full sway. Hence it is clear that all that has occurred since the first day of our era, or rather from the moment when our Saviour said to his disciples: "Go preach the Gospel to every creature," including all those attacks directed against Christianity, fits perfectly into this general idea of its influence. We have only to see Christ's kingdom reigning universally in all hearts, whether this is achieved consciously or unconsciously, voluntarily or involuntarily, to recognize the fulfilment of his prophecies. Thus, despite all that is incomplete, vicious and culpable in European society as it stands today, it is nonetheless true that the reign of God is realized in it in some way, because it contains the principle of indefinite progress and possesses the seeds and elements of all that is needed for this reign to be one day finally established on earth.

Before concluding, Madame, these reflections on the influence of religion on society, I shall transcribe here what I once said about it in a work with which you may not be familiar.

It is certain, I said, that as long as men do not see the effect of Christianity wherever human thought comes into contact with it, in any fashion, even if only to challenge it, they have no idea about Christianity at all. Wherever the name of Christ is spoken, that name alone sweeps men along, no matter what they do. Nothing reveals the divine origin of this religion better than this feature of absolute universality, which allows it to penetrate the souls of men in all possible ways and to possess their minds without their knowing it, to dominate them, to subjugate them, even when they resist it most, by introducing into the mind truths which were not previously there, by arousing in the heart emotions never felt before, and by inspiring us to feelings which place us, without our knowing it, in the general order of things. In this way the function of each individual is determined by it, and everything is made to come together for a single purpose. If we look at Christianity from this point of view, each of Christ's prophecies takes on a palpable truth. We then see clearly the interplay of all the levers which the almighty hand sets in motion to lead man to his destiny, without violating his freedom or paralyzing any of his natural powers, but, on the contrary, adding to their intensity and extending to infinity those powers he possesses...

But the effect of Christianity on society as a whole is even more remarkable. Unfold the entire picture of the development of modern society and you will see how Christianity transforms all of man's interests into its own interests, everywhere replacing material necessity with moral necessity, and stimulating in the realm of thought those great debates without parallel in the history of any other age or any other society, those fearsome struggles between beliefs when the entire life of whole peoples is concentrated in a single great idea and a single boundless feeling. You will see how everything is absorbed by it alone: private life and public life, family and fatherland, science and poetry, reason and imagination, memories and hopes, joys and sorrows. Happy are those who, in this great movement imparted to the world by God himself, are aware in their hearts of the part they must play! But not all are active instruments, not all act consciously. Necessary multitudes move blindly, like inanimate atoms or inert masses, without ever knowing the forces which set them in motion and without perceiving the goal towards which they are being urged.

It is time to come back to you, Madame. I admit that I find it hard to tear myself away from these general observations. It is from the picture which appears before my eyes from this height that I derive all consolation. It is in the sweet belief in the happiness which man has to come that I find my refuge. When I am obsessed by the unfortunate reality which surrounds me I feel the need to breathe a purer air and behold a more serene sky. I don't think, however, that I have wasted your time. I had to let you know the proper way of looking at the Christian world, and the role we Russians have to play. What I have said about our country must seem bitter to you, but I have only spoken the truth, and even then not the whole truth. Besides, Christian reason does not tolerate any sort of blindness, least of all that of national prejudice, since it is that which divides man most...

Necropolis, December 1, 1829

Ivan Vasilevich Kireevsky
A REPLY TO A. S. KHOMYAKOV

Mr. Khomyakov's article has prompted many of us to want to write a response to him.[18] For this reason I originally intended to leave this pleasure to others and offer an article on another subject. But when I thought it over I realized that our view on the relationship of Russia's past condition to her present is not one of those matters, like literature, music or foreign affairs, about which we might with impunity hold one opinion or another, but is, as it were, a fundamental part of our very being, insofar as it affects every circumstance and every moment of our lives. And when I went on to consider that each one of us holds an opinion on this matter which is quite distinct from the views of others, then I decided to put pen to paper on the assumption that my article would not prevent anyone else from having his say about the same thing, since this is a matter of importance to everyone, there is a variety of opinion about it, and agreement would be no bad thing for everyone.

The problem is usually posed in this way: was ancient Russia, where the general order of things flowed from native elements, better or worse than present-day Russia, where the order of things is subject to the predominance of Western European elements? If ancient Russia was superior to modern Russia, so the argument goes, then we must seek to restore the exclusively Russian past and do away with the Western influence which has disfigured the essential Russian character. If, however, ancient Russia was inferior then we must seek to impose the Western influence and eradicate the peculiarly Russian.

This syllogism is in my view not as clear-cut as it might appear. If the past was superior to the present then it does not necessarily follow that it would still be better today. What is appropriate for one time and one set of conditions might be inappropriate for a different time and different circumstances. If the past was inferior, then neither does it necessarily mean that the elements which determined it could not in themselves have evolved into something better had this process not been cut short by the forcible introduction of a foreign element. A young oak is, of course, smaller than a broom of the same age; the latter is more easily seen at a distance, it gives more shade, and it develops more quickly into a tree which can be used for firewood. But clearly you would not be doing the oak a service by grafting a broom on to it.

Therefore the problem itself has been unsatisfactorily posed. Instead of asking whether ancient Russia was superior, it would seem to me more useful to ask whether it is necessary for the improvement of our

contemporary life to return to the principles of ancient Russia, or whether
we should develop those Western elements which are contrary to it.

Let us see where we get by looking at the question in this way.

Let us imagine that on the basis of an impartial study we reach the
conclusion that it would best suit us to espouse one of these two opposing
ways of life. Let us suppose, moreover, that we are in a position to exercise
the strongest influence upon Russia's fate. Even in these circumstances and
despite all our efforts, we could not expect just one of these opposing
elements to prevail exclusively, since although we might decide on one *in
theory,* they both exist *in actuality.* No matter how opposed we might be to
Western culture and Western customs etc., it would be madness to think
that the memory of all that has been assimilated from the West over a
period of two hundred years could somehow be forcibly erased at some
point from the Russian mind. How could we unlearn what we have learned
or forget what we know? It is even less likely that Russia's thousand-year
heritage could be destroyed by new influences from Europe. Therefore, no
matter how strongly we might desire the restoration of old Russian
principles or the introduction of Western traditions, we can expect neither
to the exclusion of the other, and must willy-nilly postulate a third
alternative arising from the clash of these two opposing principles.
Consequently, to ask which of two elements is now exclusively of value is
also the wrong way to pose the problem. It is not a question of which of
two, but rather of how both elements should be directed to produce
beneficial results. What should we expect from their interaction and what
should we fear?

And so the question which is of essential importance to us all is one of
which direction we should take, rather than which element we should
adopt.

If we examine the basic principles of life which shape the forces of
nationality in Russia and the West, we see immediately that they have one
obvious factor in common: Christianity. The differences between them
consist in the particular forms of Christianity adopted, the particular
directions taken by their cultures, and the particular meanings of their
personal and social life. We know where their common features stem from,
but where did their differences originate and what are the characteristic
features of these differences?

We have two ways of defining the distinctive features of the West and
Russia, and each of these may be used to verify the other. We can, by going
back in history to the source of each form of development, seek the reason
for their differences in the original elements which went into their make-
up, or, by examining the subsequent development of these elements, we
may compare the results themselves. And if we find that the same
differences observed in the original elements crop up again in the end-
result of the development of these elements, then it will be clear that our

assumption is correct and we shall be able to see what further deductions can be made from it.

Three elements have formed the basis of European development: Roman Christianity, the primitive barbarian world which destroyed the Roman Empire, and the ancient, pagan, classical world.

The essence of this classical world of ancient paganism, which is absent from Russia's heritage, lay in the triumph of man's formal reason over all else to be found within or about him; the triumph of pure, naked reason, founded only on itself, which acknowledged nothing above or beyond itself and which assumed two characteristic forms: the tendency towards formal abstraction and the development of abstract sensibility. The influence of classicism on European development must have been in line with these characteristics.

But whether Christianity in the West submitted unrestrainedly to the influence of the classical world or heresy simply coincided with paganism, the fact remains that the Roman Church, in splitting away from the Eastern Church, displayed that same triumph of rationalism over the tradition of immediate wisdom and inner, spiritual intelligence. Thus, on the strength of a superficial syllogism extracted from the concept of the divine equality of God the Father and God the Son, the dogma of the Holy Trinity was betrayed, contrary to all spiritual meaning and tradition; and on the basis of another syllogism the Pope replaced Jesus Christ at the head of the Church, acquiring first temporal power and finally infallibility. The existence of God was throughout the whole of Christianity demonstrated by means of syllogisms. The entire faith relied on syllogistic scholasticism. The Inquisition, Jesuitism, in fact all of those features characteristic of Catholicism, developed on the strength of that same formal process of reason; so much so that even Protestantism, which the Catholics reproach for its rationalism, emerged as a direct result of the rationalism of Catholicism itself. In this ultimate triumph of formal reason over faith and tradition the perceptive mind will already detect in embryonic form the whole of Europe's present fate, which is the consequence of an ill-conceived principle. He will also detect in embryo Strauss,[19] the new philosophy in all its forms, industrialism as the spring of social life, the sort of philanthropy which is based on calculated self-interest, and the sort of upbringing which is expedited by stimulating envy. He will be able to discern the seeds of Goethe, that pinnacle of the new poetry, that literary Talleyrand who exchanged one beauty for another as the latter changed his governments,[20] of Napoleon, of the new hero of the modern age, that ideal of soulless calculation, of the power of the substantial majority, that fruit of rational politics, and of Louis Philippe,[21] the end result of all these hopes and all these cherished experiences!

I have no intention of writing a satire on the West. No one has a higher regard than I for those material improvements in social and personal life produced by this rationalism. To be honest, even now I still love the West—I am bound to it by many indissoluble emotional ties. I belong to the West in my education, my way of life, my tastes, my argumentative cast of mind, even in my emotional traits; but man possesses impulses in his heart, aspirations in his mind, and a sense of meaning in his whole life, which are stronger than all habits and tastes, stronger than all life's comforts and the benefits of superficial reason, and without which neither men nor nations can lead a true existence. Therefore, while paying due regard to all the individual benefits of rationalism, I believe that ultimately its painful inadequacy shows it to be a one-sided, deceptive, corrupting and treacherous principle. However, to elaborate on this here would be inappropriate. I shall merely observe that all the finest minds in Europe bemoan the present state of moral apathy, the lack of conviction, the widespread egoism, and demand a new spiritual force beyond reason, a new motivation in life higher than calculated self-interest. In a word they are seeking faith, but they cannot find it among themselves, for Christianity has been distorted in the West by individual thought.

Thus rationalism was from the start a superfluous element in European development and now it has become the sole characteristic of European life and culture. This is even more evident if we compare the fundamental principles of European social and personal life with those basic principles which, even if they were not fully developed, were at least clearly seen in the social and personal life of ancient Russia, where the influence of Christianity was direct and pure, untainted by the pagan world.

The whole of the West's social and personal life is based upon the concept of individual and private independence, which presupposes the notion of the individual as a separate entity. Hence the sanctity of external, formal relationships, property and formal decrees is more important than personality. Each individual private citizen, knight, prince or township is *within its rights* an autonomous entity, unrestricted and creating its own laws. The first step taken by each individual entity on entering into communal life is to surround itself with fortress walls, from behind which it conducts its relations with other equally independent powers.

* * *

Last time I did not finish my article, so I feel obliged to continue it now. I was discussing the differences between Russian culture and that of the West. The source of our development lay in our Church. In Europe the fertile remnants of the ancient pagan world acted together with Christianity on the development of culture. Western Christianity itself, on breaking away from the Universal Church, acquired the germ of the principle which had been the basic characteristic of the whole of Greco-pagan development, the principle of rationalism. Because of this European development was marked by the dominance of rationalism.

However, this predominance of rationalism became apparent only later, when the development of logic had already stifled the development of Christianity. At first, as I have said, rationalism appeared only in embryo. The Roman Church broke away from the Eastern Church when it changed certain dogmas rooted in the whole *tradition* of Christianity in favor of others arrived at through a process of *deduction*. It then developed these in accordance with that same process of logic, once again contrary to the tradition and spirit of the Universal Church. From the start this logical conviction lay at the very root of Catholicism, but at first the effect of rationalism went no further than this. The external and internal structure of the Church, formed earlier and in a different spirit, underwent for the time being no noticeable change—that is until the whole entirety of the Church's teaching was taken over by the intellects of the thinking clergy. This resulted in scholastical philosophy, which because of the logical principle at the very basis of the Church was able to reconcile the contradiction between faith and reason only by the force of syllogism, which thus became the sine qua non of all conviction. Naturally syllogism at first affirmed the superiority of faith over reason and subjected reason to faith on the basis of rational arguments. But this kind of faith, logically demonstrated and logically opposed to reason, was no longer a living faith, but a formal one, no longer faith itself, but merely the logical negation of reason. And so in the scholastic period of Catholicism's development the Western Church, by virtue of its very rationalism, became the oppressive, murderous and desperate enemy of reason itself. But eventually, as a result of the same logical process, this unconditional destruction of reason produced the opposite effect, resulting in the basis of modern European culture. This is what I had in mind when I spoke of the rational element in Catholicism.

Eastern Christianity experienced neither this struggle between faith and reason nor the triumph of reason over faith. Therefore its effect upon culture was quite unlike that of Catholicism.

An examination of the social structure of ancient Russia reveals many differences from that of the West. Most obvious among these is the development of society into small, so-called communes. Private and individual life, the very cornerstone of Western development, was as little known in Russia as political rule by the people. A man belonged to the commune and the commune to him. Ownership of the land, the source of individual rights in the West was collective in Russia. A person participated in the rights of ownership to the extent that he participated in communal society.

But the commune was not autonomous; it could not organize itself or promulgate its own separate laws, since it did not exist independently of other similar communes structured in the same way. The multitude of such small communes making up Russia was enveloped in a network of churches, monasteries and hermits' retreats which continually spread abroad the same ideas on social and personal relations. Gradually, but inevitably, these ideas became a universally held conviction, this conviction became custom, custom became law, and this resulted in the whole land becoming dependent on the Church and in the emergence of a single idea, a single way of looking at things, one conviction and one way of life. The universal unanimity of this tradition has no doubt been one reason for its surprising endurance; active traces of it survive even in our time, despite the intervening two hundred years of ravaging contrary influences, which have striven to replace it with new principles.

Because of this firm, unanimous and universal tradition any change in the social order which was contrary to the system as a whole was impossible. The individual's relationship to his family was defined before his birth; equally well defined were the processes whereby the family was subject to the commune, the commune as a whole to the decisions of its general meeting, and the general meeting to the popular assembly (veche), etc. Thus all were arranged like circles around a single center, the Orthodox Church. No individual idea or artificial resolution could create a different order or invent new rights and privileges. Even the word right was unknown to us in its Western sense, and meant only fairness and justice. Thus no authority, individual or class could bestow or revoke rights, since fairness and justice can be neither put up for offer nor taken away, for they exist in themselves, independent of conventional relations. In the West, on the other hand, all social relations are based on conventions, or they aspire to such an artificial basis. Beyond these conventions there are no proper relations, there is only arbitrariness, which the ruling classes call mob rule and the lower classes freedom. In both cases this arbitrariness betrays a superficial and formal development, not something which has developed from inner life. In the West all forces, interests and rights in society exist separately and in isolation. They are unified not by any natural law, but haphazardly, or by some artificial agreement. The former represents the triumph of material force, the latter a compromise between different views. But material force, physical superiority, the power of the multitude and compromise between differing views in effect form a unified principle only at certain moments in their development. It follows from this that the social contract was not an invention of the Encyclopedists, but the real ideal to which all Western societies unconsciously aspired in the past, and to which they consciously aspire today, influenced by the rational element which has gained superiority over Christianity.

We do not have a clear picture of the limits of a prince's authority in Russia in the period before the independent principalities came under the authority of Muscovy. But let us bear in mind that the force of immutable tradition did not allow despotic legislation, that the right to try and judge people, which the prince possessed in certain cases, could not be put into effect in a way contrary to universal custom, and that this custom could not for the same reason be interpreted arbitrarily. Let us remember too that the general course of affairs was determined by the communes and local authorities, again acting in accordance with time-honored tradition understood by all, and that in those extreme cases where a prince violated his proper relationships with the people and the Church he was driven out by the people themselves. If we bear all this in mind it becomes clear that in effect a prince's authority consisted in the command of his troops (*druzhina*) and in providing armed protection, not in the administration of internal affairs or mastery over his lands.

Generally speaking, Russia would appear not to have produced those local barons typical of Western history who treated society as inanimate property to be used for their own personal benefit, just as it did not produce the noble knights of the West who relied entirely on their own strength, castles and armor, recognizing no law other than that of the sword and conventional honor, based upon the notion of the autonomy of the individual.

There are, however, other reasons for the lack of the institution of chivalry in Russian history. It might at first seem strange that we did not produce such knights, if only during the Tatar period. Society was fragmented, authority had no material power, people could move from place to place, there were dense forests and the police were not yet thought of. Why, therefore, did there not arise groups of people who took advantage of their superiority in might over peaceful agriculturalists and townsfolk to steal and behave as they liked, to seize independent lands and villages and build their castles there? They could have agreed certain principles amongst themselves and thus formed a special class of the strongest, using their might to assume the name of nobility. The Church could have made use of them, forming them into different orders, each with its own charter, and using them against the unbelievers like the Crusaders in the West. Why did this not happen?

In my view this was because our Church in those days did not sell its purity in return for temporal gains. We had warriors (*bogatyri*) like these only until the adoption of Christianity. Afterwards we had brigands and organized bands of outlaws, whose exploits are still preserved in our folk songs, but these bands were repudiated by the Church and were therefore powerless. We could so easily have created crusader campaigns by adopting these brigands as servants of the Church and promising them absolution in return for their killing unbelievers. Everyone would have joined the honest brigands. This is what Catholicism did. It did not stir the people in the name of faith, but merely directed the aimless towards an aim and then called them saints. Our Church did not do this and that is why we have not had the tradition of chivalry and the aristocratic class which goes with it and which has been a major factor in the whole of Western development.

Chivalry was strongest in those parts of the West where there was most disorder; it was least established in Italy. The weaker it was, the more society inclined towards an order based upon the will of the people. Where it was strong an absolutist order tended to prevail. Absolutism itself grows out of aristocracy, when the strong prevail over the weak and the conditional ruler becomes an absolute ruler who then joins forces with the lower orders, as the people are called in Europe, against the class of the nobility. In accordance with the general rule of European social development, the lower orders then assumed the rights of the nobility, and that same force used to attain absolute power for one man was then used in the natural course of its development to transfer power to the substantial majority, which then started to create a formal social order for itself. It is still in the process of devising this order today.

Just as the Church in the West transformed brigands into knights, spiritual authority into temporal power, and the secular police into the Holy Inquisition—all of which perhaps brought it temporal advantages—so did it act in a similar fashion towards pagan science and art. It did not develop its own new Christian art from within itself, but adopted for the embellishment of its temples existing art, which was created and developed in a different spirit and for a different way of life. That is why Romantic art sparkled at first with new and brilliant life but ended up worshiping paganism, and now worships abstract philosophical formulae which cannot serve to bring the world back to true Christianity or allow the appearance of a new servant of Christian beauty.

The sciences, in their most essential form as a body of knowledge, were the same in both the pagan and Christian worlds. They differed only in their philosophical aspects. But Catholicism was unable to impart to science a Christian philosophic dimension, for it lacked such a thing itself in any pure form. Thus we see why science blossomed so intensely in the West as a heritage of paganism, but ended up in atheism, the inevitable consequence of its one-sided evolution.

Russia has shone in neither artistic nor scientific achievements, since it has not had the time to develop in this sense on its own and has not adopted foreign tradition, based on false premises and therefore inimical to its Christian spirit. But because of this, Russia preserves intact the primary requisite of a true path of development requiring only time and favorable conditions. Russia has mustered and kept alive that organizing principle of knowledge, the idea of Christianity, which alone can provide science with a true basis. All the Holy Fathers of the Greek Church, even the most profound writers, were translated and read, transcribed and studied in the tranquility of our monasteries, those holy embryos of future universities. Isaac Syrus,[22] the most profound of all philosophical writings, is still preserved in manuscripts of the twelfth and thirteenth centuries. These monasteries were in constant living contact with the people. What a rich culture we might assume among our lower orders on the basis of this fact alone! This culture might not be superficially brilliant, but it is profound; it is not resplendent and materialistic, or directed towards life's physical comforts, but is inner and spiritual. What has happened to all this? What has become of this social order without tyranny and slavery, without nobles and commoners? What has become of those age-old traditions, based not on written codes but stemming from the Church and deriving strength from the total agreement between custom and the teachings of the faith? What has happened to those holy monasteries, the breeding grounds of a Christian order which form the spiritual heart of Russia and preserve all that is necessary for a future distinctively Russian culture? Where are those hermits who shun the world's vanities and go into the forests, there to study in inaccessible ravines the writings of the most profound sages of Christian Greece, and who emerge to teach those who wish to understand them? What has become of those resolutions arrived at by whole villages, those town assemblies, that freedom in Russian life recalled in our songs? How could all this have been destroyed before it bore fruit? How could it have yielded to the force of a foreign influence? How was Peter the Great possible, that destroyer of things Russian and agent for things foreign? If the process of destruction began before Peter then how could the Principality of Muscovy, which once unified Russia, have then proceeded to crush her? Why did the unification of the different parts into one whole lead to this? Why in these circumstances did the foreign principle triumph rather than the Russian one?

One fact of our history serves to explain this unfortunate turn of events: the Council of a Hundred Chapters.[23] As soon as this heresy arose in the Church the spiritual discord was bound to be reflected in life. Factions appeared which deviated from the truth by greater or lesser degrees. The new faction overcame the faction representing the old way precisely because the old way was riven by dissension. And so with the destruction of inner spiritual unity it became necessary to create physical formal unity, which gave rise to the hierarchical system, the *oprichnina,*[24] slavery, etc. Books were distorted by delusion and ignorance, and corrected in accordance with individual understanding and arbitrary criticism. Thus, before Peter the government was out of step with the majority of the people, who were denounced as schismatics, and because of this Peter, as the leader of a faction within the state, formed a society within a society, with all that this entailed.

What follows from all that has been said? Should we wish to restore the Russia of the past? Could it be brought back? If it is true that the distinctive feature of Russian life lay in its living source in pure Christianity, and that this way of life declined as the spirit weakened, then it follows that this dead way of life could be of no value today. It would be ridiculous, if not actually harmful, to try to resurrect it by force. But only he who does not believe that one day Russia will return to that life-giving spirit which the Church breathed into her—only he would be capable of destroying the remaining features of that way of life.

We must now hope for one thing only: that some Frenchman or other will come to grasp the unique essence of the Christian doctrine, see that it is embodied in our Church and then write an article on the matter for a journal; or that some German will be persuaded by him, will study our Church in depth and will start to demonstrate in his lectures how everything which European culture now needs is quite unexpectedly revealed by the Russian Church. Then we would undoubtedly believe the Frenchman and the German and would come to appreciate ourselves what we possess.

1839

Alexei Stepanovich Khomyakov
[ON CATHOLICISM]²⁵

Papal authority, which took the place of ecumenical infallibility, was an external authority. The Christian, who had once been a member of the Church and a responsible participant in its resolutions, became subject to the Church. He and it ceased to be a single entity: he was now outside it even though he remained within its midst. The gift of infallibility conferred upon the Pope was set beyond all moral conditions which might influence it, so that neither the depravity of the whole Christian environment nor even the personal depravity of the Pope himself could have any effect on this infallibility. The Pope became a sort of oracle, devoid of all freedom, a sort of idol made of flesh and bone, worked by concealed springs. For the Christian this oracle was reduced to one of those phenomena of a material nature, the laws of which may be and should be subjected to analysis by reason alone. For the inner bond linking man with the Church had been broken. A purely external and consequently rational law took the place of that living moral law, which alone does not fear rationalism, since it embraces not only man's reason, but the whole of his being.

A temporal state took the place of the Christian Church. The single living law of unity in God was displaced by particular laws bearing the stamp of utilitarianism and legalistic attitudes. Rationalism developed in the form of authoritative definitions: it devised purgatory in order to account for prayers for the departed; it established a balance of obligations and rewards between God and man, and began to weigh up sins and prayers, misdemeanors and acts of penance; it introduced transfers from one person to another, and legitimized the barter of imaginary merits. In a word it brought into the sanctuary of faith the entire mechanism of the banking house. At the same time the Church-state introduced the language of state—Latin; it undertook judgment on worldly affairs, whereupon it took up arms and began to set up firstly disordered hordes of crusaders, then regular armies (the orders of knights), and finally, when the sword was wrested from its grasp, it put into service the disciplined troops of the Jesuits. I repeat, this is not criticism for its own sake. In seeking out the source of Protestant rationalism, I find it in the guise of Roman rationalism, and I have no choice but to trace its development. I am not speaking of abuses, but merely confining myself to principles. The Church inspired by God has for the Western Christian become something external, a sort of soothsaying authority, an authority which is somehow material. It has turned man into its slave and, as a consequence of this, has acquired in him someone who judges its actions.

"The Church is authority," said Guizot in one of his most remarkable works, and one of his critics cites these words and confirms them. In so doing neither the one nor the other suspects just how little truth and how much blasphemy these words contain. Poor Roman! Poor Protestant! No, the Church is not authority, just as God is not authority, or Christ, for authority is something extraneous to us. It is not authority, I say, but truth, and at the same time it is the life of the Christian, his inner life. For God, Christ and the Church live within him a life which is more real than the heart beating in his breast or the blood coursing through his veins. But they live only inasmuch as he lives the universal life of love and unity, that is, the life of the Church. Yet so great has been the blindness of the Western sects that to this day not one of them has yet come to understand how essentially the soil on which they stand differs from that on which the true Church has stood since time immemorial and will continue to stand for eternity.

1853

Alexei Stepanovich Khomyakov
[ON THE CHURCH]²⁶

Each of us is constantly seeking that which the Church constantly possesses. In his ignorance each seeks to understand the Church, and in his sinfulness each seeks to become part of the holiness of its inner life. Always imperfect in everything, he aspires to the perfection apparent in all manifestations of the Church: in its writs, which are the holy scriptures, in the tradition of its teaching, in its sacraments, in its prayers, and in the pronouncements which it makes whenever it is necessary to refute untruth in its midst, dispel doubt, or enunciate the truth to bolster the hesitant steps of its sons. Each of us is of this world, only the Church is from heaven.

However, man does not discover in the Church something alien to himself. He discovers himself in it, but a self which is not powerless in its spiritual solitude, but strong in its candid spiritual unity with its brethren and its Saviour. He discovers himself in his perfection or, more precisely, that which is perfect within himself—that divine inspiration, which is constantly dispersed in the coarse impurity of each separate personal existence. This purification is accomplished through the invincible power of the love of Christians united in Jesus Christ, for that love is the Holy Spirit. "But how," it will be said, "can the unity of Christians provide that which no one possesses in isolation?" And indeed the grain of sand draws no new life from the heap into which it is cast by chance: such is the situation of man under Protestantism. The brick laid in the wall in no way changes or improves as a result of the place allotted it by the bricklayer's bevel: such is man's situation in the Roman Church. But each particle of matter assimilated in a living body becomes an inalienable part of the organism and acquires in the process new meaning and new life: such is man in the Church,²⁷ in the body of Christ, the organic basis of which is love. It is clear that the people of the West cannot understand this or participate in it without first renouncing the schism which is the very negation of the Church. For the Catholic conceives of a Church unity where nothing remains of the Christian's freedom, and the Protestant clings to the sort of freedom under which the unity of the Church completely disappears.²⁸ We profess a Church which is united and free. It remains united even though it has no official representative of its unity, and free even though its freedom does not take the form of the separation of its members. This Church, if I may be permitted to use the words of the apostle, is temptation in the eyes of the judaistic Romans and holy folly for the hellenizing Protestants, but for us it is the revelation of God's infinite wisdom and grace in the world.

And so it is clear that there is an essential difference between the idea of a Church which acknowledges itself as an organic unity, the living source of which is the divine paradise of mutual love, and the idea found in Western societies, where unity is entirely conditional, consisting for Protestants solely in the mathematical sum of a given number of separate personalities with almost identical aspirations and beliefs, and for Catholics solely in the orderly motion of the subjects of a semi-spiritual state. Such differences in ideas must necessarily be echoed in the character of all manifestations of these three kinds of unity based on such critically contrasting principles. Living faith remains... the distinctive feature of the Church's manifestations, but rationalism, whether dogmatic or utilitarian, sets its seal on all the social activities of the two other opposing faiths.

1855

Alexei Stepanovich Khomyakov
TO THE SERBS. AN EPISTLE FROM MOSCOW (Extract)[29]

...In truth, O Serbs, God has bestowed great favors upon you, greater, we think, than you yourselves know. A healthy body is one of man's greatest blessings, but he realizes this only when he loses it, or when he observes the illnesses of others and compares them with his own healthy state. In the same way you can come to know your advantages only through comparison with the shortcomings of other societies (and you have not yet attended to such a comparison), or through the frank confession of such other societies, who know from experience their sicknesses and their causes. Let this knowledge serve as a warning to you, so that you might avoid the errors which other nations have not been able to avoid, and so that, in adopting what is good and useful, you will not be infected by those malignant principles which often accompany good things, unnoticed by the inexperienced eye.

The first, most important and priceless blessing which you, the Serbs, possess is your unity in Orthodoxy, that highest wisdom and highest truth, the root of all spiritual and moral growth. Such is your unity in the faith that for the Turk the words "Serb" and "Orthodox" are synonymous. You must value this finest of all blessings above all others, and guard it as you would the pupil of your eye; after all, what is Orthodoxy if not the pupil of one's inner, spiritual eye?

Christianity was not sown by force in the world; nor did it develop through violence, but by overcoming all violence. Thus it must not be preserved by violence, and woe to him who seeks to protect the might of Christ with the feebleness of human weapons! Faith is a matter of spiritual freedom, and it tolerates no compulsion. True faith is conquering the world, but it does not seek the temporal sword for its triumph. Therefore, respect all freedom of conscience and faith, in order that no one should offend against the truth by saying that it fears falsehood and does not dare compete with falsehood armed only with thought and words. Defend God's honor, not with timidity and doubt as to its might, but boldly and with a calm confidence in its victory.

But, on the other hand, always bear in mind the significance and dignity of the faith. Those who think that it is simply a matter of creed, rituals, or even the direct communion of man with God, are quite wrong. No, faith penetrates man's whole being and all his relations with his neighbor. As if with invisible threads or roots it binds together all his feelings, all his convictions and all his aspirations. It is a sort of rarefied air, recreating and transforming within him every mundane principle, or a luminous light, illuminating all his moral conceptions and all his views on other people and the inner laws which bind him to them. Therefore, faith is also the highest social principle; for society itself is precisely the visible manifestation of our inner relations with other people and our union with them.

A healthy civil society is based on its citizens' understanding of brotherhood, truth, justice and mercy; but this understanding cannot be the same among men if their faiths are different. The Jew and the Mohammedan profess one God, just like the Christian, but is their understanding of truth and mercy the same as ours? Of course, it will be said that they know neither the Sacrament of the Holy and Ever-Worshipful Trinity, nor the love of God, which is our salvation through Christ, and that consequently the difference between them and us is too great. But we know that even Christians, apart from the true Orthodox Church, possess neither a totally clear understanding nor a totally sincere sense of brotherhood. Such an understanding and such a sense develop and strengthen only in Orthodoxy. It is no accident that the commune, the sanctity of the communal verdict and the unquestioning submission of each individual to the unanimous decision of his brethren are preserved only in Orthodox countries. The teachings of the faith cultivate the soul even in social life. The Papist seeks extraneous and personal authority, just as he is used to submitting to such authority in matters of faith; the Protestant takes personal freedom to the extreme of blind arrogance, just as in his sham worship. Such is the spirit of their teaching. Only the Orthodox Christian, preserving his freedom, yet humbly acknowledging his weakness, subordinates his freedom to the unanimous resolution of the collective conscience.[30] It is for this reason that the local commune has not been able to preserve its laws outside Orthodox countries. And it is for this reason that the Slav cannot be fully a Slav without Orthodoxy. Even our brethren who have been led astray by the Western falsehood, be they Papists or Protestants, acknowledge this with grief. This principle applies to all matters of justice and truth, and to all conceptions about society; for at the root of it lies brotherhood.

1860

Konstantin Sergeevich Aksakov
MEMORANDUM TO ALEXANDER II ON THE INTERNAL STATE OF RUSSIA [31]

I

The Russian people are not political; that is to say, they do not aspire to political power, they have no desire to secure political rights for themselves, and they have not the slightest longing for popular government. The dawn of our history serves as the earliest proof of this: the Russians willingly invited a foreign power—the Varangians, Ryurik and his brothers—to rule over them. Even firmer evidence is provided by Russia in 1612, when there was no tsar, when the whole state structure lay in ruins, and when a victorious people, still under arms, rejoiced in victory over their enemies, having liberated Moscow, their capital. What did this mighty people do, having been defeated under the tsar and the boyars, but having found victory without the tsar and boyars, when they were led by the courtier Prince Pozharsky and the butcher Kozma Minin, whom they had elected themselves? What did they do? Just as in 862, the people in 1612 invited another to rule over them; they chose a tsar and entrusted their fate to him unconditionally.[32] Then they quietly laid down their arms and went their separate ways. These two proofs are so striking that it would not seem necessary to add more. But if we look at Russian history as a whole then we shall be even more convinced of the truth of what has been said. Throughout Russian history there has not been a single uprising against authority in the name of political rights for the people. Even Novgorod, once it had recognized the authority of the Tsar of Muscovy, made no further attempt to rebel and restore its former political order.[33] One does encounter in Russian history instances of rebellion in the name of lawful authority against unlawful power, and sometimes what is lawful was incorrectly understood; but nonetheless such uprisings testify to the spirit of legality in the Russian people. There has not been a single attempt by the people to win participation in government. There were pitiful attempts along these lines by the aristocracy even as long ago as the reigns of Ivan IV and Mikhail Fedorovich,[34] but they were feeble and insignificant. Then there was a more obvious attempt during Anna's reign.[35] But not a single one of these attempts found any favor among the people and all quickly faded without trace.

Such is the evidence to be drawn from history. Let us now turn from history to present conditions. Who has ever heard of the common people in Russia rebelling or plotting against the tsar? No one, of course, for such a thing has never occurred... Order in Russia is not maintained by governmental measures, nor has it ever been, and it is not in the spirit of the people to wish to disrupt it. If this were not the case, no coercive measures would help—they would merely serve as an incentive for acts of disruption. The greatest pledge of public order and governmental security in Russia is to be found in the spirit of the people. Were it at all otherwise, Russia would long ago have acquired a constitution—Russian history and her internal conditions have provided ample opportunities and possibilities for such a development. But the Russian people have no wish to govern.

This aspect of the spirit of the Russian people is beyond doubt. Some may grieve and call this the spirit of the slave, while others will rejoice and see it as a law-abiding spirit. But both will be mistaken, for they will be judging Russia on the basis of the Western concepts of liberalism and conservatism. It is difficult to understand Russia unless one can rid oneself of Western concepts, on the basis of which we expect to see in every country—and therefore in Russia too—either revolutionary or conservative elements. Both are alien to us; they are opposite extremes of the political spirit; neither is present in the Russian people, for the Russian people do not possess a political spirit. We shall leave aside for now any explanation of this absence of political spirit and the consequent absoluteness of governmental power in Russia. Suffice it to say for now that this is how the situation is understood in Russia and this is what is required in Russia.

If Russia is to fulfil her destiny she must act in accordance with her own ideas and requirements, and not with theories which are alien to her, whether borrowed from abroad or home-grown, theories which are often rendered ridiculous by history. Perhaps Russia will confound the theoreticians and reveal an aspect of her greatness which no one has suspected.

A government displays its wisdom when it does all in its power to help the country it governs to fulfil its destiny and achieve the good it was meant to achieve on earth. Such wisdom consists in understanding the spirit of the people, which should be the government's constant guide. Failure to understand the needs of the popular spirit or attempts to hinder these needs lead either to internal unrest or to the gradual exhaustion and dissolution of the powers of both people and government.

And so, the first and obvious conclusion to be drawn from the history and character of the Russian people is that they are a non-political people, neither seeking participation in government nor desiring to impose limits on governmental authority. As the Russian people lack, in a word, a political element, they have no desire whatsoever for revolution or constitutional government.

In view of this is it not strange that the Russian government is constantly taking steps against the possibility of revolution and goes in fear of some sort of political uprising, which would above all else go against the very grain of the Russian people! All such fears, whether on the part of the government or members of society, stem from not knowing Russia and being more familiar with the history of Western Europe than with Russian history. Because of this such people see in Russia specters which cannot exist here. Such precautionary measures on the part of our government— measures which are unnecessary and unfounded—are certainly harmful, as are medicines when given to a healthy person who does not need them. Even if they do not produce the very result they are needlessly seeking to prevent, they do at least destroy trust between the government and the people, and that in itself is a great and needless harm, for the Russian people, because of their very nature, will never encroach upon the authority of the government.

II

But what do the Russian people want for themselves? What is the basis, the aim, the main preoccupation of their national life, when they lack completely that political element which plays such an active role in the lives of other nations? What did our people want when of their own volition they called upon the Varangian princes to "reign and rule over them?" What did they wish to preserve for themselves?

They wanted to preserve their own inner, non-political, communal life, their customs, their mode of existence—a peaceful life of the spirit.

Even before the adoption of Christianity, our people, prepared in advance to accept it and sensing its great truths, developed a communal form of life, which was later sanctified by the acceptance of Christianity. In renouncing participation in political affairs the Russian people retained their life as a community and entrusted the state with the task of making it possible for the people to live this life as a community. Having no desire to *govern,* our people wished to *live,* not merely as animals, of course, but as human beings. Instead of political freedom they sought moral freedom, freedom of the spirit, communal freedom, freedom of the people's inner life. As perhaps the only Christian people on earth (in the true sense of the word), they remembered Christ's words: "Render unto Caesar that which is Caesar's, and unto God that which is God's," as well as Christ's other saying: "My kingdom is not of this world." Leaving, therefore, the kingdom which is of this world in the hands of the state, the Russian people, as a Christian people, chose for themselves a different path, one which led to inner freedom and spirituality, to the kingdom of Christ. "The kingdom of God is within you." This is the reason for their unparalleled submission to authority and for the absolute security of the Russian government. This is why there can be no revolutionary instinct in the Russian people and why calm prevails within Russia...

The great social feat to be performed by the government is to safeguard the people's moral life and to preserve their spiritual freedom from any violation. Heroic is he who boldly stands guard outside the temple while the divine service goes on within and communal prayers are offered up; he who guards and fends off any malicious violation of this feat of prayer...

And so the Russian people, having renounced political matters and having entrusted all authority in the political sphere to the government, reserved for themselves *life*—moral and communal freedom, the highest aim of which is to achieve a Christian society.

Although this statement requires no proof—you only have to look closely at Russian history and the Russian people as they are today— nonetheless one can point to certain particularly striking characteristics. One such feature is the ancient division in Russian thinking of the whole of Russia into *the state* and *the land* (i.e., the government and the people) and the expressions which derive from this: *affairs of state* and *affairs of the land.* By *affairs of state* was meant all matters concerning state admin- istration, whether foreign or domestic, and in particular military matters, these being the clearest expression of state power. State service is still understood by the people to mean military service. In a word, *affairs of state* referred to all matters concerning the government and the state. By *affairs of the land* was meant the people's whole way of life, their entire existence, including not only their spiritual and communal life but also their material concerns: agriculture, industry and trade. Thus those who worked for the state were known as *men of the state* or *state servants,* while the term *men of the land* was used to describe those not in government service who formed the nucleus of the country: the peasants, the settlers and the merchants...

III

And so the Russian land entrusted its defense to the state, in the person of the sovereign, so that under his protection it might lead a quiet and prosperous existence. Having separated itself from the state, as the protected is separated from the protector, the land, or the people, has no wish to cross the boundary which it has itself established: it wishes not to govern but to live... Such an attitude is an assurance of peace and tranquility, and is characteristic of Russia and Russia alone. All other peoples aspire to popular rule.

IV

Apart from the fact that such an order is consonant with the spirit of Russia—and for that reason alone, therefore, is essential to her—it may also be affirmed that such an order is in itself the only true order to be found on earth. The great question of the relationship between state and people cannot be better solved than it has been by the Russian people. Man's vocation is morally to draw ever closer to God, his Saviour; man's law is to be found within himself, and consists of the most complete love for God and one's neighbor...

When a people aspires to political power it loses sight of its inner, moral path, and its concern for outer political freedom undermines the freedom of the spirit, which is within. The exercise of governmental power then becomes the people's aim, and the higher goal—that of inner truth, inner freedom and life as a process of spiritual striving—disappears. The people should not be the government. When the people become the sovereign power, when the people become the government, the people cease to exist.

V

On the principle that the people should not interfere in matters of state authority, then that state authority should be absolute. What precise form should such absolute authority take? The answer is not difficult—it should be monarchical. All other forms, such as democracy and aristocracy, allow the participation of the people to a greater or lesser degree, and consequently limit state power. They therefore accord with neither the requirement that the people should not intrude upon governmental authority nor the need for the government to be absolute. It is clear that a constitutional monarchy, such as that of the English, will also fail to meet these requirements... Only the individual can possess absolute authority, and only the individual can free the people from all involvement in government. For this reason we need a sovereign, a monarch. Only monarchical power is absolute. Only under absolute monarchical authority can the people distance themselves from the state and avoid all participation in government and all political significance, thus reserving for themselves a communal moral life and the pursuit of spiritual freedom. Precisely such a monarchical government was chosen by the Russian people.

This attitude on the part of the Russian is the attitude of a *free* man. By recognizing the absolute authority of the state he retains his complete independence of spirit, conscience and thought. In his awareness of this moral freedom within himself the Russian is in truth not a slave, but a free man. For the Russian, absolute monarchical government is not an enemy, not something to be opposed, but a friend and defender of freedom—of that true, spiritual freedom which manifests itself in openly expressed opinion. Only when they possess such total freedom can the people be of use to the government. Political freedom is not freedom. Only when the people are completely separated from state power, only under an absolute monarchy which affords the people the full possibility of leading their spiritual life to the full, can true freedom exist on earth. This is the kind of freedom granted us by our Saviour in the words: "Wherever there is the spirit of the Lord, there is freedom."

VI

... The Russian people know that there is no authority which does not derive from God ... For this reason submission and respect for authority are firmly established among the Russians and that is why they are not capable of revolution.

VII

Such is the sober view which the Russian people have of government. But look at the West. The people there, having abandoned the inner path of faith and spirituality, have been led astray by vain longings for government by the people. Believing in the possibility of perfect government, they have formed republics, drafted constitutions of all kinds, fostered in themselves the vanity of worldly power, and their souls have become impoverished. They have lost their faith and, despite the alleged perfection of their political order, they are ready at any moment to crumble and suffer terrible upheavals, if not a decisive collapse.

VIII

We can now see clearly what the government and the people represent in Russia. In other words, we see that Russia possesses two aspects: the state and the land. Government and people, or state and land, although clearly demarcated in Russia, do nevertheless impinge upon each other, although they do not intermingle. What is the relationship between them? Above all the people do not interfere in government or administrative affairs and the state does not interfere in the life and ways of the people... Thus the relationship between government and people is primarily one of mutual *non-interference*. But such a relationship, being negative, is incomplete; it must be supplemented by a positive relationship between the state and the land... What *independent* attitude can a non-political people take towards the state? How is the state to perceive, so to speak, the will of the people? There can be only one independent way in which a powerless people can relate to an all-powerful state: through *public opinion.* There is no political element in social or public opinion; it carries no weight other than moral weight. Consequently, it is a moral, rather than coercive force. Through public opinion (which must of course be openly expressed) the state may perceive what the country desires, how it views its own purpose, what its moral needs are, and consequently, by what principles the state must be guided, for the purpose of the state is to allow the country to carry out its calling. The preservation of the freedom of public opinion as the supreme expression of the country's moral activity is thus one of the obligations of the state. At important moments in the life of the state and the land the government itself must seek the country's opinion; but only its *opinion,* which the government is free, of course, either to accept or reject. Public opinion is thus the independent means through which the people can and must serve their government, and it forms the living, moral, and in no sense political bond which can and must exist between people and government.

Our wise tsars understood this, and may we be eternally grateful to them for that! They knew that if one sincerely and wisely desires the country's happiness and wellbeing one must know, and on occasions seek, its opinion. For this purpose our tsars often convoked Assemblies of the Land, consisting of representatives of all social classes in Russia, in order to discuss some question or other concerning the state or the land.[36] Our tsars, who understood Russia so well, had no qualms about convoking such assemblies. The government knew that by doing so it would in no way forfeit or limit any of its rights, and the people knew that they would neither acquire nor extend any rights in the process. The bond between government and people was strengthened and not weakened by this. These assemblies marked an amicable relationship between government and people, one based on trust.

It was not only men of the land who participated in these Assemblies of the Land, but also state servants and men of the state such as the boyars, courtiers, court dignitaries, the service nobility, etc. But these people attended in, as it were, their land rather than state capacity, as a part of the Russian people, ready to give their advice. The clergy, essential if the Russian land were to be fully represented, also attended. Thus the whole of Russia gathered at these assemblies, giving full significance to the term *land,* and explaining why these gatherings were called *Assemblies of the Land.*

We have only to bear in mind these memorable assemblies and the statements made by the representatives who attended them to understand clearly that the purpose of these gatherings was to express *only opinion*. All statements began with the words: "It is up to you, O Sovereign, how you act in this matter. Do as you see fit, but our opinion is..." And so action was the government's prerogative, opinion the country's. In the best possible interests of the country it is essential that each side should exercise its prerogative: the land should not hinder the *actions* of the sovereign, and the sovereign should not hinder the *opinion* of the land...

IX

Now we must speak of that period when the principles of Russia's civil order were violated, not by the people, but by the government, and Russia's course was changed...

I have no intention of going into the history of Peter's social revolution; nor do I intend to impugn the greatness of that greatest of great men. But Peter's revolution, despite all its superficial brilliance, serves only to illustrate what profound internal evil can be wrought by the greatest genius as soon as he acts alone, cuts himself off from the people and looks upon them in the same way as an architect regards bricks. There began under Peter that evil which is still an evil in our age. Like all sicknesses which go untreated it has worsened with the passing of time, and has now become a dangerous and deep-rooted ulcer in the body of our Russia. I must define this evil.

If the people do not encroach upon the state, then the state must not encroach upon the people. Only then is their relationship stable and beneficial. In the West there is constant hostility and contention between the state and the people, neither of which understands its proper relationship to the other. We have never had this hostility and contention in Russia. The people and the government lived in a beneficial union without mingling; any calamities were either external or the result of imperfect human nature. They were not the result of a false path of development or confused understanding. The Russian people have remained faithful in this respect to their views and have not encroached upon the state. But the state, in the person of Peter, did encroach upon the people, intruding into their lives and customs, and forcibly changing their manners, traditions and even their dress. Attendance at public gatherings was enforced by the police. Any tailors found making traditional Russian clothing were exiled to Siberia. The men of service, who had previously, in their private rather than state capacity, been at one with the land in sharing a common understanding, a common way of life and common traditions and dress— these now bore the brunt of Peter's insistence that changes be forcibly introduced into customs and day-to-day life, and his revolution affected them most of all. Although the government made the same demands on all classes, even the peasants, it did not make them with equal insistence, so that the original intention that not a single peasant should be allowed to enter the city sporting a beard was in due course abandoned. Instead a tax was imposed on beards. In the end the people of the land were left to go about their business and live as before; but their position in Russia had changed completely. A rupture had occurred in Russian society. The men of service, the upper classes, were torn away from their Russian roots, concepts and traditions, as well as from the Russian people. They began to live, dress and speak as foreigners. Moscow no longer suited the sovereign and he transferred his capital to the very edge of Russia, to a new city built by himself and to which he gave a German name, Sankt Peterburg. There in Petersburg the sovereign was surrounded by a whole alien population of newly-transformed Russians—officials deprived even of their native soil, for the indigenous population of Petersburg is foreign.

Thus was accomplished the rift between the tsar and his people; thus was destroyed the ancient bond between the land and the state; and thus there arose in the place of the previous bond the yoke of the state over the land. The Russian land became, as it were, conquered territory and the state was the conqueror. This was how the Russian monarch was transformed into a despot and a willingly submissive people into slaves held captive on their own land!

The newly-transformed Russians, driven partly by force and partly by enticement along an alien path, soon came to terms with their situation, for the license afforded by their adopted manners, along with the vanity, the social glitter and finally the new rights accorded to the gentry, proved a strong temptation for human passions and weaknesses. Scorn for Russia and the Russian people soon became a sort of attribute of the educated Russian intent upon emulating Western Europe. At the same time, these newly-transformed Russians, whose manners and morals had fallen under government control, now found themselves in a new relationship with the authorities—that of slaves—and they began to sense within themselves the stirrings of political ambition. Aspirations towards political power now became apparent in those classes which had become estranged from the national way of life, in particular the gentry. Attempts at revolution were made and—something hitherto unheard of—the Russian throne became the illicit plaything of rival factions. Catherine I came to the throne unlawfully; so did Anna, and on that occasion the aristocracy planned a constitution, which thankfully came to nothing. Elizabeth needed the help of soldiers to claim the throne, and need one mention the deposition of Peter III? Finally the revolt of December 14 must be seen as the fruit of those un-Russian principles introduced by Peter—it was a revolt of the upper classes estranged from the people, for we know that the soldiers were deceived into acting.

This was how the upper class, which had renounced Russian

principles, behaved. But how did those people who had not betrayed their Russian roots behave: the merchants, the settlers, and in particular the peasants, who more than all others had remained faithful to the Russian spirit and the Russian way of life?

As might be expected, the people remained calm throughout this period. Does this not prove just how alien revolution is to the Russian spirit? The nobility may have rebelled, but when did the peasants ever rise up against the sovereign? The clean-shaven face and the German outfit rebelled, but when did the Russian beard and peasant smock ever rebel?

The revolt of the Streltsy in the reign of Peter is a special case: this was more in the nature of disorderly conduct than true rebellion. Moreover, the Streltsy found no support among the masses; on the contrary, it was a detachment recruited from the masses that zealously stood against the Streltsy and broke them up. In order to win the serfs over to their side the Streltsy tore up the deeds of bondage and scattered them in the streets, but the serfs declared that they did not want such freedom and set about the Streltsy. And so the people were the first to be outraged by the Streltsy's wilful disruption, and they not only refused to support the Streltsy but even stood against them.[37] In more recent times it is, I agree, possible to point to a terrible popular uprising.[38] But whose name was falsely proclaimed on the banner of this uprising? That of Peter III, the lawful sovereign. Is this not convincing enough proof that the Russian people—the true mainstay of the Russian throne—are wholly anti-revolutionary?

Yes indeed! As long as the Russian people remain truly Russian, public order and the security of the government are assured. But Peter's system and the alien spirit which is bound up with it continue to operate, and we have seen the effect they have had on the masses of Russian people who have been led astray by them... Peter's system has prevailed for 150 years, and its more frivolous, but still harmful aspects have begun at last to affect the people too. Already in a few villages Russian dress has been abandoned and the peasants are beginning to talk of fashion. Along with these superficial symptoms there comes an alien way of life with alien notions, so that Russian principles are gradually being undermined.

As soon as the government starts to take away the *inner, communal* freedom of the people it forces them in the end to seek external, political freedom. The longer Peter's governmental system lasts (even though it is on the face of it no longer so clearly defined as it was in his time), a system which is alien to the Russian people, intruding into the communal freedom of life, inhibiting freedom of spirit, thought and opinion, and turning the subject into a slave—the longer this system lasts the more will Russia be vulnerable to alien principles, the more will the people become estranged from their native Russian soil, the more will the foundations of the Russian land be shaken, and the more desperate will become those attempts at revolution. Finally they will destroy Russia when she has reached the point when she is no longer truly Russia. Yes, Russia's only danger is that *she will cease to be Russia,* and this is where the present Petrine system is leading us. God grant that this should not come to pass!

It will be said that Peter brought glory to Russia. Certainly he brought her much outward greatness, but he infected her inner integrity with the germ of corruption; he sowed in Russian life the seed of dissension and destruction. Moreover, he and his successors achieved all these glorious outward feats through the strength of that Russia which has grown and established itself on the ancient soil and on different principles. Even today our soldiers are drawn from the people, and the Russian spirit has not yet totally disappeared even among those Russians who have been transformed by exposure to alien influences. And so the Petrine state can win through with the help of pre-Petrine Russian forces; but these forces are becoming weaker as Peter's influence grows among the people, notwithstanding the fact that the government has begun to speak of Russian nationality and even to demand it.[39] But if its good intentions are to become good deeds it must comprehend the spirit of Russia and stand on Russian principles which have been neglected since Peter's time. Under the emperors Russia's outward greatness has indeed been brilliant, but outward greatness is secure only when it flows from inner greatness. The source must not be polluted, nor allowed to dry up...

X

The contemporary state of Russia is one of inner discord concealed behind a shameless lie. The government and the upper classes have become remote and estranged from the people. The people and the government are now embarked upon different courses and are guided by different principles. Not only is the opinion of the people no longer sought, but every private citizen is afraid to speak his mind. The people have no confidence in the government, and the government does not trust the people. The people see a new act of oppression in every step taken by the government, while the government constantly fears revolution and is ready to see rebellion in every independent expression of opinion. Petitions, whether signed by many or only by a few, are no longer allowed, whereas in ancient Russia they would have been respected. The government and the people no longer understand each other and their relationship is no longer amicable...

XI

All evil stems for the most part from our repressive system of government—repressive of freedom of opinion and moral freedom, since the people in Russia do not aspire to political freedom. The suppression of all opinion and all expression of thought has reached a point where some government officials even prohibit the expression of opinion favorable to the government, since they prohibit all opinion. They do not even permit praise for the actions of authority, insisting that those in authority are not concerned with the approval of their subordinates, and that subordinates should not presume to judge, even favorably, things done by their government or their superiors. Where will such a system lead? To complete apathy and the total destruction of all feeling in man. A man is not even expected to think correctly—he is expected not to think at all! This system, if successful, would reduce men to animals who obey without thinking and without conviction!..

XII

...The real remedy for the ills of modern Russia is to *understand Russia* and return to those Russian principles which correspond to her spirit. The real remedy for the disease caused by a course of action which is unnatural for Russia is to abandon that course and return to one which is in agreement with Russian ideas and the Russian essence.

As soon as the government comes to understand Russia it will learn that any desire for political power is inimical to the spirit of the Russian people; that the fear of revolution in Russia is quite unfounded; that the use of hordes of spies serves only to spread corruption; and that the government is absolute and secure precisely because the Russian people desire it so. The people wish only these things for themselves: freedom to live, spiritual freedom and freedom of speech. Since they do not intrude upon state authority, they wish the state not to interfere in their spiritual existence and their independent way of life, such as it has done so oppressively for the past 150 years—even down to such points of detail as telling the people what they must wear. The government must understand anew its fundamental relationship to the people, the ancient bond between state and land, and resurrect it...

Let the state return to the land what belongs to the land: thought and speech; then the land will return to the government what belongs to the government: its trust and its strength...

To the government—absolute freedom to *rule,* which is its exclusive prerogative. To the people—full freedom to *live* both socially and spiritually under the government's protection. The government will possess the right of action, so the law will be in its hands. The people will possess the right of opinion, and consequently the right to free speech. That is the Russian civil order! That is the only true civil order!

1855

Part III

Belinsky and Herzen

Introduction

As will become clear in the course of this chapter and the next, Westernism was a broad intellectual and political attitude which encompassed a variety of thinkers, often with fundamentally conflicting views. Its origins lay in the philosophical circle organized in Moscow in 1831 by the gifted and charismatic nobleman Nikolai Stankevich. The activities of this circle, which included Belinsky, Bakunin and Herzen, as well as the leaders of the later and more moderate wing of liberal Westernizers, Granovsky and Botkin, were abstract and philosophical. Its members met to discuss the ideas of Schelling, Fichte and, after 1837, Hegel. Stankevich's passion for German idealism and the sincere devotion he inspired among his friends bound the group together. Potential differences in political outlook among the participants were also disguised by the tendency among early Westernizers to evade directly political debate about the principles of Russian society. When the realities of Nicholaevan Russia did subsequently begin to impinge and political views came to the fore, real differences emerged between those Westernizers of essentially liberal disposition and those—most notably Belinsky and Herzen—who eventually came to espouse radical, socialist conclusions, switching their allegiance from the metaphysical abstractions of the German idealists to the social prescriptions of French political thinkers.

The career of Vissarion Grigorevich Belinsky (1811-48) perfectly illustrates the radicalization of the early Westernist intelligentsia, a process evident from a comparison of the purely philosophical Stankevich circle of Belinsky's youth with the Petrashevsky group, a political conspiracy broken up by the tsarist police within a year after Belinsky's death. The distinctive combination of extreme moral passion, total commitment to truth, a rare capacity to live ideas, genuine love of literature, and occasional gross lapses of judgement scattered the path of Belinsky's intellectual development with many obstacles. But the same qualities served to transform this sickly, lowly, shy individual into the greatest literary and social critic of his age and an inspiration to succeeding generations of radical youth.

But it was not always so: the idealism of Schelling and Fichte, which Belinsky absorbed at gatherings of the Stankevich circle, served, if anything, to detach him initially from the political and social realities of Russia, which he saw merely as the shortcomings of an imperfect and insubstantial physical world best forsaken for the world of the ideal disclosed by aestheticism and art.[1] The refinement of personal integrity rather than the pursuit of social improvement characterized Belinsky and Westernist thought in general during these years. The subsequent discovery of reality was painful, circuitous and beset by contradiction.

In 1837 Belinsky was introduced by Bakunin to Hegel's philosophy of history, which for a while he interpreted as a means for the vindication of reality. In the notion that history was the logical outcome of a supreme *Idea* evolving dialectically towards perfection Belinsky found solace, for at a stroke it accounted for the negative aspects of reality and indicated the attitude which a rational man should adopt towards that reality:

> I look upon reality, which I used to despise so much, and I tremble with mysterious ecstasy when I recognize its rationality and realize that nothing of it may be rejected, nothing reviled or spurned.[2]

Hegel's assertion that the real is rational Belinsky took to mean that the individual was bound, logically and morally, to reconcile himself with historical and social reality. This reconciliation with reality found expression in a celebrated review of F. Glinka's "Sketches on the Battle of Borodino," published in *Notes of the Fatherland (Otechestvennye zapiski)* in 1839. Belinsky called upon the individual to submit to the rationality of reality—even to such manifestations of it as the Russian tsar—or risk being crushed "under the leaden weight of its gigantic palm."[3]

Belinsky's Hegelian conservatism went hand in hand with insistence on the value of an uncommitted (i.e., non-partisan) art, for which he argued the case in an essay of 1840 on the German literary historian, Wolfgang Menzel, who had criticized Goethe for remaining aloof from contemporary political matters. The extracts from "Menzel, Critic of Goethe" given here perfectly illustrate Belinsky's championing of such a view, as well as his conception of history as a living embodiment of an eternal idea, a rational organism developing in accordance with "immutable laws which form part of its essential nature" and using great men such as Peter the Great (or, for that matter, Nicholas I) as divine envoys carrying out the universal will.

This infatuation with Hegelianism, later dismissed as an aberration by both the critic himself and his followers, did perform the important function of revealing to Belinsky the danger inherent in ignoring the world of reality. It was a significant and ultimately positive stage in his development, for in order to become a critic of reality he had first to recognize that reality as more than just a disappointing and negligible veil behind which the resplendent ideal is concealed. It was perhaps the death of Stankevich in 1840, which Belinsky found hard to accept, that focused his growing distaste for reconciliation. Soon he repudiated his Hegelian conservatism and began to make impassioned criticisms of the reality he had tried so earnestly to vindicate. The shift is marked by two articles on the poet, Mikhail Lermontov, in 1840 and 1841 in which he defends the characteristic hero of Lermontov's work, the Romantic rebel at odds with his spiritually impoverished environment, and praises the poet for exalting negation and expressing the spirit of the age. The retreat from Hegel is also documented in his private correspondence with Botkin during the same years. In October 1840 he wrote: "I curse my vile yearning to be reconciled with vile reality... For me now the human personality is higher than history, higher than society, higher than humanity." This reappraisal was matched by a growing interest in French utopian socialism. Ideas such as those of Saint-Simon and Pierre Leroux provided Belinsky with an intellectual framework through which to articulate his instinctive protest on behalf of the oppressed individual against the particular absolutism under which he lived. This in turn allowed him to develop a new view of art and a conception of the artist as having a civic responsibility in his own society. The artist, with "wonderfully artistic and profoundly truthful works," should stimulate the spirit of protest against intolerable reality, and it was this conviction which inspired his literary criticism of the 1840s. His impassioned *Letter to Gogol* of 1847, written in response to that author's unfortunate and reactionary *Selected Passages from Correspondence with Friends,* is an outstanding example of Belinsky's mature social and aesthetic position.

Belinsky never devised a socialist system of his own; indeed, in the *Letter to Gogol* he alludes to socialism in the vaguest of terms as a form of secular Christianity. In the course of the 1840s he did acquire an increasingly materialist philosophical outlook, helped by Feuerbach's *Essence of Christianity* and Max Stirner's *The Ego and its Own.* But it was through his literary criticism and the force of his personality that Belinsky exerted an unmatched influence on his contemporaries. He was one of those rare individuals whose passionate innate moral sense drives them to defend with fanatical conviction, and regardless of personal peril, whatever they believe to be truth and justice. Thus Herzen, Ogarev and Nekrasov, on the one hand, and Granovsky, Botkin, Annenkov, Kavelin and Turgenev, on the other, were unanimous in their acknowledgment of Belinsky's moral example, although the two groups were subsequently to disagree profoundly about the practical goal to which that example should properly encourage the intelligentsia to aspire.

* * *

"A kind of Russian Voltaire of the mid-nineteenth century," Isaiah Berlin's assessment of Alexander Herzen (1812-70), in what is perhaps the finest and fondest of all introductions to his work, suggests Herzen's centrality in the history of Russian thought.[4] Endowed with a keen sense of reality, a prodigious intellect and a distinctive polemical imagination, he towers above his contemporaries, discerning cant and danger where many others saw only salvation. The product of a sceptical cast of mind rare among Russian social thinkers of the nineteenth century, Herzen's writings stand, still fresh and arresting today, as a vibrant reproach to tyranny in all its forms. Ever alert to the reality of political oppression, he nonetheless warned of the intellectual and moral oppression implicit in so many of the abstract schemes for political salvation dreamed up by the would-be liberators of humanity. The enduring feature of Herzen's thought lies in this recognition that tyranny is to be found in ideas as well as in autocratic power, and among the prophets of the left as well as the gendarmes of the right.

The illegitimate, but acknowledged son of a wealthy landowner, Herzen moved among those young, rebellious, and predominantly aristocratic intellectuals who during the 1830s sought to relieve the gloom of Nicholaevan Russia through the study and discussion of Western European thought. After an association with the Stankevich circle, Herzen formed with his lifelong friend Ogarev a group with more overtly political inclinations which read the French socialist writers. This group was broken up in 1834; Herzen was arrested and exiled from Moscow for five years. When he returned early in 1840 it was to discover that many of his former friends, including Belinsky, were enduring a phase of "reconciliation with reality" as a consequence of too literal an interpretation of Hegel's famous dictum that the real is rational. Shaken by their historical passivity and fatalism, which he scorned as "German suicide,"[5] Herzen embarked upon a study of Hegel's thought with the aim of demonstrating that it was not incompatible with free historical choice and individual action.

The result of this study was the series of essays *Dilettantism in Science* (1842-43), in which Herzen attempts to define the nature and function of "science" (in the broadest sense of "learning") and the scientist in society. In roundly Hegelian terms he affirms his faith in the importance of science as "a living organism through which truth develops." But learning must not be allowed to obscure reality and become an end in itself; knowledge should always precede and lead naturally to *action*. Herzen inveighs against three broad types of scientific dilettante: firstly, there are the fashionable dabblers—the "tourists of science"—who skim the surface of learning but have no real understanding of the problems involved. Then there are the academic specialists who lose sight of the whole amongst the factual minutiae of their narrow specialisms and remain "irrelevant to any living issue." Finally, there are the formalists, or "Buddhists," who regard science as a web of abstractions in which they gladly surrender their personalities and lose the ability to relate knowledge to life. Herzen's ideal, a kind of Hegelian reconciliation of these opposites, was that of the balanced individual who uses knowledge to achieve consciousness and provide a factual basis for the kind of speculation which leads back into reality through action.

In *Letters on the Study of Nature* (1845), another work of this Hegelian phase, Herzen shows how history has produced the separation of factual science and philosophy, bringing about a contradiction between empiricism (science) and idealism (philosophy) which must be reconciled. While these two methods exclude each other "philosophy is engulfed in abstractions, while the positive sciences are lost in an abyss of facts."[6] Facts and speculation must constantly check each other; thoughts must not "recoil before the immobile strangeness of the world of phenomena."[7] Only in this way will purpose be brought to scientific study and a sense of realism to philosophical speculation. In advocating philosophical realism and the need for thought to lead to action, Herzen did much to release Russian thinkers from the abstraction and bootless idealism characteristic of the 1830s and early 1840s, and which served as extremely congenial philosophical refuges for a generation of thinkers denied activity by Nicholas's reactionary regime. In turn this was to prepare the ground for the utilitarianism of the next generation.

Herzen left Russia for good in 1847 after a further period of exile and the death of his father. He had felt stifled in Russia and hoped that the West would afford greater opportunity for political activity. He did indeed mix with the leading European socialists of the day and was to set up the first free Russian press, producing the journals *Polar Star (Polyarnaya zvezda)* and *The Bell (Kolokol),* which were regularly smuggled back into Russia. But the most significant result of Herzen's emigration was the disillusionment produced in him by the revolutionary events of 1848 and 1849, which he witnessed. The failure of these revolutions to effect socialist principles and the triumph of the bourgeoisie inspired in Herzen a profound hatred for the narrowness of the bourgeois order and a recognition of the need for radical moral, social and economic change in Europe. The vague utopianism of the revolutionaries, their fine slogans, had all dispersed upon first contact with the reality of entrenched traditional attitudes. In the making of revolution, too, idealism had to be tempered by realism. The most enlightened minds of an age might far outstrip the masses, who tend to be cautiously conservative and resistant to change, but history can progress no quicker than the masses. All attempts to press the ideals of the enlightened few upon the unenlightened masses lead to tyranny, and efforts to short-circuit the lumbering historical processes end in failure. The European revolutions failed because they represented unrealistic attempts to leap out of the bourgeois mode before bourgeois attitudes had been eradicated. These attitudes survived into the revolutionary structures and poisoned their ideals. Socialism itself was debased into bourgeois philistinism.

In 1869 Herzen warned Bakunin that "you cannot liberate people outwardly more than they have freed themselves inwardly."[8] Insisting that "the term 'gradual progress' holds no terrors for me,"[9] Herzen came to condemn those who impulsively sacrifice themselves in the present for the sake of some future utopian ideal. Progress is achieved not through vague altruism but through the gradual emancipation of the personality, through the cultivation of egoism and human dignity, leading to the ideal of the free, critically thinking individual capable of shaping the future.

The result of this realism born of disappointment was *From the Other Shore* (1848-50), a moving indictment of abstract idealism and one of the most remarkable political statements ever written. Eschewing easy solutions—"the age possesses none"—Herzen offers an inspired critique of "views that are obsolete, slavish and false" and "preposterous idols which do not belong in our time,"[10] as well as an affirmation of the importance of the independent personality, unrestrained by dogma, in the historical process.

Herzen's disillusionment with bourgeois Europe was matched by a growing belief that socialism might be more easily achieved in "backward" Russia, where communal institutions such as the peasant *mir* survived and where bourgeois attitudes had not emerged (see the extract from *The Russian People and Socialism*). This view was to find widespread favor among the Russian populists of the 1870s. But during the late 1850s and 1860s Herzen's voice, preaching caution and gradualism and coming "from the other shore" in more ways than one, carried increasingly less weight among a new generation of less tolerant, less generous, less humane and less gifted Russian thinkers.

Finally, a note on the Herzen selections: *From the Other Shore* is the cornerstone of Herzen's writings, but its effect is diminished in extracts. Moreover, it is easily available in English translation.[11] We offer instead an extract from a relatively little-known essay on Robert Owen from Herzen's memoirs, *My Past and Thoughts*. Herzen thought highly of this piece,[12] and it vividly illustrates his mature view of history and doctrine of the free individual.

Vissarion Grigorevich Belinsky
MENZEL, CRITIC OF GOETHE (Extracts) [13]

There is a particular sort of compassionate person who is more concerned with others than with himself, and who is therefore always unhappy and always burdened with anxieties and cares. For such people the whole world is going badly and their fatherland too is tottering on the brink of destruction, a victim of the way things are going. As a result of this outlook they think it is their mission to put the world to rights and to save their fatherland, which requires only that both the world and their fatherland should trust in their wisdom and steadfastly follow their advice. For these little great men the state is not a living organism whose parts are mutually dependent on each other and whose development and life are conditioned by immutable laws which form part of its essential nature. For them the state is not a single living personality, existing in itself and for itself, with its own free will which is higher than the will of individual persons. For them the state possesses neither soil, climate, geography, history, past nor present. For them it is not the living realization of a pre-existing divine idea, which has emerged from potentiality to phenomenon and is now struggling to evolve in all its infiniteness. For them there is no all-powerful providence which governs the fate of kingdoms and peoples and which in the form of free rational necessity indicates the path *which you cannot resist* ... No, for these little great men the state is an artificial machine which can be run at will by any little great man. They censure the Peters and the Napoleons, pompously point out their mistakes, and in all seriousness let it be known that had they been in the place of these men (who, incidentally, were truly great), they would not have made such a mess of things. They argue that at such-and-such a time Peter did such-and-such a thing, whereas at that time he should have done this; or that Napoleon fell because he did not stand up for the rights of man, but thought solely of his own personal power. Poor blind fools! Peter did exactly what he was sent to do, what God entrusted to him, Peter, His envoy anointed from on high. He divined the will of the spirit of the age and carried out its bidding—not his own will, but that of Him who sent him—and for this reason he was a great man. Only the little great men strive to exercise their own fortuitous will: the will of the truly great man always coincides with divine will, and this is what makes him powerful. This is why he succeeds in his undertakings. Napoleon's fall was caused by the same thing which gave rise to him in the first place: that same mighty hand which raised him also dashed him down. He had completed his task, and he fell not through weakness, but through the burden of his strength which no longer had an

outlet. How ridiculous and pitiful these little great men are! Just imagine
the sort of madman whose deranged imagination believes that the clouds
fall on the earth and crush it, that the rays of the fire-spitting sun scorch all
life on earth, and that winter then finishes it off with its pernicious cold.
Such a man imagines it is for nothing that the sun rises in such solemn
majesty each morning and awakens all creation to exultation, from the
blade of grass to man himself; that at noon it bathes the azure dome of the
sky and its beloved daughter, the bountiful earth, in the luxurious,
everlasting gold of its light; that in the evening, with renewed solemnity,
that of the victor exhausted by victory, it descends in its eternally
unchanging path and with its pale rays gives a final, dying kiss to its
beloved and sinks behind the rose-hued curtain of shimmering twilight,
sending in its place the pale moon and myriads of radiant stars... Yes, this
has all been pointless from that unknown prehistoric moment when the
Creator's "Let there be" summoned being from non-being right up to the
present day! It is meaningless that not once has the sun risen in the evening
and set in the morning, that not once has it risen in the west and set in the
east. It is all in vain that the renewal of spring always follows the soothing
death of winter, that the hot summer follows spring, and the rich fruits of
autumn the summer, only to see in turn the late, yellowed leaves and
grasses covered by the sparkling silver frost of winter. Vainly is the ocean
confined by its shores and contained in its bottomless bed; vainly do its
waves threaten the land and sky and in furious impotence, howling and
roaring, dash against the indestructible stronghold of the granite cliffs;
vainly do the rivers carry their waves like customary tribute to the sea
instead of flowing backwards. For such a man everything is without
purpose! He cannot hear the music of the spheres and heavenly bodies; he
is deaf to that harmonious chorus whose strict hierarchy, immutable laws
and inexorable progress towards the everlasting goal inspire the eternal
artist! No, he hears only dissonance and sees only discord: clouds threaten
to extinguish the light, thunder to split open the earth, and lightning to
consume every living thing. And the poor fool takes up his ax to hew his
planks and staves; and with them he tries ignominiously to prop up the
disintegrating edifice of the universe.

    You see the same thing with the little great men we are discussing.
Willing martyrs, they do not know peace, joy and happiness. Here the light
of knowledge might be threatened with extinction, here virtue and
morality might be perishing, and there a whole people might be being
crushed—and with a howl they will point to the perpetrators of such
terrible evil, as if people or any one person were in a position to halt the
world's progress or alter a nation's destiny; as if there were no providence
and the fates of mortals were subject to blind chance or the blind will of a
single individual. Madmen! You should look more closely at history—that
holy book of human destiny, that eternal "book of kingdoms"—over

which your gaze has passed superficially, clouded by prejudices and predetermined, capricious notions about your limited personality. Beautiful Greece, the land of Homer and Plato, died: its wonderful temples are now deserted, its marble statues have been pulled down from their pedestals. The temples were destroyed and their ruins were overgrown with grass; the statues were seized by the iron hand of the conquering barbarian. But has the beauty of Greece really died for us? Do not the ruins of its temples and the fragments of their columns testify to the harmony of their construction and the pristine beauty of their sumptuous forms? Did not these wonderful statues appear before the gaze of Winckelmann[14] a thousand years later in all the splendor of their eternal youth, revealing to him the hidden recesses of the vanished existence of those radiant sons of Hellas and disclosing the marvelous mysteries of creativity? Is the *Iliad* really a dead letter for us, a dumb memorial to a long-dead and now meaningless and irrelevant past, rather than a source of living joy, that supreme rational delight in a most graceful creation of world art? Has not the life of the Greeks become an element in our own life? Have we not acquired it as a legitimate inheritance? Who will say that Greece perished forever when it fell under the onslaught of barbarism and ignorance? The moments mankind has lived through do not disappear into eternity like a voice in the wilderness; instead they become forever man's lawful property in the form of his consciousness, which alone is real and which alone is the life of the spirit and not a phantom. The memory of the bright morning of infancy and the burning noon of youth forms one of the most comforting joys of age, not only for the adult but also for the old, provided that their old-age remains lucid like the evening of a fine spring day. But mankind is higher than the individual person, and moments in its life are a higher and more rational reality than moments in the individual's life. So how could it forget ancient Greece, that luxuriant flower of its infancy, or the Middle Ages, that luxuriant flower of its youth, out of which the sumptuous fruit of its maturity has formed? Omar burned down the library at Alexandria:[15] may Omar be cursed—he destroyed forever the culture of the ancient world! But wait, my dear sirs, before cursing Omar! Culture is a wonderful thing: if it were an ocean and some Omar or other turned it dry, there would nevertheless remain beneath the earth an invisible concealed spring of living water which would soon break to the surface in a clear stream and become an ocean. Culture is immortal since it has no purpose outside itself, no "use" as it is generally termed, but is its own purpose and contains its own reason for being, as the inner life of a spirit which is becoming conscious of itself. The gratification of the spirit striving towards consciousness is the intrinsic cause and purpose of culture, and its extrinsic value for mankind is already its necessary effect. Is not the sun an independent planet, a symbol of God's glory, and not a lamp to light our little world—even though it does give us light and warmth?.. Omar burned the library at Alexandria, but he did not burn Homer or Plato, Aeschylus or Demosthenes, whom we know today. And then the barbarians destroyed the Roman Empire—was that the end of civilization or of a wise civic order? No, it was not destroyed: in the eternal city which is the capital of the political world there has once again appeared an eternal city which is the capital of the spiritual world. And then the Justinian Code, which time and barbarism had concealed, was found, and the life of the ancient world became our lawful heritage and an element in our own lives. But here is the most striking example: in our time a nation particularly well-endowed with little great men forgot that it had a history and a past and that it was a modern, Christian nation and made up its mind to become Roman. A host of little great men appeared with schoolbooks in their hands, stood around a machine which they called *la sainte guillotine,* and began to turn everyone into Romans. They *ordered* poets in the name of freedom to sing the virtues of the republic, on the assumption that *art should serve society.* They *commanded* thinkers, also in the name of freedom, to prove the equality of rights. And if any poet or thinker, on the basis of free inspiration or thought, dared to sing or prove the contrary, then they chopped off his head in the name of freedom. Art and learning perished, ideas ceased to develop, and the progress of the mind was arrested for good. But don't be too quick to despair: the same unseen but powerful will which allowed the evil to arise also exterminated it, and the monstrosity fell victim to itself like the scorpion which kills itself with its own sting. The schoolboys' venture failed, their textbooks were ridiculed, the bloody comedy was hissed off the stage—and by whom? By a son of the revolution, a single man working the will of Him who sent him.[16] Who could have foreseen or foretold this? Why, everything came to nothing, but the little great men cannot see this and in their hearts they remain convinced that if the world still hangs on, it is only by virtue of their wisdom and zeal for the common good.

Menzel belongs to the ranks of such little great men. He does not like the way things are in Germany, and in his spare time he has worked out his own plan for her wellbeing... The fundamental idea of Menzel's criticism is that art should serve society. If you like, it does serve society by expressing its consciousness and feeding the spirit of the individuals which constitute it with lofty influences and noble thoughts of goodness and truth. But it serves society not as something existing only for society's sake, but as something which exists in itself and for itself, and which contains within itself its own purpose and reason for being. If we demand from art the furthering of social aims and look upon the poet as a contractor whom we can engage at one moment to celebrate the sanctity of marriage and the next to sing the joys of sacrificing oneself for one's fatherland or the need to pay one's debts honestly, then instead of works of refinement we shall inundate literature with rhymed dissertations on abstract and intellectual subjects, dry allegories which conceal not the living truth but dead reasoning, or the crazed progeny of petty passions and factional ravings...

All this only goes to show that Menzel understands neither the significance nor the essential nature of art, and if you start to talk about something you do not understand you will automatically find yourself talking nonsense. If we add partisanship and wounded pride to this, then instead of the truth you will end up mouthing abuse and curses. One thing is clear from all this: Menzel maligns Goethe because the latter did not wish to be the mouthpiece or leader of any political faction and did not demand the unification of a fragmented Germany into a single political body, which would have been impossible. Genius always has an instinct for truth and reality: it finds what exists to be rational, necessary and real, and the rational, necessary and real only in what exists. That is why Goethe neither demanded nor wished for the impossible, but liked to take delight in what necessarily exists...

So society should not sacrifice to art any of its essential interests or depart from its aim for art's sake. Art should not serve society other than by serving itself. Let each go its own way without hindering the other.

The duty of the Pitts, Foxes, O'Connells, Talleyrands, Kaunitzes [17] and Metternichs is to take part in the destiny of nations and test their influence in humanity's political sphere. The duty of the artist is to contemplate "creation filled with glory" and be its vessel, not to meddle in political and governmental affairs. Otherwise we must cry:

> Woe to the cobbler who starts to bake pies,
> And woe to the baker who cobbling tries! [18]

Everything is great in its own place, and everything has meaning, force and validity only in its own sphere. When it encroaches upon another sphere it becomes a phantom, sometimes ridiculous, sometimes repulsive, and sometimes both ridiculous and repulsive like Menzel. Perhaps Menzel would have been a good embassy official or even a deputy representing a town or class, since perhaps he understands something of these matters and is capable of achieving something. But he cannot be even a mediocre critic, since he understands precisely nothing about art and has no capacity to be impressed by the fine and graceful. He judges art as a blind man judges color or a deaf man music. You cannot measure a volume of water in linear meters or a road in bucketfuls; you cannot judge art as if it were politics, or politics as if they were art. Each must be judged on the basis of its own laws...

Everything that exists is necessary, rational and real. Take a look at nature, nestle lovingly against its maternal bosom, listen to the beating of its heart—and you will see a marvelous unity beneath its infinite diversity and a marvelous harmony in its infinite contradictions. Who can find even one mistake, even one shortcoming in the creation of the eternal artist? Who can say that this blade of grass is not necessary or that animal is superfluous? If the natural world, which is so diverse and apparently contradictory, is so rational and real, then how can that which is higher than it—the world of history—fail to be an equally rational and real unfolding of the divine idea, rather than some sort of incoherent fairy-tale filled with fortuitous and contradictory clashes of circumstances? And yet there are people who are firmly convinced that the world is not going the way it should. We have already pointed out these people, of whom Menzel serves as an example. Why do they labor under this delusion? Because they oppose their limited personalities to that of God, and measure the infinite kingdom of the spirit against the puny yardstick of their own moral postures, which they mistakenly take to be true morality. Just look at how they judge historical figures: they ignore them as historical agents and representatives of humanity and fasten like leeches on to their personal lives, which they use to try to refute their historical greatness. What business of theirs is the personal life and character of someone like Talleyrand? Perhaps such a man might be censured for many things by his confessor, the only designated and recognized judge of his conscience, but are these so-called moral people themselves beyond such censure? Would they not do better to judge Talleyrand as a state figure with regard to his influence on the destiny of France, and leave aside his personal life, which should have no place in history. Is it not surprising in view of this that for these people history appears to be a madhouse, lunatic asylum, or dungeon crowded with criminals, rather than a pantheon of glory and immortality which contains the great representatives of humanity, the executors of divine providence. History is good! Such false views, which occasionally masquerade as superior views, stem from a purely intellectual conception of reality necessarily combined with abstraction and one-sidedness. Intellectualism knows only how to abstract the idea from the phenomenon and see just one aspect of a subject. Only true intelligence can comprehend the idea along with and inseparable from the phenomenon, and vice-versa, and grasp the subject in all its aspects with all their apparent contradictions and incompatibility, grasp it in all its completeness and wholeness. Thus intelligence does not create reality but perceives it, having previously taken cognizance of the axiom that all that exists is necessary, legitimate and rational. It does not say that such-and-such a nation is good, while all others which differ from it are bad. Neither does it say that one epoch in the history of a nation or mankind is good, while another is bad. It holds that all nations and all epochs are equally great and equally important as expressions of the absolute idea evolving in them dialectically. It considers the rise and fall of kingdoms and nations not to be fortuitous, but to be the result of an inner requirement, and the age of Roman depravity to be a subject for study not censure. It does not hold, like some sort of Voltaire, that the Crusades were the result of ignorance and an absurd or ridiculous undertaking, but regards them as a rationally necessary, great and poetic event which occurred in its appointed time and expressed a moment in mankind's youth, which like all youth was filled with noble impulses, unselfish aspirations and visionary idealism. This is the way intelligence regards all the phenomena of the real world, as necessary manifestations of the spirit. Happiness and joy, suffering and despair, faith and doubt, activity and inertia, victory and decline, struggle, dissent and reconciliation, the triumph of passion and the triumph of the spirit, even crimes, no matter how heinous—all these are seen as aspects of one and the same reality, expressing necessary moments of the spirit or its departures from normality as the result of intrinsic or extrinsic causes. But intelligence does not simply stop at this objective impartiality: in acknowledging all manifestations of the spirit as equally necessary it sees in them an unending stairway, perpendicular rather than horizontal, leading from the earth to the heavens, with each step leading further upwards.

Art is a reproduction of reality. Consequently its task is not to correct or embellish life, but to show it as it really is. Only under these conditions are poetry and morality at one...

A truly artistic work elevates and opens the soul of man to the contemplation of the infinite; it reconciles him with reality rather than setting him against it, and it strengthens him for his unselfish struggle with the adversities and storms of life. Art achieves this only when it uses particular instances to reveal what is general and rationally necessary, and portrays them in their subjective fullness, wholeness and completeness, as something self-contained. If in a tragedy the ruin and death of the heroes appear as an intrinsic requirement of their characters and actions, a resolution of the disharmony produced by them in the harmonious sphere of the spirit, or the realization of moral law, then we accept this and with our hearts moved we fall into calm, profound reflection on such a striking lesson. But when the ruin and death of the heroes of tragedy come about as a consequence of the poet's passion for horrific and startling effects—as in writers like Hugo—or for some other extrinsic, fortuitous and therefore senseless reason, then this arouses revulsion and loathing in us, as when we witness an execution or torture. Yes even the sufferings of the subjective spirit can be the subject of art, and consequently not offend against morality, provided they are depicted objectively and are illuminated by the idea of the rational necessity of their appearance. But when they are the howlings of the poet himself they cannot be artistic, for whoever howls from suffering has not risen above his suffering and therefore cannot perceive its rational necessity. So he regards it as fortuitous. Yet all fortuity offends against the spirit and leads it into discord with itself; therefore it cannot be the subject of art.

1840

Vissarion Grigorevich Belinsky
LETTERS TO V.P. BOTKIN 1840-1841 (Extracts)[19]

4 October 1840

...I curse my vile yearning to be reconciled with vile reality! Long live the great Schiller, noble advocate of humanity, bright star of salvation and emancipator of society from the bloody prejudices of tradition! Long live reason, away with darkness!—as the great Pushkin exclaimed. For me now the human personality is higher than history, higher than society, higher than humanity. This is the idea and the thought of the age! My God, I shudder to think what has been wrong with me—fever or insanity; I am like a man who is recovering from an illness...

11 December 1840

...My God, how many abominations did I commit to print in all sincerity, with all the fanaticism of wild conviction... Of course, the idea I was trying to develop in my review of Glinka's book on Borodino was sound in principle,[20] but I should have developed the idea of negation as a no less sacred historical right, without which the history of mankind would become a stagnant, stinking swamp. Honor demands that if I could not express that idea then I should not have written anything at all. It is a difficult and painful memory!..I have awoken, and I am afraid to remember my dream... That forced reconciliation with vile Russian reality, that Chinese empire of bestial material life... No, may the tongue that tries to justify all this wither away—even if it is mine, I shall not complain. "Whatever exists is rational." Well the executioner exists, and his existence is rational and real, but he is no less vile and repulsive for all that. From now on the words *liberal* and *man* are one and the same to me, as are absolutist and wielder of the knout. The idea of liberalism is rational and Christian in the highest degree, for its aim is to restore the rights of the individual and reinstate man's dignity, and Christ himself came into this world and suffered on the cross for the sake of the *individual*...

The devil alone knows what zig-zags my path of development has taken and what a terrible price in delusions I have paid for the truth—and such a bitter truth: that everything in the world is vile, and particularly for us Russians... Do you remember my first letters from Petersburg? You wrote telling me how they made a painful impression on you because you could sense in them the gnashing of teeth and howls of unbearable suffering. Why was I suffering so terribly? Because of a reality which I regarded as rational and which I defended... What a strange contradiction!

1 March 1841

...I have long suspected that Hegel's philosophy is only a moment, albeit a great one, and that the absoluteness of its conclusions is not worth a ***, that it is better to die than be reconciled with them. I intended to write this to you even before I received your letter. The fools are lying when they say that Hegel has reduced life to dead schemes; but it is true to say that he has transformed the phenomena of life into ghosts clasping bony hands and dancing in the air above the cemetery. With Hegel the subject is not an end in itself but a means for the momentary expression of the universal, and this universal takes on the nature of a Moloch with regard to the subject, for when it has finished parading about in the subject it casts it off like a pair of old trousers. I have particularly good cause for being angry with Hegel, for I feel that I was being loyal to him (in feeling) in coming to terms with Russian reality, praising Zagoskin[21] and similar abominations, and hating Schiller. In the latter I was even more consistent than Hegel himself, though stupider than Menzel. All Hegel's talk about morality is utter nonsense, for there is no morality in the objective realm of thought, just as there is none in objective religion (as, for instance, in Indian pantheism where Brahma and Shiva are both gods—i.e., good and evil possess equal autonomy). I know you will laugh at me, baldy, but you can laugh as much as you like; I shall stick to my guns. The fate of the subject, the individual, the personality is more important than the fate of the whole world and the well-being of the Chinese emperor (i.e., Hegel's *Allgemeinheit*).[22] I am told to develop all the treasures of my spirit for the spirit freely to delight in, to weep in order to be comforted, to grieve in order to rejoice once more, to aspire to perfection, to climb the highest rung of the ladder of development, and if I stumble, so what—down I go, the devil take me, son of a bitch that I am. Humble thanks, Egor Fedorych,[23] and regards to your philosopher's cap; but with all due respect to your philosophical philistinism I have the honor to inform you that were I to reach the highest rung of development's ladder, I should then demand of you full account of all the victims of circumstance in life and history, all those martyrs to contingency, superstition, the Inquisition, Philip II, etc. Otherwise I should cast myself down head first from the highest rung. I do not want happiness, even for nothing, if I cannot be assured about each of my fellow men, who are bone of my bone and flesh of my flesh. They say that disharmony is a condition of harmony; that perhaps is all very advantageous and comforting for lovers of music, but not for those whose fate it is to express the idea of disharmony...

I am one of those people who see the devil's tail in everything; and that, I think, will remain my final world outlook until I die. I suffer because of this, mind you, but I am not ashamed of it. On his own a man knows nothing—everything depends on the spectacles placed upon his nose by his disposition and quirks of his nature, which are beyond the control of his will. A year ago I thought exactly the opposite of what I think now, and in all truth I do not know whether it is a good thing or not that for me to think and feel, to understand and suffer are one and the same thing. This is where we must beware of fanaticism. You know, the man I am today painfully detests my past self, and if I had the power and authority then woe betide those who are today what I was a year ago. You would see the devil's tail in everything if you saw yourself lying shrouded in your coffin, still alive, with your hands tied behind your back. What is it to me that I am convinced that reason will triumph, that everything will be fine in the future, if fate has commanded me to be a witness to the triumph of blind chance, unreason and brute force? What is it to me that all will be well for my children or yours, if I find things so awful and through no fault of my own? Would you wish me to withdraw into myself? No, better to die, better to be a living corpse!..

What a fine Prussian government in which we thought to see the ideal of rational government! What is there to say?—they are scoundrels, tyrants of humanity! A member of the triple alliance of executioners of freedom and reason.[24] There's Hegel for you!..

28 June 1841

...Alas, my friend, I am now filled with a single idea which has swallowed me up and devoured me completely. You know I am not destined to get to the core of truth, from where you can see all the points surrounding it from an equal distance. No, somehow I always seem to find myself at an extreme. So it is now: I am completely taken up by the idea of civic virtue, by the pathos of truth and honor, and I hardly notice any greatness apart from that... There has developed in me a sort of wild, frenzied, and fanatical love of freedom and the independence of the human personality, which are possible only in a society founded on truth and virtue...

It is strange, my dear Botkin: my life is sheer apathy, boredom and languor, a stagnant mire; but at the bottom of that mire there blazes a sea of fire. I always used to fear that I would slowly die with the passing of the years—but quite the opposite has happened. I have been disillusioned by everything, I believe in nothing, I love nothing and nobody, yet the interests of prosaic life absorb me less and less, and I am more and more becoming a citizen of the universe. A terrible thirst for love ever more consumes me inside, a yearning that is ever more painful and persistent. This is my problem, and only mine. But I am also keenly concerned with matters outside myself. Human personality has become an obsession which I fear will drive me insane. I am beginning to love mankind *à la* Marat: in order to make the smallest part of it happy I think I would be prepared to destroy the rest of it with fire and the sword. What right has any man, no different from me, to set himself above humanity and distance himself from it by means of an iron crown and purple robe, which, as Schiller—the Tiberius Gracchus of our age [25]—once said, bears traces of the blood of the first manslayer? What right has he to fill me with degrading fear and trembling? Why must I bare my head before him?.. Hegel dreamed of a constitutional monarchy as the ideal form of government—what a narrow concept! No, there should be no monarchs, for the monarch is no brother to humanity: he will always be separated from other men even if only for the sake of empty etiquette; they will always bow down to him even if only for form's sake. Men should be brothers and should not humiliate one another by even a hint of any kind of external, formal superiority. How clever of those two nations of antiquity to be born with such a concept! How clever of the French to understand without the aid of German philosophy what German philosophy has still failed to understand! By the devil, I must study the Saint-Simonists!..

8 September 1841

...You know my nature: it always goes to extremes and never strikes the center of an idea. I part with an old idea with difficulty and pain, and then renounce it absolutely, taking up a new one with all the fanaticism of a proselyte. And so I am now at a new extreme—this is the idea of *socialism,* which has become for me the idea of ideas, the being of being, the question of questions, the alpha and omega of faith and knowledge. It is the be all and end all, the question and answer. For me it has swallowed up history, religion, and philosophy...

Sociality, sociality or death! That is my slogan. What is it to me that the universal lives if the personality is suffering? What care I that genius lives on earth as if in heaven, if the masses are wallowing in the dirt? What is it to me that I grasp the idea, that I am allowed access to the world of ideas in art, religion and history, when I cannot share it with all those who should be my brothers in humanity, my neighbors in Christ, but who in fact are strangers and enemies to me in their ignorance? What care I that there is bliss for the elect, when the majority have no inkling of it? Away with bliss if it is given to me alone out of thousands! I do not want it if I cannot share it with my lesser brethren! My heart bleeds and shudders when I look at the masses and their representatives. I am struck with grief, painful grief, when I see bare-footed little boys playing knucklebones in the street, beggars in rags, the drunken cabman, the soldier returning from duty, the clerk running along with his briefcase under his arm, the self-satisfied officer, and the haughty big-wig. When I give a penny to the soldier I almost cry; when I give the beggar a penny I run away as if I have done something wrong, ashamed at the sound of my own footsteps. And that's what life is like: sitting in the street in rags with an idiotic expression on your face, collecting a few pennies during the day to spend in the tavern at night. And people see this and do not care! I don't know what is becoming of me but sometimes I stand for minutes on end gazing in terrible anguish at the whore, and her senseless smile, the mark of depravity in all its immediacy, tears my soul, especially if she is good-looking. Next door to me lives a fairly well-to-do official who has become so Europeanized that when his wife goes out to the baths he hires her a carriage. Recently I heard that he had smashed her teeth and lips, dragged her about the floor by her hair, and thrashed her with sticks, all because the cream she used for his coffee was not fresh enough; yet she had borne him six children. Whenever I met her I was always upset by the sight of her pale, exhausted face, stamped with the sufferings of tyranny. On hearing about this I gnashed my teeth—burning would be too good for the blackguard, and I cursed my impotence at not being able to go and kill him like a dog. So this is a society built on rational principles, a manifestation of reality! How many husbands and families are there like this! How many beautiful feminine creatures are cast from the hands of trembling parents to be corrupted by beasts for mercenary reasons or through lack of intelligence! Has a *man* the right after that to bury himself in art or knowledge! I am embittered by all those substantial principles which in the form of creeds bind the will of man! Negation is my god. My heroes in history are those destroyers of the past such as Luther, Voltaire, the Encyclopedists, the terrorists, Byron (in *Cain*), etc. Clear reason is now higher in my esteem than any immediate intelligence, and therefore I prefer the blasphemies of Voltaire to the authority of religion, society, or whatever! I am aware that the Middle Ages were a great epoch, and I understand the sacredness, poetry and grandeur of medieval religiosity; but I prefer the eighteenth century, the age of religion's decline. In the Middle Ages they burned heretics, freethinkers and witches at the stake; in the eighteenth century the guillotine chopped off the heads of aristocrats, priests and the other enemies of God, reason and humanity. And I fervently believe that there will come a time when no one will be burned and no one beheaded; when the criminal will plead for death as a mercy and deliverance and death will be denied him, for life will serve as his punishment just as death does today; when there will be no senseless uniforms and rituals, no contracts and conditions binding feeling, no duties and responsibilities, and will shall yield to love alone, not to will; when there will be no husbands and wives, only lovers... Woman will not be the slave of society and man, but, like man, will freely follow her inclinations without losing her good name or that monstrosity—her social reputation. There will be neither rich nor poor, neither tsars nor subjects; there will be only brothers and men; and according to the words of the apostle Paul, Christ will pass his power to the Father and the Father-Reason will again reign supreme, but this time in a new heaven and over a new earth. Do not think that I am being excessively rational in my thinking: no, I don't repudiate the past, I don't repudiate history—I see in them the necessary and rational development of the idea. I want the golden age, but not the former, unreasoning, animal golden age, but one prepared by society, laws, marriage, in short by everything that has in its time been essential, but which is today stupid and trite... And this will be achieved through *sociality,* and hence there is nothing higher or nobler than facilitating its development and progress. But it is ridiculous to think that this can come about on its own, simply in due course, without violent upheavals and bloodshed. People are so stupid that you have to lead them forcibly to happiness. And of what significance is the blood of a few thousand when compared to the degradation and suffering of millions. So: *fiat justitia—pereat mundus!*

1840-41

Vissarion Grigorevich Belinsky
LETTER TO N. V. GOGOL

You are only partly right in regarding my article as that of an angry man: this epithet is too weak and mild to express the state I was reduced to on reading your book.[26] But you are quite wrong in ascribing this to your indeed none too flattering references to admirers of your talent. No, there was a more important reason for it. One can put up with a sense of injured pride, and I would have had sufficient wit to let the matter pass if this had been all there was to it. But one cannot endure an outraged sense of truth and human dignity, nor keep silent when under the guise of religion and the protection of the knout lies and immorality are preached as truth and virtue.

Yes, I loved you with all the passion with which a man bound by blood to his country can love its hope, its honor, its glory, one of its greatest leaders on the road to consciousness, development and progress. And you had good cause for momentarily losing your equanimity when you forfeited your right to that love. I say this not because I consider my love to be sufficient reward for great talent, but because in this matter I speak not just for myself but for a host of people most of whom you and I have never set eyes on, and who in turn have never set eyes on you. I cannot even begin to convey to you the indignation your book has aroused in all noble hearts, or the shouts of wild joy which its appearance has provoked among all your enemies, both the non-literary (the Chichikovs, Nozdryovs and Town Mayors)[27] and the literary, whose names you know. You have seen for yourself how your book has been disowned even by those who appeared to be in sympathy with its spirit. Even if it had been written out of deep and sincere conviction it would still have had the same effect on the public. And you have only yourself to blame if it has been taken by everyone (except the few who have to be seen and known for one not to be pleased by their approval) as a cunning but all too transparent device for attaining purely wordly ends by celestial means. This is in no way surprising; what is surprising is that you find it so. I think this is because you know Russia deeply only as an artist and not as a thinker—a role you have assumed so unsuccessfully in your fantastic book. Not that you are not a thinking man, but for so many years you have been accustomed to looking at Russia from your "beautiful far-away," and as everyone knows there is nothing easier than seeing things from a distance as we would wish to see them. Moreover, in your beautiful far-away you live a life of complete estrangement, within yourself, inside yourself, or in the monotonous circle of those of similar disposition to yourself, who cannot resist your influence. For this reason you have failed to notice that Russia sees her salvation not in mysticism, asceticism, or pietism, but in the advances of civilization, enlightenment and humanism. She does not need sermons (she has heard enough of those already!), or prayers (she has repeated them for long enough!), but an awakening in the people of a sense of human dignity, buried for so long in the dirt and the muck. She needs rights and laws compatible with good sense and justice, rather than with the teachings of the Church, and the strictest possible enforcement of them. But instead of this she presents the ghastly spectacle of a country where people traffic in people without even the excuse so cunningly employed by the American plantation owners, who claim that the negro is not a human being; a country where people are not known by names, but by nicknames like Vanka, Styoshka, Vaska and Palashka; a land, finally, where not only are there no guaranteed rights of personal integrity, honor, or property, but there is not even a proper police system, only huge corporations of various official thieves and robbers. The most vital national problems in Russia today are the abolition of serfdom, the repeal of corporal punishment, and the strictest possible implementation of at least those laws which do exist. Even the government (which knows full well how the landowners treat their peasants, and how many of the former are killed each year by the latter) is aware of this, as is apparent from its timid and fruitless half-measures on behalf of our white negroes and its laughable replacement of the knout by the three-tailed whip. Such are the problems which disturb Russia in her apathetic slumber! And at such a time a great writer whose wonderfully artistic and profoundly truthful works have so powerfully stimulated Russia's self-awareness and enabled her to see herself as if in a mirror, comes out with a book which in the name of Christ and the Church teaches the barbarian landowner to squeeze even more money out of his peasants, who are criticized for their *unwashed snouts*! And am I not supposed to be indignant at this? Why even if you had made an attempt on my life I could not hate you more than I do for these shameful lines... And after all this you want people to believe in the sincerity of your book's intentions? No, if you had truly been filled with Christ's truth instead of the teachings of the Devil, you would have written something quite different to your follower among the landowners. You would have told him that since his peasants are his brothers in Christ, and since brother should not be slave to brother, he should either give them their freedom or at least make use of their labor in the way most advantageous for them, recognizing in the depths of his conscience the falseness of his position with regard to them. And the expression "Oh, you unwashed snout"! Which Nozdryov or Sobakevich did you hear this from in order to bestow it upon the world as a great discovery for the benefit and edification of the Russian muzhiks, whose only reason for not washing is that they believe their masters and do not regard themselves as human beings! And your concept of the Russian

national system of courts and punishments, the ideal of which you have
found in the words of the stupid woman in Pushkin's tale, who argues that
the innocent and the guilty alike should be flogged![28] That indeed often
happens with us, but most often it is just the innocent who are flogged if
they cannot afford to pay their way out of it—the guiltlessly guilty! And
such a book is supposed to be the result of an arduous inner process and
lofty spiritual insight? That cannot be! Either you are sick and must seek
help at once, or—I dare not finish.

Proponent of the knout, apostle of ignorance, champion of obscurantism and darkness, panegyrist of Tatar ways—what are you doing?
Look beneath your feet: you are standing over an abyss... That you can
base such a teaching on the Orthodox Church I can well understand: it has
always been a supporter of the knout and servile towards despotism. But
why mix Christ up in all this? What do you find in common between him
and any Church, let alone the Orthodox Church? He first proclaimed to
people the doctrine of freedom, equality and brotherhood, setting the seal
to it and affirming the truth of his teaching by his martyrdom. And it
remained man's salvation only until it was organized into the Church and
took as its basis the principle of Orthodoxy. For the Church was a
hierarchy and hence a champion of inequality, a flatterer of authority, the
enemy and persecutor of brotherhood among men—which it remains to
this day. But the meaning of Christ's teaching has been revealed by the
philosophical movement of the last century. That is why someone like
Voltaire who used the weapon of ridicule to extinguish the fires of
fanaticism and ignorance in Europe is, of course, more the son of Christ,
the flesh of his flesh and bone of his bone, than all your priests, bishops,
metropolitans and patriarchs, whether Eastern or Western. Do you really
not know this? Why, none of it would come as a surprise to any of today's
schoolboys.

Can it really be then that you, the author of *The Government
Inspector* and *Dead Souls,* have in all sincerity and with all your heart sung
a hymn of praise to the infamous Russian clergy, ranking it higher than the
Catholic clergy? We must assume that you do not know that the latter was
something at one time, whereas the former has never been anything apart
from the servant and slave of worldly authority. But are you really not
aware that our clergy is held in universal contempt by Russian society and
the Russian people? About whom do the Russian people tell obscene tales?
About the priest, about his wife, about his daughter, and about his hired
worker. Whom do the Russian people call "idiot species," "scoundrels,"
"stallions?" The priests. Is not the Russian priest in the eyes of all Russians
a symbol of gluttony, avarice, obsequiousness and shamelessness? And can
it be that you really don't know this? How strange!

According to you the Russian people are the most religious in the
world. That is a lie! The basis of religious feeling is pietism, reverence and

the fear of God. But the Russian speaks the name of God while scratching his behind. He says of icons: "if you can't use them for praying, use them for covering the pots." If you look more closely you will see that these people are by nature profoundly atheistic. They have many superstitions, but no trace of religious feeling. Superstition passes with the progress of civilization, whereas religious feeling often keeps pace with it. A good example is provided by France, where even now there are many sincere and fanatical Catholics among enlightened and educated people, and where many still cling stubbornly to some sort of divinity even though they might have discarded Christianity. The Russian people are not like that: mystical exaltation is not in their nature; they have too much common sense, too clear and positive a mind for that—and therein perhaps lies the greatness of their historical destiny in the future. In Russia religious feeling has not taken root even among the clergy; those few isolated and exceptional individuals who lead lives of tranquil, cool, ascetic contemplation prove nothing. The majority of our clergy have always been distinguished for their fat bellies, theological pedantry and utter ignorance. It would be quite wrong to accuse them of religious intolerance and fanaticism; rather they should be praised for their exemplary indifference in matters of faith. In Russia religious feeling has emerged only among the schismatics who are the very antithesis in spirit of the mass of the people and comparatively negligible in number.

I shall not dwell on your eulogy to the loving bond between the Russian people and their masters. I'll be blunt: this eulogy has met with sympathy nowhere and has lowered you even in the esteem of those who in other respects are very close to your way of looking at things. As far as I personally am concerned, I leave it to your conscience to revel in the contemplation of the divine beauty of autocracy (they say you find this a safe and profitable pursuit); only do carry on contemplating it judiciously from your "beautiful far-away"—it is not so lovely or so harmless at close quarters... Let me make just one observation: when the European, and particularly the Catholic, is seized by the religious spirit he becomes the scourge of unjust authority, like the Hebrew prophets who denounced the lawlessness of those who enjoyed great power on earth. With us, on the contrary, no sooner is a person (even a decent person) struck by that illness which doctors and psychiatrists know as *religiosa mania* than he starts to burn more incense to the earthly god than to the heavenly one. Moreover, he overdoes it to such a degree that the recipient would dearly like to reward him for his slavish zeal, were it not for the risk of compromising himself in the eyes of society... What a scoundrel our brother the Russian is!

I recall further that in your book you affirm as a great and incontrovertible truth that for the common people literacy is not only useless but positively harmful. What can I say to this! May your Byzantine

God forgive you this Byzantine thought, unless in committing it to paper
you were not aware of what you were doing...

As far as I can see you really do not know the Russian public at all
well. Its character is determined by the state of Russian society, in which
fresh forces are seething and trying to break through; but crushed by the
weight of oppression they can find no release and produce only despondency, anguish and apathy. Only in literature is there life and forward
movement, despite the Tatar censorship. That is why the title of writer is so
respected among us; that is why literary success comes so easily even to
those of limited talent. The titles of poet and writer have long since eclipsed
the trumpery of epaulettes and fancy uniforms in Russia. And that is why
we reward with particular and widespread attention any so-called liberal
tendency, even when accompanied by little actual ability, and why great
artists who sincerely or insincerely offer themselves in the service of
orthodoxy, autocracy and nationality [29] lose their popularity so quickly. A
striking example of this is Pushkin, who only had to write two or three
loyal verses and don the livery of Gentleman of the Bedchamber to
suddenly forfeit the people's love. [30] You are badly mistaken if you
seriously think that your book failed not because of its disreputable
opinions, but because of the harshness of the truths supposedly addressed
by you to all and sundry. Assuming this to be true of the literary fraternity,
you still have to explain the public's reaction. Did you tell it any less bitter
truths any less harshly or with less truth and talent in *The Government
Inspector* or *Dead Souls*? The public did indeed get upset with you to the
point of fury, but *The Government Inspector* and *Dead Souls* did not fail
as a result, whereas your latest book has sunk shamefully without trace.
And here the public is right: it sees in Russian writers its only leaders, its
protectors and saviours from the darkness of autocracy, orthodoxy and
nationality, and therefore although it is always prepared to forgive a writer
a bad book, it will never forgive him a harmful one. This shows what a
fresh and healthy instinct there is in our society, albeit still in embryo, and
it shows that it has a future. If you love Russia rejoice with me at the failure
of your book!..

Your conversion may, I suppose, have been sincere, but your idea of
bringing it to the attention of the public was most unfortunate. The days of
naive piety have long passed, even in our society. People now understand
that it makes no difference where you pray, and that the only people who
seek Christ in Jerusalem are those who have never borne him in their hearts
or have lost him. Whoever suffers at the sight of another's suffering or is
pained by the spectacle of other men under oppression already has Christ
in his heart and has no need to go on foot to Jerusalem. [31] The humility you
preach is nothing new for a start, and what is more it smacks of the most
terrible pride on the one hand and the most shameful debasement of one's
human dignity on the other. The idea of becoming some sort of abstract

symbol of perfection, superior to all others in humility, can only be the fruit of either pride or imbecility, and in either case it leads inevitably to hypocrisy, bigotry and Chinaism. Moreover, you have taken the liberty of expressing yourself cynically and rudely not only about others (which is merely impolite), but also about yourself, which is vile. The man who strikes his neighbor in the face arouses indignation, but the man who strikes his own face evokes contempt. No, you are beclouded rather than enlightened. You have understood neither the spirit of Christianity nor the form it has taken in our time. Your book breathes not the true Christian teaching, but a morbid fear of death, the Devil and hell...

If I were to give full rein to my feelings this letter would soon fill a thick notebook. I never intended to write to you on this subject, although I ached to do so and you yourself have gone into print inviting each and everyone to write to you without standing on ceremony and with an eye only for the truth. I could not have done this had I been in Russia, for the Shpekins[32] there open other people's letters not just for the fun of it, but in the line of duty, in order to inform. But this year the onset of consumption has driven me abroad and N. has forwarded your letter to me in Salzbrunn, from where I am leaving today with An. bound for Paris and Frankfurt-am-Main.[33] The unexpected receipt of your letter has given me the opportunity to write and tell you everything I hold against you on account of your book. I cannot say things by halves, nor can I dodge the issue; I am not made that way. If either you or time shows me that I am mistaken in my conclusions about you I shall be the first to rejoice—but I do not regret what I have written to you. What is at stake here is not my personality or yours, but something much greater than me and even than you. What is at stake is truth, Russian society and Russia herself. Let this be my final word: if you have had the misfortune to renounce your truly great works with haughty humility, then you must now with sincere humility renounce your latest book and atone for the terrible sin of having published it by producing new works reminiscent of your earlier ones.

1847

Alexander Ivanovich Herzen
DILETTANTISM IN SCIENCE (Extracts)

[The Dilettantes and the Guild of Scientists] [34]

Dilettantism is the love of science allied with a complete lack of understanding of it. It spreads its love over the whole sea of knowledge and cannot concentrate its efforts. This love which achieves nothing is enough to satisfy the dilettante, and he cares about nothing, not even whether this love is reciprocated. It is a platonic, romantic passion for science, the kind of love which begets no children. The dilettantes speak with rapture about the weaknesses and high points of science; they scorn all other discourse, leaving it to the rabble. But they are mortally afraid of questions, and they betray science like traitors as soon as logic begins to close in on them. The dilettantes are the people of the foreword, of the title page—the people who walk around the pot while others are eating...

Dilettantism is not something new. Nero was a dilettante in music and Henry VIII in theology. The dilettantes assume the outer appearance of their age. In the eighteenth century they were gay, boisterous, and called themselves *esprit fort*; in the nineteenth century the dilettante has fallen into melancholic and mysterious thought. He loves science, but is aware of its perfidy; he is a bit of a mystic and reads Swedenborg, but he is also a bit of a sceptic and dips into Byron; he often repeats with Hamlet: "There are more things in heaven and earth, Horatio, than are dreamt of in your philosophy," yet in his own mind he is sure he understands everything. Finally, the dilettante is the most harmless and useless of mortals: he meekly passes his life in communion with the sages of all times, with no regard for material concerns. Lord knows what they talk about! Even the dilettante is not sure, but he is quite at home in this half-light.

The caste of scientists (*die Fachgelehrten*) [35]—those scientists by virtue of profession, diploma and sense of their own worth—is the complete antithesis of the dilettantes. The main shortcoming of this caste is the fact that it is a caste; the second is the specialism in which these scientists are generally lost... This jealous caste wants to keep the light to itself, and it surrounds science with a forest of scholasticism, barbarous terminology and ponderous, discouraging language. In the same way the farmer sows a thorny bush around his plot, so that those who impudently try to crawl through will prick themselves a dozen times and tear their clothing to shreds. All in vain! The time of the aristocracy of knowledge has passed...

Science is a table laid out for each and every man who is hungry and craves manna from heaven. The striving for truth and knowledge in no way precludes the living of life in any particular way, whether as a chemist, physician, artist, or merchant. It is unthinkable that the specialized scientist should have a greater right to the truth; he only has greater pretensions to it. Why should a man who spends his life in the monotonous and one-sided study of some specialized subject possess clearer vision or more profound ideas than another, who is caught up in life itself and has rubbed shoulders with thousands of different people? Quite the contrary: whatever the guild scientist turns his hand to outside his field he does awkwardly. He is irrelevant to any living issue. He least of all suspects the great significance of science. Lost in the particularities of his specialized subject, he does not know science; he considers his subject to be the whole of science. Such scientists in their extremism occupy a place in society corresponding to the second stomach in the ruminant: no fresh food ever reaches them—only chewed-over food which is then chewed again simply for the pleasure of chewing. The masses act, sweating and bleeding, and the scientists come along afterwards to deliberate on events. Poets and artists create, the masses are enraptured by their creations, but the scientists write commentaries and analyses, grammatical or otherwise. All this has its value; the injustice lies in the fact that they consider themselves by right to be head and shoulders above the rest of us, high priests of Pallas, her lovers, or even worse her husbands. On the other hand, it would be even stranger to assert that the scientists are incapable of knowing the truth, or that it is beyond them. The spirit which impels man towards the truth excludes nobody. Not all scientists belong to the ranks of *guild* scientists. Many truly learned people overcome their bookishness and become genuinely *educated,* leaving the guild for humanity at large. The *hopeless* guild-scientists are those determined and desperate specialists and scholars, whom Jean Paul had in mind when he said: "The culinary art will soon reach such a state that the man who fries trout will not know how to fry carp."[36] It is these fryers of carp and trout who make up the bulk of the caste of scientists, producing all kinds of lexicons, tables, observations and all kinds of things which require infinite patience and a soul that is dead. It is hard to make people out of them. They are the one-sided development of learning in an extreme form. Not only will they die in this one-sided state, but they also impede the path of every great accomplishment not because they do not want science to progress, but because they only acknowledge achievement if it has come about through strict observance of their procedures and forms, or if they have brought it off themselves. They have only one method—the anatomical method; in order to understand an organism they must perform an autopsy. Who was it that killed Leibnitz's doctrine and turned it into a scholastic corpse, if not the learned dissectors? Who tried to turn Hegel's living, all-embracing system into a fearful, lifeless, scholastic skeleton? The professors of Berlin!

The Greeks, who knew how to develop individuality to a kind of artistic perfection and thoroughly human fullness, knew little in their heyday of scientists in our sense: their thinkers, historians and poets were first and foremost citizens, people who belonged to life, to the civic council, to the public square and the military camp. Hence that harmoniously balanced and multi-faceted development, so beautifully modulated, of great personalities and their activities in science and art: Socrates, Plato, Aeschylus, Xenophanes, and so on. But what of our scientists?..

The scientist has so departed from his age, has so withered and dried up in all respects that almost superhuman efforts are required to fit him into life's chain as a living link.[37] The truly educated man considers nothing human to be outside his field: he is in sympathy with all that surrounds him. It is quite the opposite with the scientist: everything human is alien to him apart from his chosen subject, no matter how limited that subject might be in itself. The educated man thinks as the result of a free impulse, by virtue of the nobility of human nature, and his thoughts are expansive and free. The scientist thinks out of necessity, in accordance with some vow he has taken, and there is therefore something pedantically workmanlike about his thought; it is always inhibited...

The difference between the scientists and the dilettantes is quite striking. The dilettantes love science, but don't bother themselves with it. They float about in the azure which hovers over science and which is as insubstantial as the azure of the earth's atmosphere. For the scientists science is a plot of land on which they are called upon to till their allotted strip. Preoccupied with the details of their furrow, they have no time at all to cast a glance at the field as a whole. The dilettantes observe through a telescope, and so they can see only those things which are at least as far away as the moon; they see nothing of what is near and of this world. The scientists observe through a microscope and can therefore see nothing large. For something to be noticed by them it must be invisible to the naked eye. For them there is no such thing as a clear running stream, only droplets filled with nasty homeopathic creatures. The dilettantes admire science as we admire Saturn: at a comfortable distance and content in the knowledge that it shines and has a ring around it. The scientists have got so close to the temple of science that they cannot see it, or anything else for that matter, apart from the brick against which their nose is pressed. The dilettantes are tourists in the realms of science and, like tourists everywhere, they know the lands in which they travel only through general remarks and other such nonsense, through newspaper slander, society gossip and court intrigues. The scientists are the production workers of science and, like all workers, they are devoid of intellectual agility. This does not prevent them from being outstanding masters of their own craft, but they are no use for anything else. Every dilettante is concerned with everything that is *scibile,* as well as with the unknowable, such as mysticism, magnetism, physiognomy, homeopathy, hydropathy, etc. The scientist, on the other hand, devotes himself to a single chapter or separate branch of some specialized field of knowledge, beyond which he neither knows nor wishes to know anything. Occasionally this is valuable in that it furnishes facts for genuine science. Needless to say, the dilettantes are of no use to anyone or anything. Many think that the self-sacrifice with which the scientists dedicate themselves to the academic life and to boring, monotonous and wearisome work for the good of their subject merits the eternal gratitude of society. It seems to me that work and activity are their own rewards. But without going too deeply into this, I should like to tell an old anecdote.

A good Frenchman once made a wax model of a block of houses in Paris in amazingly fine detail. On finishing this work of many years he submitted it to the Convention of the one and indivisible Republic. The Convention, as we know, was of a stern and eccentric disposition. At first it said nothing: it had enough on its plate without wax models—it had to form various armies, feed the hungry people of Paris, defend itself against the coalition, and so on... Finally it got around to the model and decreed the following: "Citizen So-and-So, whose work we cannot but concede to be exquisitely finished, is to be imprisoned for six months for spending his time on something useless while his country was in danger." In a sense the Convention was right, but the trouble was that it looked at things from only one point of view, and not a very pleasant one at that. It did not occur to the Convention that a man *capable* of devoting years on end, and such years as those, to modeling wax *could not* be put to any other use. I feel that such people should be neither rewarded nor punished. Scientific specialists are in the same position: they should be neither scolded nor praised; their activities are to be sure neither better nor worse than the daily pursuits of others. It is a strange injustice that scientists are considered superior to ordinary citizens and are spared all public burdens just because they are scientists, when they are quite happy sitting about in their academic gowns leaving all cares and effort to others. The fact that someone is obsessed by stones, medals, sea-shells or the Greek language is no justification for granting him a privileged position. Meanwhile, the scientists, spoiled by society, have nearly reached a troglodytic state of withdrawal. Nowadays everyone knows that you can't leave anything to the scientist. He is the perpetual adolescent among people; only in his laboratory or museum is he not ridiculous. The scientist even loses the primary characteristic which distinguishes man from the animal—sociability. He is embarrassed and timid in company; he can no longer speak naturally; he trembles in the face of danger; he does not know how to dress; and there is something pathetic and uncivilized about him. He is a funny kind of Hottentot, just as Khlestakov was a funny kind of general.[38] Such is the mark with which Nemesis brands the man who would wish to withdraw from humanity without the right to do so. And they demand that we recognize their superiority! They demand some sort of thank you from mankind, imagining themselves to be its vanguard! Never! The scientists are clerks in the service of the idea, the bureaucrats of science, its scribes, departmental heads and registrars...

But can science exist without specialization? Is not the sort of encyclopedic superficiality which grabs at everything precisely the weakness of dilettantism? Of course science cannot exist without specialization, but here is the point: science is a living organism through which the truth is developed. It has only one true method, namely the process of its organic plastic evolution. The outward form, the system, is predetermined in the very essence of the idea of science and is developed in accordance with contingency and the possibilities for its realization. The complete system lies in the differentiation and development of the *soul* of science, so that the soul becomes matter and matter the soul. Their unity is realized in the method. No amount of information becomes science until it grows like living flesh around a living center, that is to say until it arrives at an understanding of itself through its living form. No brilliant universality, on the other hand, constitutes complete scientific knowledge if, confined to the frozen wastes of abstraction, it lacks the power to incarnate itself, to evolve from genus into species, from the universal into the *individual,* or if the need for individualization, the transition into the world of phenomena and action, is not contained in some inner requirement which it cannot *resist.* All things living are actual and alive only as a whole, with the external and internal, the general and the particular, coexisting. Life binds together these features; it is a process of eternal transition from one into the other. Any one-sided understanding of science fragments the unity and destroys the living. Dilettantism and formalism remain within abstract universality, and thus they afford no real knowledge, only shadows. They disperse easily in the void surrounding them. To lighten their load they wished to separate life from the living, and their burden was indeed lightened, for such abstraction is tantamount to nothing at all. And this nothingness is precisely the favorite medium for dilettantes of all degrees. They see in it an infinite ocean and are delighted at such scope for dreaming and fantasy. But if there is evidently something absurd in the idea of separating life from the living organism while still hoping to preserve it, then the error made by the specialist is, of course, just as bad. He does not want to know about the universal and never aspires to it. Preserving every detail and particularity as an end in itself, he regards these as sufficient purpose. Specialism can get as far as compiling catalogues or all kinds of subsumptions, but it will never penetrate to their inner essence, to their real meaning and the truth, because to do so would mean sublimating the particular. This method is like trying to define a person's inner characteristics by means of his galoshes and buttons. The specialist's whole interest is concentrated on the particulars and with every step he gets more and more entangled. The particulars become more detailed and more insignificant, the process of dissection becomes infinite. The dark chaos of fortuity watches over him, ever ready to lure him into the mire at that extreme limit of being, where no light ever penetrates. This is his infinite ocean, the counterpart of the dilettante's. The universal, the thought, the idea, the principle from which all particulars flow, the only true Ariadne's thread—all this is lost to the specialist swallowed up in details...

[Buddhism in Science]

He who is marked out by science must sacrifice his personality, must come to see it not as something real, but as something fortuitous, and must discard it along with all personal convictions in order to enter the temple of science. This ordeal is too difficult for some and too easy for others. We have seen that science is inaccessible for the dilettantes because their personalities stand in the way. They cling on to this personality with a trembling hand and do not approach the rushing stream too closely for fear that the torrent will carry them away and drown them. And even if they do draw near then their instinct for self-preservation prevents them from seeing anything. Science cannot reveal itself to such people, because they will not reveal themselves to science. Science demands the whole man, without reservation and ready to give up all in return for the heavy cross of *sober knowledge*. The man incapable of opening his heart to anything is a pitiful creature. It is not only science which closes its doors to him: neither can he be deeply religious, nor a genuine artist, nor a worthy citizen. He will not know the deep affection of friendship or the ardent glance of reciprocated love. Love and friendship are like an echo: they can only return what they receive. In contrast to these misers and egoists of the moral world there are the squanderers and spendthrifts who set no store either by themselves or what they have. They gladly plunge into self-annihilation in the universal, and at the drop of a hat cast off both their convictions and their personality like so much dirty linen. But the bride they are wooing is capricious: she does not want the hearts of these people, precisely because they surrender them so easily and for nothing in return, as if glad to be rid of them. And she is right: what is the use of a personality which someone is ready to throw out of the window! What then is the answer? Is one to renounce the personality and then try to hang on to it, the play on words of some new cabal?

The personality perishes in science. But, apart from its affinity with the sphere of the universal, has not the personality another dimension? And if that dimension is personal then it cannot be absorbed by science, precisely because the latter disperses the personal by generalizing it. The process of the destruction of personality in science is a process of transforming the spontaneously natural personality into one that is conscious and able to think freely. The personality is checked, only to be reborn. In the same way the parabola disappears in a parabolic equation, and the numeral is lost in the formula. Algebra is the logic of mathematics: its algorithm represents general laws, results and processes in a generic, eternal and impersonal form. But the parabola is only concealed in the equation, it does not perish in it, and the same is true of the numeral in the formula. To achieve any real effect the letter must be replaced by a number, the formula must take on a living identity, it must pass back into the world of phenomena from which it was derived, developing and culminating in a practical result, without however perishing as a formula. The act of calculation realizes the formula in a practical effect so that, realized once more, it might reign in the sphere of the universal.

Examples from formal science always aid understanding as long as we do not forget that speculative science is not just formal, but that its formula is worked out in its very content. And so the personality which is resolved in science is not irrevocably lost: it must pass through this process of elimination in order to discover the impossibility of its elimination. The personality must renounce itself in order to become a vessel for the truth; it must forget itself in order not to impede the truth; it must accept the truth with all its consequences, and among these consequences it will discover its own inalienable right to retain its autonomous existence. To die in a state of natural immediacy means to be reborn in the spirit and not to perish in infinite nothingness as the Buddhists do. This victory over oneself is made possible and real only through conflict...

The personality which is powerful enough to stake itself in the game surrenders itself to science unconditionally; but science is not able to absorb such a personality, nor will it disintegrate of its own accord in the universal—there is too much space. He that loseth his life *shall find it*. [39] He who suffers in this way for science will master it not only as a framework for the truth but as the living truth itself, unfolding through the living organism of science. He will feel at home in it, no longer surprised by either his own freedom or science's light. But science's reconciliations will not be enough for him; he will find little satisfaction in serene contemplation and insight. He will want the fullness of rapture and suffering. He will want to *act,* for action alone can satisfy man fully. Action is the personality itself...

The Buddhists of science, who have somehow or other reached the sphere of the universal, never leave it. You won't tempt them into the world of action and life for love or money. Who could command them to trade their spacious temple where they live in honorable inactivity for our life with its raging passions, where we must work and sometimes perish? The specific gravity of some bodies is greater than water and they sink, while splinters and straws float importantly on the surface. The formalists have found reconciliation in science, but it is a false reconciliation. They are more completely reconciled than science permits. They have not grasped *how* reconciliation is accomplished in science. Approaching with their feeble sight and meager desires they were blinded by science's light and abundant gratification. They are drawn to science as unfoundedly as the dilettantes are repelled by it. They imagine that it is enough simply to *know* reconciliation and that there is no need to put it into effect. Having withdrawn from the world they look negatively upon it and have no desire to rejoin it. They think that simply knowing that quinine cures fever is enough to effect a cure. It does not occur to them that for man science is but a point in the flow of life. Life flows towards it, naturally spontaneous, and then flows away from it, conscious and free. They have not grasped that science is a heart into which the dark blood from the veins flows, not in order to remain there, but in order that it might combine with the fiery element of air and flow out as crimson arterial blood. The formalists thought they had arrived safely in harbor when in actual fact they should have been casting off. They stood with folded arms when strictly speaking they should have been rolling up their sleeves. According to them knowledge was sufficient payment to compensate for life; they needed life no longer. They saw science as an end in itself and imagined it to be the sole object of man's aspirations. The reconciliation offered by science is a renewed conflict resolving itself in the realm of the practical. This reconciliation is in thought, but "man is not merely a thinking, but also an acting being!"[40] This reconciliation is universal and negative, and therefore it does not involve the personality: positive reconciliation is possible only through free, intelligent and conscious action...

When science reaches its highest point it quite naturally transcends itself. In science thought and being are reconciled. The necessary prerequisites of the world are created by thought, the completed world by action. "Action is the living unity of theory and practice," said the greatest thinker of the ancient world over two thousand years ago.[41] In action the mind and the heart are subsumed in the act of realization, fulfilling in the phenomenal world that which exists in potentiality. Are not the universe and history eternal such actions? The action of the mind in the abstract is thought which annihilates personality: man is infinite in it, but he loses himself. He is eternal in thought, but *he is not he.* The action of the heart in the abstract is a particular act incapable of evolving into the universal. In his heart a man is himself, but he is transient. Only in intelligent, morally free and passionately energetic action does man attain the actuality of his personality and immortalize himself in the world of phenomena. In such action man is eternal in his transience, infinite in his finiteness, representing both his kind and himself, a living and conscious organ of his age...

Thought must assume flesh, descend to life's bazaar, and unfold in all the splendor and beauty of transient being, without which there can be no vital, passionate and absorbing action... Man's vocation is not logic alone, but also the socio-historical world of moral freedom and positive activity. He possesses not only the facility for aloof understanding, but also will, which may be regarded as positive, creative reason. Man cannot refuse to participate in the human affairs which go on around him. He must act in his own place and time. This is his universal vocation, his *conditio sine qua non*. The personality emerging from science no longer exclusively belongs to either personal life or the sphere of the universal: in such a personality the personal and the universal are combined in the unity of the civic individual. Having achieved reconciliation in science it longs for reconciliation in life. But this requires the creative realization of the moral will in all practical spheres.

The fault of the Buddhists is that they do not feel this need to go out into life and realize the idea in actuality. They see reconciliation in science as reconciliation in everything, not as a stimulus to action but as complete and self-sufficient satisfaction in itself. Let the world beyond the covers of their books go hang. They will endure anything for the futility of the universal. The Buddhists of India strive to purchase freedom in Buddha *at the price of existence*. And for them Buddha is an abstract infinity, a nothingness. Science has conquered the world for man; what is more it has conquered history, and not merely so that man should be able to rest content... Taking only the letter of science, its words, [the formalists] have used them to stifle all compassion and warmth of feeling. Deliberately and with great effort they have reached a point of complete indifference to everything human and regard this as the height of truth. They don't always need to believe that they are without a heart; sometimes they just pretend to be so (a new kind of *captatio benevolentiae*). They always take formal solutions to be real ones. They believe that the personality is a bad habit which it is time to give up. They preach reconciliation with all the dark aspects of contemporary life, regarding as real and therefore worthy of recognition every fortuitous incident, everything routine and obsolete, everything in short that they find in the street. This is how they have understood the great idea that "everything real is rational." They stamp every noble urge with the name *Schönseeligkeit*[42] without understanding the sense in which the term was used by their master.[43] If we add to the results of this their pompous and absurd language and the arrogance of their narrow-mindedness, then we shall be giving due credit to society's good sense in regarding with mistrust these buffoons of science. Hegel took every opportunity to beg and implore people to beware of formalism and to show how even the truest proposition, if taken literally or to extremes, would lead to trouble. In the end he railed against people, but all in vain. His words were taken literally and to extremes. The formalists could not get used to the idea that truth is in eternal motion; they could not recognize once and for all that every situation is negated in favor of something higher, that it is only through the continuous succession of such situations, conflicts and negations that the living truth emerges, and that these are but the snakeskins which it sheds to emerge freer and freer. Despite the fact that they harp on about something similar, they cannot get used to the idea that there is nothing to lean on in the development of science and that salvation lies only in rapid, headlong motion. They clutch at every passing moment as if it were the truth. They regard any one-sided manifestation as all manifestations of the object. They demand maxims and ready-made laws. Every time they get through to a given stage they, in their ridiculous credulity, assume that they have reached the absolute and settle down to rest. They keep strictly to the text and for that reason they cannot grasp its meaning. It is not enough to understand what is said and written: you have to understand the spirit of the thing, what lies between the lines. You must assimilate the book so as to be able to get out from it. This is how the *living* understand science; understanding is the process of exposing the pre-existing homogeneity. Science is passed to the living in a living way and to the formalists in a formal way...

Immediacy and thought are two negations resolved in the act of history. Their unity has been dissolved into opposites in order to be reconciled in history. Nature and logic are subsumed by history and realized. Everything in nature is particular, individual, and exists separately, hardly enveloped by any essential bond. In nature the idea exists corporeally, unconsciously, subject to the law of necessity and obscure influences which have not been negated by free understanding. Quite the reverse is true in science: the idea exists in a logical organism, everything particular is starved and everything is infused with the light of consciousness. The *implicit* thought, which agitates and impels nature, frees itself from its physical existence through development and becomes the *explicit* idea of science. No matter how complete science might be, its completeness is abstract and its relationship to nature negative. Science has been aware of this since Descartes, who clearly contrasted thought and fact, spirit and nature. Nature and science are two concave mirrors eternally reflecting each other. The focus, the point where the complete worlds of nature and logic intersect and come together, is the personality of man. Concentrating on each point and becoming ever more intensified, nature culminates in the human ego; here it reaches its aim. Man's personality, opposing itself to nature and struggling against natural immediacy, develops within itself the generic, the eternal, the universal, the mind. The completion of this process is the purpose of science. The whole of man's past existence has consciously or unconsciously aspired towards the achievement of intelligent self-cognition and the elevation of the human will to the level of God's. Throughout the ages mankind has aspired to morally good and free action. But history has never witnessed such action, nor could it. For such action must be preceded by science: without knowledge, without full consciousness there can be no truly free act, and man's past has been without such full consciousness... Moral freedom begins where consciouness begins, and every personality realizes its vocation in its own way, thus leaving the stamp of its individuality on events... The history of the spirit's activity is, as it were, its personality, for "it is what it does"... [44] From the moment man comes to understand the truth it will remain in his heart, and at that point the business of education is complete and conscious activity begins. Mankind will leave the temple of science with his head held high—proud in the knowledge that *omnia sua secum portans*— to erect the divine city.

1843

Alexander Ivanovich Herzen
THE RUSSIAN PEOPLE AND SOCIALISM
(Extract) [45]

The thinking Russian is the most independent person in the world. What is there to stop him? Respect for the past? But what serves as the point of departure for modern Russian history if not the denial of nationality and tradition? [46]

Perhaps then the tradition of the Petersburg period? That tradition imposes no responsibilities upon us; on the contrary, that "fifth act of a bloody drama staged in a brothel" [47] relieves us completely of all obligation.

On the other hand, the past of the Western European nations serves us only as a lesson, that is all; in no way do we consider ourselves to be the executors of their historical testaments.

We share your doubts, but we derive no comfort from your faith. We share your hatred, but we do not understand your attachment to what your ancestors have bequeathed you; we are too oppressed, too unfortunate to be satisfied with half-freedom. You are bound by scruples and held back by inherited notions. We have neither inherited notions nor scruples; we lack only strength.

This is the source of our irony, of that anguish which eats away at us, drives us to fury, and urges us on until we reach Siberia, torture, exile, or untimely death. We sacrifice ourselves without hope, from bitterness and boredom. There is indeed something reckless about our lives, but there is nothing banal, nothing stagnant or philistine.

Do not accuse us of immorality just because we do not respect what you respect. Can one reproach the foundling for not respecting its parents? We are independent because we are starting life anew. We have nothing legitimately ours apart from our nature, our national character. This is our essence, our flesh and blood, but in no way is it a binding authority. We are independent because we have nothing. We have hardly anything to love. All our memories are filled with bitterness and spite. We received our education, our learning, at the end of a knout.

What do we care for your sacred duties, we who are your younger brothers deprived of inheritance? And could we in all conscience be satisfied with your worn-out morality, which is neither Christian nor human, but which exists only in rhetorical exercises and procurators' speeches! What respect can be inspired in us by your Roman-barbarian law, that god-forsaken, clumsy edifice without light and air, which was renovated in the Middle Ages and whitewashed by the emancipated middle classes? I agree that the daily brigandage of the Russian law-courts is even worse, but it does not follow from this that your laws and your courts are just.

The difference between your laws and our decrees lies only in the formula which introduces them. Imperial decrees begin with the crushing truth: "The Tsar has been pleased to command"; your laws begin with a disgusting lie—the ironical abuse of the name of the French people and the words: "Liberty, Equality, Fraternity." Nicholas's code is drawn up against the interests of the people and for the sake of autocracy. The Napoleonic code is absolutely the same. We already bear too many chains to fetter ourselves with new ones voluntarily. In this respect we are on exactly the same level as our peasants. We yield to brute force. We are slaves because we have no possibility of freeing ourselves; but we accept nothing from our enemies.

Russia will never be Protestant.

Russia will never be *juste milieu.*

Russia will never make a revolution with the aim of doing away with Tsar Nicholas only to replace him with tsar-members of parliament, tsar-judges and tsar-policemen.

Perhaps we demand too much and will achieve nothing. That may be so, but nevertheless we do not despair; before 1848 Russia neither should nor could have entered the revolutionary field. She had to learn her lesson, and now she has learned it.[48] The Tsar himself has realized this and is raging against the universities, ideas and learning; he is trying to cut Russia off from Europe and destroy enlightenment.[49] He is doing his job.

Will he succeed in this?

I have already answered this. There is no point in blindly believing in the future; every embryo has the right to develop, but not every one succeeds. The future of Russia does not depend on Russia alone. It is bound up with the future of Europe. Who can foretell the fate of the Slav world if reaction and absolutism finally triumph over revolution in Europe?

Perhaps it will perish?

But in that case Europe too will perish.

And history will pass over to America...

1851

Alexander Ivanovich Herzen
ROBERT OWEN (Extract)[50]

The contrast between Robert Owen and Gracchus Babeuf[51] is very
remarkable. In a hundred years' time, when everything will have changed
on this terrestrial globe, it will be possible by means of these *two molar
teeth* to reconstruct the fossil skeletons of England and France down to the
last little bone. The more these two mastodons of socialism belong in
essence to the same family, and pursue the same aim in response to the
same stimuli, the clearer is the difference between them.

The one saw that, despite the execution of the king, the proclamation
of a republic, the destruction of the Federalists,[52] and the democratic
terror, the people were still neither here nor there; the other that, despite the
enormous development of industry, capital, machinery, and increased
productivity, "Merry England" was more and more becoming sorry
England, and greedy England more and more hungry England. This
persuaded both of them of the need to change the basic conditions of
political and economic life. Why they (and many others) happened upon
this way of thinking at more or less the same time is understandable. The
contradictions in social life had become neither greater nor any worse than
before, but by the end of the eighteenth century they stood out more
distinctly. Elements of social life, developing separately, had destroyed that
harmony which had previously existed among them in less auspicious
circumstances.

Having found themselves so close together at the point of departure,
they both went off in opposite directions.

Owen sees in the fact that social evil is coming to be acknowledged the
latest achievement, the latest victory, in a hard and complex historical
campaign. He greets the dawn of a *new* day, which has never existed or
been possible in the past, and he calls upon the children to cast off their
swaddling clothes and leading-strings as soon as possible and stand on their
own two feet. He has peered through the doors of the future and, like a
traveler who has reached his destination, he no longer gets cross at the road
or curses the stationmasters and the worn-out horses.

But the Constitution of 1793 thought otherwise, and so did Gracchus
Babeuf. It decreed *the restoration of the natural rights of man, long
forgotten and lost.* The social order was the criminal fruit of usurpation,
the consequence of a villainous conspiracy of tyrants and their
accomplices, the priests and aristocrats. They had to be punished as
enemies of the fatherland and their property returned to the lawful
sovereign, who had nothing and was therefore called *sansculotte.* It was

time to restore his old *inalienable rights* ... What has become of them? Why should the proletariat be the sovereign? Why should all the property seized by others belong to it? Ah! You have your doubts, you are a suspicious individual; the nearest sovereign will take you off to the citizen judge, who will send you to the citizen executioner, and you won't be doubting any more!

The practice of the surgeon Babeuf could not hinder the practice of the *accoucheur* Owen.

Babeuf wanted to use force, that is authority, to destroy what had been created by force, to smash what had been wrongfully gained. To this end he laid a plot: if he had succeeded in making Paris his own, the insurrectionary committee would have *prescribed* a new social order for France, just as the victorious Osmanlis did for Byzantium. It would have forced upon the French its *tyranny of general prosperity,* and of course with such violence that it would have provoked the most fearful reaction, in the struggle against which Babeuf and his committee would have perished, leaving the world with *a great idea in an absurd form*—an idea which even now smoulders beneath the ashes and confounds the complacency of the complacent.

Owen, seeing that the people of the developed countries were growing towards a transition to a new epoch, had no thought of coercion, and merely wished to help the process of development. As consistent in his own way as Babeuf was in his, Owen set about the study of the embryo, the development of the cell. Like all natural scientists, he took a particular instance as his starting point: his microscope, his laboratory, was New Lanark. His study grew and matured along with this cell, and it led him to the conclusion that the main path to the establishment of a new order was *education.*

Owen had no need of a plot, and an uprising would only have harmed him. He was able to get on not only with the best government in the world, the English government, but also with any other. He saw in the government an outmoded historical fact supported by backward and undeveloped people, not a band of outlaws to be caught red-handed. Not seeking to overthrow the government, neither did he in any way seek to *correct its defects.* If the pious shopkeepers had not prevented him, there would now be hundreds of New Lanarks and New Harmonies in England and America; the renewed strength of the working population would have flowed into them, and gradually they would have drawn off the best vital juices from the obsolete cisterns of the state. Why should he have struggled against something which was dying? He could leave it to die naturally, knowing that every child brought to his schools—*c'est autant de pris* from Church and government!

Babeuf was executed. During his trial he grew into one of those great personalities, one of those martyrs or crushed prophets before whom a man involuntarily bows. He was extinguished, but on his grave there grew and grew the all-consuming monster of *Centralization*. Before it individuality was effaced, the personality withered, paled and vanished. Never on European soil, from the time of the Thirty Tyrants of Athens[53] to the Thirty Years' War, or from then to the end of the French Revolution, has man been so caught in the spider's web of government, so ensnared by the meshes of administration, as in the most recent period in France.

Owen was gradually sucked into the mire. He moved while he still could, and spoke while his voice lasted. The mire shrugged its shoulders and shook its head; the irresistible wave of philistinism grew. Owen grew old and sank even deeper in the quagmire; little by little his efforts, his words, his teachings, all disappeared in the swamp. Sometimes little violet will-o'-the-wisps seem to skip above the swamp, frightening the timid souls of the liberals—but only the liberals: the aristocrats despise them, the priests hate them, and the people know nothing of them.

"But then what of their future!"

"What will be will be."

"For pity's sake, what does history all amount to after this?"

"Yes, and what indeed is the point of everything on earth? As far as history is concerned, I do not make it, and therefore I cannot answer for it. I am like Sister Anne in *Bluebeard:* I look out along the road for you and tell you what I see.[54] There is only the dust on the high road, nothing else in sight.. Now they are coming, I think it is they! No, it is not our brothers, it is sheep, many sheep. At last two giants approach by different roads. First one then the other tries to pull Raoul by his blue beard. Nothing doing! Raoul does not heed Babeuf's menacing decrees, nor does he go to Robert Owen's school. Instead he has sent one to the guillotine, and drowned the other in a swamp. I don't commend this at all—Raoul is no kin of mine. I am merely stating the fact, nothing more!"

* * *

About the time that the heads of Babeuf and Dorthès fell into the fatal sack at Vendôme,[55] Owen was living in the same lodgings as another unrecognized genius and pauper, Fulton, and giving him his last shillings so that he might make models of machines which would enrich and benefit the human race. It happened that a certain young officer[56] was showing off his battery to some ladies. In order to be as obliging as possible, he quite needlessly fired off a few shells (he tells this story himself); the enemy replied in kind, a few men fell dead, and some others were wounded. The ladies were thoroughly pleased with the shock to their nerves. The officer felt a few pangs of conscience: "Those people," he says, "perished for no purpose at all." But it was a matter of war and the thought soon passed.

Cela promettait, and the young man went on to spill more blood than all revolutions taken together and to demand in a single conscription more soldiers than Owen needed pupils to transform the entire world.

He had no system, and he neither wished the people well nor promised them it. He wished well only for himself, and by this he meant power. Just look how feeble Babeuf and Owen are compared to him! His name alone was enough thirty years after his death to get his nephew recognized as emperor.

What was his secret?

Babeuf wished to *enjoin prosperity* and a communist republic upon the people. Owen wished to *educate* them into a different economic way of life which would be incomparably more advantageous for them.

Napoleon wanted neither the one nor the other. He realized that the French people did not in fact wish to live on Spartan soup or return to the morality of Brutus the Elder, that they did not relish the thought that on public holidays "citizens will gather to discuss the laws and teach the children civic virtues." But, on the other hand, *they did like* fighting and boasting of their bravery.

Instead of preventing them or irritating them by preaching everlasting peace, Lacedaemonian fare, Roman virtues and myrtle wreaths, Napoleon, seeing how passionately they loved bloody glory, began to set them against other nations, and he went hunting with them himself. There is no point in blaming him; even without him the French would have been the same. But this coincidence of tastes entirely explains the people's love for him. He was not a reproach to the mob, he did not offend it by his own purity or virtue, and he did not offer it some lofty, transfigured ideal. He appeared as neither chastising prophet nor sermonizing genius. He himself was one of the mob, and he showed it *itself,* with its deficiencies and sympathies, its passions and inclinations, elevated to the point of genius and bathed in the light of glory. That is the key to his power and influence; that is why the mob wept for him, lovingly brought his coffin home, and hung his portrait everywhere.

If he fell, it was in no way because the mob had abandoned him, or discerned the emptiness of his designs, or tired of sacrificing its last son and spilling human blood for no good reason. He provoked other nations to ferocious resistance and they began to fight desperately for the sake of their own slavery and their own masters. Christian morality was satisfied: one could not have defended one's enemies with greater frenzy!

On this occasion a military despotism was vanquished by a feudal one.

I cannot pass with indifference the engraving which portrays the meeting of Wellington and Blücher[57] at the moment of victory at Waterloo. Each time I look long at it, and each time my heart is seized with a cold fear. That calm British figure, promising nothing bright—and that grey, gruffly good-natured German condottiere. The Irishman in the service of England, a man without a fatherland—and the Prussian, whose fatherland is in the barracks. They greet each other gladly, and indeed how could they not be glad? They have just turned history off the high road and up to its hubs in mud, mud from which it will not be dragged in half a century... It was dawn... At that time Europe was still asleep, unaware that its destiny had been changed. And why? Because Blücher had hurried and Grouchy[58] had been late! How many misfortunes, how many tears that victory cost the people! Yet equally, how many misfortunes and how much blood would victory by the other side have cost?

"So what conclusion may be drawn from all this?"

"What do you mean by 'conclusion'? A moral, such as *fais ce que doit, advienne ce que pourra,* or a maxim like:

> Blood has always flowed in rivers
> And men have always wept?

Understanding of what is going on—that is the conclusion; emancipation from lies—that is the moral."

"But where is the profit in this?"

"What avarice! Especially now when everyone is crying out about the immorality of bribes. 'Truth is like religion,' says Owen. 'You must not expect it to be more than it is.' "

For everything we have endured, for the broken bones, for the hearts that have been trampled, for all our losses, our mistakes, our delusions—just to be able to make out a few letters of the mysterious writing, to grasp the general sense of what is going on around us. That is an awful lot! The childish nonsense we forfeit is no longer of any interest; it is dear to us only out of habit. What is there to regret? The Baba Yaga,[59] or the life-force? The fairy tale of the Golden Age behind us, or that of infinite progress in the future? The miracle-working phial of St Januarius,[60] or a meteorological prayer for rain? The secret design of conspiratorial chemists, or *natura sic voluit?*

The first minute is frightening, but only the first minute. Everything around one quivers and rushes past. You either stand still, or go wherever you wish: there are no barriers, no roads and no authority. No doubt the chaos of the sea was frightening at first, but as soon as man came to understand its aimless bustle, he forged a way for himself and sailed across the oceans in a sort of dug-out.

Neither nature nor history are going anywhere, and for this reason they are ready to go *wherever* they are directed, *if at all possible,* that is to say, if nothing prevents them. They are the outcome of the gradual accumulation of a multitude of particles, acting upon and encountering each other, checking and attracting each other. But man is in no way lost because of all this, as the grain of sand is lost in the mountain; he is no more subject to the elements, nor more firmly bound by necessity. By coming to understand his situation, he grows into a helmsman proudly cleaving the waves with his boat, and making the bottomless abyss serve as a path of communication.

Having neither program, nor set theme, nor inevitable dénouement, the tattered improvisation of history is ready to go with anyone; anyone can insert into it his own line of verse, and if it is sonorous it will remain *his* line until the poem is broken off, and for as long as the past ferments in its blood and its memory. A host of possibilities, events and discoveries lie dormant at every step in history and nature. You only have to touch the rock with science for water to flow out—and what a thing water is! Just think what has been achieved with compressed steam and what is being done with electricity, since man, rather than Jupiter, took them into his hands. Man's contribution is great and filled with poetry; it is a kind of creation. The elements and matter are indifferent: they can slumber for a thousand years without waking up; but man sets them to work for him, and off they go. The sun has long patrolled the sky, but all at once man intercepted its light, preserved its trace, and the sun began to make pictures for him.

Nature never struggles with man. This is a base religious calumny. Nature is not intelligent enough to struggle: she is quite indifferent. "Insofar as man knows nature, he can control her," said Bacon, and he was quite right. Nature cannot thwart man as long as he does not contradict her laws: she will unwittingly do his bidding while going about her own business. Men know this, and on this basis they rule the land and sea. But man does not have this same respect when faced with the objectivity of the historical world. Here he feels at home and is less diffident. In history he finds it easier to be carried along passively by the flow of events, or to burst upon it armed with a knife and a cry of "General prosperity or death!"[61] than to look closely at the ebb and flow of the waves carrying him, or to study the rhythm of their fluctuations and thus discover for himself endless channels to navigate.

Of course man's position in history is more complicated: here he is at one and the same time *boat, wave and helmsman.* If only there were a chart!

"But if Columbus had had a chart, it would not have been he who discovered America."

"Why not?"

"Because it would have to have been discovered already to get on the chart."

Only when you deprive history of every predetermined course do man and history become something serious, real and filled with profound interest. If events are stacked in advance, if the whole of history is the unfolding of some ante-historic plot and leads only to its realization, to its *mise en scène,* then at least let us too take up wooden swords and shields of brass. Are we to shed real blood and real tears for the sake of playing out some providential charade? If it has a preordained plan, history is reduced to the insertion of figures in an algebraic formula, and the future is sold into bondage before it is born.

Those people who spoke with horror of Robert Owen's having deprived man of free-will and moral valor are reconciling predestination not only with freedom, but also with the hangman! If only on the basis of the text: "The son of man *must be* betrayed, but woe unto him who shall betray him."[62]

From a mystical point of view all this is as it should be, and here it has its artistic side, which is missing in doctrinairism. In religion a whole drama unfolds: there is struggle, revolt and its pacification; there are the eternal Messiahs, the Titans, Lucifer, Abadonna, the banished Adam, Prometheus bound, those punished by God and those redeemed by the Saviour. It is a romance which stirs the soul, but it is just this which has been discarded by the science of metaphysics. Fatalism, in making the transition from church to school, has lost all its sense, even that sense of verisimilitude which we demand of a fairy-tale. From a bright, scented, intoxicating Asiatic bloom the doctrinaires have dried a pale straw for the herbarium. Spurning fantastic forms they are left with a naked logical error, an absurdity before the *arrière-pensée* of history, which takes form whatever the cost and reaches its goal by means of people and kingdoms, wars and revolutions. Why, if it already exists, does it realize itself again? If, however, it does not exist, but is only *becoming* and *being affirmed* by events, then what kind of new immaculate process of conception is it which gives birth in the temporal world to some pre-existing idea, which on emerging from the womb of history proclaims immediately that it existed previously and will exist in times to come? This is a new, summary immortality of the soul, which works in two directions and is not personal, not anyone's own, but generic... The *immortal soul* of the whole of humanity—this is worth dead individual souls! Might there not be an immortal birch tree of all birch trees?

Is it surprising that with such elucidation the simplest everyday subjects are made quite incomprehensible by scholastic interpretation? Can there, for example, be a fact more obvious to everyone than the observation that the longer a man lives the more opportunity he has of making a fortune; the longer he looks at an object the better he sees it, provided nothing disturbs him and he does not go blind? And yet from this fact they have contrived to create the idol of *progress,* a sort of golden calf, incessantly growing and promising to grow to infinity.

Is it not simpler to understand that man lives not for the *fulfilment of destiny,* not in order to embody an idea, not for progress, but solely because he was born, and he was born *for* (however bad the word)... for the present, which in no way prevents his either receiving the heritage of the past or bequeathing something to the future. This seems humiliating and crude to the idealists: they have no wish whatsoever to recognize that the whole of our great significance, notwithstanding our puniness and the barely discernible flicker of each individual's life, lies in the fact that while we are alive, and until the knot we hold together has unwound into its component elements, *we are for all that ourselves,* and not dolls destined to endure progress or embody some stray idea. We should be proud that we are not needles and thread in the hands of fate, as it weaves the richly-colored cloth of history. We know that this cloth will not be woven without us, but it does not constitute our purpose, our calling, or some lesson set out for us, but is the consequence of that complex mutual guarantee which binds together all that exists in a web of endings and beginnings, causes and effects.

And not only that: *we can change the pattern of the carpet.* There is no master watching over us, no set design, only a foundation, and we are left entirely to ourselves. Previous weavers of fate, all those Vulcans and Neptunes, have departed this world. Their executors concealed their testament from us, but the deceased have bequeathed us their power.

"But if, on the one hand, you give man free rein over his fate, and, on the other, relieve him of responsibility, then on the basis of your teaching he will sit with arms folded and simply do nothing."

If that were the case would not people stop eating and drinking, loving and producing children, delighting in music and the beauty of women, when they found out that they eat and listen, love and take pleasure for themselves, and not for the fulfilment of higher designs or in order to expedite *as soon as possible* the *infinite* development of perfection?

If religion, with its oppressive fatalism, or doctrinairism, with its cheerlessness and coldness, have not reduced people to inertia, then we need not fear that this will come about as the result of a view which liberates men from these tombstones. The mere whiff of life and its inconsistency was enough to save the people of Europe from such religious mischief as asceticism and quietism, which always remained words and never became deeds. Will reason and consciousness really turn out to be any weaker?

Moreover, the realistic view has its own secret; he who sits with arms folded in the face of it will never understand this secret or embrace it. He will still belong to another age in the brain's development: he will still need to be spurred on by the devil with his black tail on one side, and an angel with a white lily on the other.

Man's aspiration towards a more harmonious way of life is quite natural. Nothing can stop it, just as nothing stops hunger and thirst. That is why we have no fear that people will simply sit with their arms folded, no matter what the teaching. Whether this better life will ever be found, and whether, if it is, man will be able to control it, or will go astray in one place and make a mess of things in another—that is a different question. In saying that man will never lose his appetite, we are not saying that there will always be provisions for everyone, let alone nourishing ones.

There are people who are satisfied with little, who have meager requirements, a narrow outlook and limited desires. There are also nations with limited horizons and strange ideas, who find contentment meagerly, falsely and sometimes even in the banal. China and Japan are without doubt two nations which have found the most appropriate civil forms for their way of life. That is why they remain so unalterably one and the same.

It seems to us that Europe too is close to "satiation," and in her tiredness she tries to settle down and crystallize, finding her enduring social situation in a *petit-bourgeois way of life*. She is prevented from composing herself by monarchico-feudal relics and the principle of conquest. The petit-bourgeois order represents a great success when compared to the oligarcho-militaristic—there can be no doubt about that. But for Europe, and especially for Anglo-Germanic Europe, it represents not only a great success, but also *sufficient* success. Holland has outstripped the others: she was the first to settle down for the rest of time. The cessation of growth is the start of maturity. The life of a student is more full of incident and proceeds much more impetuously than the sober working life of a family man. If over England there did not hang the leaden shield of feudal landowning, if she, like Ugolino, did not constantly step on her children who are dying from hunger,[63] and if she, like Holland, could achieve for all the prosperity of small shopkeepers and middling proprietors of modest means, then she would settle down in her pettiness. And together with that the level of intelligence, breadth of vision and refinement of taste would sink still further; and a life without incident, enlivened occasionally by external stimuli, would yield to a monotonous roundabout, a hardly changing *semper idem*. Parliament would assemble, the budget would be presented, business-like speeches would be made, the form of things would be improved... and the same thing the next year, and in ten years' time. It would be the calm rut of the adult man, his everyday business life. Even in natural phenomena we observe that the early stages are often eccentric, but the settled continuation of the process proceeds quietly; not the turbulent comet, tracing with the flowing tresses of its tail its unknown paths, but a tranquil planet, orbiting with its satellites like lamps around its well-worn and oft-repeated track, any small eccentricity serving only to highlight even more the general order. The spring might be wetter or drier than usual, but it is always followed by summer and preceded by winter.

"For pity's sake! So the whole of humanity will get as far as the petit-bourgeois state and then get stuck?"

"I don't think all of it, but some parts certainly. The word 'humanity' is most repugnant. It expresses nothing definite, and serves only to add to the confusion of other concepts yet another sort of piebald demi-god. What sort of entity is understood by the word 'humanity'? Is it the same as we understand by any other collective noun, like caviare, etc.? Who on earth would be bold enough to claim that there is any sort of order capable of satisfying in identical fashion the Iroquois and the Irish, the Arab and the Magyar, the Kaffir and the Slav? We can only say that for some nations the petit-bourgeois order is repugnant, whilst others are at home in it like fish in water. The Spanish, the Poles, and to a certain extent the Italians and Russians contain very few petit-bourgeois elements; the social order under which they would come into their own is higher than anything the petit-bourgeois order could offer. But it in no way follows from this that they will *achieve* this higher state, or will not turn off on to the bourgeois road. Aspiration alone ensures nothing—we cannot emphasize enough the difference between the possible and the inevitable. It is not enough to know that such and such an order is repugnant to us; we must know what we do want, and whether it can ever be achieved. There are many possibilities ahead: the bourgeois nations might fly off in an entirely different direction, and the most poetic peoples might turn into shopkeepers. Quite a few possibilities will come to nothing, aspirations abort, and developments fade. What could be more evident, more palpable than those possibilities—and not just possibilities, but the beginnings of personal life, thought and energy—which die in every child. Note that neither is there anything inevitable in this premature death of children: the lives of nine-tenths of them could no doubt be saved if the doctors knew anything about medicine, or if medicine itself were truly a science. We must pay particular attention to this *influence of man and science,* for it is extraordinarily important.

Note too how the apes (chimpanzees, for instance) constantly verge upon the further development of their intellect. This can be seen in their restless and preoccupied look, in the way they wistfully keep a melancholic eye on all that happens, in their distrustful and fidgety anxiety and their curiosity, which on the other hand never allows their thought to concentrate, but constantly dissipates it. Generation after generation aspire time and again to some kind of understanding; their place is taken by others who also aspire, but die without attaining anything. And so tens of thousands of years have passed, and tens of thousands more have yet to come.

Men have a great advantage over the apes: their aspirations do not fade without trace; they are cloaked in words and embodied in images; they live on in tradition and are handed down from age to age. Every man is supported by an enormous genealogical tree, whose roots go back almost to the paradise of Adam. Behind us, as behind the wave as it breaks on the shore, we can feel the pressure of an entire ocean—that of world history. The thought of all the centuries is in our brain at this moment, and it cannot exist save in the brain, but with it we can be a power.

There are no absolutes in anyone, but each person can be an irreplaceable reality; the doors are open before each of us. If a man *has something* to say, let him say it; he will be listened to. If his soul is tormented by a conviction, let him preach it. People are not as submissive as the elements, but we must always concern ourselves with the masses of our particular time. They are not something distinct, and neither are we independent of the common *background* of the picture, of the same antecedent influences. There is a common bond. Now do you understand on whom the future of men and nations depends?"

"On whom?"

"What do you mean, on whom! Why, on YOU AND ME, for instance. Now how can we sit with folded arms!"

1861

Part IV

Liberal Westernizers

Introduction

The preeminence of Belinsky and Herzen in Russian intellectual life in the 1840s was acknowledged by the majority of their contemporaries, and subsequent developments in nineteenth-century Russian thought tended to confirm their importance. Nevertheless both owed much to a Pleiad of other men of letters—notably Granovsky, Botkin and Annenkov, as well as emerging writers such as Turgenev and Nekrasov—whom it is customary to describe as "Westernizers" and whose contribution to Russian thought, though not of such lasting impact as Belinsky's and Herzen's, did help significantly to generate the sudden exuberant growth of an intelligentsia committed to the spread of enlightenment and civilized values in tsarist Russia.

"Westernism," it is true, cannot be considered a coherent doctrine, nor even a set of sharply defined ideas. The term does have a usefulness, however, if it is taken to imply a receptive attitude to certain Western European philosophical and cultural currents and acceptance of certain shared beliefs which Granovsky, Botkin, Annenkov and others helped to disseminate. All of the major Westernizers, with the partial exception of Annenkov, had imbibed the philosophy of Hegel in one form or another in the late 1830s (they had been close to the saintly Stankevich, who played such an important role in the introduction of German philosophy into Russia), and, although they were quickly to reject Hegelianism, they tended throughout the remainder of their lives to cling to certain Hegelian conceptions, notably: that history is a spiritual development, the unfolding of some idea, the Absolute; that "world-historical individuals," such as Alexander the Great, are instruments of the will of this Absolute; and that art may serve as a vehicle for the perception of this idea, manifested as a beauty superior to anything to be found in everyday reality.[1] The Westernizers also enthusiastically read Feuerbach's *Essence of Christianity,* first published in 1841, in which it was argued that man's God was not a perfect being with an objective existence of His own, but rather a subjective creation of man's own consciousness, and from which a far-reaching humanism could be derived. They turned again to French culture and read writers such as George Sand and Eugène Sue, whose works could be construed as socially critical and radical. And they became acquainted with the socialist doctrines and utopian schemes being elaborated by Pierre Leroux, Fourier, Cabet and Louis Blanc[2] (though the significance of these thinkers seemed to the Russian intelligentsia of the 1840s to be primarily moral rather than political). Finally, shape was given to this vague Westernism by a shared hostility to Slavophilism with its insistence on the decadence of Western civilization and the vitality of Russia, its exaltation of the collective at the expense of the rights of the individual, its veneration of spiritual rather than rational truth and of moral rather than juridical law. In opposition to the Slavophiles, the Westernizers advocated a rationalistic approach to knowledge and greater social equality, on the moral and legal planes at least, if not on the material plane; they believed in the necessity of the rule of law and in the advantages of industrial progress; and, most importantly, they had a deep—though not undiscriminating— respect for the Western European countries in which these blessings of civilization found expression.

As the Westernizers clarified their own values and attitudes in the course of the 1840s, however, so they began to discover differences of opinion among themselves that were eventually to prove as fundamental as their differences with the Slavophiles. It became clear that Granovsky, Botkin and Annenkov—together with Turgenev and others—were of an essentially liberal disposition and could not follow Belinsky and Herzen— and Nekrasov and others—to socialist conclusions. An early indication of this rift was a disagreement of 1842 between Granovsky and Belinsky on the subject of the character and significance of the Jacobin Robespierre. Towards the middle of the decade, however, the rift became more apparent. Whereas Herzen's enthusiasm for Feuerbach led him towards a philosophical materialism incompatible with the preservation of religious faith, Granovsky refused to accept Herzen's "dry, cold idea of the unity of soul and body" and clung to a belief in the immortality of the soul.[3] Both Granovsky and Botkin disliked Herzen's bitter denunciation of the French bourgeoisie in his *Letters from the Avenue Marigny* and, together with Annenkov, advocated scepticism and toleration. These differences were not much debated in the period 1848-55, the last years of the reign of Nicholas I, when the government, frightened by the revolutionary disturbances in the West in 1848, inhibited the free expression of ideas to an even greater extent than before, and in any case Herzen had emigrated in 1847 and Belinsky had died in the following year. But in the freer atmosphere that prevailed after the death of Nicholas I and the accession of Alexander II to the throne the rift between surviving liberals and a new generation of more militant socialists widened and took on a more overtly political character. Faced with the challenge of Chernyshevsky and then Dobrolyubov as well, the "men of the 40s" struggled to resist the new utilitarian values and in particular to defend their belief in the importance of a free art unconstrained by any political commitment. And, although they all deplored Russia's almost feudal social structure, the corruption of her officials and the obscurantism encouraged by the *ancien régime,* nevertheless none of them could contemplate the destruction of that regime with equanimity. They hoped for gradual, peaceful change, to be effected by means of moderate reform, rather than for a sweeping social and political transformation wrought by violent revolutionary action.

The most important of the liberal Westernizers of the 1840s was indisputably Timofei Granovsky (1813-55), one of the "most luminous and remarkable personalities" of the period, as Herzen described him,[4] and a man whose "pure, noble soul" and generous, loving nature[5] equipped him for a conciliatory role. It was principally through the medium of historical scholarship and in his capacity as Professor of World History at the University of Moscow that Granovsky made his contribution to Russian thought. Out of his academic discipline he created what Annenkov called a "flourishing oasis of science," a piece of territory on which he could propagate enlightened values and make pronouncements which had a bearing on the life and *mores* of Russia in his own day.[6] His series of public lectures delivered in Moscow University in the winter of 1843-44 on the apparently remote subject of the Merovingian and Carolingian Kings attracted a large section of the educated public of the capital and secured his reputation as a humanist intellectual as well as a leading Russian historian. In his scholarship he laid emphasis on the civilizing value of moral ideas which, he believed, found expression in Western Europe both in an enlightened form of Christianity and in dispassionate legal systems that had developed in post-feudal times on the foundations of Roman law. In defiance of the deterministic tendencies in nineteenth-century thought he upheld the view that the great historical individual—whom Granovsky tended to regard as an instrument of Providence—played a crucial role in directing the destinies of nations and had the capacity to propagate some unifying ideas which might promote the ideals of national and, ultimately, universal harmony. With regard to Russian historical development he combined admiration of Peter the Great—the ruler who had given Russia the chance to absorb the benefits of Western European civilization—with a belief in the importance of the enlightened intellectual, the Russian *intelligent,* who clearly radiated something of the chivalrous spirit of the medieval knights-errant (in whom Granovsky took a keen scholarly interest).

Vasily Botkin (1814-69), though not a prolific writer, also played an important role in the intellectual life of the 1840s and 1850s, by virtue of his intimate friendship with Belinsky—he was one of Belinsky's main sources of information on German philosophy, both Hegelian and post-Hegelian—his extensive knowledge of foreign languages and cultures, his wide experience as a traveler in Western Europe and his popularity as conversationalist and *bon viveur* in the circles of the 1840s (where, as Herzen tells us in *My Past and Thoughts,* ideas that had originated in the mind of one person would in the course of discussion become the common property of all).[7] Botkin's most original contribution to Russian literature is undoubtedly his collection of *Letters on Spain,* the widely acclaimed product of his journeyings in Spain in the summer of 1845. Here Botkin not only described Spanish life and culture with acuity and infectious enthusiasm, but also implicitly suggested some similarities in the destinies of Spain and Russia (both countries stood at the periphery of European civilization, and both had suffered a long period of subjection to an infidel invader). By praising the chivalrous Spanish *caballero* Botkin seemed, like Granovsky, to point an example for the Russian nobleman to follow, while his allusions to the common sense, lucidity and dignity of the Spanish common people and the harmony of their relations with the aristocracy served to underline the superiority of a society in which the masses were not oppressed by serfdom.

The original contribution of Pavel Annenkov (1813-87) to Russian intellectual life was small, but like Botkin Annenkov was a central figure in the literary circles of the 1840s and 1850s where he was highly respected for his artistic judgement, erudition and first-hand knowledge of the West as well as for his gregariousness and amiability. As a memoirist he has left an invaluable account, in his work *The Extraordinary Decade,* of the sudden magnificent flowering of Russian intellectual life in the 1840s. He also wrote a biography of Pushkin, which constituted the first volume of his highly acclaimed edition of the poet's works (1855-57). It was this edition that precipitated the debate between the representatives of the so-called "Pushkin" and "Gogol" schools of Russian literature about the purpose and function of art in general and the course that should be taken by Russian literature in particular. Annenkov's sympathies in this debate lay with the "fathers," and when members of the intelligentsia were compelled in the late 1850s to make choices of a more or less political nature he naturally found it impossible to accept a militant socialism that might lead to the sort of social upheavals which he himself had witnessed—and by which he was lastingly frightened—in Paris in 1848. His humane liberalism found expression in his nostalgic love of Italy—in which he had traveled widely—and it underlay his attempt to depict Italian life in idyllic terms as relatively untouched by the social antagonisms and political turmoil that seemed increasingly to afflict the modern world.

Alexander Druzhinin (1824-64), who was close to Botkin and Annenkov and other leading Westernizers in the late 1840s and 1850s, established his literary reputation with his epistolary novella, *Polinka Saks* (1847). Written in the humanitarian spirit of the Westernist intelligentsia of the 1840s, the novella portrays an altruistic hero who sacrifices his happiness by leaving his wife when he discovers that she loves another. It was in literary criticism, however, that Druzhinin made his main contribution to Russian letters and in the second half of the 1850s he emerged as the leading representative of the "Pushkin school" of Russian literature, arguing in defense of an art free of political partisanship or any other utilitarian commitment and complaining that Russian writers, as a result of the injunctions of Belinsky in his last years, had become too preoccupied with satirical or critical depiction of the dark sides of Russian life. As an "antidote" to this tendency, which, rightly or wrongly, had come to be associated with the name of Gogol, Druzhinin advocated emulation of Pushkin, the supreme example of the detached poet who, paradoxical as it might seem, brought more practical benefit to mankind, in Druzhinin's opinion, than any poet writing with the specific intention of serving his society. In the conditions of Russia in the late 1850s, however, Druzhinin's insistence on the need for a dispassionate art inevitably struck many contemporaries, including such close friends of his as Turgenev and Tolstoi, as cold and uncaring and therefore in some degree reactionary. Together with Botkin and Annenkov, he retreated from the center of the stage at the end of the 1850s and thereafter found himself more at odds with the young *raznochintsy* than with the tsarist government and its supporters, against whom he himself had helped in the 1840s to generate an honorable opposition.

Timofei Nikolaevich Granovsky
[ON SLAVOPHILISM][8]

You can't imagine what sort of a philosophy these people have. Their main premises are these: the West has decayed and nothing more can be expected of it; Russian history was spoiled by Peter, we have been forcibly torn away from our native historical foundation and live a random existence; the only advantage of our present life lies in the possibility of our dispassionately observing foreign history; this is even our mission in the future; all human wisdom was used up in the work of the holy fathers of the Greek Church writing after its separation from the Western Church. One needs only study them: there is nothing to be added, all has been said. Hegel they reproach for not respecting facts. Kireevsky says these things in prose, Khomyakov in verse. What is vexing is that they are spoiling the students: a lot of good youth is gathering around them and imbibing these fine ideas.

1839

Timofei Nikolaevich Granovsky
[ON THE FRENCH REVOLUTION]⁹

Botkin read me your letter, furious Roland.[10] The letter is very good, because it came pouring out of the soul in a moment of warmth, but there is no historical truth in it. Your lisping friend[11] is right when he says that Robespierre[12] was a shallow, worthless person, the organ and instrument of other people's wills. I should like to write an article on this subject, for you alone, of course, but let's be brief for now. You like Robespierre's personality because by his deeds he satisfies your hatred for aristocrats, etc. But, my God, how many petty personal motives impinge on Robespierre's general views. How infinitely far above him stands Saint-Just,[13] a limited fanatic but a noble man with deep convictions. Robespierre's eloquence, notwithstanding the passages you cite, falls a long way short of the eloquence of the Girondins,[14] not to mention that of Mirabeau.[15] As a statesman, in the great sense of the word, Robespierre is insignificant, just like Saint-Just. Carnot, Merlin and other gifted Montagnards[16] worked for him. He was a practical person, because he knew how to vulgarize and apply to actual conditions higher questions which it is evidently for a future age to solve. That is to say, he derived private benefit for himself and his party from general questions. His virtue, the main feature of which was the fact that he did not steal or seek profitable appointments, is very praiseworthy in the French bourgeois, but in itself it is rubbish. The Gironde is superior to him precisely because it lacked so-called practical sense. It understood the significance of the revolution, which was not merely to change external political forms but to resolve all the social problems and contradictions that had afflicted the old world for so long. The Gironde defined and pointed out all the questions which Europe is now pondering, the Gironde declared that the revolution was not a French event but a universal one, the Gironde went to the grave pure and holy, having fulfilled its theoretical mission. Robespierre looked on the revolution as an exclusively political and French event, although he said the opposite; it was he who gave the middle estate[17] a position from which it could only be ousted by a new revolution.

Early 1840s

Timofei Nikolaevich Granovsky
[ON SCEPTICISM AND HISTORICAL SCHOLARSHIP][18]

I don't agree with your last letter and strongly uphold my right to scepticism. I can remember its birth and growth in me. It was a natural consequence of my almost exclusive study of history. There is no science more inimical to every sort of dogmatism than history. You say that scepticism is by its nature mocking, that it strikes to right and left. This definition is too narrow. It may contain at least as much sorrow as irony, and it does not always strike to right and left but more often looks distrustfully at both sides. Mockery is a personal thing, a capacity which man brings to bear. I do not have it. You are wrong to attribute to me shabbiness of the sort which says "Don't touch me and I shan't touch you." But I do indeed have a profound hatred for every sort of intolerance that is not capable of respecting the intellectual individuality which in any thinking person who is at all intelligent is the outcome of a whole course of development, a whole life. I do not boast of my scepticism, but I speak about it as a fact: I know that it is something unhealthy, perhaps a sign of impotence, but I am grateful to it for nurturing in me a true, humane toleration. Intolerance is useful and excusable only in a youth who thinks that he has mastered the truth just because he has read some clever and noble book and ardently taken it to heart, and also in people with limited and rigid minds, such as (for example) the Protestant theologians of the seventeenth and even the nineteenth centuries. The more limited the mind, the more easily it takes up some small conviction which enables it to sleep easily. Yes, history is a great science, and, whatever you say about the natural sciences, they will never give man that moral strength which history furnishes.

1847

Timofei Nikolaevich Granovsky
[ON TAMERLAINE] [19]

The subject of our lectures will be descriptions of Tamerlaine, [20] Alexander the Great, [21] Louis IX, [22] and Chancellor Bacon. [23] We shall not find a great deal that is similar in their inner lives, still less in the external history of their exploits; the exploits of each of them are marked by a special character all of his own. But they do have one thing in common: namely the title of great men given to them by their contemporaries and confirmed by posterity. What do we associate with that title? What is the calling in history of people designated by the name "great"? That is the question with which I shall permit myself to begin these lectures. This question is not without a certain topicality. Not long ago voices were raised denying the necessity of great men in history, asserting that their role was finished, that peoples themselves can fulfil their historical mission without their mediation. One might as well say that one of the forces operating in nature had lost its significance, that one of the organs of the human body had now become unnecessary. Such a conception of history is only possible if one takes the most casual and superficial view of it. But he for whom history is not a dead letter, he who is wont to heed its mysterious growth, sees in great men the chosen ones of Providence, those who are called to earth to accomplish what resides in the requirements of a given epoch, in the beliefs and wishes of a given time and people. A people is something collective. Its collective thought, its collective will must, in order to reveal themselves, be turned into the thought and will of one individual endowed with an especially sensitive moral hearing, an especially perspicacious intellectual vision. Such men clothe in the living word that which before them lay hidden in the mind of the people and they convert the vague aspirations and wishes of their compatriots or contemporaries into visible exploit. But together with the opinion to which I have already referred goes another, equally lacking in foundation, according to which great men are something coincidental, something which one can do without. Let us note in this connection that chance may only play a great role in epochs of intellectual and moral debilitation, when man ceases to believe in the legitimate movement of events, when he loses sight of the divine link which comprehends the whole life of mankind. Of course, the place which belongs to the great man in the chain of phenomena is not always clear to us, nor is the purpose of his activity. Centuries pass and he remains a bloody and doleful enigma and we do not know why he came, why peoples were stirred by him. The things said about him are so much at variance with one another that it is impossible even to determine with precision the effect of what he has revealed. But surely that which is incomprehensible to us today must not remain incomprehensible tomorrow? Does not each new event shed light on events which to all appearances are long since over and done with? The sense of separate phenomena is sometimes only revealed when centuries and even millennia have passed. In such cases science is not capable of stepping ahead of life itself and must patiently await new facts without which the range of a certain course of development would not be complete. The historical significance of Socrates has only been properly appreciated in the nineteenth century at a distance of twenty-two centuries from the sentence pronounced on him by the people of Athens.

1851-52

Timofei Nikolaevich Granovsky
[ON ALEXANDER THE GREAT][24]

On the other side of the Tigris, not far from Arbela, Alexander gave battle to Darius for the last time.[25] Darius had at least ten times as many troops as his opponent. The Greek mercenaries and the most bellicose tribes of the Persian state were again called upon to defend together the monarchy of Cyrus.[26] The bold and experienced Parmenio[27] quailed at the sight of the numerous enemy. He advised Alexander to begin the battle at night and received a reply to the effect that victory should not be concealed. Alexander's enemies and those who envied him said that he owed his glory for the most part to commanders whom Philip[28] had trained for him. Alexander was entitled to say about his victory at Arbela, the most difficult of those he had thus far gained, that he won it himself. The cause was lost when the personal courage and leadership of the young ruler revived the battle and turned it to the advantage of the Macedonians. The success was all the more considerable for the fact that the Persians fought with greater bravery than ever before. Their cavalry burst into the ranks of the Macedonian infantry; their phalanx was broken; the left flank under the command of Parmenio was almost destroyed. Bold pressure from the right flank, marshaled by the ruler himself, changed the course of the battle and brought about the complete defeat of the Persians. On this occasion envy had to remain silent and acknowledge in Alexander a worthy leader of the victors. The war seemed almost at an end. The best lands of Darius were in the power of his enemies; behind him there remained only the poor regions of north-eastern Persia, albeit inhabited by bellicose tribes. The exhausted Macedonians and Greeks demanded that the rich spoils already at hand be shared out. But other plans were ripening in Alexander's mind. He summoned the Persian nobles and declared that in his kingdom there could be no distinction between victors and vanquished, that both the former and the latter must merge into one nationality, under the protection of a single, higher civilization. The idea was infinitely great: but could his contemporaries rise to it, not to mention the Macedonian officers who were grumbling loudly about one who had in their opinion taken away from them the spoils they had bought with blood, and who were used to looking on the Persians as slaves? From Greece itself accusing voices resounded, full of reproof. Even Aristotle thought it necessary to caution his pupil and wrote him an epistle in which he tried to demonstrate the impossibility of equality between Greeks and barbarians. The philosopher of Stagirus[29] expressed the same thought, only more clearly still, in his celebrated work on politics. He says that nature herself has drawn a sharp distinction between peoples, "consigning some to domination and others to eternal servitude." One could not better express the attitude of the Hellene to men of other races, from the point of view of the former; Alexander understood these relations differently and in a higher sense. For him, who had already stepped across the frontier of cherished Greek conceptions, the distinction between the Hellene and the barbarian signified only the possession of a higher or lower level of culture. He wished to apportion to his new subjects a part of those spiritual blessings which before him had been the exclusive property of a single people. It goes without saying that such a course of action was bound to bring him the love and gratitude of the tribes he had subjugated; yet it could not help but cause deep dissatisfaction among the Macedonians and Greeks who were offended by a leveling of political rights which was incomprehensible to them.

1851-52

Timofei Nikolaevich Granovsky
[ON LOUIS IX][30]

Louis IX paid particular attention to France's judicial system. Nowhere were the defects of the feudal state clearer than in this field. The basic principle of the medieval court, founded on the deep division of estates,[31] was very simple: each must be judged by a court of his peers, that is to say people equal to him by birth. The cases of vassals were heard at the seat of their feudal lord, and with him presiding, by a court made up of the peers of the plaintiff and the defendant. But the barons did not willingly fulfil this part of their feudal obligations and tended to evade judicial gatherings which entailed various inconveniences and even danger. A defendant who was dissatisfied with the sentence he had received would not infrequently challenge not only his opponent but also the witnesses and judges to a duel. The majority of law-suits were resolved by the judicial duel which gained the upper hand over all other forms of proof. Louis prohibited recourse to this means in his own and ecclesiastical domains. The power of the feudal courts was limited by definition to those cases which were subject exclusively to hearing by the royal courts. Moreover, individuals dissatisfied with the decision of local feudal courts received the right of complaint, that is to say appeal to the royal courts. If any of the first Capetians[32] had devised such an innovation he would have met with stubborn resistance which he would probably not have been able to overcome. However, Louis's measures, which I have listed, did not provoke strong opposition, because he personally inspired unlimited trust and nobody suspected him of ambitious calculations or intent to increase his own power to the detriment of others. Closely connected with the judicial duel was the right of feudal war. When two lords quarreled and started a war, then generally all their relatives and friends took part in it. In this way a petty feud which had flared up at one end of France would quickly find an echo at the other. Putting into practice, it seems, an idea which had belonged to his grandfather, the King decreed that henceforth forty days (*la quarantaine du roi*) should elapse between the *casus belli* and the war's beginning; anyone who infringed this ordinance was liable to punishment as a state traitor. Nor did the legislator stop at this: he granted every member of the feudal estate the right to address himself directly to the supreme power in the event of his facing a contest with a stronger or wealthier opponent. It goes without saying that such a revolution in the deeply rooted customs of the medieval aristocracy could not be accomplished all at once: a great deal of time and effort was needed for this, but Louis IX set an example, from which his successors were not to deviate.

His decrees concerning judicial duels and private wars underpinned subsequent legislation. The people who helped Louis with these reforms were learned jurists, who enjoyed his special respect and trust. The reforms of which they were the authors were not of course envisaged by the King, who thought only about the ennoblement and consolidation of feudal institutions through greater justice and morality. He knew that the knights were bad judges and replaced them as far as possible by people who had studied law as a science. The consequences came to light after Louis's death. The jurists whom he had set on a career of practical activity constituted a whole estate inimical to the ideas and forms of the Middle Ages. They opposed the strictly logical and generally applicable decisions of Roman law to the local and idiosyncratic customs which had developed in the states of Western Europe which had been founded by the Germans. They indicted the medieval papacy in the person of Boniface VIII,[33] and the spiritual knighthood in the form of the Templars. Feudal gentry and commoners alike felt their influence. The fate of the French jurists of the fourteenth and fifteenth centuries is not without a certain tragic grandeur and poetry. Endeavoring to create a strong and orderly monarchy on the model of the Roman Empire, they had to wage a constant and fierce struggle with the forces of a world of feudal lords and commoners who were not accustomed to subordinating themselves to the objectives of the state. Almost every new King was compelled to sacrifice the most trusted advisers of his predecessor to the hatred of vassals who dimly understood that it was their independence that was in question. But the places thus vacated in the King's council and courts did not remain empty for long. The son of an executed clerk would boldly take the place of his father and act in the same spirit and direction, apparently unconcerned about the fate which awaited him. Louis IX could not foresee the political significance which the experts in Roman law subsequently acquired, and valued only their judicial activity. I do not consider it necessary to repeat to you Joinville's[34] all too familiar story about how the King, surrounded by men experienced in the science of law, himself resolved the law-suits of his subjects and passed sentences under the famous oak of Vincennes. King and justice became synonymous words for France at that time. In the whole state there was not an impartial judge except for him, because he alone stood outside, or it would be better to say above, all mercenary ambitions. The idea of monarchical power was invested with the moral radiance of incorruptible justice.

1851-52

Timofei Nikolaevich Granovsky
ON THE CONTEMPORARY STATE AND SIGNIFICANCE OF UNIVERSAL HISTORY (Extract)[35]

Even in its present, far from complete, state universal history more than any other science develops in us a sure sense of reality and that noble toleration without which there is no true evaluation of people. It shows the distinction between eternal, absolute principles of morality and the limited understanding of these principles in a given period. Only by means of such a yardstick may we measure the deeds of bygone generations. Schiller[36] said that death was a great conciliator. These words may be applied to our own science. In the case of every historical misdemeanor it adduces circumstances which mitigate the guilt of the criminal, whoever he might be, a whole people or an individual. And may we be permitted to say that he is not a historian who is not capable of transferring a living sense of love for his neighbor to former times and of recognizing a brother in a man of another race many centuries removed from himself. He is not a historian who has not been able to read the truths inscribed in vivid letters in the chronicles and documents he has studied: in the most shameful periods in the life of mankind there are redeeming features which are apparent to us at the distance of many centuries, and in the depths of the heart adjudged most sinful by contemporaries there yet lurks some better and purer feeling. Such a conception cannot prejudice the strict justice of the sentences passed, for it requires not vindications but explanations and addresses itself to individuals themselves rather than to those of their deeds which are subject to judgment. One of the main obstacles impeding the salutary effect of history on public opinion lies in the disdain with which historians generally treat the majority of their readers. They appear to write only for scholars, as if history could admit of such a restriction, as if it were not by virtue of its very essence the most popular of all sciences, summoning all and everyone. Fortunately narrow notions arising in the stifling atmosphere of the studies of German scholars—notions concerning the supposedly spurious worth of a science which degrades itself by seeking elegant form and accessible exposition—are foreign to the Russian mind, which loves light and space. A parochial science, proud of its exclusiveness, is not entitled to count on the sympathy of that mind...

1852

Timofei Nikolaevich Granovsky
[ON PETER THE GREAT]³⁷

On Sunday evening I was at Pogodin's[38] and my visit was not in vain. I saw at his place a portrait he has bought recently of Peter the Great. This portrait was painted from the dead man, evidently immediately after his demise, and was kept in the Makarov family whose forbear was private secretary in Peter's time, in the last years of his life. The artist is unknown. I am not a connoisseur or even a lover of painting; but I think I should be capable of standing for hours on end in front of this picture. I should willingly give up my favorite books, a part of my library, in exchange for it. Imagine the head of the deceased on a red pillow which increases the pallor of the face. The upper part of the divinely beautiful face bears a stamp of majestic tranquility—the sort of tranquility which may be the result of holy, pure, infinitely noble thought. There is no longer any thought, but the expression of it has remained. Such beauty I had never seen. But it was as if the life had not yet gone from the lower part of the face. The lips are compressed with anger and sorrow. It is as if they are quivering. The whole evening I looked at this portrayal of the man who gave us a right to a history and almost single-handedly announced our historical calling. . .

1855

Vasily Petrovich Botkin
[FROM A LETTER OF 12 OCTOBER 1847 TO ANNENKOV][39]

Incidentally I read Herzen's three "Letters from the Avenue Marigny"[40] in No. 10 of *The Contemporary* and I read them with keen pleasure. The first letter is inferior to the others: one even detects in it a certain effort to be witty, not everywhere of course, but here and there a witticism isn't in unison with the movement of the pen or the phrasing. As for his view of the theater and the city, for all his superiority, for all his brilliance and perspicacity, it is in my opinion nevertheless a *first* and *visual* impression. *Je ne cherche pas chicane à sa manière de voir*[41] but, while fully acknowledging his right to look at things from his own angle, all the same I stick to my previous opinion and am not going to emulate the Slavonic intolerance of Herzen, who took me to task for having the audacity to be at odds with him. I repeat, I read his "Letters" with enjoyment: they are so engaging, so playful, an arabesque in which jest and profound thought, heartfelt impulse and nimble witticism are intertwined! What concern is it of mine that I think quite differently about many things! Everyone has a right to look at things in his own way, and Herzen looks at them in such a lively and engaging way that I altogether lose any desire to argue with him: enjoyment outweighs any other feeling. But in my opinion their main shortcoming lies in a lack of definition in their point of view; yes, I think Herzen has not clearly appreciated either the significance of the old nobility, which he so admires, or the significance of the bourgeoisie which he so despises. So what is left for him? The worker. But what about the peasant-farmer? Surely Herzen doesn't believe that a lowering of the electoral qualification will alter the position of the bourgeoisie? I don't believe that. I am no admirer of the bourgeoisie, and the coarseness of its *mores* and its overwhelmingly prosaic outlook make me as indignant as the next man, but it is fact that is important to me in the present instance. I am a sceptic; seeing that on each of the contending sides there is sense and vacuousness in the same degree, I am not able to adhere to either one, although the working class, as the oppressed class, undoubtedly has all my sympathies. But I can't help adding at the same time "God grant that we may have a bourgeoisie!" *Cet air de matador* with which Herzen solves everything in France is very sweet and engaging and I couldn't possibly love it more in him, precisely because I know the gentle dove-like heart of this matador; but really Herzen's solution doesn't explain anything at all: it only skates over the surface of things. All these questions are so complex that it is impossible to raise one of them without raising several others as well. . .

1847

Vasily Petrovich Botkin
LETTERS ON SPAIN (Extract)[42]

I am still in Madrid, in spite of its stifling heat and burning air, in spite of its incessant disturbances. The more closely I look at people and events here the more convinced I become that in order to form any judgement of Spain and the disturbances which affect her one must first of all put aside any comparison of her with Europe. A general European point of view, applied to Spain, can lead only to a false conception of her. Has not Europe looked on Spain as the country of the staunchest monarchic institutions, has it not regarded the Spanish people as exemplifying the most sensitive and touching national feeling? And yet this people with complete equanimity watched Ferdinand, who had deprived the Infante Don Carlos of his legitimate inheritance of the Spanish throne, bequeath it to the foreigner Maria-Cristina, and looked on indifferently as the Spanish Infante wandered in the mountains of Navarre.[43] Europe regarded Spain as the most Catholic country in the world, and yet the Spanish people slaughtered their monks, or at least permitted them to be slaughtered, allowed the secular power to plunder their churches and monasteries and finally, with the same indifference, watched their monasteries being destroyed and are not in the least concerned at the fact that about ten years ago the Pope broke off all spiritual relations with Spain. True, this country is a living riddle to which Europe has hitherto been quite unable to find the solution. Thrown into revolution it moves through it like a slave of higher instincts, which forcibly direct it towards the fulfilment of its destiny. But what destiny is this? Spain herself does not know. She goes not knowing whither her road will lead her, without a definite goal, without any plan and in complete ignorance of the morrow. Never has Europe been confronted with such a spectacle![44]

If people are so often mistaken about Spain, and if it is so difficult not to be mistaken about her, is it not because people look on Spain not from her own point of view, not in the light of her own history, but from the vantage point of the general history of Europe; whereas Spain, while appearing to be almost entirely like all unlimited monarchies, has in fact undergone a historical development quite different from that of the rest of Europe; besides, the elements from which Spanish society has been formed are quite different, both in principle and in the direction they have taken, from those which lie at the foundation of other European states. Look, for example, at the position and significance of the Spanish gentry. In France, the country of equality, the people regard the gentry and aristocracy with hostility; in Spain, where the sense of equality is considerably stronger, the aristocracy not only excites neither hatred nor envy, but actually enjoys the people's respect. This circumstance seems rather curious to me, and I should like to make use of certain evidence which I have to hand in order to say a few words about the gentry in Spain and about its relations with the people. I believe that if we understand these relations we shall be better able to understand current events in Spain and shall be all the more willing to excuse her people for their indifference to them.

After the fall of the Roman Empire (forgive me for beginning so far in the past) the whole of Europe was conquered and occupied by barbarians; the vanquishing tribe and the vanquished settled on the same land, some as masters, others as vassals. For the history of France and England is nothing but the gradual liberation of the conquered tribe. It would seem that the French Revolution, having proclaimed political, civil and religious equality, was bound to obscure the very memory of the former conflict and hatred; yet such was the depth of this hatred that it outlived even the cause of the quarrel itself. To this day one still sometimes hears voices raised against the aristocracy in France; and, however senseless and hollow these voices might sound, they still awaken a vague irritation in the people. O aristocracy, the memory of centuries is not wiped out in a single day! But let us leave this excusable touchiness of a young society and return to Spain.

In Spain you will find nothing of the kind; here the nobleman is not proud and haughty, the commoner is not envious of him; between them there is only one distinction, wealth, and no other. Complete equality of tone and the most delicate intimacy of address reign here between the estates. And not only the citizen, but also the peasant, the unskilled laborer and the water-carrier deal with the nobleman on an absolutely equal footing. If the entrance to the house of a Spanish grandee is open to them, they go in, sit down and talk to their noble host in a tone of absolute equality. The reason for relations which are so surprising to us must lie in Spanish history itself, to be precise in the fact that there was never a class of plebeians or common people in Spain, that the Spanish peasant does not belong to the conquered tribe while the nobles belong to the conquering one. The new Spain began with the expulsion of the Moors;[45] it is only from that time that landowning rights date. But this expulsion itself shows that only the victors have remained in Spain. It is common knowledge that after the Moorish conquest of the whole of Spain a handful of bold and unyielding people, entrenched in the mountains of Asturias, subsequently became the salvation and standard-bearer of national independence. As their strength grew so they gradually conquered the provinces of Leon, Castille and Aragon, pressing the Moors further and further back, and finally the taking of Granada[46] destroyed the political significance of the Moors in Spain. At the same time the clergy set about the elimination of every trace of Islam. The Inquisition took the conquered Arabs under its jurisdiction, subjected them to torture, compelled them to renounce their costume and language and finally expelled them all from Spain. To be of low origin, in the conception of a Spaniard, meant to have Arab blood in one's veins, the blood of a race doubly despised as the infidel and the defeated. For the same reason nobility for a Spaniard consists above all in being a Christian of long standing; and this quality alone, of being a long-standing Christian, if the humblest porter considers it to belong to his own stock, then he is proud of it[47] and in his eyes it puts him on a level with the most important people in the state. Among the local *aguadores* (water-carriers), who are almost all from Asturias, there are many nobles; they know this and glory in their origin. *Yo soy mejor que mi amo* (I am more of a nobleman, I am more noble than my lord),[48] says the *aguador,* taking on a proud air and holding his bucket of water on his shoulder. And indeed the oldest and most noble families try to trace the beginning of their stock primarily in Asturias. But since people in other provinces took part in the expulsion of the Arabs as well everyone is proud in his own way and all deal with one another among themselves on an equal footing because, I repeat, the main and greatest event of Spanish history is the struggle against Islam; both property and nobility are derived from it and it is only on the basis of it that one can explain the political power of the clergy in Spain and the huge possessions of the gentry.

The cause of the universal respect which the gentry has always enjoyed among the people lay in the fact that its forbears were the original liberators of Spain from the yoke of the Arabs. While the people were engaged in agriculture, the gentry fought the infidels and extended the frontiers of Spanish Christendom. Hence the respect in which the people hold the gentry, but again there was no sense of subjection in this respect, for the very reason that between the nobleman and the humblest peasant there was not the abyss of conquest, as in the rest of Europe, but merely a difference in the degree of activity and bravery.

1847-51

Pavel Vasilevich Annenkov
[ITALY][49]

Thus an hour before sunrise, when the dampness of the spring night still lingered in the mountains, we would begin our journey, wrapping ourselves up in our coats and huddled in our corners; but gradually, with the increasing warmth of the day, which would often come vividly into sight over the peaks, we would cast off our coats together with the last vestiges of slumber. Then we would come to a halt in some hollow in the mountains at the entrance to one of those stony shacks built of roughly hewn cobble-stones where the owner's family live downstairs around the hearth, attending there to all their needs—and there we would breakfast. Sitting outside some secluded inn I often happened to look at a patch of sky visible from the gorge and delight in the clouds that scudded overhead like Chinese shadows rolling on a narrow canvas and here and there leaving shreds which had been torn off and spots of transparent mist on the mountain slopes. Sometimes we would drive in for lunch and a rest to some little medieval town with a gloomy turret by a bridge which had been thrown across a precipice, and with a Romanesque cathedral in the center and the remains of a half-destroyed castle at one end where some aristocrat's keep was sometimes still preserved... And, the more menacing such a town seemed on the outside, the more pervasive was the dead and drowsy stillness that reigned in its streets. Bustling medieval life seemed to have departed in order to leave a void only occasionally filled by gusts of modern life which sometimes momentarily and tempestuously blow over these places forgotten by history and then again leave them to sleep and unruffled calm. There was something similar about our slow and lazy journey and this lethargic way of life, which has no care for time and does not rush after it with frantic passion, like the rest of Europe, but lets it flow past with equanimity... It is as if one experiences this state of mind oneself and rejoices at having been able to experience it. I derived an inexpressible pleasure from those happy valleys which intersect the Apennines, leaving in one's imagination only the memory of their gardens. The reader may find in Mr. Mittermaier's splendid book on Italy a description of the remarkably humane, gentle relations between the landowners of this country and their tenant-farmers, between the farmers and their laborers, relations which have removed the ulcer of that enmity between different estates which afflicts Western Europe.

1857

Alexander Vasilevich Druzhinin
A.S. PUSHKIN AND THE LATEST EDITION OF HIS WORKS (Extract)[50]

No one who is interested in Russian prose should, in our opinion, pass over *The Tales of Belkin* in silence. *The Tales of Belkin* were Alexander Sergeich's[51] first experiment in the narrative mode; these tales had great success among the reading public; and the influence they have had is partially reflected in almost all our novels and novellas. *The Tales of Belkin* is a captivating book, beautiful and radiant like the best chapters ever written by Goldsmith and, like the best pages in Goldsmith's works, it bears the reader away into the realm of serene feelings. If we are delighted by poets who acquaint us with the comic and dark side of life, then what right do we have to withhold our acclaim from a writer who unfurls before us another side of that same life, a tranquil, joyful side dear to our hearts? If we enjoy rereading several times the quarrel of Ivan Ivanych and Ivan Nikiforych,[52] "The Nose," "The Carriage" and other tales of that sort, then what right do we have to deny that there is content in *The Tales of Belkin*? If Pushkin looked with fondness at our rural life and if his jest had no malice then on what grounds may we be so bold as to demand satire and chastising humor of him? If Pushkin, a man who experienced much in life and suffered as a result of the slander of friends and the insults of a cold society, a man who struggled, repented, went astray and many times in the course of his life spent sleepless nights shedding bitter tears, finds a means of looking on life with serene amiability, are we to condemn Pushkin for this? We shall go further; we should love him for precisely this reason. Happy is the man who derives from life's experience such a power of forgiveness, such a capacity to smile, such cordiality towards people, such a perspicacious view of the whole serene side of life! Sometimes one needs more strength for an idyll than for a drama in the misanthropic vein; very often satire comes more easily than sweet jest. But we still refuse to acknowledge this truth, for in accordance with our mocking Slavonic nature we are always prepared to become enamored of a man who amuses himself at our expense and who is not hard put to find an unkind word.

One of our contemporary men of letters put it very well when, talking of the essence of Alexander Sergeich's gift, he said: "If Pushkin had lived to our time, his works would have counteracted the Gogolian tendency which, in certain respects, needs such counteraction." This judgment is absolutely just and very much to the point. Even in our time, even so many years after the death of Pushkin, his works must play their part. Studying the prose of Pushkin, his *Onegin*—where our everyday way of life, rural as well as urban, is depicted—his verse, inspired by village scenes, the rural way of life, we shall embark upon that counteraction, that reaction which is so essential in our current literature. Whatever the ardent admirers of Gogol might say (and we ourselves are not among those readers who are cool towards him) a whole literature cannot live on *Dead Souls* alone. We need poetry. There is little poetry in the followers of Gogol and no poetry in the excessively realistic tendency of many of the latest writers. This tendency itself cannot be called natural,[53] for the study of one side of life is not nature. We shall say what we think without beating about the bush: our current literature is worn out and weakened by its satirical tendency.

Against that satirical tendency, to which immoderate emulation of Gogol has brought us, Pushkin's poetry may serve as the best weapon. Our eyes clear, we breathe more freely: we are borne from one world into another, from artificial illumination into the simple light of day, which is better than any bright illumination, although illumination, at the proper time, also has its attractions. Before us stands the same way of life, the same people—but how calm, tranquil and joyful it all looks! Where previously we saw along the roadside only drab fields and all sorts of other rotten things, now we feast our eyes upon rural scenes of Russian antiquity, on dry and many-colored valleys, with all our heart we hail the first days of spring or a poetic night by the river—the night on which Tatyana visited Evgeny's deserted house. The road itself, on which we recently thought, as we traveled along it, only of jolts and the drunken Selifan, takes on a different aspect and our journey seems not so fatiguing as before. The unknown plains have something fantastic about them; the moon illuminates the passing darkness like an invisible man, little sparks and imaginary leagues rush up before the coachman's eyes, and before the poet's eyes the spirits of the road, howling mournfully, begin their poetic flight. Winter has come; winter is the season of frost-bitten noses and of the misfortunes of Akaky Akakievich, but for our singer and those who venerate him winter brings with it the previous radiant scenes, the very thought of which makes our heart pound. The peasant triumphantly tears over the new path on his wooden sledge; the heavy red-footed goose steps carefully on the bright ice, preparing to swim, slips, and to its utter astonishment falls over. Happy is he who can seek out this poetry, who celebrates winter and autumn in his verse, and on a frosty late October's day sits by the fireside calling together in his imagination the dear friends of his heart, the faithful companions of his school-days, and repaying their friendship with sweet songs, remembering not the evil in life but exalting the good alone!...[54]

Pushkin's spirit was the spirit of an unusual, highly developed, loving and highly enlightened man. That is why his work is so beautiful, that is why his experience of life did not bear bitter fruit. In the mountains of the island of Sardinia there is an unusual vale, in which all the plants, as a result of certain deficiencies in the soil, have the taste of bitter wormwood: that vale is like the spirit of many a poet, but quite unlike the spirit of Pushkin. Not one of his descendants will address himself to this singer with the well known bitter lines from Goethe's "Prometheus": "Do you wish me to revere you? For what services should I revere your name? Were you able to wipe away the tears of those who weep, to diminish the anguish of those who are afflicted?" "The name of Pushkin will for ever be worshiped by the world, for he piously fulfilled the poet's calling, scattering about him the blessings of poetry, causing his brethren, by means of his verse, to smile brightly, weeping together with those who are downcast, and by his gaiety increasing the joy of those who are happy." And that is why we should utter a word of eternal praise over the remains of our forgiving, loving, great poet; that is why we must remember every word ever spoken by him and boldly hasten after him, down the road he indicated!

1855

Alexander Vasilievich Druzhinin
THE CRITICISM OF THE GOGOLIAN PERIOD OF RUSSIAN LITERATURE AND OUR ATTITUDE TOWARDS IT (Extract)[55]

All critical systems, theses and outlooks which ever stirred the world of ancient and modern poetry may be reduced to two eternally counteracting theories, one of which we shall call the *artistic,* that is to say having as its slogan pure art for art's sake, and the *didactic,* that is to say striving to have an effect on man's *mores,* way of life and concepts through its direct instruction...

The *artistic* theory, which preaches that art serves and must serve as an end in itself, rests on ideas which are in our view irrefutable. Under its guidance the poet, like the poet extolled by Pushkin, acknowledges himself to have been created not for everyday concerns but for prayers, sweet sounds and inspiration. Firmly believing that the interests of the moment are transient, that although mankind is constantly changing, there is one area in which it does not change, that of ideas of eternal beauty, goodness and truth, he sees his eternal anchor in the disinterested service of these ideas. His song has no preconceived, mundane, moral or any other conclusions applicable to the advantage of his contemporaries; it serves as its own reward, object and meaning. He portrays people as he sees them, and since he does not stipulate how they might mend their ways he gives society no lessons, or, if he does give them, then he gives them unconsciously. He lives in his elevated world and comes down to earth, as the Olympians once came down to it, remembering full well that he has his home on lofty Olympus. We intentionally depict the poet imbued with the extreme artistic theory of art in the way that the opponents of this theory are wont to depict him.

At first sight the position of the didactic poet seems incomparably more brilliant and enviable. For the writer who has broken away from the eternal and unchanging laws of the beautiful, for the poet who has thrown himself, in Gogol's marvelous expression, into the waves of *turbid modernity,* the path is apparently broader and the sources of inspiration incomparably more numerous than for the servants of pure art. He boldly turns his gift to the interests of his fellow citizens at the given moment; he serves political, moral and scientific ends of paramount importance; he exchanges the role of calm singer for that of stern mentor and goes among the crowd of agitated contemporaries with his lyre not as a guest of the world and a dweller on Olympus but as a toiler and worker for the common weal. A judicious poet of a practical bent, having given himself up to didacticism, may effect much that is useful for his contemporaries—that we shall not deny...

Having set out as far as possible the gist of both theories, let us turn to their historical significance. At all times, in all ages and in all countries we see one and the same thing. Poets, those who revere pure art, stand firm and steady, their voice resounds from century to century, while the voices of the didactic writers (often noble and strong voices) die almost before they have succeeded in shouting something out and are sunk in the abyss of utter oblivion. Didactic writers who are moralists do, in spite of the satires and gibes aroused by their works, play a certain part in a literature owing to the *eternal* moral-philosophical element in their work, but didactic writers who sacrifice their poetic talent to the interests of so-called *modernity* wither and fade together with the modernity they have served. In the great onward movement of man and society the tens of years which constitute the life-span of a whole human generation are but an atom, a minute, the briefest term of an eternally transitional epoch. What was new, bold and fruitful today is tomorrow old and inapplicable and, what is sadder still, unnecessary to society! Woe to the poet who has exchanged an eternal goal for one rooted in a given time; woe to the mariner who has trustingly cast his only anchor not in the firm ocean floor but in a weak and shifting bank of sand. And a strange thing—and strange is the power of pure genius—poets who are Olympians, poets who are so imperturbable, poets who have forsaken mundane cares and have no thought of instructing man become man's leaders, his mentors, his teachers, his prophets at that very time when the high priests of modernity lose all their significance! It is to them that peoples come for spiritual pabulum and from them that they go away lighter in spirit, having moved forward along the path of enlightenment. Posterity reveres them long after it has forgotten the cries of the didactic poets, the servants of the ephemeral. Their every word soothes the mortal's soul, they make the story of Orpheus come true, Orpheus to the accompaniment of whose inspired songs cities built themselves, battles came to an end, people gave each other their hand and even wild animals forgot their savagery. Good, beauty and truth, which inspired these poets, were reflected in all their works. And these works, sung in a moment of inspiration, jotted down for pleasure alone, without any instructive purpose, have become the germ of the education of all, the basis of our knowledge, of our good intentions, of our great deeds!..[56]

From the time that the Russian criticism of the Gogolian period[57] adopted the didactic sentimentality of the representatives of the latest French literature,[58] its influence, we say with sadness, began visibly to decline. We hasten to say, however, that this was not a hopeless decline, the decline of senility, a decline remarkable for impotence alone. A sacred love of poetry and truth continued to burn on the altar; only the brightness of this flame suffered from the clouds of mist which blew over it. We are convinced with all our heart and soul that the criticism we are now examining would have emerged from under the yoke of false theories if fate had deigned to prolong the life of its main exponents, to make them witnesses of what we have witnessed. The criticism of the 1840s left the stage without by any means having uttered its last word: no one will persuade us otherwise. It had everything necessary for further progress and further beneficial activity, and given its talent, perspicacity, receptivity, readiness to admit to its mistakes it was not capable of going hand in hand with the didactic sentimentalism of France and Germany for long. If we, figures of minor importance, have learned so much from the experience of the last few years, then how must that criticism have been affected by this experience? If we, who once followed the literary schools of modern Germany and modern France with affection, have learned so much from the decline of these schools, then how much would our criticism of the Gogolian period necessarily have learned if it had lived through what we have lived through?

Be that as it may, before us we have what is done, not that which might have been accomplished subsequently. The didactic errors of the criticism of the Gogolian period were manifested above all in the current literature in the journals and in second-rate writers. Our imaginative literature, encouraged by the approval of its judges and by models that were pointed out to it, was rapidly inundated with a flood of the strangest works. Realism, sentimentality of the new style, a didactic tendency in the basic idea—these are three factors, of which one had only to make nimble use in order to get into print and receive acclaim. In all literatures the work of the imaginative writer is well rewarded and serves as the best means to the attainment of an enviable reputation, and for that reason it is no wonder that in any literature we see a large number of people who set about the creation of works of art without having the slightest aptitude for it. The first sign of a didactic tendency in literature is when purely scientific work, or at least the work of people capable of it, seeks expression in art, to the detriment of writers called to an artist career. Wherever poetry is transformed into the servant of unpoetic ends (however noble these ends might be), everyone considers himself entitled to use the form of the poetic work as a vehicle for his ideas, his treatises, his views. Economists aspire to lyricism, historians begin to imitate novelists, and the literary confusion, which has begun with the invasion of a scientific element into art, ends with poets and novelists going over to scientific work. Where the scholar Gervinus[59] starts writing verse the poet Heine will see it as his right to compile a book on the history of German literature,[60] and both the verse of the professor and the scholarly work of the poet will turn out to be unsatisfactory. If the historian Michelet[61] is going to produce pages in the style of chapters from the *Mysteries of Paris*[62] the versifier Lamartine,[63] in turn, will take to historical work. The very principle of literary didacticism, which admits of, even encourages, the mixture of the ephemeral with the eternal, the scientific with the poetic, the artistic with the edifying, leads to such oddities, which are deleterious to art. No sooner had our criticism of the 1840s been carried away with the new didacticism than it lost the right to be artistically demanding. If the work it was examining was directly instructive for the contemporary reader, developed an idea of great topicality and did not offend against the rules of grammar, then it was deemed satisfactory and noteworthy. Our literature seethed with writers who were perhaps fit to compose pamphlets or economic booklets, but who preferred to dress their idea up in artistic form and who instructed the public through tales and even poetry. Men of letters, in turn, whose talent suited them for purely artistic work, considered it their duty to deviate from their calling, by adhering to transient ideas and views in their artistic things. A factional spirit and the intolerance inseparable from it began to flare up in literature...

1856

Part V

Polemics of the 1850s and 1860s

Introduction

In the new atmosphere which prevailed in Russia after the death of Nicholas I and Russia's defeat in the Crimean War intellectual life was suddenly reinvigorated. One manifestation of the new vitality was the blossoming of imaginative literature again after the "seven dismal years" with which the reign of Nicholas I had ended, and indeed a remarkable crop of works appeared between 1855 and 1861, among them Turgenev's novels *Rudin* (1856), *A Nest of Gentry* (1859) and *On the Eve* (1860), Tolstoi's *Sebastopol Stories* (1855-56), Pisemsky's novel *A Thousand Souls* (1858), Goncharov's *Oblomov* (1859), Ostrovsky's play *The Thunderstorm* (1860) and Dostoevsky's *Notes from the House of the Dead* (1860). Publicism began to flourish again too: the journals *The Contemporary (Sovremennik)* and *Notes of the Fatherland* achieved a circulation of approximately 4,000, which was very large for the time, and others, such as *Russian Herald (Russkii vestnik),* sprang up in response to the increased public interest in topical, cultural and social questions. As the attention of the educated public came at last to rest on concrete practical questions, however, so debate took on a more political character than it had had before and a clear fissure developed in the intelligentsia between the surviving "men of the 40s," liberal Westernizers such as Botkin, Annenkov and Druzhinin, on the one hand, and younger men of more plebeian origin, socialists such as Chernyshevsky and Dobrolyubov, on the other.

Nikolai Chernyshevsky (1828-89), the son of a priest *(popovich)* from Saratov province and the main spokesman for the young radical wing of the intelligentsia in the late 1850s, made perhaps the greatest single contribution in nineteenth-century Russia to the socialist stream of thought that was to find expression in revolutionary Populism and later in Marxism, and in important respects he lays foundations for Bolshevism. (He was greatly admired, incidentally, by Lenin.) Chernyshevsky and his disciples belong to the rationalist, scientific tradition in European thought, and in many ways they are the heirs of the rational *philosophes* of the eighteenth century. Like Western thinkers such as Comte, they admire the rigor and exactitude of the natural sciences, reject *a priori* hypotheses and accept only what they believe can be empirically demonstrated. The scientific method, which had been applied to such effect in physics, chemistry, biology, astronomy and geology in the first half of the nineteenth century, seemed to Chernyshevsky to be applicable also to other areas of enquiry which had not previously been considered amenable to rigorous rational analysis, namely the study of man's art, his society, institutions, behavior and moral life. It is not surprising, therefore, that scientific allusions and mathematical formulae abound in Chernyshevsky's writings. Admittedly their purpose appears on occasion to be to dazzle the reader with the author's erudition, and they tend either to tire or to amuse the modern reader; but such allusions are also undoubtedly intended to point up by analogy the supposed accuracy of the conclusions Chernyshevsky draws.

Chernyshevsky's intellectual challenge to the established beliefs of both the conservative and the liberal wings of the intelligentsia in the late 1850s and early 1860s is very wide-ranging. His first attack is mounted against the old aesthetic beliefs, for in the mid 1850s, when he began to make his mark in journalism in St. Petersburg, imaginative literature and literary criticism were still the realms in which debate was mainly conducted. In his dissertation, "The Aesthetic Relations of Art to Reality," presented for a master's degree and published in book form in 1855, Chernyshevsky set out to demolish the idealist conception, derived from Hegelian aesthetics, that there coexisted a real world—the mundane, concrete actuality of everyday life, with all its joys and sorrows—and a superior, enduring world of perfect forms to which man aspired in his religion and philosophy and the beauty of which might be captured for posterity by the great artist. This traditional conception rested on an intuitive assumption concerning the unverifiable existence of a higher reality, which Chernyshevsky, as a devotee of scientific method, could not accept. Moreover, the idealist aesthetic had deeply conservative implications repugnant to the socialist. For insistence on the comparative imperfection of everyday actuality and the exhortation to the artist to seek beauty in a transcendent reality encouraged an attitude of resignation towards earthly suffering and thus permitted the creation of an art devoid of any fierce sense of civic responsibility. In order to combat this indifferentism Chernyshevsky sought to redefine the concept of beauty as that which reminds us most vividly of real life, thus focusing the attention of the artist on reality with all its defects and topical problems. He also sets art the goal of being useful to the artist's contemporaries.

Chernyshevsky's arguments for a utilitarian and politically committed art—which provoked heated objections from outside the radical camp—found further expression in his long series of "Essays on the Gogol Period of Russian Literature" (1855-56). After 1857, however, Chernyshevsky turned his attention to political, socio-economic, ethical and other questions. In 1858, for example, as the controversy between the radical and liberal wings of the intelligentsia intensified, he produced a series of articles, ostensibly on the remote subject of French political history, in which he accuses the liberals of a lack of real concern for the working class and takes them to task for apparently ineffectual advocacy of changes that struck Chernyshevsky, the socialist, as unimportant. Thus, in an article on

Cavaignac, the French general who had ruthlessly suppressed the workers' uprising in Paris during the "June days" of 1848, he condemns the betrayal of the workers by "moderate republicans," whose political ambitions the workers had helped to realize, and dismisses these liberals as indecisive and unpractical people who "behind the glitter and noise of their abstract formulae" see and hear nothing. An even clearer statement of Chernyshevsky's view of liberalism, however, was contained in his article on the "Struggle of Parties in France in the Reign of Louis XVIII and Charles X" which deals ostensibly with the restoration of the Bourbon monarchy in France after the Napoleonic Wars, when moderate republicans clashed with loyalist supporters of the monarchy, but which has a clear pertinence for Russia in the years immediately following the Crimean War.

As he attacks contemporary liberals Chernyshevsky also begins to explore the forms that a future socialist society might assume, and, like Herzen after 1848, he comes to fix his attention on the peasant commune. In numerous articles written while the emancipation of the serfs was being considered by the government he tried to underline the practical advantages as well as the moral virtues of communal landholding, taking issue, for example, with those who saw the commune as an unproductive and inefficient agricultural unit. And in his most notable essay on the subject, "A Critique of Philosophical Prejudices against Communal Landholding" (1858), he advanced the view—which was to provide an important foundation for revolutionary Populism—that backward nations do not have to pass through all the stages of development through which other nations have passed in order to reach higher levels of development. In other words, Russia might arrive at a socialism based on the commune without passing through the protracted capitalist phase of development, with all its attendant social misery, which had developed in the West after the collapse of feudalism there.

Of all Chernyshevsky's essays, however, perhaps the most wideranging and influential is his "Anthropological Principle in Philosophy" which was published in 1860. Chernyshevsky attempts in this essay to popularize the materialist and determinist views with which the Russian intelligentsia was becoming familiar through the work of German thinkers such as Vogt, Moleschott and Büchner. Following these writers, Chernyshevsky denies the existence of a spiritual aspect in man, thus carrying out a simplification analogous to that which he had carried out in aesthetics: in both instances two conventional planes of reality are reduced to one. He then proceeds to assert that thought is the product not of intuition or innate impulse but of sensation and stimuli, and to belittle the role of the will in human affairs. Character he treats as molded by circumstances, and crimes, or "bad actions" as he calls them, are explained accordingly as the product of poverty. Finally, Chernyshevsky puts forward a utilitarian ethic. Whereas it was conventional to attribute to man altruistic as well as selfish impulses, Chernyshevsky again rejects dualism, contending that man's actions are invariably dictated by self-interest. At the same time man is a rational creature, Chernyshevsky contends, and is thus amenable to the argument that his own best interest lies in the last analysis in co-operation with his fellows. According to Chernyshevsky's doctrine of "rational egoism" man must therefore be taught to derive his selfish satisfaction from performing actions that are useful to others. As to the question of how we may judge which actions are good and which are bad, Chernyshevsky abandons absolute moral standards and applies a relativistic criterion. An act is good or bad in relation to its consequences; it is good if it is useful, and the greatest good is that which is useful to the greatest number.

Although Chernyshevsky was arrested in 1862 and his publicistic career brought to a premature end, he did manage while in prison to write a long novel *What is to be done?* (1863) which, despite its incoherence and frequent banality, exercised an immense influence on the radical youth for the next thirty years and more. Towards the end of the novel we glimpse Chernyshevsky's vision of the socialist future, when his heroine, Vera Pavlovna, who runs an efficient co-operative of seamstresses, beholds in one of her dreams a communistic rural utopia housed in a building reminiscent of that monument to scientific progress, London's Crystal Palace.

One of the reasons why Chernyshevsky was able from 1857 to turn his attention away from art was the emergence of another *popovich*, Nikolai Dobrolyubov (1836-61), as a major critic to whom the literary section of *The Contemporary* could be entrusted. Dobrolyubov's thought is close in most important respects to that of Chernyshevsky, but his literary criticism is perhaps more vigorous and his influential reviews of many of the major works of Russian fiction that came out in the late 1850s secure him a prominent place of his own in the history of Russian thought. He is notable as one of the most articulate exponents of the method of literary criticism that Belinsky had helped to establish in Russia and that required the critic to examine not so much any merits or defects inherent in a work of art as the social factors which had supposedly given rise to it. Many of Dobrolyubov's most famous essays—for instance those on Goncharov's *Oblomov,* Ostrovsky's play *The Thunderstorm* and Turgenev's *On the Eve*—take the work of art as a starting point from which the critic may set out to explore social conditions and the mood and characters they have helped to create. Dobrolyubov is primarily interested, then, in the social processes which an author has perceived (though the author who faithfully observes reality may not always be conscious himself of the full meaning of his work or approve of the course he shows society to be taking) and in the literary characters, "types," who best exemplify these social processes. No work of art is of great significance for Dobrolyubov unless it can be made to yield such social meaning. Content therefore has more importance for him than the form in which it is couched and he is dismissive of critics whose main aim is to discuss a work from the aesthetic point of view. Nor are political implications ever very far from the surface of Dobrolyubov's writings. Thus his impatience with the liberal wing of the intelligentsia is apparent in his scorn for the latterday "superfluous men," the Oblomovs, who stand idly by, unable to bestir themselves, when the order which has nurtured them is in need of fundamental change. Similarly his sympathy for the socialist revolutionary, who has no ties with the old order and will therefore be uninhibited in his assault on it, finds expression in his discussion of Turgenev's "positive hero" Insarov, the Bulgarian harbinger of Russia's own men of action.

The attack mounted by Chernyshevsky and Dobrolyubov on cherished values was vigorously resisted in the late 1850s and early 1860s, and not merely by the liberal Westernist section of the intelligentsia, but also by the surviving Slavophiles and the so-called *pochvenniki,* native soil conservatives who were intellectually and spiritually close to the Slavophiles in many respects and whose position was formulated by Grigorev, Strakhov and Dostoevsky. Indeed it was in contributions to the polemics of the early 1860s, and in response to the propositions being advanced by Chernyshevsky and Dobrolyubov in particular, that Fyodor Dostoevsky (1821-81) clarified many of the views which were to find fictional expression in his four great novels, beginning with *Crime and Punishment* (1866). In numerous articles published in the journals *Time (Vremya)* and *The Epoch (Epokha),* of which he was *de facto* editor, Dostoevsky rejected the young radicals' utilitarian view of art, their belief that all subjects were amenable to scientific investigation, their determinism, their faith in man's rationality, their assertion that all human actions were in the last analysis prompted by self-interest, their denial of the existence of altruism and their optimistic vision of a socialist utopia. All these objections of Dostoevsky's to the radical outlook found expression not merely in his *Notes from the Underground* (1864), a credo of irrationalism which is often seen as a sort of prologue to his major fiction, but also in his *Winter Notes on Summer Impressions* (1863), a scathing depiction of the Western European countries Dostoevsky had visited in 1862, in which the Crystal Palace, Chernyshevsky's symbol of technological progress, prosperity and social harmony, is presented in quite another light, as a monument to man's spiritual degradation in the brave new world promoted by scientific advancement and Victorian capitalism.

As both the liberal Westernizers and the *pochvenniki* contested the new radical outlook, however, so other thinkers of the younger generation were giving this outlook a still more militant and destructive quality. Most notable among these new iconoclasts, who wrote in the main for the journal *The Russian Word (Russkoe slovo),* was Dmitry Pisarev (1840-

68), many of whose articles were written in the Peter and Paul Fortress where he was incarcerated from 1862 to 1866. Like Chernyshevsky, Pisarev preaches materialism and believes that man is governed by self-interest. He too asserts that it is to one's advantage to behave in socially useful ways, and he praises the exponents of this doctrine, the rational egoists whom Chernyshevsky had portrayed in his novel *What is to be Done?* He also propounds an extreme utilitarian view of art. But whereas Chernyshevsky, in 1855, had undertaken a careful examination of the old aesthetic values, Pisarev, in 1865, advocates the "destruction of aesthetics," and throughout his brief career he demands that old values, all obstacles to progress, be simply destroyed without further ado. In a famous article of 1861, "Scholasticism of the Nineteenth Century," for instance, he invites writers to liberate man "from the various constraints imposed on him by the timidity of his own thought, by caste prejudices, by the authority of tradition" and "by all the obsolete lumber that prevents a living man from breathing freely and developing in every direction," and he urged the destruction of that "artificial system of morality" which crushed people from the cradle. The freedom from traditional restraints which Pisarev advocated found its fictional representation in Bazarov, the central character of Turgenev's *Fathers and Sons* (1862) and the literary prototype of the new rebel, to whom Turgenev applied the title "nihilist." Pisarev gladly accepted Bazarov as an example for the radical section of the young generation to follow (though he preferred to dub him a "realist"). Freed of any of the constraints which old moral and religious values tended to impose and therefore rising far above the common herd, Bazarov possessed great power and freedom to destroy whatever seemed obsolete.

Nikolai Gavrilovich Chernyshevsky
THE AESTHETIC RELATIONSHIP OF ART TO REALITY (Extracts)[1]

The sensation brought about in man by the beautiful is one of radiant joy similar to that with which we are filled by the presence of a being dear to us. We *love* the beautiful in a disinterested way,[2] we admire it, we rejoice in it as we rejoice in a person dear to us. From this it follows that there is in the beautiful something dear, precious to our heart. But this "something" must be something extremely comprehensive, something capable of taking on the most diverse forms, something extremely general; for extremely diverse objects, beings utterly dissimilar to one another seem beautiful to us.

The most general thing of all that is dear to man, and the thing most dear to him on earth is *life;* in the most immediate way the life he would like to lead; then any life, because it is better in any case to be alive than not to be alive: everything that lives is by its very nature fearful of perishing, of non-being, and loves life. And it seems that the definition: "the beautiful is life"; "beautiful is that being in which we see life as it should be according to our concepts; beautiful is that object, which manifests life in itself or brings life to our minds"—it seems that this definition satisfactorily explains all instances which arouse in us a sense of the beautiful. Let us trace the main manifestations of the beautiful in different areas of reality in order to verify this.

"A good life," "life as it ought to be" consists for the common people in eating one's fill, living in a good *izba*[3] and having enough sleep; but the idea of work always goes together with this in the peasant's conception of life: to live without work is impossible, indeed it would be tedious. A consequence of a life of contentment filled with hard work—though not work leading to exhaustion—on the part of the young peasant or peasant girl will be an extremely fresh complexion and rosy cheeks—the first prerequisite of beauty as it is conceived by the common people. As she does a lot of work and is therefore strongly built the peasant girl, if she eats squarely, will be quite stout—this is also a prerequisite for the rural beauty; the "flimsy" beauty of high society seems to the peasant downright "unattractive," and even makes an unpleasant impression on him because he is accustomed to looking on "thinness" as a consequence of sickliness or a "bitter lot in life." But work will not allow one to grow plump: if the peasant girl is fat this is a type of sickliness, a sign of a "podgy" build, and the people consider great corpulence a defect; the rural beauty cannot have tiny little hands and feet because she does a lot of work—these attributes of beauty are not mentioned in our songs. In short, one will not find in descriptions of a beautiful woman in folk songs a single mark of beauty which is not an expression of radiant health and that equilibrium in the organism which always accompanies a life of contentment filled with constant and serious, but not excessive, work. The beauty of high society is quite another matter: her ancestors have already lived for several generations without working with their hands; an inactive way of life makes for poor circulation of the blood at the extremities; with each new generation the muscles of the arms and legs grow weaker, the bones become thinner; tiny little hands and feet are an inevitable consequence of all this—they are signs of a life which seems the only life for the upper classes of society, a life without physical work; if a woman of high society has large feet and hands that is a sign either of the fact that she is badly built or that she is not of an ancient good family. By the same token a beauty of high society must have small ears. Migraine, as is well known, is an interesting ailment and not without reason: as a result of inactivity blood remains entirely in the organs in the middle of the body, it rushes to the brain; even without that the nervous system is tense as a result of the general weakening of the organism; prolonged headaches and various sorts of nervous disorder are an inevitable consequence of all this; what is one to do? Even illness is interesting, almost enviable, when it is a consequence of a way of life which we like. Health, it is true, can never lose its value in man's eyes, because even in contentment and luxury it is bad to live without good health—consequently a rosy glow on the cheeks and the freshness of radiant health continue to be attractive even for people in high society; but sickliness, weakness, lack of vigor and a languid look also have the status of beauty in their eyes as soon as they seem a consequence of a luxurious and inactive way of life.

* * *

Here are the main conclusions to which this research has led us:

1. The definition of the beautiful: "the beautiful is the complete manifestation of a general idea in an individual phenomenon" does not stand up to scrutiny; it is too broad, being a definition of the formal aspiration of any human activity.

2. The true definition of the beautiful is this: "the beautiful is life," a beautiful being seems to man to be one in which he sees life as he conceives of it; a beautiful object is one which brings life to his mind.

3. This objective beauty, or the beautiful in its essence, must be distinguished from perfection of form, which consists in the unity of idea and form or in the object's entirely fulfilling its purpose.

4. It is not by arousing the idea of the Absolute that the sublime affects man; it hardly ever does arouse it.

5. Man perceives as sublime that which is much bigger than the objects or much stronger than the phenomena with which he compares himself as a man.

6. The tragic has no essential link with the idea of Fate or necessity. In real life the tragic is for the most part fortuitous, it does not flow from the essence of preceding factors. The form of necessity with which art invests it is a consequence of the usual principle of works of art: "the denouement must flow from the opening,"[4] or an inappropriate submission on the part of the poet to notions of Fate.

7. In the conception of modern European culture the tragic is "that which is terrible in man's life."

8. The sublime (and its element, the tragic) is not a modification of the beautiful; the ideas of the sublime and the beautiful are quite different from one another; there is neither any inner link nor any inner antithesis between them.

9. Reality is not only more vigorous but also more perfect than the fantasy. The images of the fantasy are merely a pale and nearly always unsuccessful remolding of reality.

10. The beautiful in objective reality is completely beautiful.

11. The beautiful in objective reality satisfies man absolutely.

12. It is not any need on man's part to make up for the deficiencies of beauty in reality that engenders art.

13. The artistic creation is inferior to the beautiful in reality not only because the impression made by reality is more vigorous than the impression made by artistic creations: artistic creations are inferior to the beautiful (in exactly the same way as they are inferior to the sublime, the tragic, the comic) in reality from the aesthetic point of view as well.

14. The sphere of art is not confined to the sphere of the beautiful in the aesthetic sense of the word, the beautiful by virtue of its living essence and not merely by virtue of the perfection of its form: art reproduces everything that is of interest for man in life.

15. Perfection of form (unity of idea and form) is not a characteristic of art in the aesthetic sense of the word (of the fine arts); the beautiful as unity of idea and image, or as a complete realization of an idea, is the object of art's striving in the broadest sense of the word or of "craft," the object of any of man's practical activity.

16. The need which gives rise to art in the aesthetic sense of the word (the fine arts) is the same one which is so clearly displayed in portrait painting. A portrait is painted not because the features of the living person do not satisfy us but in order to assist our recollection of the living person when he is not before our eyes and to give some idea of him to people who have not had occasion to see him. Art by means of its reproductions only

brings to our minds that which is interesting to us in life and attempts to some extent to acquaint us with those interesting facets of life which we have not had occasion to experience or observe in reality.

17. The reproduction of life is the general, characteristic mark of art, it is its essence; works of art often have another function too—explanation of life; they often also have the function of passing a verdict on the phenomena of life.

1855

Nikolai Gavrilovich Chernyshevsky
[ON LIBERALISM] [5]

...In spite of the fact that the word "liberalism" is widely used everywhere its meaning, both in Western Europe and all the more in our country, remains very inconsistent. Liberals are quite unjustly lumped together with radicals and democrats. Our article would be obscure or would seem absurd to one who was accustomed to lumping together these parties, which differ very greatly from one another. We do not need to say very much here about either the radicals or the democrats because they did not play leading roles in the age of the Restoration [6] and, one may say, did not yet constitute solid political parties in France; it will be sufficient to mention them only in so far as is necessary to show how they differ from liberals and thereby to define liberalism in the exact sense of the word.

The fundamental wishes, the basic motives of liberals and democrats are essentially different. Democrats intend as far as possible to destroy the domination of the lower classes by the upper classes in the state system, to diminish the power and wealth of the higher estates, [7] on the one hand, and to give more weight and prosperity to the lower estates, on the other. It is almost a matter of indifference to them by what means the laws should be changed to this end and by what means the new social order should be supported. Liberals, on the contrary, will never agree to grant superiority in society to the lower estates, because these estates, as a result of their lack of education and their material poverty, are indifferent to the interests which for the liberal party stand above all other things, namely the right of free speech and a constitutional order. For the democrat our Siberia, in which the common people enjoy prosperity, is considerably superior to England, in which the majority of the people suffer great hardship. The democrat is implacably opposed to only one of all the political institutions, the aristocracy; the liberal almost always finds that society can attain to a liberal order only if a certain degree of aristocratism is present in it. This is why liberals generally harbor a mortal enmity towards democrats, saying that democratism leads to despotism and is ruinous for freedom.

Radicalism, properly speaking, consists not in adherence to one political order or another but rather in the belief that a certain political order, the establishment of which seems useful, is incompatible with the fundamental laws already in existence, that the main defects of a certain society may be eliminated only by a complete refashioning of its foundations, not by minor adjustment of details. In North America a radical would be a monarchist, in China he would be an adherent of European civilization, in the East Indies an opponent of the caste system. [8]

Of all the political parties the liberal party alone cannot come to terms with radicalism because the latter is disposed to carry out reforms with the help of material force and is prepared for the sake of reforms to sacrifice both freedom of speech and constitutional forms. Of course, the liberal may become a radical in despair, but this state of mind is not natural in him; it costs him constant struggle with himself and he will constantly seek grounds for avoiding the need for fundamental breaks in the social order and for promoting his cause by means of small adjustments which do not occasion the need for any extreme measures.

Thus liberals are almost always opposed to democrats and are hardly ever radicals. They desire political freedom, but since political freedom almost always suffers when great upheavals take place in civil society, even freedom itself, the highest goal of all their aspirations, they wish to introduce gradually and to extend little by little without, as far as possible, any tremors. Freedom of the printed word and the existence of parliamentary government seem to them a necessary condition of political freedom; but since freedom of speech, given the present condition of Western European societies, generally becomes a vehicle for democratic, impassioned and radical propaganda, they wish to keep freedom of speech within fairly narrow boundaries lest it should turn against them. Parliamentary debates are also bound everywhere to take on a radical-democratic character if parliament is to consist of representatives of the nation in the broad sense of the word, and so liberals are compelled also to restrict participation in parliament to those classes of the people who are quite well off or even very well off under the present Western European social orders.

From a theoretical point of view liberalism may seem attractive to a person spared by good fortune from material need: freedom is a very pleasant thing. But liberalism conceives freedom in a very narrow, purely formal way. It sees freedom as an abstract right, as permission on paper, as the absence of legal prohibition. It will not understand that legal permission only has any value for a man when he has the material means to take advantage of this permission. Neither I nor you, reader, is forbidden to dine off a golden dinner service; unfortunately neither you nor I has or, in all probability, ever will have the means with which to put this refined idea into practice; for this reason I say frankly that I place no value whatever on my right to have a golden dinner service and am ready to sell this right for a silver ruble or even less. All those rights for which liberals plead are exactly like that for the common people. The people are ignorant and in almost all countries the majority of them are illiterate; having no money with which to obtain an education, having no money with which to give their children an education, how are they to value their right of free speech? Need and ignorance deprive the people of any opportunity to understand the affairs of state and to devote themselves to them—so tell me now, will the people place any value on the right to hold parliamentary debates, and will they be able to make use of it?

There is no European country in which the vast majority of the people is anything but quite indifferent to the rights which are the object of liberalism's desires and efforts. Consequently liberalism is everywhere doomed to impotence: argue as one might, only those aspirations have force, only those institutions have durability which are supported by the mass of the people. From the theoretical narrowness of the liberal concept of freedom as simple absence of prohibition flows the weakness of liberalism in practice, lacking as it does any solid support in the mass of the people who place no value on rights of which they cannot, for lack of the necessary means, make use.

Unless one ceases to be a liberal one cannot break out of this narrow concept of freedom as simple absence of legal prohibition. A practicable conception of freedom, in which the actual means to the utilization of the right are supplied by a more consequential element than the mere abstract absence of legal prohibition, lies quite outside the ambit of liberalism's ideas. Liberalism pleads for abstract rights without worrying about the worldly prosperity of the masses which alone makes possible the real implementation of a right.

These brief remarks would seem to suffice for the time being as a preliminary explanation to the reader of the sense in which we are using the word "liberalism."

It goes without saying that the theoretical bankruptcy of liberalism is felt only by those who need material means as well as legal permission. But of course it doesn't enter the head of a person who has these means to plead for them. Hence liberalism was for very long a system which completely satisfied people with independent material means of livelihood and with highly developed intellectual needs. "He who has a full stomach does not understand the hungry man"[9] and they were quite unable to arrive by a theoretical path at the notion that the needs of the common people might consist in something other than liberal tendencies. They imagined that they were truly doing people a service by trying to deliver freedom of speech and parliamentary government to them. Bitter experience has begun to disillusion the liberals. The failure of practical ventures is gradually opening the eyes of the most sensible among them to the theoretical shortcomings of their system and with every passing year the number of true liberals in Europe is decreasing. But the delusions of political parties are long-lasting; indeed how could they be otherwise? If a single individual needs whole years to acquire healthy notions about life on the basis of experience, then of course a collection of many people supporting one another in their common delusions needs decades. For this reason liberals still continue to exist and plead their case in France, as in all the other countries of Western Europe, and one could not say that France or

Western Europe in general was out of danger from their pleadings; indeed they themselves, unfortunately, are still not prudent enough to spare themselves from calamity and persecution by completely handing over the concern about the common people to others. No, they are still prepared to "sacrifice themselves for the good of freedom."

There is no more sad spectacle than to see honest people who love you doing their utmost to confer on you a blessing that you emphatically do not need, putting their lives at risk by climbing Mont Blanc to bring down an Alpine rose for you to enjoy—poor fellows! How much money and time has been squandered and how many honest necks have been broken in this journey undertaken beyond the clouds for your pleasure! And it didn't enter these people's heads that what you needed was not an Alpine rose but a piece of bread, because a hungry man doesn't care for the flowers of nature or eloquence, and they looked at you with wonder and showered you with reproaches to the effect that you were ungrateful to them and indifferent to your own happiness because you looked coldly at their exploits and didn't climb after them over the crags and chasms and didn't hold them up when they fell down into the abyss from their pinnacle up above the clouds. Poor blind wretches, they didn't realize that it would have been much easier for them to get you a piece of bread, they didn't realize it because they didn't suppose that anyone could need such a prosaic thing as a piece of bread.

One is sorry for them because they've nearly all broken their necks with hardly any benefit for the nations on whose behalf they were pleading. One is even sorrier that nations have not always been cold towards their aspirations, but have sometimes been seduced by the eloquence and boldness of these "progressive people" and have followed them and fallen after them into the chasms.

1858

Nikolai Gavrilovich Chernyshevsky
A CRITIQUE OF PHILOSOPHICAL PREJUDICES
AGAINST COMMUNAL LANDHOLDING
(Extracts)[10]

Before the question of the commune[11] acquired practical importance with the beginning of the business of changing rural relations, the Russian commune was an object of mystical pride among the exclusive admirers of Russian nationality who imagined that other peoples had nothing like our communal order and that it should therefore be regarded as an innate distinctive feature of the Russian or Slavonic tribe, of exactly the same sort as, for example, broader cheekbones than other Europeans have, or a language which calls a man *muzh* rather than *Mensch, homo* or *l'homme* and which has seven cases rather than six like Latin or five like Greek.[12] Eventually learned and impartial people[13] showed that a communal land order in the form in which it now exists in our country exists among many other peoples who have not yet emerged from relations close to a patriarchal way of life and existed among all others when they were close to that way of life. It turned out that the Germans, and the French, and the ancestors of the English, and the ancestors of the Italians, in a word all European peoples, had communal landholding; but then as history moved further forward it gradually fell into desuetude, giving way to private landed property. The conclusion from this is clear. There is no reason for us to consider communal holding a distinctive innate feature of our nationality, rather we should look on it as the common human attribute of a certain period in the life of each people. Nor do we have any reason to take pride in the preservation of this vestige of primitive antiquity, just as in general no one should take pride in any antique things, because the preservation of antique things bears witness only to the slowness and sluggishness of historical development. The preservation of the commune as an institution on the land which has disappeared as such among other peoples proves only that we have lived considerably less than those peoples. Thus for the purposes of showing off in front of other peoples its preservation is of no use at all.

This view is absolutely correct; but our economists and foreign ones of the old school come along and take it into their heads to draw the following conclusion from it: "Private landed property is a later form which ousted communal landholding, which proved inadequate in the face of it when social relations developed historically; therefore we must abandon it as other peoples have done if we wish to go forward on the path of development."

This conclusion is one of the most fundamental and common grounds for the rejection of communal landholding. Hardly a single opponent of communal landholding will be found who doesn't repeat with all the others: "Communal landholding is a primitive form of relations on the land, whilst private landed property is a secondary form; how then can one fail to prefer the higher form to the lower?" Just one thing strikes us as strange here: many of the opponents of communal landholding belong to the followers of modern German philosophy; some boast of the fact that they are Schellingians, others firmly adhere to the Hegelian school; and what puzzles us about them is that they haven't noticed that in laying emphasis on the primitive nature of communal landholding they are singling out precisely that aspect of it which should most strongly dispose in the favor of communal landholding all those who are familiar with the discoveries of German philosophy concerning the succession of forms in the process of universal development; how have they failed to notice that the argument advanced by them against communal landholding is bound, on the contrary, to bear witness to the correctness of the view that communal landholding is to be preferred to the private landed property which they defend?

We shall pause at some length on the consequences to which the primitive nature of a thing, when taken as a particular form, must lead, because it is precisely this primitive nature that our opponents, through a curious lack of native wit, have used as one of their favorite and most fundamental arguments.

We are not followers of Hegel, still less followers of Schelling. But we cannot but acknowledge that both these systems have performed great services for science by their revelation of common forms through which the process of development moves. The basic result of these discoveries is expressed in the following axiom: "The highest stage of development is similar in form to the beginning from which it proceeds." This idea contains the fundamental essence of the Schellingian system; it is revealed with still greater precision and detail by Hegel, whose whole system is an application of this basic principle to all the phenomena of the life of the world from its most general conditions to the tiniest details of each separate sphere of being...[14]

The general course of planetary development, the progressive scale of the classes of the animal kingdom in general, the higher classes of animals in particular, the physical life of man, his language, dealings with other people, his clothes, his manner of comporting himself, all his social institutions—administration, armed forces and warfare, legal procedure, foreign trade, commercial traffic in general, the notion of justice—each of these factors is subject to the norm about which we are speaking: everywhere the higher stage of development is in form a return to the primitive form which was replaced by its antithesis in the intermediate stage of development...

The norm which we have set out, and which to any person in the least familiar with the modern position concerning notions about the general laws of the world is indubitable, inevitably leads to the following formulation of relations on the land:

Primitive condition (beginning of development).[15] Communal ownership of the land. It exists because man's labor does not have secure and precious connections with a certain plot of land. Nomads have no agriculture and do no work on the land. Also agriculture is connected in the first instance with hardly any expenditure of capital on the land itself.

Secondary condition (intensification of development). Agriculture requires expenditure of capital and labor on the land itself. The land is improved by many different methods and labors, of which the most common and ubiquitous necessity is fertilization. A man who has expended capital on the land must have inalienable ownership of it; the consequence of this is the passing of the land into private property. This form achieves its purpose because landholding is not the subject of speculation but the source of a regular income.

These are the two stages which the opponents of communal landholding talk about, but there are only two, aren't there, so where is the third? Surely the course of development does not end with them.

Industrial and commercial activity intensifies and gives rise to a huge development of speculation; speculation, having engulfed all other branches of the people's economy, addresses itself to the basic and most extensive branch of the economy, agriculture. Hence personal landed property loses its former character. Previously the land was owned by the man who worked it, who expended his capital on its improvement (the system of small proprietors tilling their plot with their own hands, also the system of emphyteusis[16] and hereditary sharecropping with serfdom or without it); but now a new system appears: contract farming; under this system the rent, which goes up as a result of the improvements made by the farmer, passes into the hands of another person who has either not contributed his capital at all to the improvement of the land or has only contributed it to the most insignificant extent but who nevertheless enjoys all the profit which the improvements furnish. Thus personal landed property ceases to be a means of rewarding expenditure of capital on the improvement of the land. At the same time the working of the land begins to require amounts of capital in excess of the means of the vast majority of farmers, and the agricultural enterprise requires a size that far exceeds the resources of the individual household and, as a result of the large area of agricultural plots, also excludes (under a system of private property) the vast majority of farmers from enjoyment of the benefits furnished by the running of the holding, and turns this majority into hired laborers. The factors by virtue of which private landed property was formerly superior to communal landholding are destroyed by these changes. Communal landholding becomes the only means of furnishing the vast majority of farmers with a share of the rewards rendered up by the land for the improvements effected in it by means of labor. Thus communal landholding is necessary not only for the prosperity of the agricultural class but also for the success of agriculture itself; it proves the only rational and complete means of linking the advantage of the farmer with the improvement of the land and methods of production with conscientious performance of one's work. And without this link entirely successful production is not possible...

Is that high stage, of which communal landholding must be an attribute, really attainable by our civilization at the present time? This question, solved not with the aid of logical induction and deduction from general universal laws but by an analysis of facts, has been partially examined by us in previous articles about communal landholding and will be more fully re-examined by us in future articles which will address themselves to a statement of special data about agriculture in Western Europe and in our country.[17] The present article, which has a purely abstract character, must content itself merely with a logical development of concepts, knowledge of which is one of the prerequisites for a correct view of the matter and distortion or ignorance of which has been a basic cause of error for the best among the opponents of communal landholding.

From these general concepts the concept as to whether each separate manifestation of the general process must pass in actuality through all the logical moments with their full force follows directly upon the position of modern science which we have set out concerning the succession of forms. Or can circumstances favorable to the course of a process at a given time and in a given place bring it in actuality to a high stage of development, altogether bypassing the intermediate moments or at least greatly shortening their duration and removing from them any palpable intensity?

By means of the method of modern science the solution of a question relating to complex phenomena is facilitated by examination of it in the simplest manifestations of the same process. In accordance with this method one always endeavors to begin an analysis with physical facts in order to pass on to the moral facts of the life of the individual which are considerably more complicated and, finally, to social life, which is yet more complicated, and social life one endeavors to examine as far as possible in its initial least complicated phenomena, in order thereby to facilitate analysis of the extremely involved phenomena of the civilization of our countries.

...Let us see how man, by himself, without any outside help, progresses to the use of the...phosphorous match.

At first man is not only unable to kindle fire but cannot even keep alight what has been kindled: travelers speak of savages who, like monkeys, love to warm themselves by a tree which has been set alight by lightning and are upset when it begins to go out but do not have the sense to add some brushwood to the fire. Then man learns to set fire to wood by rubbing two pieces of wood together—what a triumph for life! But then a means is devised of making them catch light more quickly, by putting a piece of tinder between them. Next steel is devised and tinder put on flint. But tinder doesn't take spark reliably and quickly enough, so its receptivity is increased by dousing it with saltpeter. The tinder is splendid now; but still it's so much trouble to extract flame from its smoldering condition: one must blow it over a piece of coal, then blow two pieces of coal over a splint placed between them. But now the sulphur match is invented, catching light itself directly on contact with the tinder: another great triumph! But steel and flint seem too much trouble now. Whereupon a means is found of coating the sulphur tip of the match with phosphorous and stabilizing the phosphorous in an atmospheric environment with other coatings and additives.

What a long path! Man needed not less than 7,345 years to cover it.[18] What are the results for each individual person of the fact that certain people arrived by such a long and difficult process at the use of phosphorous matches? All other people are given the chance to attain the same thing without having to cover this terribly long path; and the deductions for the phenomena of individual human lives are the same as those we obtained previously for the phenomena of the physical world:

1. When a certain process (for example a means of procuring fire) has reached in a certain person a certain stage of development (for example, the use of phosphorous matches), the attainment of this stage can be greatly speeded up in other people (right now savages who are unable to kindle fire no longer need 7,345 years in order to attain to phosphorous matches— anyone can teach them how to use them in two seconds and how to make them in two hours).

2. This speeding up is brought about when a person who needs to attain a higher stage of a process comes into contact with a person who has already attained it (a man from Paris comes to Central Africa with phosphorous matches or a savage from Central Africa comes to one of the settlements where they already have phosphorous matches).

3. This speeding up consists in the fact that the process of development passes from the lower stage through all the intermediate stages to the higher one with extreme rapidity. (Savages don't have to be taught first how to use steel, then how to use a sulphur match—they take up the phosphorous match directly).

4. When this speeding up of a process takes place the intermediate stages are revealed only in theory, they take on only a theoretical existence as logical moments and hardly take on a real existence or do not take it on at all.[19] (Savages who are now able to procure fire only by rubbing two pieces of wood together, once they have learned directly how to use

phosphorous matches, will in general know only from stories that before phosphorous matches there existed sulphur ones, with flint and steel.)

5. If these intermediate stages omitted by a speeded up course of development do take on a real existence then it is only on a scale quite insignificant in size and still more insignificant in the practical importance of its role. (It is very possible that strange fellows will be found among the slaves who will take it into their heads to play around with steel and sulphur matches even when they have learned to use phosphorous ones; but this quirk would hardly afflict one person in ten thousand and even he will play around with steel and sulphur matches only if and when he has nothing to do, and as soon as he needs to work or obtain fire quickly he will abandon his quirk and strike a phosphorous match on the wall.)

1858

Nikolai Gavrilovich Chernyshevsky
THE ANTHROPOLOGICAL PRINCIPLE IN PHILOSOPHY (Extracts)[20]

The natural sciences serve as a basis for that part of philosophy which examines questions concerning man just as they do for the other part which examines questions concerning external Nature. The idea, formulated by the natural sciences, of the unity of the human organism serves as a principle of the philosophical view of human life and all its phenomena; the observations of physiologists, zoologists and physicians have removed any idea of dualism in man. Philosophy sees in man what medicine, physiology and chemistry see in him; these sciences demonstrate that no dualism is apparent in man and philosophy adds that if man did have another nature, besides his real one, then this other nature would necessarily reveal itself in some way, and since it does not reveal itself in any way, since everything that occurs and manifests itself in man occurs in accordance with his real nature alone, he has no other nature. (This proof is absolutely unquestionable.)[21] It is as compelling as those grounds[22] on the basis of which you, reader, are sure, for example, that there isn't a lion in the room in which you are sitting at this moment as you read this book.[23] You think this, firstly, because you can't see it with your eyes, you can't hear it roaring; but is that the only thing that makes you certain that there isn't a lion in your room? No, there is another thing that makes you certain of this: the fact that you are alive makes you certain; if there were a lion in your room it would pounce on you and tear you to pieces. There are none of the consequences which would inevitably attend the presence of a lion and so you know that there's no lion here. Again, say why you are convinced that a dog cannot speak. You've never heard one speaking; this would not be enough by itself: you've seen many people who were saying nothing at the time when you saw them; they simply didn't want to speak, it wasn't that they couldn't: perhaps the dog too just doesn't want to speak and it's not that it isn't able to? That's what backward people think, who believe fairy-tales in which animals have conversations and who explain their assumption thus: the dog is very clever and cunning and it knows that words often lead to no good, so it keeps quiet, reckoning that it is much safer to keep quiet than to talk. You are laughing at such intricate explanations and understand the matter more simply: you have seen cases in which a dog would have been bound to speak if it had had the capacity to do so; for instance, the dog is being killed, it yelps as loud as it can, clearly it cannot refrain from expressing the thought that it is in pain, that it is being cruelly treated. It seeks any means of expressing this, and finds one—yelping, but it finds no words; which means that it does not have the gift of speech; if it had had that gift it would have acted differently. A circumstance has been given in which the existence of a certain element in a certain object would necessarily have had a certain result; this result is lacking, so the element too is absent. Let us take another case. How do you know, for instance, that Mr Hume, who caused such a stir among us in St. Petersburg with his tricks a couple of years ago, was really just a magician and could not actually know the future and secrets which he hadn't been told, and read books and papers which he did not have before his eyes? This is how you know: if he had been able to know the future, he would have been made a diplomatic advisor at some court or other and would have told the ministers of this court everything that would happen in certain situations... In all such cases it is not enough to say that we do not know whether a certain element exists; no, reason obliges us to say straight out: we know that this element does not exist; if it did exist things would have happened differently from the way they have.

* * *

The first effect of the entry of the moral sciences into the field of the exact sciences was the strict differentiation of what we know from what we do not know. The astronomer knows that the size of the planet Mars is known to him and he knows just as positively that the geological composition of that planet, the nature of the flora or fauna on it and the very question of whether flora or fauna exist on it are unknown to him. If anyone took it into his head to assert that clay or granite are found on Mars, that birds or molluscs exist there, the astronomer would say to him: you are asserting something which you do not know. If some dreamer were to go further in his assumptions and say, for example, that the birds which live on Mars are not susceptible to diseases and the molluscs do not need food, the astronomer, with the help of a chemist and a physiologist, would prove to him that this just could not be so. In exactly the same way the known is now strictly differentiated from the unknown in the moral sciences too, and on the basis of what is known the inadequacy of some former assumptions about what still remains unknown has been proved. We know positively, for example, that all phenomena of the moral world derive one from another and from external circumstances in accordance with a law of causality and on these grounds every assumption about the emergence of any phenomenon that is not the product of previous phenomena and external circumstances has been accepted as false. Current psychology therefore does not allow, for example, of such assumptions as: "a man acted badly in a given instance because he wanted to act badly and acted well in another instance because he wanted to act well." It says that a bad act or a good act was necessarily the product of some moral or material fact or combination of facts, and "wanting" here was only a subjective impression, which attends the emergence in our consciousness of thoughts or acts out of previous thoughts, acts or external facts. The most commonly presented example of actions based on nothing but our will is a fact of the sort: I am getting out of bed; which foot shall I get out on? If I wish, the left, or if I wish, the right. But it only seems like this if one looks at it superficially. In reality it is facts and impressions that determine which foot a man gets up on. If there are no special circumstances and if he has no special thoughts he gets up on to the foot which it is most comfortable for him to get on to given the anatomical position of his body on the bed. If there are particular motives which are strong enough to overrule this physiological comfort, the result will change in accordance with the change in the circumstances. If, for instance, a man has the thought: "I shan't get up on the right foot, but on the left," he'll do that; but all that has taken place here is a simple replacement of one cause (physiological comfort) by another one (the thought of proving one's independence) or, to put it better, the triumph of a second, stronger cause over the first. But whence has this second cause come, whence the thought of showing one's independence of external conditions? It could not have arisen without a cause, it is the product either of the words of someone he has been talking to, or of a recollection of some previous argument, or something of the sort. Thus the fact that a man may when he wishes step out of bed not on to the foot which it is comfortable for him to step on to, given the anatomical position of his body on the bed, but on to the other one—this fact doesn't show at all that a man can step on to one foot or the other without any cause but merely that the act of getting out of bed may be carried out under the influence of causes that are stronger than the influence of the anatomical position of his body before the act of getting up. The phenomenon which we call the will is itself a link in a series of phenomena and facts linked by a causal connection. It very often happens that a thought is the immediate cause of the appearance of a will to a certain act in us. But a definite disposition of the will is also only a product of a definite thought: whatever the nature of the thought, the will is the same; if the thought is not of that nature then the will is not of that nature either. But why exactly did such and such a thought and not another appear? Again, as a result of some thought or other, some fact, in a word, some cause. Psychology says the same thing in this case as physics or chemistry in such cases: if a certain phenomenon has occurred, then one must seek causes for it, not content oneself with the empty answer: it occurred by itself, without any particular cause—"I did that because that's what I wanted to do." Fine, but why exactly did you want to do that? If you answer: "simply because I wanted to" that is the same as saying: "the plate broke because it broke; the house was burnt down because it was burnt down." Such answers are not answers at all: they merely conceal a lack of resolve to try to ascertain the real cause, a lack of any desire to know the truth.

*　*　*

Thus, the theoretical questions which remain unresolved with the moral sciences in their present state are in general such as do not even enter the head of anyone except specialists; the non-specialist has difficulty even understanding how learned people can occupy themselves with the study of such trivia. On the other hand, those theoretical questions which usually seem important and difficult to non-specialists have in general ceased to be questions for present-day thinkers because they are solved beyond all doubt with the greatest ease as soon as the powerful resources of scientific analysis are brought to bear on them. Half of such questions turn out to have sprung simply from the fact that a person is unaccustomed to thinking, the other half have an answer which may be found in phenomena familiar to everyone. Where does the flame go, which flickers over the wick of a burning candle, when we extinguish the candle? No chemist is going to agree to call these words a question, is he? He simply calls them nonsensical verbiage arising out of unfamiliarity with the most basic and simplest facts of science. He says: the burning of the candle is a chemical process; flame is one of the phenomena of this process, one of its sides, one of its qualities, to put it in plain language; when we extinguish the candle, we end the chemical process; it is self-evident that when it ends its qualities disappear; to ask what happens to the flame of the candle when the candle goes out is the same as asking what remains of the figure 2 in the number 25 when we cross out the whole number—absolutely nothing remains of the figure 2 or the figure 5, for they are both crossed out; only a person who himself doesn't understand what it means to write a figure and what it means to cross it out can ask this; there is only one reply to all the questions asked by such people: my friend! you have no idea about arithmetic and will do well to start studying it. The really brain-teasing question is put, for example: is man good or bad? A large number of people toil away trying to find an answer to this question, and nearly half the toilers decide: a man is good by nature; others, also representing nearly half of the toilers, decide otherwise: man is by nature bad. There are in addition to these two opposing dogmatic parties a number of sceptical individuals who laugh at both and decide the question is insoluble. But as soon as scientific analysis is applied the whole thing turns out to be simple in the extreme. Man likes what is pleasant and does not like what is unpleasant—this does not seem open to question, because the subject is simply repeated here in the predicate. A is A, what is pleasant for man is pleasant for man, what is unpleasant for man is unpleasant for man. Good is he who does good for others, bad is he who does harm to others—this seems to be simple and clear as well. Let us now join together these simple truths and we shall get the conclusion: a man is good when in order to gain pleasure for himself he has to do what is pleasant for others; he is bad when he is forced to derive his pleasure from the infliction of what is unpleasant on others. Human nature should not be taken to task here for one thing or extolled for the other; everything depends on circumstances, relations, (institutions).[24] If certain relations have a constant character, then in a man who has been formed under them there is formed the habit of acting in a way which accords with them.[25] One might therefore find that Ivan is good while Peter is bad; but these judgments apply only to individual people, not to man in general, just as notions about the habit of cutting pieces of wood or being able to forge metal and so forth apply only to individual people and not to man in general. Ivan is a carpenter, but one cannot say what man in general is, a carpenter or not a carpenter; Peter knows how to forge iron, but one cannot say of a man in general that he is a blacksmith or not a blacksmith. The fact that Ivan became a carpenter while Peter became a blacksmith shows only that in certain circumstances which obtained in Ivan's life a man becomes a carpenter while in certain circumstances which obtained in Peter's life he becomes a blacksmith. In exactly the same way man in certain circumstances becomes good and in others bad.

* * *

When you speak without plan you yourself have no idea where you will end up. And so now we see that we've got round to talking about moral or lofty feelings. On the subject of these feelings the practical conclusions drawn from ordinary everyday experience are completely at variance with the ancient hypotheses that used to ascribe to man a great variety of unselfish aspirations. People have seen from experience that every person thinks all the time only about himself, worries about his own interests more than other people's and nearly always sacrifices the interests, honor and life of others to his own advantage, in a word everyone has seen that all people are egoists. In practical matters all sober-minded people have always been guided by the belief that egoism is the only impulse that governs the actions of anyone they have dealings with. If this view, for which the experience of each and every one of us provides daily corroboration, did not have rather a lot of other everyday facts running counter to it then it would, of course, have quickly gained the upper hand in theory too over the hypotheses which asserted that egoism is but a corruption of the heart and that an uncorrupted man is guided by impulses opposed to egoism, that he thinks about the welfare of others, not about his own, is prepared to sacrifice himself for others and so forth. But it was precisely in this that the difficulty lay, that the hypothesis about man's unselfish endeavor to serve the welfare of others, disproved though it was by hundreds of experiences in everyone's daily life, seemed to be corroborated by quite numerous instances of unselfishness, self-sacrifice and so forth: there we have Curtius[26] hurling himself into the abyss in order to save his native town, here we have Empedocles[27] hurling himself into a crater in order to make a scholarly discovery, here we have Damon hurrying to his execution in order to save Pythias,[28] here Lucretia[29] stabs herself with a dagger in order to restore her honor. Until recently there were no scientific means of deriving both these categories of phenomena in an exact way from a single principle, of subsuming facts that were contrary to one another under a single law. A stone falls to the ground, steam rises, and in ancient times they thought that the law of gravity which operates on a stone did not operate on steam. It is now known that both these movements, which take place in opposite directions, the falling of a stone to the ground and the rising of steam away from the ground, stem from a single cause, in accordance with a single law. It is now known that the force of attraction, which generally impels bodies downwards, manifests itself in certain circumstances by making some bodies rise upwards. We have said many times that the moral sciences have not yet been so fully developed as the natural sciences; but even with them in their present far from brilliant state people have already solved the problem of subsuming all human actions and feelings, which often conflict with one another, under a single principle, just as they have solved in general nearly all the moral and metaphysical problems in which people were tangled up before the moral sciences and metaphysics began to be developed in accordance with strict scientific method. In man's motives, as in all aspects of his life, there are not two different natures, two fundamental laws which are different from or contrary to one another, but all the diversity in the way in which human motives manifest themselves stems, as in all human life, from one and the same nature, in accordance with one and the same law.

We are not going to talk about those actions and feelings which everybody accepts as egoistic, self-interested, and stemming from personal calculation; we shall concentrate only on those feelings and acts which seem to have the opposite character: generally one need only look a little more closely at an act or feeling which seems unselfish to see that they are grounded all the same on the same thought of one's personal gain, personal satisfaction, personal welfare, they are grounded on the feeling called egoism. Very few instances will be found when this basis for the act or feeling would not thrust itself on the attention even of a person who was not much accustomed to psychological analysis. If a husband and wife have lived together happily, the wife will quite genuinely and very deeply grieve about the death of her husband, but just listen carefully to the words with which her grief is expressed: "To whom have you abandoned me? What am I going to do without you? Without you my life on earth is sickening!" Underline the words "me, I, my"; it is in them that the sense of the lamentation, the basis of the grief reside. Let us take a feeling that is much higher and purer still than the highest conjugal love, the feeling of a mother for her child. Her lament over its death is exactly the same: "My angel! How I loved you! I took such delight in you, how I cared for you! How many sleepless nights you cost me! My hope has perished in you, all my joy has been taken away!" And here we have the same thing all over again: "my, I, me." An egoistic basis is revealed just as easily in the most sincere and tender friendship. Nor do instances in which a man makes a sacrifice for something he loves give much more difficulty; even if he sacrifices his life itself for it, still personal calculation or a passionate surge of egoism underlies the sacrifice. The majority of instances of so-called self-sacrifice do not deserve to be called self-sacrifice: that name is unbecoming for them. The inhabitants of Saguntum[30] slew themselves so as not to deliver themselves alive into Hannibal's hands, an act of heroism at which one might marvel but of which egoistic calculation entirely approved: they were accustomed to living as free citizens, to putting up with no injuries, to having self-respect and the respect of others; the Carthaginian commander would have sold them into slavery, their lives would have been a series of the most intolerable torments; they acted in the same way as a person who tears an ailing tooth out of his mouth: they preferred one moment of frightful mortal anguish to never-ending years of torment; in the Middle Ages heretics who were being burned on a slow fire of damp wood tried to break their chains to throw themselves into the flames: it is easier to choke to death in a minute than to be suffocating for several hours. Indeed the position of the inhabitants of Saguntum was like that. We were wrong to suggest that Hannibal would have been content to deliver them into slavery: they would have been killed just the same, by Carthaginian hands if not by their own, but the Carthaginians would have subjected them at length to barbaric tortures, and their sound calculation rightly preferred a quick and easy death to a slow and hard one. Lucretia stabbed herself when Sextus Tarquinius[31] defiled her: she too acted in a very calculating way; what awaited her in the future? Her husband might have spoken many soothing and affectionate words, but all such words are absolute nonsense, are they not, nonsense which testifies to the nobility of the person who speaks them but does not in the least change the inevitable consequences of the deed. Collatinus[32] might have said to his wife: I consider you pure and love you as before; but given the concepts of the time, which have changed all too little up to our own day, he did not have the power to vindicate his words with deeds: whether he wished it or not he had already lost a very great deal of his former respect, his former love for his wife; he might have concealed this loss by treating her with deliberately increased tenderness;

but tenderness of that sort is more offensive than coldness, more bitter than blows and curses. Lucretia rightly found it much less unpleasant to lose her life than to live in a position that was degrading by comparison with the position to which she had been accustomed. An upright person will more willingly endure hunger than touch food contaminated by some filth; for a person who has been wont to hold himself in respect, death is much easier than degradation.

The reader appreciates that we are not saying all this in order to lessen the great praise which the inhabitants of Saguntum and Lucretia deserve: to demonstrate that an heroic act was also an intelligent one, that a noble deed was not an imprudent one, is by no means tantamount, in our view, to devaluing heroism and nobility. From these heroic deeds let us turn to a more ordinary form of actions, though still a form all too rare; let us look into cases such as the devotion of a person who renounces all pleasures, all freedom to dispose of his time, in order to look after another person who is in need of his care. A friend who spends weeks on end at the bedside of a sick friend is making a much harder sacrifice than if he had given him all his money. But why does he make such a great sacrifice and for the sake of what feeling does he make it? He sacrifices his time, his freedom to his feeling of friendship—*his* feeling, let us note; it is so highly developed in him that he derives greater contentment from satisfying it than he would from any other pleasures or from freedom itself; whereas if he were to go against it, leave it unsatisfied, he would feel greater discontent than he would derive from constraining himself in any other needs. It is exactly like this in cases where a person renounces all enjoyment and interests in order to serve science or some belief. Newton and Leibnitz,[33] who denied themselves love for a woman in order to give their undivided time and thoughts to scholarly research, spent their whole lives, of course, accomplishing a sublime feat. One must say exactly the same thing about politicians who are usually called fanatics. Here again we see that a certain need is so highly developed in a person that he finds it pleasant to satisfy it even if it means sacrificing other very strong needs. These cases differ very greatly in nature from those facts of calculation in which a person sacrifices a very great sum of money in order to satisfy some base passion, but as far as their theoretical formula is concerned they all come under one law: the stronger passion prevails over the less strong leanings and sacrifices them in pursuit of its own satisfaction.

If one carefully examines the motives which guide people it turns out that all deeds, good and bad, noble and base, heroic and pusillanimous, stem in all people from one source: man acts as it is most pleasant for him to act, is guided by calculation which dictates the renunciation of the lesser advantage or the lesser pleasure so that he may obtain the greater advantage, the greater pleasure. Of course, the difference between bad and good actions is in no way diminished by this uniformity of the cause from which they stem: we know that a diamond and coal are the same pure carbon, but nevertheless a diamond is a diamond, an extremely valuable thing, while coal is coal just the same, a thing of very little worth. The great difference between good and evil deserves our full attention. We shall begin with an analysis of these concepts in order to see by what circumstances the good is developed or weakened in human life.

It was noted very long ago that different people in the same society call things good or fine which are different, even contrary to one another. If, for example, someone bequeaths his legacy to people outside his family, these people find his act good but his relatives who have lost the legacy find it very bad. There is the same difference between concepts of good in different societies and in different epochs in the same society. For a very long time people drew the conclusion from this that the concept of good has nothing constant about it, nothing independent, nothing liable to common definition, but that it is a purely relative concept that depends on people's opinions, on their whim. But if we examine in a more precise way the relationship between acts which are called good and the people who give them that name, we find that in this relationship there is always one common, necessary feature from which the inclusion of the act in the category of good acts also stems. Why do people outside a person's family who have received the legacy call the act which has given them this property a good deed? Because this act was useful to them. On the other hand it was detrimental to the relatives of the testator who had lost the legacy, so they call it a bad deed. War against infidels for the propagation of Islam seemed a good deed to Mohammedans because it brought them benefit, gave them spoils; this view was supported in particular by the clergy among them, whose power was extended by the conquests. It is those deeds of other people's which are useful to an individual that he calls good acts; in the view of society it is that which is useful for society as a whole or for a majority of its members that is taken to be good; finally, it is that which is useful for man in general that people in general, irrespective of nation or estate, call good. Cases in which the interests of different nations and estates are contrary to one another or to the general interests of mankind are very common; and just as common are cases in which the interests of some individual estate are contrary to the national interest. In all these cases argument arises over the nature of the act, institution or relationship which is advantageous to some interests but detrimental to others: the adherents of the side for whom it is detrimental call it bad, evil; the defenders of the interests who derive benefit from it call it fine and good. To decide who has theoretical justice on their side in such cases is not at all difficult: the interest of mankind in general stands above the interests of an individual nation, the general interest of a whole nation stands above the interests of an individual estate, the interest of a numerous estate is above the interests of a numerically small one. In theory this gradation is beyond any doubt, it is merely an application of geometrical axioms—"the whole is greater than a part of it," "the greater quantity is larger than the smaller quantity"—to social problems. A theoretical falsehood necessarily leads to harm in practice; those cases in which an individual nation tramples for its own advantage on the interests of mankind in general or in which an individual estate tramples on the interests of a whole nation always prove harmful not only for the side whose interests were infringed but also for the side which thought to win some advantage for itself by infringing them: it always turns out that a nation ruins itself by enslaving mankind, that an individual estate brings itself to a bad end if it sacrifices a whole people in pursuit of its own interest. From this we see that when national interest conflicts with the interest of an estate, the estate which thinks to derive benefit for itself from harm done to the people is wrong from the very outset and is blinded by false calculation. [34]

1860

Nikolai Gavrilovich Chernyshevsky
WHAT IS TO BE DONE? (Extract)[35]

Now you know who I am; find out what I am...

"I embody the sensual pleasure that Astarte[36] embodied: she is the ancestor of all of us other queens who have taken her place. I embody the delight in contemplation of beauty which Aphrodite[37] embodied. I embody the veneration of purity that was embodied in 'Chastity.'

"But in me all these things are different from what they were in them, more complete, elevated and intense. What was embodied in 'Chastity' is coupled in me with what was embodied in Astarte and with what was embodied in Aphrodite. And each of these forces, being coupled in me with other forces, is the more powerful and the better for the union. But in me each of these forces is lent more, much more power and charm still by something new which I embody and which none of the previous queens embodied. This new element which I embody and which makes me different from them is the equality of lovers, an equal relationship between them as people and by virtue of this one new element everything that I embody is much, so much more beautiful than it was in them.

"When a man acknowledges that a woman has the same rights as himself he rejects the view of her as his property. Then she loves him as he loves her, merely because she wants to love, and if she doesn't want to then he has no rights over her, nor she over him. Consequently I embody freedom.

"Even that which I embody, and which was embodied in former queens, takes on, by virtue of equality of rights and freedom, a new character, a higher charm, a charm which people did not know before I appeared and before which everything that people knew before my appearance pales into insignificance.

"Before I appeared people did not know completely sensual pleasure because without the free attraction of both lovers neither of them feels joyous ecstasy. Before I appeared people did not know the full pleasure that comes of contemplation of beauty because unless beauty is revealed through free attraction there is no joyous ecstasy in its contemplation. Without free attraction both pleasure and delight are miserable by comparison with what they are in me.

"My chastity is purer than that 'Chastity' which spoke only of the purity of the body: I embody purity of heart. I am free because there is no deceit in me, no pretense: I shall speak no word which I do not feel, I shall give no kiss in which there is not fondness.

"But that which I embody and which is new and gives a greater charm to what previous queens embodied, that by itself amounts to a charm in me which is greatest of all. A master is constrained in the presence of his servant, the servant is constrained before his master; only with one's equal is one completely free. With one's inferiors one is bored, only with one's equals does one find complete gaiety. That is why before I appeared even man did not know the full happiness of love; what he felt before I appeared did not deserve to be called happiness, it was only momentary intoxication. As for woman, how pitiable was woman before I appeared! She was a dependent being then, dwelling in a condition of servitude; she lived in fear, before I appeared she was too little aware of what love was: where there is fear, there is no love.

"Consequently, if you want to express in a single word what I am, then that word is equality. Without it physical pleasure, delight in beauty are boring, miserable, vile; without it there is no purity of heart, there is only the illusion of purity of body. From it, from equality, comes the freedom which I embody and without which I do not exist.

"I have told you everything that you can tell others, everything that I am now. But at present my realm is still small, I must still guard my own from the calumny of those who do not know me, I cannot yet voice my whole will to everybody. I shall speak it to everybody when my realm holds sway over all people, when all people are beautiful in body and pure in heart, then I shall reveal my full beauty to them. But you, your fate, are especially fortunate; I shall not upset you, I shall not harm you by having said what I shall be when not a few, as now, but all will be worthy of acknowledging me as their queen. You alone I shall tell the secrets of my future. Swear to be silent and listen."

7^{38}

* * *

8

"O, my love, now I know your whole will; I know what it will be; but how will it be fulfilled? How will people live then?"

"I alone cannot tell you this, for this I need the help of my elder sister, the one who appeared before you long ago. She is my sovereign and my servant. I can be only what she makes me; but she works for me. Sister, come to my aid."

The sister of her sisters, the bride of her grooms appears.

"Greetings, sister," she says to the queen, "are you here too, sister," she says to Vera Pavlovna, "do you want to see how people will live when the queen, my pupil, rules over all? Look."

A building, an enormous, enormous building such as one finds at present only in small numbers in the largest capitals—or rather no, there is no such building at present! It stands amid cornfields and meadows, orchards and groves. The cornfields contain our crops, only they are not like ours but thick, thick, abundant, abundant. Can this be wheat? Who ever saw such ears? Who ever saw such grain? At present one could only grow such ears with such grains in a hothouse. The fields are our fields; but they contain flowers such as grow at present only in flower beds in our country. The orchards, the lemon trees and orange trees, the peach trees and apricot trees, however do they grow in the open air? Oh yes, there are columns around them, they are opened for the summer; yes, these are hothouses uncovered for the summer. The groves, these are our groves: oak and lime, maple and elm, yes, the groves are the same as they are at present; they are tended with great care, there isn't a single ailing tree among them, but the groves are the same—they are the only things that have remained the same as at present. But this building—what is it, what architecture is this? There is no such building at present; or rather, there is already one hint at it—the palace which stands on Sydenham Hill;[39] cast iron and glass, iron and glass and only that. Or rather, not only that: this is just the casing of the building, its outer walls; inside is a proper house, the most enormous house: it is covered by this building of iron and glass as by a case; the building forms broad galleries round it on all floors. How light the architecture of this inner house is, how small are the piers between the windows—but the windows are huge, broad, the whole height of each storey! Its stone walls seem like a row of pilasters forming a frame for the windows which look out on to the gallery. But what sort of floors and ceilings are these? What are these doors and window frames made of? What is it? Silver? Platinum? And even the furniture is nearly all the same—wooden furniture is just a whim here, it's just for variety, but what is all the other furniture made of, the ceilings and floors? "Try and move this armchair," says the elder queen. This metal furniture is lighter than our walnut furniture. But what sort of metal is this? Ah, now I know, Sasha showed me a little slab like this, it was light as glass and there are already earrings and brooches like it; yes, Sasha said that sooner or later aluminum would replace wood, perhaps even stone. But how opulent all this is! Everywhere is aluminum, aluminum, and all the spaces in between the windows are taken up by huge mirrors. And what carpets on the floor! In this hall half the floor is uncovered and one can see here that it's made of aluminum. "See, it's got a matt finish here so as not to be too slippery—children play here, and grown-ups with them; and in that hall the floor is also uncarpeted, it's for dancing." And everywhere there are trees and flowers of the south; the whole house is an enormous winter garden.

But who lives in this house which is more magnificent than palaces? "Many, very many people live here; come, we'll see them." They go out on to a balcony which extends from the top floor of the gallery. How had Vera Pavlovna not noticed this before? "Groups of people are scattered over the cornfields; everywhere there are men and women, old people, young people and children all together. But there are more young people; there aren't many old men and even fewer old women, more children than old men though not very many all the same. More than half the children have stayed at home to do the housework; they do nearly all the housework, they greatly enjoy it. There are some old women with them. But there are very few old men and old women because people become old very late in life here, life is healthy and tranquil here; it preserves one's freshness." The groups working in the fields are almost all singing; but what work are they doing? Ah, they are gathering in the grain. How quickly the work is done! But it would be surprising if it were not done quickly, it would be surprising if they weren't singing! Machines are doing nearly everything for them, reaping, and binding the sheaves and carting them off—the people are doing virtually nothing but walking around, driving around, driving the machines. And how comfortable they have made things for themselves; the day is scorching, but that doesn't trouble them of course: over that part of the cornfield where they are working a huge awning has been set up; as the work moves on so the awning moves too—how cool they have made it for themselves! It would be surprising if they didn't work swiftly and merrily, it would be surprising if they didn't sing! I would have done the same! And there are songs all the time, songs all the time—unfamiliar, new ones; but they are reminiscent of one of ours; I know it:

> We shall live like lords, you and I;
> These people are our friends,
> Whatever you desire
> We shall get it for you...[40]

But now the work is done and they are all going towards the building. "Let's go back into the hall and watch them having dinner," says the elder sister. They go into the largest of the huge halls. Half of it is taken up with tables, the tables are already laid, how many of them there are! How many people will be having dinner here? About a thousand or more: "Not everybody is here; whoever wishes dines separately, in his own place." Those old women, old men and children who didn't go out into the fields have cooked all this: "to cook the meals, do the housework, clear up the rooms—this work is too light for other hands," says the elder sister, "it must be done by those who cannot yet or can no longer do anything else." All the crockery and cutlery is magnificent. Everything is of aluminum and glass; down the middle of the wide tables vases with flowers are set out, the dishes are already on the table, those who were working having come in, everybody sits down at table, those who were working the fields and those who were cooking the dinner. "But who is going to serve?" "When? At table? Why? For there are only five or six courses in all: those which have to be kept hot have been put in places where they won't get cold. Do you see these recesses? These are pans filled with hot water," says the elder sister. "You live well, you like to eat well; do you often have a dinner like this?" "A few times a year." This is normal for them: anyone who wishes to has something better, whatever he wishes, but in that case he pays separately; but anyone who doesn't require anything different from what is made for everybody makes no payment. And it's like that with everything: what everybody can afford given the means at the company's disposal is free; for every special thing or personal whim a charge is made.

"Surely they can't be us? Surely this can't be our land? I heard our song, they are speaking Russian." "Yes, you can see a river not far away, that's the Oka; these people are us, for I am Russian like you!" "And have you made all this?" "All this has been made for me, and I inspired people to make it, I inspire people to perfect it, but it's she, my elder sister, who makes it, she is a working woman, I just enjoy it." "And will everybody live like this?" "Everybody," says the elder sister, "for everybody there is eternal spring and summer, eternal joy."

1863

Nikolai Alexandrovich Dobrolyubov
WHAT IS "OBLOMOVSHCHINA"? (Extracts) [41]

... Goncharov set to work differently. He did not want to lose track of a
phenomenon, once he had cast his eye on it, without following it through
to the end, without seeking out its causes, without understanding its
connection with its whole environment. He wanted to elevate the
incidental image that flashed before him to the status of a type, to lend it a
generic and permanent significance. Consequently in all that concerned
Oblomov there was nothing that seemed pointless or trivial to him. He did
everything with affection, he drew everything distinctly and in detail. Not
just the rooms in which Oblomov lived, but even the house in which he
merely dreamed of living; not just his dressing-gown, but also the gray
frock-coat and bristly whiskers of his servant Zakhar; not just Oblomov's
writing of a letter, but also the quality of the paper and ink in the village
elder's letter to him, everything is brought in and depicted with complete
precision and clarity. The author cannot even pass by a certain Baron von
Langwagen who plays no role in the novel; so he writes a whole splendid
page about the baron too, and would have written two or four had he not
managed to exhaust the subject in one. This does, if you like, slow down
the action and it tires the unsympathetic reader who demands to be
constantly entertained by thrills. But this is nevertheless a precious quality
in Goncharov's talent, and one which very greatly enhances the artistic
merit of his portraits. When you start to read him you find that many
things do not seem to be strictly necessary, or to be in harmony with the
eternal requirements of art. But before long you start to fall in with the
world he depicts, you are compelled to admit that all the phenomena he
describes are legitimate and natural, you put yourself in the position of his
characters and somehow feel that in their place and position one could not
behave in any other way and indeed, it would seem, should not behave in
any other way. The little details which the author constantly introduces
and which he draws with such affection and uncommon skill, ultimately
have a certain allurement. You are completely transported into the world
into which the author is leading you: you find something familiar in it, it is
not just the external form but the inner life as well, the spirit of every
character and every object that opens up before you. And when you have
finished reading the whole novel you feel that something new has been
added to the sphere of your ideas, that new images and new types have
deeply penetrated your being. [42] They haunt you for a long time, you would
like to ponder over them, you would like to clarify [their] significance and
the bearing they have on your own life, character and inclinations. Where

is your sluggishness and weariness going? More spirited thoughts and
fresher feelings are stirring in you. You are prepared to reread many pages,
to ponder over them and debate them. That's how Oblomov affected us, at
any rate: "Oblomov's dream" and some of the scenes we have read several
times; the whole novel we have read twice almost right the way through
and the second time we liked it almost more than the first. Such is the allure
of the details with which the author enfolds the course of the action and
which some people think make the novel *too long-drawn-out!*

Thus Goncharov emerges first and foremost as an artist able to
express the fullness of life's phenomena. Their depiction is his vocation and
his pleasure; no theoretical prejudices or preconceived ideas disturb his
objective creation, it yields to no exclusive sympathies. It is calm, sober
and unimpassioned. Is this the highest ideal of artistic creation or is it
perhaps even a shortcoming which betrays a weakness in the artist's
perception? It is difficult to give a categorical answer and it would in any
case be unfair to do so without reservations and qualifications. Many
people do not like the poet's calm attitude towards reality and they are
prepared straightaway to deliver a harsh verdict to the effect that such a
talent is unattractive. We do realize how natural such a verdict is and are
perhaps ourselves inclined to wish that the author would stir our senses a
little more and arouse greater feeling in us. But we recognize that this wish
is of a rather Oblomovian nature, and stems from an inclination always to
have guidance, even where one's feelings are concerned. It is unjust to
ascribe a low level of perception to the author merely because impressions
do not send him into lyrical raptures but rather lie silent in the depths of his
being. On the contrary, the sooner and more impetuously an impression is
voiced the more often it proves to be superficial and transient. We see a
host of examples at every turn in people who are possessed of a boundless
enthusiasm for words and mimicry. If a person is able to bear the image of
an object and nurture it in his heart and then present it vividly and in its
fullness, it means that he combines a fine perception with depth of feeling.
He does not speak out until the time is right, but nothing in the world
eludes him. For him everything that lives and moves around him,
everything that abounds in nature and human society, all this

> dwells in some miraculous way
> in the depths of his being.[43]

All life's phenomena, at any given moment, find reflection in him as in a
magic mirror, and come to a stop there as he wills it, and set and are cast in
solid motionless forms. He seems to be able to stop life itself, forever to fix
and put before us its most elusive instant so that we may behold it for all
time for our edification or our pleasure.

Such power, developed to the full, is of course worth everything that we call attractiveness, charm, freshness or vigor in a talent. But this power too has its gradations and, besides, it may be applied to objects of various sorts, which is also very important. Here we differ from the adherents of so-called *art for art's sake,*[44] who think that a superb depiction of a little leaf on a tree is just as important as, for example, a superb depiction of a person's character. Perhaps this would be fair enough from a subjective point of view: two authors might actually have talents of equal power and merely operate in different fields. But we shall never agree that the poet who expends his talent on exemplary descriptions of little leaves and brooks could be equal in importance to one who is able with a talent of the same power to reproduce, for example, the phenomena of social life. We believe that the question of what the artist's talent is used for, what it finds expression in, is far more important for criticism, literature and society itself than the matter of what dimensions and qualities it has in itself, in abstraction, in potentiality.

So how has Goncharov's talent found expression, what has it been expended on? For an answer to that question we shall have to analyze the content of the novel.

Goncharov would seem not to have chosen to depict a very broad area. The story of how the good-natured idler Oblomov lies around and sleeps and how neither friendship nor love can rouse him and get him to his feet is hardly a very momentous one. But Russian life finds reflection in it, before us stands a living, contemporary Russian type chiseled with ruthless rigor and accuracy; a new word in the development of our society is spoken in it and it is uttered clearly and firmly, without despair or the sanguine expectations of a child, but in full awareness of the truth. This word is *oblomovshchina;* it provides a key to many of the riddles of Russian life and it lends Goncharov's novel far more social significance than all our accusatory novellas[45] possess. In the type of Oblomov and in all this *oblomovshchina* we see something more than just the felicitous creation of a powerful talent; we find in it a product of Russian life, a sign of the times...

In all that we have said we have had in mind *oblomovshchina* rather than the personality of Oblomov and the other heroes.[46] As far as personalities are concerned, we could not help but see the difference in temperament between, for example, Pechorin[47] and Oblomov, in exactly the same way that we cannot help but see this difference between Pechorin and Onegin,[48] or Rudin[49] and Beltov[50]... Who is going to dispute that differences in personality exist among people (though perhaps they do not exist to nearly such an extent or have nearly such importance as is generally supposed)? But the point is that over all these people hangs the same *oblomovshchina* which indelibly brands them as idle spongers who are absolutely superfluous on earth. It is highly probable that in other conditions, in another society, Onegin would have been a really good chap,

Pechorin and Rudin would have accomplished great deeds and Beltov would have turned out to be a quite splendid person. But in other conditions, perhaps, Oblomov and Tentetnikov[51] too would not have been such loafers and would have found some useful employment... The point is that at the moment they all have one common feature—a futile yearning for activity, an awareness that much might have come of them but that nothing would... In this respect they are strikingly similar to one another...

There is a great difference in the actual ages of Oblomov and the other heroes. We are not speaking about their years: they are almost of the same age in that sense, Rudin is even two or three years older than Oblomov; we are speaking about the times at which they appeared. Oblomov belongs to a later period, so that to the young generation, to people today, he is bound to seem much older than previous Oblomovs... When he was at university, at some seventeen or eighteen years of age, he felt the same yearnings, was imbued with the same ideas which inspired Rudin at the age of thirty-five. From then on there were only two paths for him to go down: either activity, real activity, not tongue-wagging but the engagement of the head, heart and hands all together, or simply lying around twiddling his thumbs. His apathetic nature led him to take the latter course; this is shabby, but at least there is no falsehood in it, no pulling the wool over people's eyes. If he had started, like his brethren, to talk for all to hear about things which he now dares only to dream of, he would have experienced every day distress like that which he experienced when he received the letter from his village elder or the request from his landlord to clear out of his flat. Formerly people listened with affection and reverence to phrase-mongers who spoke of the need for this or that, of higher aspirations and so forth. Then, perhaps, Oblomov too might not have been averse to saying a thing or two... But now any phrasemonger or castle-builder is greeted with the question: "so would you like to have a go?" And this the Oblomovs cannot bear...

Indeed how one senses the breath of a new life when one thinks, after reading Oblomov, what has brought this new type into being in literature. One cannot attribute this just to the personal talent of the author and to the breadth of his outlook. We find both a powerful talent and the broadest and most humane outlook in those authors too who created the earlier types which we have mentioned above. But the fact of the matter is that from the time when the first of them, Onegin, appeared to the present thirty years have elapsed. What was then in embryo, what found expression only in an obscure whispered hint, has by now assumed a definite and solid form, and has been voiced openly and loudly. Words have lost their importance; society itself feels the need for real deeds. Beltov and Rudin, people who had aspirations that really were lofty and noble, not only felt no need to enter into terrible mortal combat with the conditions which were oppressing them but could not even imagine that such combat was feasible in the near future. They were entering a dense, unknown forest, they were passing through a dangerous, marshy bog, they saw various reptiles and snakes underfoot and they climbed a tree, partly in order to have a look to see whether they could spot any roads and partly in order to have a rest and avoid the risk, if only for a while, of sinking in or being bitten. Those who were following waited for them to say something, and looked up at them respectfully as at trail-blazers. But these leaders saw nothing from the great height to which they had climbed: the forest was too vast and thick. Besides, in climbing up the tree they had scratched their faces, hurt their legs over and over again, and damaged their hands... They are in pain, they are worn out, they must have a rest, perched as comfortably as possible in the tree. They are not doing anything for the common good, they have not made anything out or said anything, it is true; those standing down below must cut a road through the forest and clear the way themselves, without their help. But whoever could bring himself to cast a stone at these poor wretches to make them fall from the great height which they have clambered up to and established themselves on with such difficulty and with the common good in mind? People feel pity for them, people do not even demand for the time being that they take part in the clearing of the forest; it is another job that has fallen to their lot and they have done it. If nothing has come of it that is not their fault. Each of our authors was able formerly to look on his Oblomovian hero from this point of view, and he was right. To this was added the fact that the hope of spotting a way out of the forest on to a road somewhere persisted for a long time among the whole band of travelers, just as people long remained sure of the far-sightedness of the leaders who had climbed up the tree. But now gradually things have become clearer and taken another turn: the leaders have grown to like it up the tree; they discourse very eloquently about various ways and means of getting out of the bog and out of the forest; they have even found certain fruits up the tree and enjoy them and throw the skin down below; they invite one or two other people chosen from the crowd to come up and join them and these people come and they stay up the tree, but without looking for a road any more, just devouring the fruit. These are already Oblomovs in the proper sense of the word... And the poor travelers standing down below are sinking into the bog, the snakes are biting them, the reptiles are scaring them, the boughs are lashing their faces... At last the crowd resolves to get down to business and wants to call back those who were the last to climb the tree; but the Oblomovs say nothing and gorge themselves on the fruit. Then the crowd addresses itself to its former leaders as well and asks them to come down and help in the general labor. But the leaders again repeat the phrases they had spoken before about how they have to look for a road and to the effect that there is no use in toiling away at the job of clearing the forest. Then the poor travelers see their mistake and with a wave of the hand say, "Oh, you're all

Oblomovs!" And then they get down to work in earnest, tirelessly: they fell the trees, use them to make a bridge over the bog, form a path, and kill the snakes and reptiles which they find on it, without worrying any more about these wiseacres, these powerful natures, the Pechorins and the Rudins, on whom they used to rely, whom they used to admire so much. At first the Oblomovs look down calmly on the general stir but then, as is their wont, they get scared and start shouting... "Hey, hey, don't do that, stop," they shout, seeing that the tree they are sitting in is being hacked down. "For pity's sake, we could be killed, and all our beautiful ideas, our lofty feelings, our humane aspirations, our eloquence, zeal, love of everything that is beautiful and noble, all these things which we have always kept alive will perish with us... Stop, stop! What are you doing?"... But the travelers have heard all these fine phrases a thousand times before and carry on working without paying any attention to them. There is still one way for the Oblomovs to save themselves and their reputations: to climb down from the tree and set to work together with the rest. But they have gone to pieces, as usual, and they do not know what they have to do... "How has all this come about so suddenly?" they say over and over in despair and they carry on addressing futile imprecations to the stupid crowd which has lost all respect for them.

But the crowd is right, isn't it? Once it has recognized the need for real action, then it could not care less whether it is faced with a Pechorin or an Oblomov. We are not saying, we repeat, that Pechorin would have started to act exactly like Oblomov if placed in the given circumstances; he might have developed as a result of these circumstances in a different direction. But the types created by a powerful talent are long-lasting: even today there are people who would seem to be a chip off Onegin, Pechorin, Rudin and so forth, and not in any form which they might have assumed in other circumstances but exactly in the form in which they are presented by Pushkin, Lermontov and Turgenev. Only in the public consciousness are they all being transformed more and more into Oblomov. It cannot be said that this transformation has already taken place: no, even now thousands of people spend their time conversing and thousands of others are prepared to take conversations as deeds. But that this transformation is beginning is proved by the type of Oblomov whom Goncharov has created. It would not have been possible for him to have appeared had there not matured an awareness, if only in a certain section of society, of how insignificant all these quasi-talented natures were whom people used to admire so much. They used to attire themselves in various cloaks, do themselves up in various hair-styles and attract people with their various talents. But now Oblomov stands before us exposed, as he is, silent, brought down from a beautiful pedestal to a soft sofa, attired in just an ample dressing-gown instead of a cloak. The question *"What does he do, what is the sense and purpose of his life?"* is put bluntly and clearly, and is not cluttered up with any peripheral questions. That is because the time for active service for the good of the community has now come or is fast approaching... And that is why we said at the beginning of the article that we see in Goncharov's novel *a sign of the times*.

1859

Fyodor Mikhailovich Dostoevsky
MR. —BOV AND THE QUESTION OF ART (Extract)[52]

The main point is that art is always true to reality in the highest degree—its deviations are fleeting and transient; it is not only always true to reality, but it cannot be unfaithful to contemporary reality. Otherwise it would not be art. It is the measure of true art that it is always contemporary, urgent and useful. If it concerns itself with anthologies [of ancient poetry] then this means that ancient poetry is still needed; mistakes and deviations may happen but, we repeat, they soon pass. Art which is not contemporary, which does not correspond to contemporary needs, cannot possibly exist. If such a thing does exist, then it is not art: it becomes petty and degenerates, losing all force and artistic value. In this respect we go even further than Mr.—bov in his idea: he still recognizes the existence of useless art, of pure art which is neither contemporary nor urgent, and he takes up arms against it. But we do not acknowledge the existence of such art at all, and we remain calm, because there is nothing to take up arms against. If there are occasional deviations, they are nothing to get upset about: they will pass away of their own accord, and quite quickly too.

"But excuse me," we shall be asked, "on what do you base this view, and how do you reach the conclusion that true art cannot be un-contemporary or unfaithful to modern reality?"

We reply:

First of all, if we take all the historical facts together, from the beginning of the world to the present day, we shall see that art has never abandoned man, but has always responded to his requirements and ideals, has always helped him in his quest for these ideals. It was born with man, it has developed parallel to his historical existence and died along with his historical life.

Second (and most important): creativity, the basis of all art, lives in man as a function of part of his total being, but it is inseparable from him. Consequently, creativity can have no aspirations other than those pursued by man's whole being. If it were to go off in another direction it would mean that art was at odds with man and had broken with him. This would mean it had betrayed the laws of nature. But for as long as mankind is in a sound and healthy state it cannot die out or betray the laws of nature (generally speaking). Consequently there is no need to fear for art; it too will not betray its purpose. It will always live man's true life along with him: it can do nothing else. For this reason it will always remain true to reality.

Of course, during his life man may deviate from normality, from the laws of nature; in this case art will deviate with him. But this serves to show art's close and indissoluble link with man, its constant loyalty to man and his interests.

But all the same, art will only be faithful to man when its freedom of development is not inhibited.

It is therefore of primary importance not to hinder art with various aims, not to prescribe laws for it, and not to confuse it, for even without this it is already confronted by many submerged rocks, many temptations and deviations inseparable from man's historical existence. The more freely it develops, the more normal its development will be and the sooner it will find its true and *useful* path. And since its aims and interests are identical to those of man, whom it serves and with whom it is inseparably united, the freer its development, the greater the benefit it will bring humanity.

Let me be clear: what we want is for art always to correspond to man's aims, not to be at odds with his interests; and if we desire the greatest possible freedom for art it is out of the belief that the freer its development, the more useful it will be to man's interests. We must not prescribe aims and sympathies for art. Why should we? Why doubt art when if it is allowed to develop normally, according to the laws of nature, it cannot possibly go against man's needs even without your prescriptions? It will not get lost; it will not lose its way. It has always been true to reality and has always gone shoulder to shoulder with man's development and progress. The ideal of beauty and normality cannot perish in a healthy society. Therefore leave art to pursue its own path and trust it not to go astray. Even if it does go astray *it will immediately retrace its steps* in response to man's first need. Beauty is normality, health. Beauty is useful because it is beauty and because man has a constant need for beauty and its highest ideal. If a people preserves an ideal of beauty and a need for it, it means that the need for health and normality is also there, and this in itself guarantees the highest development of that people.

1861

Fyodor Mikhailovich Dostoevsky
WINTER NOTES ON SUMMER IMPRESSIONS
(Extract)[53]

And so here I am in Paris... However, don't think that I shall be telling you much about the city of Paris itself. I imagine you have already read so much about it that you have finally tired of such reading. Moreover, you have been there yourselves and no doubt noticed more than I did. What is more, when I am abroad I cannot bear guided tours or sightseeing to order, or to feel obliged to see all the things a traveler is expected to see, and so in some places I missed things which I am ashamed to admit. Even in Paris. I am not saying that I exactly overlooked it, but I will say this: I formed an impression of Paris and found an epithet to describe it, and I am prepared to stand by that epithet: namely, that Paris is the most moral and virtuous city in the whole world. Such order! Such prudence! And such well-defined and firmly established attitudes! How assured and cut-and-dried everything is; how contented everyone is, and how they keep trying to convince themselves that they are contented and perfectly happy, until they reach the point where they do indeed convince themselves—and then they settle for that. There is no further to go. You won't believe that they have settled for that; you will cry out that I am exaggerating, that this is all acrimonious patriotic calumny on my part, that in reality it is not possible for everything to stop completely like that. But, my friends, I have already warned you in the very first chapter of these notes that I might lie terribly. Don't interrupt me. You know very well that if I lie I do so secure in the knowledge that I am not lying. And as far as I am concerned that is more than satisfactory. So leave me be.

Yes, Paris is an amazing city. Such comfort, such unlimited convenience for those who have a right to it, and, as I have already mentioned, such order, such, as it were, *ordered tranquility*. I keep coming back to order. Indeed, just a little more and Paris with its population of a million and a half would turn into a sort of German professorial town, something like Heidelberg for example, petrified in its calm and its order. It seems to be longing to do so. And what is impossible about the idea of a Heidelberg on an enormous scale? And what regimentation! Do you know what I mean? Not so much outward regimentation, which is negligible (comparatively speaking, of course), but a colossal, inner, spiritual regimentation, stemming from the very soul. Paris is becoming narrow, as if of its own volition; it is diminishing gladly, gently huddling into its own shell. But look at London, for example, in this respect. I was in London only eight days, and superficially at least what sweeping pictures, what vivid maps, all distinctive and drawn to different scales, it etched in my memory. Everything is so huge and distinct in its originality. You might even be deceived by this originality. Each distinctive feature, each contradiction gets along with its antithesis and they stubbornly go hand in hand with each other, each contradicting the other, yet apparently without eliminating each other. Everything appears stubbornly to stand up for itself and go along in its own way, without apparently getting in the way of everything else. But meanwhile here too there is that persistent, smoldering, and already chronic struggle: the fight to the death between the principle of individuality common to Western man and the necessity somehow or other to live together in harmony, to form a community and settle down in the one ant-hill; yes, even to become an ant-hill, just so long as things can be organized without people eating each other—otherwise people will turn into cannibals! On the other hand, in this respect you see the same thing as in Paris: the same desperate urge to cling desperately to the status quo, to tear out from oneself all desires and hopes, to curse one's future, in which perhaps even the champions of progress themselves lack sufficient faith, and to bow down to Baal. However, please don't be carried away by this elevated style: all this is consciously noticed only in the souls of the most progressive and conscious, and sensed instinctively in the day-to-day functions of the masses as a whole. But the bourgeois, in Paris for example, is consciously almost quite contented and convinced that all is as it should be. He will even flatten you if you doubt that all is as it should be, because even now he is still rather afraid of something, despite all his self-confidence. It might well be the same in London, but to make up for it what sweeping, overwhelming pictures! How different to Paris even superficially. This city, bustling day and night, and boundless like the sea; the screeching and howling of machines, the railways built above the houses (and before long beneath them too), the boldness of enterprise, the apparent disorder which is in fact the very height of bourgeois order, the polluted Thames, the air impregnated with coal dust, the magnificent squares and parks, those terrible districts like Whitechapel with its half-naked, wild and hungry inhabitants. Then there is the City with its millions and world trade, the Crystal Palace, the World Exhibition... Yes, the Exhibition is staggering. You can sense the terrible force which has brought all these innumerable people from all over the world together into one fold; you are conscious of a huge idea; you feel that here something has already been achieved, a victory, a triumph. You even begin to feel a little afraid. No matter how independent you are, for some reason you become fearful. You begin to think "Is this not indeed the attainment of the ideal? Is this not indeed the end of the line? Is this not in fact the 'one fold'? Should you not indeed accept it all as the whole truth and hold your peace?" It is all so solemn, triumphal and proud that it begins to get you down. You look at these hundreds of thousands, these millions of people obediently flocking here from the four corners of the world, all coming with the one idea, calmly, deliberately and silently crowding into that colossal palace, and you feel that here something final has come to pass— and come to an end. It is a sort of biblical image, something like Babylon, a prophecy from the Apocalypse, taking place before your eyes. You feel it will take a great deal of constant spiritual resistance and denial not to give in, not to succumb to the illusion, not to bow to the fact and worship Baal; not, in other words, to accept what exists as the ideal.

1863

Dmitry Ivanovich Pisarev
BAZAROV (Extracts) [54]

... As an empiricist Bazarov recognizes only that which may be felt by the hands, seen by the eyes or placed on the tongue, in a word only that which may be attested by one of the five senses. All other human feelings he reduces to the activity of the nervous system; as a result of this, enjoyment of the beauty of nature, of music, painting, poetry and a woman's love seems to him no higher and purer at all than enjoyment of a substantial dinner or a bottle of good wine. What ardent youths call the ideal does not exist for Bazarov; he calls all this "Romanticism" and sometimes uses the word "nonsense" instead of "Romanticism." In spite of all this Bazarov does not take the shirt off other people's backs, does not extract money from his parents, works assiduously and is not even averse to doing something worthwhile with his life. I anticipate that many of my readers will ask themselves what it is that holds Bazarov back from ignoble acts and what prompts him to do something worthwhile. This question raises a doubt as to whether Bazarov might not be pretending to himself and to others. Is he not striking a pose? Perhaps in his heart of hearts he accepts much of what he says he rejects, and perhaps it is precisely those things which he accepts and which lie deep in his being that save him from moral downfall and moral nullity. Although Bazarov is no relation of mine and although perhaps I do not even sympathize with him, nevertheless I shall attempt in the interests of abstract justice to answer the question and quell this nagging doubt.

One may berate people like Bazarov as much as one wishes, but it is absolutely essential to recognize their sincerity. These people may be honest or dishonest, public servants or inveterate swindlers, depending on circumstances or personal tastes. Nothing but personal taste prevents them from killing and robbing and nothing but personal taste prompts people of this stamp to make discoveries in the scientific field or in public life. Bazarov will not take the shirt off someone else's back for the same reason that he will not eat a piece of tainted beef. If Bazarov were dying of starvation he would probably do both things. The agonizing sense of an unsatisfied physical need would overcome his feeling of revulsion at the foul smell of the rotting meat and at the underhand infringement of somebody else's property. There is another guiding force in Bazarov's life, apart from immediate attraction, and that is calculation. When he is sick he takes medicine even though castor oil or asafoetida hold no immediate attraction for him. He acts in this way as a result of calculation: at the cost of a small unpleasantness he buys greater comfort or the avoidance of greater unpleasantness in the future. In a word, he chooses the lesser of two evils, although even the lesser evil holds no attraction for him. In mediocre people calculation of this sort proves for the most part ineffectual; they dissemble as calculation dictates, they behave shabbily, they steal, they get themselves in a mess and eventually make fools of themselves. People who are very clever act differently; they realize that it is very much to one's advantage to be honest and that any crime, starting with a simple lie and ending with murder is dangerous and consequently inconvenient. People who are very clever may therefore be honest because calculation dictates it and may act without equivocation where limited people will prevaricate and try to throw people off the scent. In working tirelessly Bazarov was following an immediate inclination, a taste, and, moreover, was acting in accordance with the soundest calculation. If he had sought patronage, bowed and scraped and behaved shabbily instead of laboring away and comporting himself proudly and independently then he would have been acting improvidently. Careers carved out by dint of one's own efforts are always more secure and wide-ranging than those built by means of low bows or the intercession of an important uncle. One may by the last two means become a bigwig in the provinces or the capitals, but no one, since the world began, has succeeded by virtue of them in becoming a Washington[55] or a Garibaldi[56] or a Copernicus[57] or a Heinrich Heine.[58] Even Herostratus[59] carved out a career by his own efforts, and it was not as a result of patronage that he went down in history. As for Bazarov, it is not his aim to become a bigwig in the provinces: if in his imagination he sometimes pictures a great future for himself then the bounds of this future are ill-defined; he works without an end in view to earn his daily bread or through love of the process of work, and yet at the same time he has a vague feeling, which comes of the abundance of his powers, that his work will leave its mark and lead to something. Bazarov holds himself in very high regard, but his self-regard is not noticeable precisely because it is so immense. He is not preoccupied with those trivia out of which the everyday relationships of human beings are shaped; one cannot make him happy by according him signs of respect; he is so full of himself and has such an unshakably high opinion of himself that he grows almost completely indifferent to the opinions of others. Kirsanov's uncle,[60] who closely resembles Bazarov in his cast of mind and character, calls his self-regard "Satanic pride." This expression is very aptly chosen and sums up our hero absolutely. Bazarov really could only be satisfied by a whole eternity of constantly expanding activity and constantly increasing enjoyment, but, to his misfortune, Bazarov does not accept that the human personality exists forever...

Thus, Bazarov acts everywhere and in all things only as he wishes or as seems advantageous and convenient to him. He is governed only by personal whim or personal calculations. Neither over himself, nor outside himself, nor within himself does he acknowledge any regulator, any moral law, any principle. Ahead there is no great aim; in his mind there is no grand design, yet for all that he has immense power. "But this is an immoral person! A rogue, a depraved monster!" I hear indignant readers exclaiming on all sides. Well, all right, a rogue, a depraved monster; go on, abuse him, persecute him with satires and epigrams, with outraged lyricism and scandalized public opinion, with the fires of the inquisition and the executioner's ax, but you will not destroy him, you will not slay this depraved monster, you will not put him in spirit for the respectable public to marvel at. If *bazarovshchina*[61] is a disease then it is a disease of our time, and one has got to suffer it regardless of any palliatives or amputations that may be necessary. Look on *bazarovshchina* as you please, that is your business, but try and arrest it and you will not succeed; it is a cholera too...

Thus, here are my conclusions. A person from the mass lives according to the established norm, which falls to his lot not as a result of any free choice but because he was born at a certain time, in a certain town or village. He is enmeshed in various relationships, in the family, at work and in everyday and social life; his thought is fettered by accepted prejudices; he himself does not like either these relationships or these prejudices, but they represent for him a "boundary which thou shalt not cross" and he lives and dies without displaying his personal will and often without even suspecting the existence of such a will in himself. If a rather cleverer person appears in this mass then one way or another, according to the circumstances, he will stand out from the mass and deal with things in his own way, as he finds most advantageous, convenient and pleasant. Clever people who have not had any serious education cannot stand the life of the mass because it is colorless and bores them; they themselves do not conceive of a better life and so once they have instinctively shied away from the mass they dwell in a void, not knowing where they should go, what they should live for on earth or how they are to dispel their anguish. Here we have the individual tearing himself away from the herd but not knowing how to take himself in hand. Other people, who are clever and educated, are dissatisfied with the life of the mass and consciously subject it to criticism; they have formed an ideal for themselves; they want to march towards it, but all the time they look over their shoulders and timorously ask one another whether society will follow them, whether they will be stranded on their own with their aspirations, whether they will make fools of themselves. With these people, who are wanting in firmness, matters do not go beyond words. Here we have the individual recognizing his individuality and fashioning some conception of an independent life, but not daring to budge and cleaving his existence in two by separating the world of thought from the world of life. People of the third category go further—they recognize their dissimilarity to the mass and boldly mark themselves off from it by their acts, habits and whole way of life. Whether society will follow them is not their concern. They are full of themselves and of their inner life and they do not inhibit it to suit accepted customs and rituals. Here we have the individual attaining his full self-liberation, his full uniqueness and independence.

In a word, the Pechorins[62] have will without knowledge, the Rudins[63] have knowledge without will; the Bazarovs have both knowledge and will, thought and action merge in a solid whole.

1862

Part VI

Revolutionary Populism

Introduction

The radical thinkers of the 1850s and 1860s had mounted a wide-ranging attack on the aesthetic, ethical, religious and political beliefs of conservatives and liberals alike, but their rebellion was a mainly intellectual one and did not as yet give rise to a widespread revolutionary movement, even though revolutionary groups did appear in the 1860s (for example, the first "Land and Liberty" organization of 1861-64, the group founded by Zaichnevsky and Argiropulo in 1861 and the network of circles built up by Nechaev in 1868-69 in the higher educational institutions of Moscow and St. Petersburg). By the end of the 1860s, however, different historical conditions obtained. The age of reform had come to an end and there had begun a new period of reaction, inaugurated by the brutal repression of the Polish uprising of 1863 and marked by numerous arrests and the final closure of *The Contemporary* in 1866 after the attempt of a student, Karakozov, on the life of Alexander II. Chernyshevsky was in Siberian exile, Dobrolyubov and Pisarev were dead. The journal, *Notes of the Fatherland,* taken over in 1868 by the poet and publicist Nekrasov and the satirist Saltykov-Shchedrin, became the center of an intellectual and cultural renaissance, which found expression in imaginative literature, painting and music, as well as thought. Questions long since broached— for example, the place of the commune in Russian life, the nature of the Russian people and Russia's historical path—now assumed greater prominence and a new importance. It is in this period that revolutionary Populism, in its classical form, may be said to have taken shape.

Implicit in the Populist credo which underpinned the intense revolutionary activity of the 1870s were perhaps as many as six fundamental and inter-related assumptions. Firstly, the Russian peasant commune was an egalitarian and democratic institution and would serve as a basis for socialism in Russia. Secondly, the Russian peasant was instinctively socialistic, or at least he had qualities which made him amenable to socialist collectivism. Thirdly, given these advantages, Russia could bypass the capitalist stage of economic development currently afflicting the advanced nations of Western Europe and thus pass directly from a semi-feudal condition to socialism. Fourthly, the educated man had a compelling moral responsibility to devote himself to the task of transforming his society in the name of the socialist ideal. Fifthly, the individual—or at least the individual who belonged to the ranks of the intelligentsia—possessed, as did his nation as a whole, the freedom and the capacity to exercise a significant degree of control over his own destiny.

And, sixthly, the forthcoming revolution would not only promote the interests of the popular masses, but would also give expression to their wishes and even be carried out mainly by them. The classical exponents of Populism thus defined were Lavrov, Mikhailovsky and Bervi-Flerovsky, though Bakunin, broadly speaking, shared most of these assumptions and even Tkachev, for all his isolation among the revolutionaries of the 1870s, subscribed to some of them.

Of the many writers of this period who were attentive to the plight of the Russian masses and hopeful that they might be the beneficiaries of a unique historical development, none more forcefully articulated the mood of the moment than the eccentric economist and publicist Vasily Bervi (1829-1918). (That is not to say that Bervi's writings were lucid; on the contrary, a sense of urgency and indignation mars his writing, and indeed Populist publicism in general, if we were to judge it purely from the point of view of the quality of its style and argumentation, represents a further stage in that degeneration that can be traced back through Chernyshevsky to Belinsky.) Bervi is now little remembered and receives less attention than Mikhailovsky, Lavrov, Bakunin and Tkachev, and yet his major work, *The Condition of the Working Class in Russia,* first published in 1869 under the pseudonym N. Flerovsky, seems to have affected Populist revolutionaries more deeply than any other work with the exception of Lavrov's *Historical Letters.* On one level the work is an exhaustive chronicle of the people's misery, based on Bervi's first-hand study of the life of the people during his enforced wanderings in periods of political exile and on a mass of statistical evidence which helps to make it still a useful factual source for the study of the economy of post-reform Russia. On another level the work contains a powerful reassertion of the arguments concerning Russian national distinctiveness on which Populism rested. Bervi contends, for example, that the poverty of the masses could not be due to any defects such as a proclivity to drunkenness or indolence in the national character, since the masses drank little and were hard-working to a fault. He also praises the peasant for preserving the communal system of landholding. That the peasant community was being divided into rich and poor groups he did not doubt, but he shared the faith widespread at the period that the commune would serve as an antidote to burgeoning capitalism and urged his contemporaries to preserve at all costs the "shoots" out of which Russia's future distinctiveness would grow. Finally, like Mikhailovsky and other classical Populists, Bervi makes a strong appeal to the moral sensibility of his readers. It is as if revolution for him will entail not only a radical improvement in the economic condition of the masses, but also a moral regeneration for an intelligentsia which has resolved to sacrifice itself for the welfare of others.

Nikolai Mikhailovsky (1842-1904), who was instrumental in the revival of the journal *Notes of the Fatherland* in the late 1860s and early

1870s, and who was one of the most prolific publicists in the Populist camp, is perhaps most important as one of the founders, together with Lavrov, of the "subjective" school of sociology. The radicals of the early 1860s, particularly Chernyshevsky, had used a crude materialism derived from such foreign thinkers as Feuerbach and Büchner in order finally to prohibit passive acceptance of social conditions as divinely preordained and had thus prepared the ground for revolutionary political opposition to the established order. But by their attempt to explain man's behavior in the light of rigid, supposedly scientific laws as a product of environment or physiological factors over which man had no control, these materialists had tended, albeit unintentionally, to deprive man of the free will to change his society. Such determinism, however, was deeply disturbing to thinkers of a slightly later period, who were alarmed by the advance of capitalism and impatient to transform society in accordance with their own ideals. It was important to the theoreticians of the early Populist period, therefore, to free ethical and sociological speculation from the jurisdiction of an inflexible scientific method. They wished to assert that man had freedom to make moral choices and to change his society, indeed they demanded that he do so, and this is the burden of Mikhailovsky's long essay *What is Progress?* It was neither intellectually nor morally acceptable, Mikhailovsky argued, to apply the objective method of the natural sciences to sociology, for the sociologist did not have the right to remove from his work man as he really was with all his "sorrows and desires." Mikhailovsky did not wish altogether to abolish the "objective" method, it is true; but he did insist that the "subjective" method should serve as a "higher control," and towards the end of his essay he began to anticipate— as did many imaginative writers from the late 1850s on—the appearance of individuals of high moral caliber who might rightfully exercise such control.

A similar position was adopted by Pyotr Lavrov (1823-1900) in his *Historical Letters,* which were published in serial form in 1868-69 and in a separate edition in 1870, and which had an almost evangelical significance among the revolutionaries active inside Russia in the 1870s. Having attempted to establish that history is a field of human enquiry at least as important as the natural sciences, and that a subjective method, unacceptable in the latter, is inevitable, legitimate and indeed obligatory in the former, Lavrov proceeds in his fourth letter, entitled "The Price of Progress," to frame a vigorous appeal to the intelligentsia to pursue the ideal of social justice. An enormous price had been paid by the toiling majority of mankind, Lavrov argues, for the conditions which had made possible the development of the privileged "critically thinking minority" who cherished that ideal. A member of that minority could only absolve himself from his share of the blame for the sufferings of the masses if he repaid his debt to them by attempting to reshape society for their benefit in accordance with the ideal which he had had the leisure and the education to formulate. Unlike Mikhailovsky, though, Lavrov also made an important contribution to the development of revolutionary strategy. Having escaped from exile in the remote Russian province of Vologda, he set up, with the help of a number of young supporters, an emigre journal *Forward! (Vpered!),* which was printed, first in Switzerland and then in London, between 1873 and 1877. Fearing the imminent development of capitalism in Russia and the division of the peasantry into a small class of rich peasants, or *kulaks,* on the one hand, and a large landless proletariat, on the other, Lavrov exhorted the radical intelligentsia to "go to the people" without delay in order to prepare the masses for a socialist revolution by transmitting the socialist ideal to them. This task the intelligentsia would carry out by means of patient and scrupulously honest propaganda. Lavrov was insistent, however, that it was the masses themselves, not the intelligentsia, who would in the last analysis have to make the socialist revolution. Socialist ideals should not be imposed on the mass from above by a small minority claiming to represent the people's interests; such a strategy would produce only a new struggle for power and a further imposition of "consciousness" on the masses by a minority alien to them. The revolution that Lavrov envisaged was therefore, in the terminology of the time, an "economic" rather than a "political" one. For the most part Lavrov's recommendations accorded with the general mood of the time, though his gradualist approach could not satisfy more impatient spirits and there was some concern lest the painstaking self-preparation of the propagandist demanded by Lavrov in a famous article, "Knowledge and Revolution," should render the revolutionary movement ineffectual.

Mikhail Bakunin (1814-1876), like Lavrov, believed that the revolution should be carried out by the masses who were to be its beneficiaries, but he disagreed radically with Lavrov over the strategy which the revolutionary intelligentsia ought to pursue. Certainly the intelligentsia should move closer to the people, Bakunin believed. But the object of this "going to the people" should not be to inculcate in the people a socialist ideal formulated by the intelligentsia; rather it should be to erode those factors, such as the patriarchal quality of Russian peasant life and a misplaced faith in the tsar, which prevented the people from properly expressing their own innate socialist leanings. Revolutionaries, therefore, should foment the hostile attitude which Bakunin thought the people harbored towards the Russian state and its authorities, and he glorified those figures, such as the leaders of the great peasant revolts in Russian history and all who lived outside the law, who had most clearly and violently expressed this hostility. As to the best means of inciting peasant rebellion, Bakunin advocated agitation, the emotional advertisement of specific grievances, rather than the more rational explanation of the faults of the whole social and political system that the peaceful propagandists recommended, and he scoffed at the "sociological faculties" which, it seemed to him, the supporters of Lavrov hoped to set up in the countryside. Both in his extreme opposition to the contemporary state, in all its forms, and in his exaltation of the destructive aspect of revolution, Bakunin consistently preached right up until the end of his life the violent anarchism that had first found expression in his writings and utterances in the 1840s and that had made him one of the most prominent European revolutionaries, a major opponent of Marxian socialism. All the most typical elements in his thought find expression in his last major work, *Statism and Anarchy,* and the addendum to it, printed under the title "Appendix A," in which his most influential contribution to Russian revolutionary strategy was made. Like all his writings, however, these works are impassioned streams of revolutionary consciousness and are as a result deficient in coherence and lucidity.

It is indisputable that the overwhelming majority of the revolutionaries who went "to the people" in the 1870s and who from 1876 joined the ranks of the second "Land and Liberty" organization accepted the revolutionary strategy of either Lavrov or Bakunin. But it is important to consider too the thought of Pyotr Tkachev (1844-86), who made a number of challenging assertions which threw into relief the more widely accepted assumptions of the Populists and which took on a new significance when it became apparent at the end of the 1870s that the Populist revolutionaries had achieved none of their objectives. Tkachev's thought reveals the perplexity of one who was attracted by the deterministic notions popular in the early 1860s but at the same time was anxious to modify them in order that they should not inhibit the revolutionary activist. Thus in a review, published in 1868, of a book dealing with peasant movements in sixteenth-century Germany, he attempts to marry the determinism of the "objective" thinker with the voluntarism of the revolutionary by arguing that, while it was not possible to disrupt the logical development of the economic principle underlying a given social order, it was nevertheless possible entirely to alter the governing principle of a society, to replace it with a new one, to accomplish a "historical leap" from one order to another.

Such voluntarism underpinned Tkachev's revolutionary strategy. Fearing the imminent development of capitalism and the transformation of the state into an instrument of the bourgeoisie, and placing no hope on the peasantry, which he saw as a benighted mass oppressed by poverty, Tkachev urged revolutionaries to organize themselves into a highly centralized, disciplined, conspiratorial party capable of mounting an attack on the autocratic government and seizing political power. Having carried out a *coup d'état* the revolutionaries would then implement their socialist ideals by decree, from above. They would need at least the passive support of the masses and the masses might make their wishes known to the revolutionary party; but all the same a socialist order would come into being, in Tkachev's schema, through the agency of the rulers of the revolutionary, authoritarian state, not through the agency of the popular masses. Nor should the revolutionaries convinced of the rectitude of their cause, be squeamish in their choice of tactics: like the Machiavellian conspirator Nechaev they would approve that which brought nearer the socialist goal and deprecate that which hindered its attainment. Tkachev's revolutionary strategy—which was known by his contemporaries as "Jacobinism" or "Blanquism"—earned him and his small emigre group of Russian and Polish collaborators great notoriety among Populist revolutionaries in general. Indeed it is tempting to view the desire of the majority of the Populists of the 1870s to repudiate Tkachev's basic premises as a final formative influence on the Populist outlook.

With the failure of the Populists of the 1870s and early 1880s to stir the Russian peasantry by means of propaganda and agitation or to wring concessions from the government by means of terrorism, revolutionaries began to consider the merits of other streams of socialist thought and to search for new strategies. In fact Russian revolutionaries proved extremely reluctant in the 1880s to reject the basic premises of Populism, not least because the activists who had accepted them in the 1870s were remembered with veneration. A few individuals did question these premises, however, and in 1883 set up in Switzerland the "Emancipation of Labor" Group which dedicated itself throughout the 1880s to the rather thankless task of undermining Populist theory and propagating Marxism in its place. The leading theoretician of the group, Georgy Plekhanov (1856-1918), argued in his major work of the decade, *Our Differences,* that the Populists were wrong to assert that Russia might follow an independent historical path different from that of the Western European nations. Russia could not avoid the capitalist development which had reached an advanced stage in the West; indeed capitalism was already well established in Russia in both town and country, and under its impact a new class structure was developing. It followed, Plekhanov believed, that revolutionaries could no longer pin their hopes on the commune as the base for socialism in Russia, but should turn their attention instead to the proletariat that was developing in the towns and that would, so Marx predicted, eventually expropriate the bourgeoisie and establish a dictatorship of its own.

N. Flerovsky (Vasily Vasilevich Bervi)
THE CONDITION OF THE WORKING CLASS IN RUSSIA (Extracts)[1]

I have said a great deal about the things which stand in the way of the wellbeing and development of the Siberian peasant, and now I shall say a few words about what serves as a guarantee that he has the capacity for this development. This guarantee I see in the Russian's natural wit, vigorous, enterprising nature and instinctive striving for civilization. Take a series of portraits of peasants and compare it with a series of portraits of scholars and statesmen; the same spiritual strength will be expressed in both series alike; but in any given selection of faces the peasants will come out best. I have carried out experiments and communicated great ideas formulated by European science[2] to people from the peasantry and the gentry and, to my no small surprise, the peasants repeatedly grasped what was expressed in language they could understand more profoundly and quickly. Such an observation may seem partial and paradoxical, but it is confirmed by very significant data; most of what has been done in Siberia to make it a better place to live has been done by people from the peasantry,[3] people who are not only uneducated but even illiterate; people who were considered the most advanced in Russia have been unable to compete with the illiterate intelligentsia of the region. The majority of the most adventurous and famous owners of gold-mines and factory-owners in Siberia belong to the peasantry and have emanated from the lowest strata of society; the people who are the spirit of the shipping companies, which have again been set up in Siberia, include in their number people of the lowest origin who have received no education; the most famous mechanic and builder of distilleries in Siberia is a person who cannot read or write Russian. Wealthy Russian nobles who have attempted to compete with the enterprising spirit of the Siberian *muzhik*[4] have become completely bankrupt and have ended up having to turn to people of peasant origin and ask them for a large grant of money to put their affairs in order; their learned chemists and mechanics have had to give way to the illiterate peasant intelligentsia. I left Siberia full of respect for the intellectual capabilities of the peasantry; I am convinced that there lies within that estate[5] the hope of Russia, the guarantee of her future glory and greatness. Whoever holds dear the glory of the Russian fatherland, whoever wants Russia to stand in the ranks of the great civilizing nations of mankind, must try with all the means at his disposal [to ensure] that literacy spreads among the peasantry and that they develop intellectually. How often did I admire the soundness of the peasant intelligentsia's judgment, its knowledge of its strength and its understanding of its affairs, which was so profound that its calculations were impeccable! With the spread of enlightenment in its midst the results will become clearer. In order to gain an impression of the bold and enterprising spirit of the peasant one should acquaint oneself with the life of the native *taiga*[6] dweller. Imagine a village consisting of a few houses with a chapel in the middle. All around is impenetrable *taiga*. Sometimes its inhabitants belong to some sect or other, sometimes they are of the Orthodox creed. In each *izba*[7] you find a rifle of most strange appearance with a butt so awkward that you cannot imagine how anyone could fire such a gun. Get into conversation with these inhabitants of the virgin forests and they will tell you how they hunt bear and elk; the elk is an animal which is so strong that it can split a tree with a blow of its foot, and it is also unusually quick, and people whom it strikes with its foot or antlers rarely survive. Non-Russian people go on such hunting trips in groups of five to twenty and more; but the Russian hunter of the *taiga* prefers to go hunting alone, it is more profitable and pleasanter that way; tales about how bears have torn to pieces non-Russians who have attacked them in a whole crowd don't scare him in the least. You have already seen his gun, you want to see a bullet and a dog; the bullet is a small piece of lead, sometimes of irregular shape, and the dog is an ordinary mongrel of small stature. It is impossible not to feel respect for the courage and nerve of a man who kills the strongest bear or elk single-handed with such resources and without fear. He is a sort of heroic figure as mighty and majestic as the endless *taiga* that surrounds him...

Have you ever happened to hear a good, unfortunate person, a person whom you love passionately and have good grounds for holding in great respect, being disparaged for his misfortunes? (And the disparaging is often done by those who are themselves the principal cause of these misfortunes.) This is what I feel every time the Russian worker, and particularly the Russian peasant farmer, is accused of being indolent, ignorant and poor; when our poverty and destitution are compared with foreign wealth, when our peasant farmer is set alongside the German settler and when people talk about the iron nerve of the latter, about his inflexible will and inexhaustible industry. I can assure the reader that there is no iron in the nerve of the settler that would make it exceptionally strong, it is of the same material as the nerve of the Russian peasant farmer, and the Russian would be just as rich as the settler if his lot was such a happy one. It is easy for settlers to grow rich, they get seven pounds of bread per person a day and to each person there are about five head of livestock; the settler will always have something to sow his fields with, however many fields he might have, he will have enough manure to make the soil fertile; and besides, he himself is full and his horse has strong muscles and is well fed. But how is the Russian peasant farmer to live, who has every day to fight against hunger in order to keep the seeds he needs for sowing; he keeps livestock, but the meat from this livestock he only ever sees on sale, it never turns up in his pot, for whenever there is the slightest difficulty he has to start selling off his livestock at a great rate, its quantity decreases and not infrequently he has to sell the whole lot down to the last animal. A peasant who has a relatively large number of animals has so little manure all the same that the soil on which he sows becomes exhausted; as soon as the number of his cattle decreases his farm is bound to go into complete decline. The harvests in his fields will be bad, and even when there are good harvests he is barely able to pay his taxes, or get enough to eat and keep by as much as he needs for seeds. The greater the privations to which he will subject himself, his family and his horse in striving to keep enough grain for seeds, the more slowly his work will proceed and the less he will profit from it. Let anyone try to starve himself and his family for two or three days while he is keeping rye close at hand for seeds and the hungry family besieges him with its wails and cries and demands that he grind the rye and feed them. Heroism is needed to resist such pressures, and in Russia we have millions of such heroes.

* * *

One must be very unfamiliar with the Russian worker or look on him with eyes which are prejudiced to the point of blindness to believe the reproaches to the effect that he is indolent, which people living at his expense so love to shower on him. The main failing of the Russian worker is not indolence but an excessive love of work—a love of work which wears out his body and renders his labor unproductive. The English worker has come to believe that the most productive labor is eight hours with abundant meat in one's diet; our worker, who feeds only on black bread, labors fourteen hours and more. Everywhere he is burdened by an enormous amount of work for which he receives very little reward. He staggers hundreds and thousands of *versts*[8] along the Russian roads during the muddy seasons of spring and autumn in search of a meager wage. He takes on work at the cheapest rate and yet at this rate he not infrequently does one and a half times as much work as he need under the terms of his agreement: when he is working on the land they move the markers about and deceitfully increase the size of his task, and at the same time it happens that the quality of his food is cut down, so that his strength is completely sapped; when he is fishing the price he is offered for his fish is inordinately low; the agricultural laborer is given infertile land and high quitrents[9] are demanded of him; and either he is forced to buy the things he needs from the landlord at twice the proper price or he is paid in defective goods. It would be much better for his own good and for the wellbeing of Russia if this worker valued his labor more highly and did not consent to work on unprofitable terms. There is not an employer who will not tell you how the workers go boozing and abandon their work and what losses this causes. Of course there are such cases, but they are not infrequently encountered in England and France too; the best workers go on a binge, stay away from work three or four days a week and because of them all work comes to a standstill, but this happens there in exactly the same way as in Russia with skilled workmen who receive good pay; ordinary workers do not have the wherewithal for such extravagances. In the proper place, when I speak about industrial Russia, I shall paint a grim picture of the pitiful consequences of an excessive love of work; immoderation is always harmful, but immoderation in work is one of the most harmful forms of all...

* * *

As soon as we find enough courage to make up our minds to do this [accept our destiny with dignity and take our path without turning aside, with an open, fearless gaze], we shall see that we have not lost the prospect of not only putting our affairs in order but even playing a great historical role; for England has overtaken Spain, which in the fifteenth century stood incomparably higher, was defended from its enemies by the Pyrenees, could command both the Mediterranean and the Great Ocean and possessed incomparably richer parts of America and in every respect had better chances of occupying the place in world affairs that England now occupies. If we are really going to have such spiritual greatness that we shall wish to play such a great and glorious role then we must not forget that only a people which has nurtured finer feelings in its soul and created a finer outlook may stand at the head of civilization and lead mankind. Great empires without an idea, such as the powers created by Chingis Khan, Tamerlaine and Cyrus,[10] have disappeared without trace and left behind them only the most unenviable reputation, whilst India, Athens, England and the United States will ever be preserved in the memory of history as leaders of mankind... [We] may reason thus: Europe has passed down that same path along which we are traveling, it has lived through the same phases; if we go in its tracks we shall get ourselves out of trouble in the same way that it has done; why should we wring our hands and rack our brains over the laying down of a new road when there is an old, well-trodden path. Thus have we reasoned up until now, thus have we tried to act; but even here we were constantly afraid of taking an unnecessary step or taking a step too quickly... If we continue to go down the path which we have been on up until now, then we are inevitably bound always to remain at the tail-end of the civilized world; if I follow a person and go timidly step after step down the track he has left then I shall without any doubt always remain behind. The national pride of every Russian is bound to take offense at such a state of affairs, and it would be a different matter if there were really nothing more for us to do. But it is not so, is it? We see in modern civilization, at the head of which stand Europe and the United States, a fundamental defect, one of those defects which have dug the graves of civilizations and have made it inevitable that new leaders with fresh forces have come to take the place of the old ones. A normal civilization should nurture in people concepts and feelings which would enable them to help one another, to attain to development and wellbeing, not prevent one another from doing so. Only when people have such an upbringing may a society be deemed healthy...

* * *

As far as general measures are concerned, attention must of course be paid above all to the attitude towards the land. Here we see that our peasant has shown incomparably more tact and common sense than his Western European counterpart. He has understood a great truth which the Western European worker has never understood. He has comprehended that one must above all take care that no peasant farmer be deprived of his own holding. To manage one's own holding is not a trivial matter, one must adapt to it and get accustomed to it from one's childhood. The Western European rural proletarian will not manage to do this in the near future, indeed he may never manage it, and on Western European soil we can again see the Roman latifundia. Western European political economy vainly preaches that the most productive land is that which is in the hands of the peasant farmer; it will never achieve its goal so long as the principle of large-scale and small-scale private property exists. The small property-owner will always be a privileged worker perched on his brother's neck. Communal ownership leads, at least within the commune,[11] to a rational distribution of the land among the workers. Each receives all the plots which he needs to run a complete holding, he will be given a share of the meadows too, and of the forest and of the hemp-field and of every sort of land, and he will be given as much as can possibly be given without upsetting another worker. The small-scale property-owner receives land at the whim of Fate. The father has all he needs; if he is the only son he will be happy, but if there are three sons—then he'll be done out of his fair share of something or other. How many tears are shed by small-scale property-owners over this; the farmer who has received a plot which does not have all he needs for farming would be glad to exchange a part of his land for what he needs, but the opportunity to do this rarely presents itself to him. When they distribute the land at the time of a partition, the peasants have the opportunity to give to each not only all he needs but the most suitable things too. In communes with a lot of land, where the distant lands are left to be used in a random fashion without partitions, the nearby lands are shared out afresh; sometimes only the best lands are involved in the partition, sometimes a forest is involved so that it can be saved from felling. If the Western European community, consisting of small-scale property-owners, were able to partition its lands in this way, it would consider itself the most fortunate in the world: among small-scale property-owners one hears nothing but complaints about the impossibility of augmenting one's estate, but unfortunately the community never manages [to do] this; in order to do this one needs the habit of partitioning, and the ability to adapt oneself, qualities and ways which the small-scale property-owner, who never partitions his lands, can in no way acquire.

1869

Nikolai Konstantinovich Mikhailovsky
WHAT IS PROGRESS? (Extracts) [12]

This whole muddle which we have described in Spencer's exposition and ideas hinges on his inappropriate use of the objective method. Once we have erased from our mental make-up the belief that there is good sense in the ordering of the universe, we must also stop applying the word and concept "progress" to the way in which natural phenomena successively supplant one another, or else we must make no distinction between development and decomposition. Why should we not regard the decomposition of a dead body as a progressive phenomenon, a stage in its further development? Perhaps "Nature's interests," "Nature's economy," "Nature's aims," "Nature's aspirations" require a circular development, with the moment of decomposition turning out to be just one of the phases of development. But we know that Nature, which neither laughs nor cries, has no aims, no aspirations, no interests, and so we look on the decomposition of the corpse as a fact liable to objective evaluation. But man does have aims; these aims are facts of our consciousness every bit as real as the fact of the decomposition of the dead body. This fact requires evaluation in exactly the same way, only the evaluation must be subjective. And not merely because an exclusively objective evaluation cannot give a complete picture of the facts of social life, since there is in these facts an element which is encountered only in them and does not lend itself to objective evaluation, but also because an exclusively objective evaluation is unthinkable and impossible here.

* * *

Just as absolute justice is impossible for man, just as an art devoid of any tendentiousness is impossible, so too an exclusively objective method in sociology is impossible. In spite of the apparently fundamental distinction between the first two species of eccentricity and the latter one, they are all products of the same cause, the same historical phenomenon, namely the economic division of labor (not economic in a special sense, but I use the expression in contradistinction to the physiological division of labor) and social differentiations. And as such they all have similar qualities and similar results. All of them, in the first place, represent attempts to get away from a certain mental make-up; they all want to be impartial and all are equally partial, all sanction facts in equal degree, all alike are silenced by reality's contingencies. All of them make the mistake of thinking to attain to objectivity by examining the phenomena of social life from the point of view of an abstract category—pure beauty, pure justice, pure truth, whereas all these points of view are too narrow for such a complex phenomenon as man in society. They are narrow to such an extent that it is man in society who at every turn clambers out of pure justice, pure art and pure truth, that is to say man with certain feelings, certain aspirations, and, finally, a certain preconceived opinion. In most cases man emerges ugly from these integuments, the illusion of purity crumbles to dust. But one can hardly deplore this: there is nothing more beautiful to man than man himself and the least good man is still better than the best camera, the best gibbet and the best calculating machine...

1869

Pyotr Lavrovich Lavrov
HISTORICAL LETTERS [13]
[Fourth Letter: The Price of Progress]

In the course of its long existence mankind has produced a number of individuals of genius, whom historians proudly call mankind's representatives, its heroes. In order that these heroes might operate, in order even that they might appear in the societies which were fortunate enough to have them, there had to arise a small group of people who consciously strove to cultivate human virtue, extend their knowledge, clarify their ideas, strengthen their characters, and establish a social order that was more propitious for such heroes. In order that this small group might arise, there had to emerge, among the majority struggling hour by hour to exist, a minority protected from the most onerous everyday concerns. And in order that the majority which had to struggle for its daily bread, its shelter and its clothing might produce this *flower of the people,* these *sole representatives of civilization,* this majority had to survive; and that was not nearly such an easy matter as it might seem at first sight.

In the primeval struggle for survival with his brothers, the animals, man came off badly. He does not have such powerful natural weapons of attack and defense as other species which have grown up surrounded by enemies precisely by virtue of such weapons; and in physical contest he was devoured by the strongest animals. He lacks the organs for climbing, jumping, flying or swimming which would enable him more easily to escape danger, whilst other, weaker species probably owe their survival to precisely these organs. Man has to *learn* everything, adapt himself to everything; otherwise he perishes. The young of man, in the opinion of some writers, are a helpless burden to their parents for, on average, a fifth of their lives, whilst for other species this figure never exceeds a twentieth. Even if one accepts that in man's primeval phase this difference was expressed in figures that were closer to one another,[14] still it was inevitably not in man's favor. Consequently man has in general found it extremely hard to survive in the animal kingdom.

One organ in his gradual evolution *did* enable man to triumph in this struggle, making up for the advantages which all other species had and surpassing them. This was the organ of *thought.*[15] Probably an innumerable multitude of bipeds perished in a hopeless struggle with their enemies, wild animals, before those fortunate individuals appeared who were capable of thinking *better* than these enemies, capable of inventing means of safeguarding their existence. They *defended* themselves at the cost of consigning all the rest to ruin, and this *first,* absolutely *natural* aristocracy among the bipeds *created* mankind. The ability to inherit characteristics or to pick them up made it possible for the inventions of these original individuals of genius to be transmitted to the small minority who were in the most favorable position to pick them up. Mankind's survival was assured.

If man had fought man even before this, as he had fought every other animal, in order to take food away from him or to devour him, now the only struggle that was important for the future was that between people themselves. Here the odds were more even, so the struggle was bound to be more dogged and protracted. Every improvement in bodily agility, in the use of weapons of attack and defense in emulation of man's first teachers, the wild animals, every invention which an individual managed to devise brought about the ruin of many individuals. Abandoned offspring perished, females of the species perished when they were pregnant or just after they had given birth, the weakest, the least agile, the least inventive, the least careful, the least receptive perished. The child survived who was sturdy enough to get by sooner than the rest without being looked after, or who, being fortunately placed, could be looked after for longer; the one most able in body and mind survived and the one who was luckiest among those of equal ability. He got better food; he slept more peacefully; he knew more; he had time the *better to consider* his actions. These fortunate people made up the second aristocracy of the human species who were able to survive at the cost of the destruction of their brethren.

Defense of the pregnant female while she was asleep, so that pleasure or help could be had from her in future, was probably the first and greatest matter in man's moral development. This was the first utilitarian *bond* between people and the first lesson about how profitable bonds between individuals are for both of them. It was bound to lead sooner or later to caring for the young, the formation of the family, traditional transmission of knowledge and thought, the emergence of peoples. Faced with these united forces, all those who did not hit upon union in some form or other in good time or who for some reason did not take up this invention, disappeared with no chance of saving themselves. The destructive struggle of families against lone individuals and of families against one another was bound to be even more implacable than previous ones, because each healthy adult, in order to care for his children and provide for them, and also while the womenfolk were pregnant, had to obtain *more* food than just for himself. At the cost of this destruction of the majority man bought the *possibility* of uninterrupted progress for his culture; by transmitting it from one generation to another he bought the habit of social life and attachments and the tradition of knowledge and belief.

The struggle continued between families and clans. Vanquished opponents were mercilessly destroyed so long as it was only a matter of the struggle for survival; but the first lesson about the use that could be made of the life of another for one's own *convenience* could not pass unnoticed. The desire to increase one's own pleasure compelled people to think whether it was not *sometimes* more advantageous not to kill the vanquished. Was it not more advantageous for the victor to cultivate only the agility of his body and mind and to load the job of obtaining what he needed on to someone else? Those men of genius from the prehistoric period who hit upon this utilitarian principle laid a foundation among mankind for respect for another person's life and for one's own worth. At the same time they made physical and intellectual development, culture and science, a responsibility, a moral ideal for themselves and their descendants. They assured themselves and posterity of *leisure* for progress. They *created* progress[16] among mankind just as their predecessors, individuals of genius or good fortune, created mankind among the beasts, created the human species in the struggle with human individuals and created the *possibility* of progress in the future. But this progress achieved by a small minority was bought by the *enslavement* of the majority, by depriving it of the chance of acquiring that agility of body and thought which was the virtue of the representatives of civilization.

Awareness of the great importance of culture and science, as forces and pleasures, led of its own accord to a desire to monopolize this force and this pleasure. Downright coercion, the organization of society, the law's retribution, religious fear, the habit of tradition instilled from the cradle, set the minority, people with breeding, knowledge and cultivation, off from all the rest. At the cost of tireless labor and the struggle for survival on the part of *all these others,* the few were able to choose the best women for themselves, produce the best families and feed them and bring them up better; they were able to use their time for observation, thought and reflection without worrying about food, shelter or the most basic comforts; they were able to strive for truth and ponder justice, seek technical improvements and a better social order, they were able to cultivate a passionate love of truth and justice, and a readiness to sacrifice their life and wellbeing for them and a determination to preach the truth and bring about justice.

The message of truth and justice passed from individuals with conviction and understanding to a small group of people for whom cultivation was a pleasure, and in this circle it found receptive followers to whom the believers from among the protected minority would attach themselves. Force or consent would instil the doctrine of truth and justice in law and custom. Just as cultivated individuals strove as a result of some inner need to implement justice and to disseminate truth, so the reasoning minority found it best, for their own good, to share *some* of the comforts of life with the majority and to extend somewhat the number of people with knowledge. I have already said that civilization depended for its security on an awareness of the need for such an extension. But understanding spread slowly; petty calculation always induced people to give up as few comforts as possible to others and to restrict as far as possible the sphere of knowledge to which they might have access. A reluctance to think induced people to see in all new topical demands something at odds with the social order, something criminal and sinful, and so the monopolists of knowledge for the most part opposed its progress by every means. The feebleness of this progress inevitably gave rise to a poor understanding of human virtue and the forms of justice. Hence the long insecurity of civilizations; hence too their constant tendency to stagnate; hence, finally, that extreme paucity of progress among mankind to which reference was made in the preceding letter, in spite of the fact that the few great men down the millennia and the progress of a barely appreciable minority have been paid for with thousands of millions of lives, oceans of blood, countless sufferings and the interminable labor of many generations.

Mankind has paid dearly in order that a few thinkers might sit in their studies and speak of *its progress*. It has paid dearly for the few seminaries where it has fostered its teachers, who have as yet, however, brought it little benefit. If one were to count the educated minority of our own time and the number of lives lost in the past in the struggle for that minority's survival and if one were to assess the labor of all those generations which have toiled just to subsist themselves and to cultivate others, and if one were to calculate how many human lives had had to be lost and what amount of labor had needed to be expended for each individual who lives a life that is *in some degree* human—if all this were done, then probably some of our contemporaries would be horrified to discover how much capital, in terms of blood and labor, it had cost to nurture them. Their sensitive consciences may be put at ease by the fact that such calculations are impossible.

Perhaps, though, one should be horrified not so much at the fact that the minority's progress has cost a great deal but rather at the fact that it has cost *so* much and that *so* little has been done for that price. If the minority had taken greater pains, and at an earlier date, to spread its attainments in the field of culture and thought, then the number of lives lost and the amount of labor expended would not have been so great; the outlay on each of us would have been smaller and it would not have increased so greatly from one generation to the next. We have no control over the laws of natural necessity and so a man of good sense must come to terms with them, confine himself to a calm study of them and, in so far as possible, make use of them for his own ends. Nor do we have control over history:[17] the past furnishes us only with facts which may enable us to improve the future. We are responsible for the sins of our fathers only in so far as we perpetuate these sins and take advantage of them without attempting to rectify their consequences. We have a certain degree of control only over the future, since our thoughts and our actions are the material out of which the whole content of truth and justice will in the future be fashioned. Each generation is responsible to posterity only for what it *could* have done and did not do. Consequently we too, when we come to be judged by posterity, shall have had to have solved these questions: what amount of unavoidable, natural evil resides in the process to which we give the high-sounding name of historical progress? To what extent did our forbears, who have made it possible for us, the civilized minority, to take advantage of the benefits that this progress can confer, needlessly increase and prolong the sufferings and labors of the majority, who were never able to take advantage of these benefits? In what event may the responsibility for this evil fall on us too in the eyes of future generations?

The law of the struggle for survival is so universal in the animal world that we have not the slightest grounds for indicting mankind in its primeval stage, when this law applied to mankind too, before a sense of mutual solidarity awakened in people and before they felt a need for truth and justice. Since this sense could hardly awaken while people were busy destroying one another and before they replaced killing with exploitation, we have to look on both the incalculable period of struggle among individuals and perhaps a considerable part of the period of struggle among families as merely a zoological fact.

One can hardly imagine the accumulation of knowledge, the development of notions of rights and obligations in the beginning as anything other than a process taking place in individuals placed in particularly advantageous circumstances, that is to say in individuals who had leisure, better food and a better upbringing at the expense of other individuals who furnished the former with this leisure, food and upbringing by themselves giving more labor, if not at the cost of their own lives or by dint of considerable sufferings. Before one can study, one must have teachers. The majority can become cultivated only through undergoing the influence of the more cultivated minority. Consequently mankind either had to forego any cultivation or the majority had to bear the fortunate minority on its shoulders, labor for it, and suffer and perish because of it. This would also appear to be a law of nature. In view of it we have either to say we just do not want cultivation bought at such a price, or to look on this too as an anthropological fact. But at the beginning of the preceding letter we agreed on the moral needs which progress presupposes, so we should be contradicting ourselves if we were to accept that we might repudiate cultivation in general. Let us come to terms with the fact that humanity, in order to cultivate itself, had to get ready, at very, very high cost, a pedagogical seminary and a more cultivated minority so that science and life's many-sided practical work, the thought and technology, accumulated in these centers, might constantly spread to a greater and greater number of people.

The necessary, natural evil in progress is confined to the aforegoing, and beyond the bounds of these laws the responsibility of mankind, and of the civilized minority in particular, begins. All the blood shed in history that was shed not in the straight struggle for survival, but in the period when man's right to live was more or less clearly recognized, is blood shed criminally and the generation which shed it is accountable for it. Every civilized minority which did not wish to *civilize,* in the broadest sense of the word, bears responsibility for all those sufferings, of its contemporaries and of posterity, which it *could* have eliminated if it had not confined itself to the role of *representative* and *custodian* of civilization but had instead taken on the role of civilization's *moving force.*

If we assess history's panorama up to the present time from this point of view then we shall probably have to admit that every historical generation has shed rivers of blood without even having the struggle for survival as an excuse, and that almost always and everywhere the minority, while taking pride in its civilization, has done very little indeed to spread this civilization. A few individuals have taken pains to extend the field of knowledge among mankind; a still smaller number to strengthen thought and to seek the most just forms for society; but the individuals from the civilized minority who have striven to put such forms into effect are to be found in the most inconsequential numbers. Many brilliant civilizations have paid with their downfall for this inability to link the interests of a large number of individuals to their survival. In all civilizations without exception a large proportion of the people who have enjoyed the comforts of culture have had no thought for all those who have not enjoyed that culture and could not enjoy it, and still less have they thought about the price at which the comforts of life and thought which they have acquired have been bought. But there have always been plenty of people who, at each stage of civilization, have deemed this stage the limit of social development and have bridled at any critical attitude towards it, any attempt to spread the benefits of civilization to a larger number of people, to diminish the toil and suffering of the majority who did not enjoy this civilization and to instil a greater element of truth into thought and a greater element of justice into social forms. If these proponents of stagnation have only on very rare occasions succeeded in putting up an effective obstacle in the way of social progress then they have often managed to slow it down and intensify the sufferings of the majority.

In view of this we must accept that the benefits of modern civilization have been paid for not merely with *unavoidable* evil, but also with an enormous amount of completely *unnecessary* evil, the responsibility for which rests with previous generations of the civilized minority, partly because they have been unconcerned and partly because they have directly opposed any civilizing activity. This evil in the past we can no longer remedy. The suffering generations of the majority have died without relief from their labor. The present civilized minority is taking advantage of their labor and sufferings. Moreover, it is taking advantage still of the sufferings and labor of an enormous number of its contemporaries and can have an influence on the increase in the labor and sufferings of their descendants. Since we bear and shall bear a moral responsibility before posterity for this last circumstance, historical examination of the price of the progress that has been achieved leads one to ask the following practical question: what means does the present generation have to reduce its responsibility? If living individuals of different degrees of cultivation were to ask themselves what they might do in order not to have to answer to posterity for the new sufferings of humanity and if they all *clearly understood their business,* then the replies would of course be different.

A member of the majority, struggling every day for physical survival, as his ancestors did in the early periods in the life of mankind, would say to himself: "Fight as you know how and as best you can! Uphold your right to live and the right of those to whom you are attached! That was the law of your forefathers; your position is no better than theirs was; this is the only law for you too."

A less fortunate member of the same majority, in whom civilization had awakened a sense of his human worth, but who had gone no further than that, would say to himself: "Fight as you know how and uphold your worth and that of others as best you can, die for it if necessary!"

A member of the civilized minority, who wished only to increase his own pleasure and make certain of it, but was inclined to see it more in the field of life's comforts than in the field of thought, would say to himself: "The position of the majority needs to be improved if you are to prosper: what you sacrifice out of today's benefits with this end in view will come back to you in as much as everything else will be more secure, you will have great tranquility in which to enjoy those benefits which you have retained, and you will have great influence on the majority which, in spite of its unfortunate position, is all the same a force. So study where your *real* advantage lies: strive to improve the position of others: that is the most useful thing you can do."

A member of that small group among the minority who see their pleasure in their own cultivation, in seeking out truth and implementing justice, would say to himself: "Each comfort which I enjoy, each idea which I have had the leisure to acquire or formulate has been bought with the blood, sufferings or toil of millions. The past I cannot rectify, and however dearly my cultivation might have been bought I cannot renounce it: it is the very ideal that prompts me to act. Only an ineffectual and undeveloped person is crushed under the responsibility which lies upon him and flees from evil to the Thebaids[18] or to the grave. Evil must be remedied as far as possible, but this may be done only in life. One must *redeem* evil by one's deeds in life.[19] I shall absolve myself from responsibility for the bloody price of my cultivation if I use this very cultivation to reduce evil in the present and the future. If I am a cultivated person, then I am *obliged* to do this and this obligation is not at all onerous for me, since it coincides with what I find pleasurable: by seeking and spreading more truths, clarifying my ideas about the most just social order and striving to put it into effect, I am increasing my own pleasure and at the same time doing everything I can for the suffering majority in the present and the future. And so my job is defined by one simple rule: live in accordance with the ideal which you yourself have set yourself, as the ideal of a *cultivated* man!"

This would all be so easy and simple if all individuals understood the matter, but the trouble is that very few do understand it. Only a part of those people in the first category and a few of the remainder comply with the aforegoing rules. Others among those who struggle for their physical survival do not defend themselves sufficiently energetically; not because they do not know how to do so or are not able to do so, but because they lack the determination and are apathetic. A majority of people in the second category sacrifice their dignity for their daily bread and demean themselves in their own estimation without all the same having any chance to get out of their predicament. A majority of the people in the third category do not understand where their own advantage lies, act in accordance with routine and are not able to enjoy their *pleasure in peace,* that is to say, do exactly what they aspire to. And the majority of people in the last category either set up idols in place of truth and justice, or they confine themselves to truth and justice in thought, not in life, or they refuse to see how tiny is the minority that enjoys the benefits of the progress of civilization.

And the price of this progress keeps rising...

1868-69

Pyotr Lavrovich Lavrov
PROGRAM OF THE JOURNAL "FORWARD!" ("VPERED!") (Extract)[20]

Paramount for us is the premise that the reconstruction of Russian society must be carried out not only with the welfare of the people *as its objective,* not only *for the benefit* of the people, but also *by* the people. The contemporary Russian activist must, in our opinion, abandon the obsolete view that revolutionary ideas formulated by a small section of the more highly developed minority may be imposed on the people, that socialist revolutionaries, having successfully overthrown the central government, may take its place and introduce a new order by means of legislation, thus conferring benefits on the unprepared mass. We do not want any new coercive authority to take the place of the old, whatever the source of the new authority might be. The future Russian social order, which we have resolved to promote, must put into effect the demands of the majority, demands acknowledged and understood by the majority itself. Given the unpreparedness of the majority and its low level of literacy we cannot address ourselves directly to it. We address ourselves to that portion of the civilized Russian minority which understands that the future belongs to the people, that the exploitation of the people must end and will inevitably end one way or the other, and that they have merely to join the ranks of the people or give up the idea of any progressive activity of which they might be capable. It is the responsibility of this section of the civilized Russian minority not to impose its own ideas on the people, with a view to conferring benefits on the majority, but to explain to the people their true needs and the best ways of satisfying these needs and to point out to them the force which resides in them but of which they are not aware and therefore cannot use to crush their enemies and secure a better situation for themselves. Anyone who has the welfare of the people at heart should seek not to set himself up in authority with the help of a successful revolution and lead the people towards some goal clearly perceived only by the leaders; rather he should seek to make the people consciously set themselves goals and consciously strive towards these goals and he should seek to become no more than the instrument of these social strivings when the time comes.

1873

Pyotr Lavrovich Lavrov
KNOWLEDGE AND REVOLUTION (Extracts)[21]

We are, I hope, agreed that nobody has the right to foist on the people his own program, to seize power and set up on the basis of his own lofty individual reason a new and better order which would *grant* the Russian peasants autonomy for the commune and socialist ownership of the land and a federation of free peasant centers and all those benefits which can be so deftly and smoothly drawn up on paper, when one is alone with one's brimming thoughts, in the absence of all real obstacles, all the real multiformity of the conditions in which the people dwell, all the real routine which weighs so heavily on our people as on any other society. I think I shall not be mistaken if I say that you too grant us—us, who are separated from the people by one and a half centuries of history, estranged from them by virtue of our way of thinking and way of life, and by the tradition of serfdom, estranged still more as a result of their mistrust which is so difficult to overcome—a single role, the role of initiators, expounders, assistants to the people; the movement which must make them masters of the Russian land you expect to come from the people themselves; the program for the new order which will determine the future of Russia must come from the people themselves and the regulations, statutes and declarations which will give shape to the order we expect will be written at the people's bidding. Do we not agree on all this?

And it is not only in these theoretical fundamentals that we do not differ. I think we go further, in certain practical effects which flow from these things.

You do not belong to that group who intend to help the Russian people by setting up schools, rural banks, hospitals, consumers' and producers' associations as *efficacious* medicines which might at the present time safeguard the people from the ills which are wearing them out. People infected by this sickly illusion belong to another type of contemporary pathological phenomena among our youth, to another category of infected people. Some day I may have occasion to return to them but now, in addressing myself to you, I need not dwell on these illusions. We are both agreed, I think, that these *are* illusions; that you cannot drain the sea by scooping it out with a spoon, or cure the people by giving microscopic local aid. We are agreed that all this is perhaps not bad as a temporary palliative to reduce acute pain at a particular moment and in a particular place among a particular small group of people; but not only is all this not essential, rather it distracts the people from meditation on the real, general cause of their sufferings and encourages them to think that these elemental social ailments can be cured by trivial local medicines; this reduces the force of their annoyance with the whole order which oppresses them and puts off the moment when they will erupt. For you and me assistance for the people consists in one thing alone: making them realize the cause, the real, basic cause of their sufferings, pointing out to them that they have it in their power to eradicate this cause and then sharing with them the fortunes and dangers of struggle for a better future. This is the only possible cure for their sufferings, the only cure that gets to the root of the matter. Schools and hospitals and associations may be *means* in this activity, but such activity is the only essential thing.

Thus we are agreed too that the role of the leading members of our youth, who desire the wellbeing of the people, consists, firstly, in getting close to the people; secondly, in preparing them for the moment when they will be able to throw off the yoke of the state which crushes them, to destroy the old restrictive forms of social life and to found a new society in accordance with their *own* requirements, in conformity with their *own* tasks; finally, thirdly, the role of the leading members of our youth will consist in helping the people, *with all the forces the youth has acquired,* to found, in the difficult time of struggle, an order of things that is not ephemeral but *durable.* I hope that you will not contradict me in this.

But one step further and we differ; our disagreement begins.

I told you that our Russian youths must prepare themselves for this important morally binding role by cultivating their minds in the most serious way; but only thorough knowledge provides this preparation, and therefore anyone who seriously desires the wellbeing of the people, anyone who gets close to them with a view to conducting *fruitful* revolutionary propaganda, anyone who has it in mind to take part in the future revolution in order that the people may establish their supremacy in the Russian land *in a lasting way* must cultivate his mind by means of scientific critical thinking,[22] and enrich his thought with thorough knowledge. Knowledge, I repeat, is a necessary preparation for revolutionary activity, a necessary tool if this activity is to yield lasting victory as opposed to momentary success. Knowledge is the basic force of the revolution which is being prepared, the basic force by which the revolution is put into effect.

* * *

Let us take the people's revolutionary in the three phases of his activity...: as propagandist of the revolution before the eruption of the people, as participant in the revolution during the struggle itself and as participant in the creation of a new social order after the conclusion of this struggle.

You are among the people. You have won their trust. You are listened to and believed. You want to shake their diffidence about their own strength, you want to explain to them the real purport of the sufferings which they experience, which they sense but do not understand; you want to point out to them their real enemies, the real root of the evil which hangs over them; you want to point out the means at their disposal, tell them how to act to throw off, trample on and destroy this evil. What are you going to tell them about and how are you going to speak to them?

You will point out to them the ailments which are destroying them, the mortality rate among their children, the violent shortening of their life-span, the sapping of their strength, the degeneration that is threatening them. You will tell them that it is not the laws of nature that have sent them this evil, that by comparison with them rich folk rarely fall ill, that the average life-span of rich folk is longer, that the offspring of the rich have a better future, that the roots of this evil lie in the social situation, the social environment, social injustice.

But in order to explain this one must know it oneself, and not by hearsay, not from a conversation with a student friend from the medical faculty, not from some popular booklet read in haste. You must understand and assimilate the findings of social hygiene, understand the forms of illness which occur among the people, know statistics about their incidence and their characteristics, know the physiological processes of falling ill, infection, exhaustion; know the social conditions which give rise to typhus[23] and mortality among the new-born. Unless you know all these facts clearly enough not merely to understand them yourself but to put them across to an ignorant, illiterate person, to put them across in a graphic, tangible and intelligible way, then your propaganda will have no effect, or else you will have to make up facts, to think up comparisons, you'll have to lie to the people... And to make things up, *to lie to the people*... To lie to the people?.. No, no man or woman among the best representatives of our youth can sink so low that he or she could even countenance this...

You will talk to the people about their economic ruin, about the impossibility of their escaping the fateful process of pauperization or avoiding the oppressive force of capital by dint of their personal labor; about the fact that it is not a particular instance, or a bad year, or a rogue of a contractor, or a district constable that is to blame for this; that the people suffer everywhere, are ruined everywhere and exploited everywhere; that it is the very social foundations of the order that are to blame for this, the injustice of the order for the weak, the poor, the majority.

You will talk about the state of affairs in Russia, the limitless arbitrariness of the tsar, the obsequious ministers, the servility of the courtiers, the rapacious officials, injustice in the courts, the lawlessness of the Russians, about the way in which Russia has arrived at its present position and what has been done to the Russian people by the Muscovite tsars and Petersburg emperors and predatory boyars and dull-witted priests and bribe-taking scriveners and tyrannical provincial governors.

But all this too one needs to find out for oneself if one is to explain and recount it. And for this too one needs to study, to understand the laws by which capital is accumulated and rent produced, the laws of the fluctuation of prices; one needs to know about the distribution of labor and have statistics about it; one needs to know about the life of the worker and the exploiter in Russia and abroad; one needs to know the history of Russia, and not from text-books which speak merely of "glorious conquests," "wise tsars," "valiant generals" and the "prospering people" but from the works of specialists who are more serious and therefore less constrained in what they say.

Everywhere knowledge and science are needed, otherwise propaganda will have no effect or else *lies* will be told to the people to whom you are preparing to devote your whole life and work.

* * *

I am not going to list the other possible subjects of revolutionary propaganda, but all of them, with very few exceptions, require study, all of them require of you, members of the progressive Russian youth, time and labor devoted to serious intellectual preparation of yourself for the role of prophet of the people's freedom, for the role of one who explains to the Russian people their rights and strength, and the injuries done to them and their duty to put up with these injuries no longer. Anyone who has picked up some "new ideas" from a fleeting conversation or got hold of some of the information he needs at third hand, from popular booklets, will realize his complete inadequacy for the job he has undertaken at his first attempt actually to conduct propaganda among the people; he will realize to what extent he would be acting in good faith [i.e., to a very small extent] if he were to face the people as one who could explain things that were not clear to him, as a preacher of principles which he had not properly thought about himself, as a propagandist of ideas he himself had not digested. If in this eventuality he is not much troubled by his conscience—I hope that there are not many among you who would be thus untroubled—if he resolves to *pretend* to know and understand, then he may very easily come to grief. Our people are ignorant but quick on the uptake and, most importantly, distrustful. They'll quickly catch the slightest lie if they have a chance to check it, and once a preacher has plainly given himself away he has lost credit in the estimation of his listeners. One thing and one thing alone sustains people from civilized society in their dealings with the people, and that is trust. Once the masses have ceased to trust them, these people become in the eyes of the masses lying little *barin*'s sons[24] who come to them for God knows what purpose. Any such lying, once exposed, is not only morally wrong but is also a social evil which does great harm to the general revolutionary cause in Russia. The success of the revolution depends on the alliance and mutual trust of the people and our radical intelligentsia. Anything that shakes or weakens this alliance directly undermines revolutionary propaganda. Any slip made by our youth on this path may have a very bad effect. It is difficult for the youth of the civilized classes to get close to the people and inspire their trust, but if you have overcome this difficulty then you must, in the name of the success of the revolutionary cause, take the field fully armed, having inspected your armor and prepared yourself properly for your difficult role.

But let us turn to the second phase of revolutionary activity.

Let us suppose that the popular uprising has begun. Let us suppose that the struggle is going on in various parts of Russia, on the Volga, the Oka and the Dnepr.[25] The Russian state, be it in the form of the present unlimited Empire or in a constitutional form after the model of one of the European states, is harnessing all its energies to survive, to crush the people, to keep power and ownership in the hands of the *ruling* classes. It has tradition on its side. It has routine on its side. It has organization on its side. It also has on its side the not inconsiderable intellectual forces of all those who are nourished by the juices of power, live off the state organization and see that the sources of their wellbeing will be destroyed come the popular revolution. All these things represent very serious obstacles, enemies with which one has to reckon, enemies which may on more than one occasion place the revolutionary party in a difficult position. The struggle will not be easy. Victory will be uncertain. Among the ranks of our enemies there will be opponents who are dangerous and clever and who understand the ways in which we can be hurt. And we shall need all of our forces, in their entirety, for we should not delude ourselves into believing that they will be immense. We have already agreed above that it is quite impossible to rectify the lack of education among the people while the present state of affairs obtains, until the popular revolution has succeeded. One can hardly count on a particularly significant portion of our intelligentsia accompanying the people into a struggle which is extremely dangerous and, what is more, incompatible with the interests of the intelligentsia as a class. Only those with conviction will accompany the people, those who have developed morally and become aware that this *must* be done; those who sense with particular acuity Russia's distress, the sufferings of her people and the immoral position of a civilized class which has grown up at the expense of the majority and cannot help but exploit that majority in the present state of affairs. But there never was a very great number of such people, nor will there be a very great number of them.

Thus, in the forthcoming struggle every unit, every extra bit of strength, every extra resource will be important. The future of Russia, the future of the people is at stake; consequently every kopeck must count. Every one of us, fighters for these priceless benefits, not only will give and must give *all of himself* when the difficult moment comes, but must also arm himself as best he can, with whatever he may; he must lay in store every possible weapon for this struggle; he must forge for himself whatever arms he lacks; he is bound to procure every force that is available to him.

But we have already agreed, I think, that one of the mighty historical forces is *knowledge*. We shall follow M. A. Bakunin in saying "ignorance is the source of social impotence." And surely this force, whose importance is acknowledged by ourselves and by all those who are like-minded whatever faction of the socio-revolutionary movement they belong to, surely this force should not be willingly and needlessly rejected out of some unhealthy fear that it will corrupt you and make you into the likeness of those philistines who count fishes' scales, measure the angles of crystals, record the number of lines at a given point on the spectrum, argue until they are foaming at the mouth about some Sanskrit root and walk with indifference past the outrages perpetrated by the state or past the sufferings of the people?[26] Come, come! What is there in common between young people who study science in order to solve life's problems and who wish to understand truth in the serious sense of the word in order that they may bear the fruits of this truth to the people, that they may apply them in their struggle for the people—[what is there in common between these people] and these snails of knowledge for whom some microscopic little fact which they have discovered can overshadow the whole world and all life's questions? They are the impotent slaves of science, chained in one of the dark corners and obediently turning one of the millions of millstones on which science prepares man's pabulum. Revolutionaries with a scientific training are science's free and mighty lovers to whom she gladly gives everything that she can at a particular moment, with whom she goes hand in hand towards bold enterprises, whom she heartens with magical words at times of danger and whom she infuses with redoubled strength in the moment of struggle. Love her, live with her; she, real science, will never make you indifferent to the sufferings of the people, rather she will show you where to find the most effective means with which to treat them and she will point out the charlatanism of those empiricists who offer the people toxic salves and soporific potions; she, real science, will never counsel resignation in the face of the outrages perpetrated by authority, rather she will help you to descry the weak spot of this authority and to discover how to burrow under it, where it might best be struck and by what it might best be shaken. And do you want lightly to reject this faithful friend and mighty assistant, this huge force, at a time when you face such a difficult struggle, when you are threatened by so many hardened, skillful and well armed enemies? I beg your pardon, but I think this is some sort of inexplicable madness.

There will come, I hope, a third phase to your revolutionary activity. The oppressive state will collapse. The people will become masters of their actions, their forces, their resources, masters of the Russian land. At that

point will come the moment which will be most difficult for you, just as it
has been the most critical for all revolutions, for all history's combatants.
Surrounded by a generation which has grown up with the ways of the old
state and is deeply affected by the old cultural practices, the victorious
combatants, bearing the inevitable traces of the social order in which they
have grown up, must promote a form of social organization in which
desirable ideals must be brought into being given the *possible* conditions
obtaining and in accordance with the *necessary* laws of things. The victors
know too that they are surrounded by enemies, people plotting against
them and people who are apathetic; that every mistake they make in the
building of the new will bring forth bitter criticism, provide ammunition
for their opponents and represent a weak spot on which blows will shower
down from all sides. These blows must be foreseen and averted. One must
adopt an objective and critical attitude to the cause one passionately loves,
to the task of putting into effect the idea that has filled one's life, and calmly
weigh up the possibilities, bowing to necessity. And at the moment when
the people triumph, a people inevitably lacking knowledge, inevitably
lacking the habit of formulating a critical, comprehensive view of things,
inevitably capable of making mistakes about the means needed to attain an
aim they clearly see—on whom does the responsibility to give counsel lie,
the responsibility to make criticisms, the responsibility to point out
possible mistakes, if not on those who consider themselves called upon to
help the people as representatives of the progressive intelligentsia, as
representatives of moral conviction arrived at through critical thought? On
whom, if not on you and your comrades?

But where might you find pointers in this eventuality if not in science
and its findings, arrived at by its methods? If knowledge has furnished you
with the material necessary for the preparation of the revolution, if it has
served you as your most trusty assistant in the course of the struggle, then it
becomes your master, your only leader, the very essence of your activity
when it comes to promoting the organization of the new order. While
revolution is being preached ardent love of the cause and talent and quick-
wittedness may on occasion—though more rarely than people think—
make up for gaps in one's knowledge. In the course of the revolutionary
struggle vigorous determination plays the greatest role, and although
knowledge is a very important force, which it is unforgivable to disregard,
nevertheless it is not in any event the only force. But when it becomes
necessary to foresee and evaluate, to weigh up the odds and examine the
possibilities critically, then nothing can replace science, nothing can even
make up for gaps in it. The victorious revolutionary who has not sharpened
his thinking by critical methods, and enriched his mind with the proper
information, must, if he is acting in good faith, stop trying to do anything
for the cause he loves as soon as the struggle is over and the enemy
overthrown and the last blow struck. The more passionately he loves his
social ideal the more he jeopardizes calm discussion of the new

organization of society if he has not made a critical study of the ways in which social ideas in general may be put into effect. It is precisely his sincerity and his passion that make him liable to be carried away and prone to error; for this passion makes it the more probable that he will not be able calmly to discuss the obstacles and difficulties that arise. It is precisely this passion that increases the danger that the building erected by the victorious revolutionaries will be an insecure one.

1873

Mikhail Alexandrovich Bakunin
STATISM AND ANARCHY: Appendix A (Extracts)[27]

Among the Russian people there exist on the largest scale the first two elements to which we may point as prerequisites for social revolution. They can boast extreme poverty and also exemplary slavery. Their sufferings are countless and they bear them not patiently but with a deep and passionate despair which has already expressed itself historically on two occasions, in two terrible explosions, the revolt of Stenka Razin and the Pugachev revolt,[28] and which right up until the present time continues to manifest itself in a constant series of individual peasant revolts.

What prevents them from carrying out a victorious revolution? Is it the lack of some ideal common to the people as a whole which would give sense to a popular revolution, give it some definite object and without which, as we said above, a simultaneous and general uprising of the whole people is out of the question and the very success of revolution consequently out of the question too? But it would hardly be true to say that no such ideal had yet taken shape among the Russian people.

If there were no such ideal, if it had not taken shape in the people's consciousness, at least in general outline, then one would have to give up all hope of a Russian revolution because such an ideal emerges from the very depths of the people's life and is inevitably the result of the people's historical experience, their aspirations, sufferings, protests and struggle and is at the same time a sort of graphic and generally comprehensible expression, always simple, of their real needs and hopes.

Of course, if the people do not themselves fashion such an ideal then nobody will be in a position to give it to them. In general we should note that no one, no individual, society or people, can be given something which does not already exist in them not merely in embryo but even in a certain stage of development... One would have to be an absolute idiot or an incurable doctrinaire to imagine that one might give the people anything, bestow on them any sort of material benefit or new intellectual or moral content, any new truth, and lend their life at will some new direction or, as the late Chaadaev said thirty-six years ago with precisely the Russian people in mind, write on them what one pleased, as on a blank sheet of paper.[29]

* * *

Does any such ideal exist in the mentality of the Russian people? There is no doubt that it does exist and one does not even need to delve too far into the historical consciousness of our people in order to define its main features.

The first and main feature is the conviction, which is universal among the people, that the land, all the land, belongs to the people who water it with their sweat and make it productive with the labor of their own hands. The second, and equally important, feature is that the right to the utilization of the land belongs not to the individual but to the whole commune, the *mir*,[30] which periodically divides it up among individuals; the third feature, of equal importance to the two preceding ones, is a quasi-absolute autonomy, communal self-government, and, as a result of this, the thoroughly hostile attitude of the commune towards the state.

Those are the three main features which underlie the Russian popular ideal. In essence they fully correspond to the ideal which has of late been taking shape in the consciousness of the proletariat of the Latin countries, which are now incomparably closer to social revolution than the Germanic countries. However the Russian popular ideal is obscured by three other features which distort its character and very greatly hamper and slow down its realization; features which we must therefore fight against with all our strength, and against which struggle is the more possible for the fact that it is already being waged among the people themselves.

These three obscuring features are: 1) the patriarchal quality of Russian life; 2) the absorption of the individual by the *mir;* 3) faith in the tsar.

One might add as a fourth feature the Christian faith, in its official Orthodox or its sectarian forms; but, in our view, this question has nothing like the same importance in Russia that it has in Western Europe, even in Protestant as well as Catholic countries. Social revolutionaries do not of course disregard it, and make use of every opportunity while in the presence of the people to deliver a deadly truth to the Lord God of Sabaoth and to his theological, metaphysical, political and legal representatives, and his representatives among the police and bourgeois economists, on earth. But they do not give priority to the religious question, for they believe that the people's superstition, naturally linked with ignorance, is all the same rooted not so much in this ignorance as in the people's poverty, in their material sufferings and in the unprecedented oppression of every sort which they endure each day; that religious notions and fables, this fantastic susceptibility to the absurd, are a practical phenomenon rather than a theoretical one and so less a delusion of the mind than a protest of the life will, and passion against life's unbearable constraints; that the Church is for the people a sort of heavenly ale-house, just as the ale-house is something of a heavenly church on earth; in the ale-house, as in the church, the people forget just for a moment their hunger, their oppression and their degradation, and endeavor to deaden the memory of their daily misery in mindless faith, in the one case, and in wine in the other. One form of intoxication is worth about as much as the other.

Social revolutionaries know this and therefore believe that religiosity among the people can be killed off only by social revolution, and certainly not by the abstract and doctrinaire propaganda of so-called free thinkers. These gentlemen, the free thinkers, are bourgeois from head to toe, incorrigible metaphysicians in their ways, habits and style of life even when they call themselves positivists and imagine themselves to be materialists. All the time they think life is derived from thought, that it is some sort of realization of a preconceived idea, as a result of which they contend that thought, including of course their own barren thought, should govern life itself; and they do not realize that thought, on the contrary, is derived from life and that in order to change thought one must first of all change life. Give the people an ample human life and you will be surprised how rational their ideas are.

* * *

The common people are not doctrinaires and they are not philosophers. They have neither the leisure to concern themselves with many questions at one and the same time nor the habit of doing so. Once they are carried away by one question they forget all others. Consequently our direct responsibility is to place before them the main question on whose solution more than any other the people's liberation depends. But this question has been indicated by the very position of the people, by their whole life—this is an economic and political question, economic in the sense of social revolution and political in the sense of the destruction of the state. To preoccupy the people with the religious question is to distract them from the real cause, to betray their cause.

The business of the people is solely to realize the popular ideal, making such corrections as may be possible because they are rooted in the people themselves and lending this ideal the best course which leads most directly and rapidly towards the goal.[31] We have pointed to the three unfortunate features which mainly obscure the ideal of the Russian people. Let us now note that the last two (the absorption of the individual in the *mir* and veneration of the tsar) are essentially derived, as natural results, from the first, that is to say, from the patriarchal quality of Russian life, and that this patriarchal quality is therefore the main historical ill, though unfortunately one that is entirely popular in character, which we are obliged to combat with all our strength.

It has distorted the whole of Russian life, and has given it that quality of obtuse immobility, impenetrable filth, fundamental falsehood, grasping hypocrisy and, lastly, slavish servitude which make it unendurable. The despotism of the husband, the father and then the elder brother have turned the family, already immoral as a result of its legal and economic principles, into a school for triumphant coercion and tyranny, for everyday domestic meanness and depravity. The whited sepulcher[32] is an excellent expression with which to define the Russian family. The good Russian family-man, if he is really a good man but one without character, is simply a genial swine, innocent and meek, a being who is alive to nothing, who wants nothing definite and does good and bad indiscriminately and thus seemingly unintentionally at almost one and the same time. His actions are determined far less by any aim than by circumstances, by the disposition of the moment and chiefly by environment; having grown used to obeying in the family he carries on obeying and bending with the wind in society too; he was created to be and to remain a slave, but a despot he will not be. He will not have the strength for that. He will therefore not do any flogging himself but he will certainly detain the unfortunate person, guilty or not guilty, whom authority has a mind to flog, authority presenting itself to him in three main and sacred forms: as father, *mir* and tsar.

If, though, he is a difficult person, and one with fire, he will be at one and the same time both slave and despot, a despot behaving tyrannically towards everyone who is beneath him and who depends on his whim. His lords are the *mir* and the tsar. If he himself is head of a family, he will be an unbridled despot in his own home but a servant of the *mir* and a slave of the tsar.

The commune is his world.[33] It is nothing other than a natural extension of his family, his clan. Therefore the same patriarchal principle prevails in it, the same vile despotism and the same ignoble obedience, and for that reason the same fundamental injustice and the same complete denial of every personal right that prevails in the family itself. The decisions of the *mir,* whatever they might be, are law. "Who will dare to go against the *mir*?", the Russian peasant exclaims with surprise. We shall see that apart from the tsar, his officials and nobles, who really stand outside the *mir* or rather above it, there is among the Russian people itself one person who dares to go against the *mir*: that is the brigand. This is why brigandage is such an important historical phenomenon in Russia—the first rebels, the first revolutionaries in Russia, Pugachev and Stenka Razin, were brigands.

In the *mir* only old men, heads of families, have the right to vote. Young people who are not separated from their parents, be they unmarried or even married, must carry out orders and obey. But over the commune, as over all communes, stands the tsar, the universal patriarch and founder of the clan, the father of all Russia. His power is therefore limitless.

Each commune is a self-contained whole, as a result of which—and this is one of Russia's main misfortunes—no commune has or even feels the need to have any independent organic link with other communes. They are united to one another only through the mediation of the tsar, the people's father,[34] only by dint of his supreme, paternal power.

We say that this is a great misfortune. Clearly such disunity enfeebles the people and dooms all their revolts, which are almost invariably local and unconnected to one another, to inevitable defeat and by that token ensures the triumph of despotic power. This means that it must be one of the main duties of the revolutionary youth to establish, by every possible means and at all costs, vigorous rebellious connections between the disunited communes. It is a difficult task, but not an impossible one, for history shows us that at times of troubles, for example during the internecine strife at the time of the False Dmitry,[35] in the Stenka Razin and Pugachev revolutions, and also in the Novgorod rebellion[36] and at the beginning of the reign of Emperor Nicholas,[37] the communes themselves, with a momentum of their own, attempted to establish this saving connection.

The number of communes is incalculable, and their common tsar, the people's father, stands too far above them, only just below the lord God, for him to deal with them all personally. For the lord God himself, in order to rule the world, needs the service of innumerable heavenly officials and forces, seraphim, cherubim, archangels, six-winged angels and two-winged ones, so it is that much more impossible for the tsar to do without officials. He needs a whole military, civilian and judicial administration and police force. Thus between tsar and people, between tsar and commune, there stands the state with its military, police and bureaucratic apparatus, which is inevitably highly centralized.

Thus the imaginary tsar-father, the guardian and benefactor of the people, is placed high, high up almost in the far, celestial distance, while the real tsar, the tsar-knout, the tsar-thief, the tsar-destroyer, the state,[38] occupies his place. From this the strange fact naturally arises that our people at one and the same time worship the imaginary, fantastic tsar and hate the real tsar who is embodied in the state.

Our common people have a profound and passionate hatred of the state, a hatred of all its representatives in whatever guise they present themselves to them. Until quite recently this hatred was divided between the nobles and the officials, and sometimes it even seemed as if the people hated the former more than the latter, though essentially they hated them both to an equal degree. But since the gentry, as a result of the abolition of serfdom, started to show signs of economic ruin and collapse and to revert to its original condition of a purely service class, the people have enveloped it in their general hatred of the whole official class. Does one need to demonstrate how legitimate their hatred is!

The state has utterly crushed and corrupted the Russian commune which had in any case already been corrupted by its own patriarchal principle. Under the oppression of the state even communal voting has become a fraud and the persons temporarily elected by the people themselves, headmen, elders, peasant police, foremen,[39] have been turned into tools of authority on the one hand, and suborned servants of the rich kulaks[40] peasants on the other. In such conditions the last vestiges of justice, truth[41] and simple love of one's fellow human-beings were bound to disappear from the communes, which had in any case been ruined by state taxes and obligations and squeezed to the limit by the arbitrary behavior of the authorities. Brigandage has more than ever before become the only outlet left to an individual, and a general revolt, revolution, the only outlet left to the people as a whole.

What can our intellectual proletariat, the honest, sincere, totally committed, social-revolutionary Russian youth do in this sort of situation? It must go to the people, undoubtedly, because nowadays it is everywhere the case, and especially in Russia, that there is no longer life, or any cause or future outside the people, outside the multi-million masses of unskilled laborers. But how and for what purpose should one go to the people?

At the present time, following the unhappy outcome of the Nechaev venture,[42] opinions among us on this score seem to be sharply divided; but out of the general mess of ideas two principal and opposite tendencies already stand out. One is of a more pacific and preparatory nature; the other is rebellious and aspires directly to the organization of a force for the people's defense.

The champions of the first tendency do not believe in the real possibility of this revolution. But since they do not wish to and cannot stand by as calm onlookers while the people suffer they resolve to go to the people in order to share these sufferings with them in a brotherly way and at the same time to teach them, to prepare them, not theoretically but in practice, by their own living example. Some will go among the factory workers, and working on the same level with them will try to spread a spirit of communion among them...

Others will try to set up rural colonies in which, besides common utilization of the land which is already so familiar to our peasants, they will promote and apply a principle as yet quite unknown to them, albeit an economically necessary one, the principle of collective cultivation of common land and equal division of their produce or the value of their produce among themselves on the basis of the strictest justice, not juridical but human justice, that is to say requiring more work from the able and strong and less from the less able and weak, and apportioning earnings not according to work but according to the needs of each.[43]

* * *

All this is fine, extremely magnanimous and noble, but hardly practicable. And if the odd individual here and there does succeed, this will be a drop in the ocean, and a drop is far from enough to prepare, stir up and liberate our people; a lot of resources and a lot of vitality will be needed and the results will be too insignificant.

* * *

The other way is the fighting way, the way of rebellion. It is in this way that we believe and it is only from this way that we expect salvation.

Our people plainly need help. They are in such a desperate position that one could raise up any village with no trouble at all. But although any uprising, however unsuccessful, is always useful, nevertheless individual eruptions are not enough. All the villages must be raised up at once. That this is possible is proved by the huge popular movements led by Stenka Razin and Pugachev. These movements prove to us that the ideal which our people strive to realize is really alive in their consciousness, but from their failures we conclude that there are important defects in this ideal which have prevented and are preventing success.

We have named these defects and stated our belief that it is the direct responsibility of our revolutionary youth to counteract them and use every effort to overcome them in the consciousness of the people themselves, and in order to prove that such struggle is possible we have shown that it has long since begun among the people themselves.

War against the patriarchal quality of Russian life is now being waged in almost every village and almost every household: the commune and the *mir* have by now been transformed to such an extent into tools of state power and the arbitrariness of officialdom, things so hateful to the people, that a revolt against the latter becomes at the same time a revolt against the despotism of the commune and the *mir*.

There remains veneration of the tsar; we think that it has very much lost its appeal and weakened in the popular consciousness over the last ten or twelve years, owing to the magnanimous Emperor Alexander's wise policy, which betrays such love of the people. The land-owning, serf-owning noble no longer exists, and he was a lightning-conductor who himself mostly attracted the full force of the storm of the people's hatred. There remains the nobleman or land-owning merchant, the big *kulak,* and most of all there remains the official, the tsar's angel or archangel. But the official carries out the tsar's will. However befuddled our peasant might be by the mindless historical faith in the tsar, he himself is at last beginning to realize this. And how could he fail to realize it! For ten years he has been sending his petitioners and deputies to the tsar from all corners of Russia, and all of them hear from the mouth of the tsar himself just one answer: "You will get no other emancipation!"[44]

No, say the Russian peasant is a boor, if you will, but he is not a fool. But he would have to be a complete fool to fail to see finally, after so many glaring facts and experiences which he has borne himself, that he has no greater enemy than the tsar. To drum it into him, to use every possible means to make him feel this, to use all the lamentable and tragic instances with which the daily life of the people is brimming to show him how all the brutalities, robberies and plunderings which have been carried out by the officials, land-owners, priests and *kulaks* and which make life impossible for him, emanate directly from the power of the tsar, derive support from it and are possible only because of its existence, to prove to him, in a word, that the state which is so hateful to him is the tsar himself and nothing but the tsar—that is the direct responsibility, and the main responsibility now, of revolutionary propaganda.

1873

Pyotr Nikitich Tkachev
[ON HISTORICAL LEAPS]⁴⁵

The fact of the matter is that the causes which brought the Order[46] into being and prepared the ground for its downfall should be sought not in the personal activity of its members but in the general conditions of the economic situation in Europe at that time. The sixteenth century was distinguished by two revolutionary movements that ran parallel to one another: a purely democratic movement, the peasant wars, and a purely bourgeois movement, the uprising of the towns. The first of these movements was suppressed and destroyed; the second was also defeated and arrested, but only for a while and only partially. The defeat of the first was a matter of pure chance; it could have taken place or not taken place; the people's party had just as much chance, or even more, of being victorious as of being defeated: in examining Zimmerman's history of the peasant war,[47] we tried to prove our idea with facts, so there is no need for us to return to this question again now. But, as far as the victory of feudalism over the bourgeoisie is concerned, that was not a simple matter of chance but a fatal, logical, inescapable inevitability. We would appear to be making absolutely contradictory statements, we would appear to be defending obvious paradoxes. In the one case we are trying to prove the possibility of *historical leaps,* in the other we are upholding the theory of *gradual* historical development. Why should the peasants have been able to triumph in the sixteenth century and completely rebuild society according to their own social-democratic program, while the urban bourgeoisie had patiently to wait another two whole centuries for its victory? If a historical leap was possible in the first case, then why was it not possible in the second? This is why: the peasantry was fighting for a change of the very principle that lay at the basis of the social order in question, while the bourgeoisie, leaving the principle untouched, was concerned only to hasten some of its logical consequences. But in as much as the first was possible the second was impossible. Any given economic principle develops according to the laws of its own logic and it is as impossible to change these laws as it is to change the laws of human thought or the laws of our psychological and physiological functions. In the sphere of logical thought it is impossible to proceed from the first premise to the last, passing over the middle one, and in exactly the same way it is impossible in the sphere of the development of a given economic principle to leap directly from a lower rung to a higher one over all the ones in between. Anyone who attempts to make such a leap can count on failure before he starts; he will merely overstrain himself and will waste his strength to no purpose. It is quite a different matter if, leaving aside the old principle, he is going to seek to replace it with a new one. His strivings may very easily be crowned with success, and there will be absolutely nothing utopian about his activity. Thus we come to a conclusion, which appears to be extremely paradoxical but is in essence absolutely correct, that those people whose views are generally regarded as extremely utopian are in fact much more practical than those timid reformers who have the reputation of being the most moderate and supposedly far-sighted politicians. Jan of Leiden[48] and Thomas Müntzer[49] were less utopian than, for example, Wendel Hipler[50] or Weigand;[51] the aspirations of the peasantry were less utopian than the aspirations of the bourgeoisie.

1868

Pyotr Nikitich Tkachev
PROGRAM OF THE JOURNAL "THE TOCSIN" ("NABAT") (Extracts)[52]

The time has come to sound the tocsin. Look! The fire of "economic progress" has already touched the foundations of the life of our people.[53] Under its influence the old forms of our communal way of life are already crumbling, the very "principle of the *obshchina,*" a principle which is supposed to be a cornerstone of the future social structure we all dream of, is being destroyed.

On the ruins of those forms which are being burnt down new forms, the forms of bourgeois life, are coming into being, a class of *kulaks* and people who live off others is developing; the principle of individualism, of economic anarchy, of heartless, grasping egoism, is setting in.

Each day brings us new enemies and creates new social factors which are inimical to us.

The fire is creeping up even to the institutions of our state. Now they are dead, lifeless. Economic progress will stir life in them, breathe new spirit into them and give them the power and strength which they as yet lack.

Today our state is a fiction, a legend which has no roots in the people's life. It is odious to all; in all, even its own servants, it inspires blind malice and servile fear mixed with the lackey's scorn. People are afraid of it because it possesses material strength; but once it loses this strength not a single hand will be raised in its defense.

But tomorrow all today's enemies will stand up for it, tomorrow it will express their interests, the interests of the *kulaks* and bloodsuckers, the interests of private property, the interests of trade and industry, the interests of the bourgeois world which is coming into being.

Today it is absolutely absurd and absurdly absolute.

Tomorrow it will become constitutional and modern, thrifty and prudent.

So hurry!

Sound the Tocsin! Sound the Tocsin!

Today we are a force.

You see, the state, despairing of controlling us, is calling bourgeois society, the intelligentsia, to its aid.

But alas! Its allies refuse to serve it, at least for nothing, and through the mouths of their publicists they say to it: "We hate you ourselves; if you want us to serve you, share all your rights with us; otherwise we had better follow the utopian revolutionaries. They are utopians, we are not afraid of them. If only we could control you, but we shall get the better of them!"

And they send their children into our ranks, while their intelligentsia, with very few exceptions among whom it is considered "base and shameful" to be numbered, stands firmly on our side.

The people, languishing under the yoke of a coarse, barbaric and arbitrary despotism, oppressed, plundered, ruined and deprived of absolutely all human rights, heed us and are in sympathy with us and if it were not for their servile habits, which have been formed historically under the influence of the conditions of their environment, if it were not for their panic when faced with "the powers that be," they would rise up openly against their exploiters and plunderers.

Today our enemies are weak and divided. Only the government with its officials and soldiers stands against us. But these officials and soldiers are no more than soulless automata, senseless, blind and often unconscious instruments in the hands of a few autocrats. Destroy them, and instead of a disciplined and well organized army of living enemies you will find yourself face to face with a disorderly crowd of headless corpses. Consequently, the only strong and dangerous enemy we face today is this insignificant handful of autocrats.

But our whole society is hostile to it too; however heterogeneous the elements of that society may be, it has for long felt the oppressive weight of the present order of things; the toleration of even the most patient is exhausted by uncertainty as to their personal safety and by capricious and absolutely senseless arbitrariness.

Wherever you turn you hear the same phrases: "No, things can't go on like this for long! An end must be put to this! This can't be borne any longer!"

That is today.

But what will things be like tomorrow?..

Do not rely too much on the stupidity of our enemies.

Make use of every moment. Such moments are not frequent in history. To let them slip by means voluntarily to put back the possibility of social revolution for a long time, maybe for ever.

So do not delay!

Sound the Tocsin! Sound the Tocsin!

You've talked for long enough about "preparation" and "preparation." To prepare revolution is not the job of the revolutionary at all. It is prepared by the exploiters—the capitalists, land-owners, priests, police, officials, conservatives, liberals, progressives, etc.

The revolutionary must merely make use of and arrange in a certain way all the given revolutionary elements which are already ripe, which have been shaped by history, which have been nourished by the economic life of the people, which are growing strong and developing thanks to the dull-wittedness of the "protectors," the absurdity of governments with their gendarmes and troops, and thanks, finally, to the sedulous cultivators of the garden of "peaceful" progress and their bourgeois science.

The revolutionary does not prepare revolution; he "makes" it.

So make it! Make it soon! All vacillation, all procrastination is criminal!

Sound the Tocsin! Sound the Tocsin![54]

* * *

We acknowledge anarchy (or, to be more accurate, *what* is usually understood by this word), but only as a desirable "ideal" of the distant future. However, we contend that the word *anarchy* does not fully express the ideal of this future: it indicates only one side of it, one feature—and by no means the essential one—of the future social structure.

Anarchy means *absence of power*. But absence of power is only one of the inevitable, logical consequences of a more fundamental and profound cause, equality.

In exactly the same way that power is not a cause, as anarchists contend, of existing social evils, but merely an inevitable outcome of them.[55]

All social calamities, all social injustice[56] are caused by and derive solely from the inequality of people, physical, intellectual, economic, political and every other sort of inequality.

Consequently, so long as inequality exists in any sphere of human relations whatever, power too will exist. Anarchy is inconceivable, logically inconceivable (not to mention its practical impossibility) unless absolute equality is first established among all members of society. And for that reason the most essential, the most characteristic feature of the society of the future must be expressed not by the word *anarchy* but by the word *equality*. Equality presupposes anarchy, and anarchy freedom; but *equality* and *anarchy* and *freedom* are all concepts which merge into one concept, one word, the word *brotherhood*. Where there is brotherhood, there we find equality too, and where there is equality there we find also absence of power, and freedom.

It follows that no revolution can establish anarchy without having first established brotherhood and equality.

But in order to establish brotherhood and equality, it is necessary in the first place to change the given conditions of a society's way of life, to destroy all those institutions which introduce inequality, enmity, envy and competition into people's lives and to lay a foundation for institutions which introduce into it the opposite principles; in the second place, to change man's nature itself, to re-educate him. This great task can be accomplished, of course, only by people who understand it and who sincerely aspire to carry it out, that is to say people who are highly developed intellectually and morally, that is to say the minority. This minority, by virtue of its higher intellectual and moral level of development, always has and is bound to have intellectual and moral power over the majority.

Consequently the revolutionaries are the people of this minority, and, embodying as they do the best intellectual and moral forces of society, they necessarily possess and, while they remain revolutionaries cannot help but possess, *power.*

Up until the revolution this power has a purely moral, so to speak, spiritual character, and that is why it is quite ineffectual in the struggle with an order of things in which everything is based on crude material strength, and all is subordinated to the advantage of a grasping, self-seeking rapacious egoism. Revolutionaries understand this and seek by means of a revolution involving the use of force to turn their intellectual and moral strength into material strength. It is in this metamorphosis of strength that the basic essence of any true revolution resides. Without it revolution is inconceivable. Intellectual strength, in isolation from material strength, can create only so-called *peaceful progress.* On the other hand, any attack on the existing order of things which is not governed and disciplined by intellectual strength can generate only a chaotic ferment, a senseless, aimless movement that is ultimately always reactionary.

But since in modern societies in general, and in Russia in particular, material strength is concentrated in the hands of the state power, consequently a true revolution—the actual metamorphosis of moral strength into material strength—can be effected only if one condition obtains: if revolutionaries seize state power into their own hands; in other words the immediate, direct aim of the revolution must be nothing other than the capture of governmental power and the transformation of the given *conservative* state into a *revolutionary* one.[57]

* * *

Thus the immediate aim of the revolution must be the seizure of political power, the creation of a revolutionary state. But the seizure of power, while it is a necessary condition of the revolution, is still not the revolution. It is only its prelude. The revolution is effected by the revolutionary state which, on the one hand, struggles with and destroys the conservative and reactionary elements of society, and abolishes all those institutions which impede the establishment of equality and brotherhood, and, on the other hand, brings into being institutions which promote their development.

Thus the activity of the revolutionary state must be twofold: revolutionary-destructive and revolutionary-constructive.

The essence of the first is struggle, and consequently *force*. Struggle can be waged with success only when the following conditions are brought together: centralization, strict discipline, speed, decisiveness and unity in actions. Any concessions, any vacillations, any compromises, the absence of clearly defined spheres of authority and the decentralization of the forces engaged in the struggle weaken their energy, paralyze their activity and remove any chance of victory.

Revolutionary-constructive activity, while it must go hand in hand with destructive activity, must by its very nature rest on principles absolutely opposite to the latter. If destructive activity rests primarily on material strength, constructive activity rests primarily on moral force; the former envisages first and foremost speed and concerted action, the latter the durability of the changes which are being put into effect and the ease with which they can be brought about. The former is effected by force, the latter by conviction; the *ultima ratio* of the one is victory, the *ultima ratio* of the other is the people's will, the people's reason.

* * *

The organization of revolutionary forces.

If the revolutionaries' short-term task, which may in practice be accomplished, amounts to a violent attack on the existing political power with the purpose of seizing this power into their own hands, then it follows that all the efforts of a truly revolutionary party must be directed to the fulfilment of precisely this task. It is easiest and most convenient to fulfil it by means of a state conspiracy. Thus a state conspiracy is, if not the sole means, then at any rate the main and most expedient means of carrying out violent revolution. But anyone who acknowledges the need for a state conspiracy must by the same token acknowledge too the need for a disciplined organization of revolutionary forces.

Not the illusory, impossible, fictitious organization which bourgeois revolutionaries and revolutionary anarchists recommend to the youth but a real organization, an organization which tightly unites the unco-ordinated revolutionary elements into a single living body acting according to a single common plan and subordinated to a single common leadership, an organization based on the centralization of power and the decentralization of revolutionary functions. Only an organization satisfying these conditions can create and carry out a state conspiracy. Only if they have an organization of this sort will revolutionaries, once they have seized power, be in a position to defend it from the claims of hostile parties, intriguers and ambitious politicians, only such an organization will give them any chance of crushing the conservative and reactionary elements of society, and only that sort of organization fully answers to the needs of the struggle, and is entirely in keeping with the type of the *fighting organization.*

The organization recommended by the utopian revolutionaries, on the other hand, an organization which repudiates all subordination and centralization and accepts only a federative link between autonomous revolutionary groups acting independently of one another—an organization of that sort satisfies none of the requirements of a fighting organization. It is not capable of speedy and decisive actions, it leaves the way wide open for mutual animosities and altercations, for all sorts of vacillations and compromises, it is constantly tied in its movements, it cannot pursue any single common plan in a strictly consistent way, and its activity can never have balance, or harmony, or unity.

Not being a fighting organization, it consequently cannot be a revolutionary one either. Indeed it is anti-revolutionary by virtue of its basic principle, the purely bourgeois principle of *individualism* which sets the *personal* above the *general,* the *particular* above the *whole, egoism* above *selflessness.*

This organization, running counter to the basic principle of revolutionary morality and quite unsuitable for revolutionary struggle, does not even satisfy the most elementary requirement of any so-called unlawful society. It cannot and is by its nature bound not to be completely and unconditionally clandestine.

Consequently, its existence in Russia is possible only in the event that it pursues ends which are not only peaceful and legal (in which case it could exist only in constitutional states) but also conservative and reactionary...

Having grouped themselves into a fighting organization and having made the seizure of political power their basic task, the revolutionaries, without losing sight of the aim of conspiracy, must not forget for a moment that this object cannot be successfully achieved without the direct or indirect support of the people.

Hence the activity of the revolutionary party must even before the violent revolution have the same dual nature that it will have (as we said above) after the revolution. On the one hand, it must prepare the seizure of power at the top, on the other the popular uprising at the bottom. The more closely these two activities are linked, the sooner and more successfully each of them will achieve its object. A local popular uprising unaccompanied by a simultaneous attack on the center of power has no chance of success in just the same way that an attack on the center of power and the seizure of power into revolutionary hands, unaccompanied by a popular uprising (albeit a local one), can lead to positive, durable results only in extremely propitious circumstances.

1875

Georgy Valentinovich Plekhanov
OUR DIFFERENCES (Extract) [58]

[The commune]

If one listens to our Populists then one really might think that the Russian commune was an organization quite exceptional in its durability. "Neither the intestine strife of the period of appanage principalities, [59] nor the Mongol yoke, [60] nor the bloody age of Ivan the Terrible, [61] nor the troubled years of the interregnum, [62] nor the reforms of Peter and Catherine [63] which introduced the principles of Western European culture into Russian life—nothing rocked or changed this cherished institution of peasant life," says one of the most excitable Populists, Mr. K-in, [64] in a book about the "forms of landholding among the Russian people," "serfdom could not erase it: neither the voluntary exodus of peasants to new lands, nor forcible resettlement" contributed to its destruction, etc., etc., in a word,

> The centuries passed, and all aspired to happiness.
> Everything in the world changed several times over, [65]

but the Russian commune remained unchanged and unalterable. Unfortunately this eulogy, for all its indisputable eloquence, proves absolutely nothing at all. Rural communes exhibit unquestionable vitality until such time as they emerge from the conditions of a natural economy. "The simplicity of the organization of production in these self-sufficing communities which constantly reproduce themselves in the same form and, when accidentally destroyed, spring up again on the same spot and with the same name—this simplicity supplies the key to the riddle of the unchangeability of Asiatic societies, which is in such striking contrast with the constant dissolution and refounding of Asiatic states, and their never-ceasing changes of dynasty. The structure of the fundamental economic elements of society remains untouched by the storms on the political horizon." [66]

But that same basic element of barbarian societies which steadfastly withstands the storms of political revolutions proves powerless and defenseless before the logic of economic evolution. The development of a monetary economy and commodity production gradually undermines communal landholding. [67] To this is added the destructive effect of the state which by force of circumstances is compelled to support the principle of individualism. It is driven down that path by pressure from the upper estates, whose interests conflict with the communal principle, as well as by its own ever increasing needs. The development of a monetary economy which is in turn a consequence of the development of productive forces, that is to say of the growth of social wealth, calls into being new social functions which it would have been inconceivable to sustain with the help of the former system of collecting taxes in kind. The need for money makes the government support all those measures and all those principles of social economy which increase the flow of money into the country and quicken the pulse of socio-economic life. But these abstract principles of social economy do not exist just by themselves, rather they are but the general expression of the actual interests of a certain class, namely the commercial-industrial class. Consisting partly of former members of the commune and partly of individuals from other estates this class is essentially interested in mobilizing both immovable property and property-holders themselves in so far as the latter are workers. The principle of communal landholding impedes the achievement of both of these aims. That is why it becomes an object first of antipathy and then of more or less determined assaults from the bourgeoisie which is coming into being. But even these blows do not immediately destroy the commune. Its downfall is prepared gradually. For a long time the external relations of the members of the commune appear to remain quite unchanged while the internal nature of the commune undergoes drastic metamorphoses which finally bring about its complete decay. This process sometimes takes place over a very long period, but once it has reached a certain degree of intensity it can no longer be halted by any "seizures of power" on the part of this or that secret society.[68] The only serious rebuff to triumphant individualism can be delivered by those social forces which are called into being by the process of decay in the commune itself. The commune's members, who once had equal positions as far as their property, rights and obligations were concerned, are subdivided, owing to the process indicated, into two strata. One gravitates towards the urban bourgeoisie, striving to merge with it into a single class of exploiters. All the land of the *mir*[69] accumulates little by little in the hands of this privileged stratum. The other stratum is partially cast out of the commune and, wrenched from the land, takes its working hands to the market-place, and partially forms a new category of communal members who are pariahs and whose exploitation is facilitated, incidentally, by convenient features of communal organization. Only where historical circumstances produce a new economic basis for the reconstruction of society in the interests of this lower class; only when this class begins consciously to address itself to the root causes of its servitude and to the essential conditions of its emancipation—only there and then may one "expect" a new social revolution without sinking into *manilovshchina*.[70] This new process also takes place only gradually, but, once it has begun, it goes forward to its logical conclusion, in exactly the same way, with the same undeviating certainty as astronomical phenomena. Social revolution hinges, in this case, not on the "possible" success of conspirators but on the sure and irresistible course of social evolution.

Mutato nomine de te fabula narratur, [71] we may say, if we turn to the Russian commune. It is precisely the fact that a monetary economy did not develop long ago in Russia that explains the durability which was displayed by our commune *until very recently* and which continues *to this day* to move people who are a bit weak when it comes to thinking. Until the elimination of serfdom almost all Russia's social economy and to a considerable extent the state economy too was a natural economy favorable in the highest degree to the preservation of the commune on the land. That is why the commune could not be destroyed by the political events of the times of the appanage structure and the *veche* [72] and Muscovite centralization, [73] the Petrine reforms and the "tub-thumping enlightenment" of the St. Petersburg autocrats. However severe the effect of many of these events on the wellbeing of the people, nevertheless there is no doubt that in the last analysis they themselves were not harbingers of fundamental revolutions in the social economy but only a consequence of the mutual relations in which individual communes stood among themselves. At the base of Muscovite despotism lay precisely those "ancient foundations of the life of the people" which our Populists admire. This was clearly understood by the reactionary Baron Haxthausen [74] and the revolutionary agitator Bakunin alike. Had Russia been isolated from the economic and political influences of Western European life it would have been difficult to foresee when history would have finally undermined the economic foundation of her political structure. But the influence of international relations has hastened the natural, albeit slow, process of the development of a monetary economy and commodity production. The reform of the 19th February [75] was a necessary concession to the new economic current and, in turn, gave it new force. The commune did not know how and indeed was unable to adapt to the new conditions. Its organism broke down and only the blind now fail to notice the signs of its decay.

1884

NOTES

PART 1

1. R. Pipes, *Karamzin's Memoir on Ancient and Modern Russia* (Cambridge, Mass., 1959), pp. vii-viii.

2. A. Walicki, *A History of Russian Thought: From the Enlightenment to Marxism* (Oxford, 1980), p. 55.

3. M. Raeff, *Origins of the Russian Intelligentsia* (New York, 1966), p. 168.

4. This extract is a note from Radishchev's translation of Mably's *Observations sur l'histoire de la Grèce*, published in 1773 by the Academy of Sciences. Translated from A. V. Kokorev, *Khrestomatiia po russkoi literature XVIII veka* (Moscow, 1965), p. 669.

5. Translated from Kokorev, *Khrestomatiia po russkoi literature XVIII veka*, pp. 669-76. The quaintness and awkwardness of our translation are inherent in Radishchev's original Russian and are characteristic of his style.

6. Alexander of Macedonia: Alexander the Great (356-323 BC), King of Macedonia. Alexander's education was undertaken by Aristotle (384-322 BC).

7. Translated from Kokorev, *Khrestomatiia po russkoi literature XVIII veka*, pp. 676-711.

8. The Russian word for "glory" is *slava*.

9. A reference to the Pugachev revolt of 1773-75. Emelyan Pugachev was a Cossack who claimed to be the Emperor Peter III. His manifesto, which promised the emancipation of the serfs, attracted large numbers of peasants, Cossacks and nomads, and for a while the revolt posed a real threat to the regime of Catherine II. When the revolt was eventually put down, Pugachev was executed. Pushkin gives a fictional account of the affair in his historical novel, *The Captain's Daughter* (1836).

10. Translated from the Russian text in Pipes (ed.), *Karamzin's Memoir on Ancient and Modern Russia*, pp. 41-119.

11. In Karamzin's view the main achievement of the reign of Catherine the Great (1762-96) was that she had "softened autocracy without emasculating it" and "cleansed autocracy of the stains of tyranny." His somewhat idealized account of her reign earlier in the *Memoir* emphasizes Catherine's firmness, confidence and respect for national customs, as well as her enlightenment and zeal for honor. The dark reign of Catherine's successor, the mad Paul I (1796-1801), is treated with appropriate harshness by Karamzin who accuses Alexander's father of violating "the ancient covenant between authority and obedience" by his tyranny and use of political terror, which severed any bond between the progressive gentry and the autocracy established by Catherine.

12. A reference to the emergence of Muscovy from Mongol overlordship in the 14th-15th centuries and the formation of a national unified state under the autocrats Ivan III and Ivan IV. Karamzin may also have in mind the conferment of autocratic power on Mikhail Romanov in 1613, following the rupture of national unity during the Time of Troubles.

13. Montesquieu, *De l'esprit des lois*, Book 2, Chapter 4.

14. The creation of a State Council in 1809 was part of Mikhail Speransky's project for widespread constitutional reform with the ultimate aim of transforming Russia into a constitutional monarchy. After 1812 Alexander's reforming zeal was exhausted and Speransky was dismissed, his reforms unfinished. Consequently many existing institutions remained unreformed, and in particular the relationship of the Council to the Senate was

confused. Under the edict establishing the Council, the tsar was not obliged, as Karamzin implies, to abide by its decisions.

15. The purchase of a *recruit,* that is, a peasant bought from a private landlord to serve in the army as a substitute, was a widespread practice which allowed state peasants in particular to avoid military service for themselves or their sons. Alexander tried to prohibit the practice by a law of 1804.

16. Soul-tax. Introduced by Peter the Great in 1724, this was a capitation tax imposed upon adult males of the peasant population. Also called poll-tax.

17. A reference to the two traditional ways in which a landowner benefited from the labor of his serfs who either worked the landowner's own fields when required or paid him a quitrent (*obrok*) derived from the sale of their own produce. Sometimes the two systems were combined.

18. In 1597 Boris Godunov issued an edict calling for the return, by force if necessary, of all peasants who had left estates since 1592. In effect this bound the peasant to a single master. The law code of 1649 consolidated serfdom by abolishing Godunov's five-year limit (which had already in 1642 been extended to ten).

19. The Table of Ranks, instituted by Peter the Great in 1722, created fourteen grades in the military, court and civil services. Those who reached grade eight were entitled to ennoblement.

20. Translated from the Russian text in I. Ia. Shchipanov and S. Ia. Shtraikh, *Izbrannye sotsial'no-politicheskie i filosofskie proizvedeniia Dekabristov* in 3 vols (Moscow, 1951), I, pp. 295-329.

21. *Economic peasants*—a category of state peasant working on land originally owned by the church but secularized in 1764. *Appanage peasants*—peasants working on land set aside by a law of 1797 for members of the tsar's family.

22. *Appanage administration*—a reference to the *Udel'noe vedomstvo,* which was set up in 1797 to administer appanage property.

23. This article contradicts Muravyov's earlier provision (Article 101) for the Emperor to act as Commander-in-Chief of Russia's armed forces at home and abroad. Muravyov was aware of this inconsistency and remarked on it in a marginal note in the manuscript of his *Constitution.*

24. In entitling his draft constitution *Russian Law (Russkaia Pravda)* Pestel no doubt wished his reader to recall the original *Russkaia Pravda,* the first Russian law code, drawn up in the eleventh century during the reign of Yaroslav. These extracts are translated from the Russian text in Shchipanov and Shtraikh, *Izbrannye sotsial'no-politicheskie i filosofskie proizvedeniia Dekabristov,* pp. 75-83, 89-92, 99, 100-105, 120-21, 135-36.

25. The appanage system evolved from the form of succession adopted on the death of Yaroslav in 1054 and lasted until the emergence of Muscovy as a unified Russian state. The land was divided into principalities and shared among Yaroslav's heirs. Further subdivision took place with succeeding generations until all semblance of national unity was lost in dissension and internecine feuds. The system prevented any unified attempt to resist the Mongol invasion in the thirteenth century.

PART II

1. Belinsky uses this phrase in his essay of 1841, "The Idea of Art." See V. G. Belinskii, *Polnoe sobranie sochinenii,* 13 vols (Moscow, 1953-59), IV, p.586.

2. I. Berlin, "The Birth of the Russian Intelligentsia," in *Russian Thinkers* (London, 1978), p.122.

3. Cited in N. V. Riasanovsky, *A Parting of Ways* (Oxford, 1976), pp. 107-8.

4. See Herzen's article "A New Phase in Russian Literature," A. I. Gertsen, *Sobranie sochinenii v tridtsati tomakh* (Moscow, 1954-65), XVIII, p. 189.

5. A. S. Khomiakov, *Polnoe sobranie sochinenii,* 8 vols, fourth edition (Moscow, 1904), V, p. 217.

6. Raeff, *Russian Intellectual History: An Anthology* (New Jersey, 1978), p. 230.

7. Chaadaev is writing to Ekaterina Dmitrievna Panova in reply to a letter in which she voices her religious fears. This translation is from the French in M. Gershenzon's edition *Sochineniia i pis'ma P. Ia. Chaadaeva* (Moscow, 1913-14), I, pp. 75-93.

8. John, 17: 21.

9. The Mongol overlordship.

10. Peter the Great.

11. Alexander I during the Napoleonic campaign. Russian troops entered Paris in April 1814.

12. The Decembrist revolt of 1825.

13. Byzantine Christianity was adopted by Russia in 988, during the reign of Vladimir.

14. Photius (Chaadaev's note). Chaadaev's reference is to the "Photian Schism," the ninth-century dispute between the Patriarch of Constantinople, Photius, and Pope Nicholas I (858-67).

15. Chaadaev has in mind the establishment of autocracy and the development of serfdom in Muscovite Russia.

16. Torquato Tasso (1544-95). The reference is to Tasso's epic based on the events of the First Crusade, *Gerusalemme Liberata.*

17. A reference to eighteenth-century rationalism.

18. Kireevsky's article, written in 1839, is a response to Khomyakov's "O starom i novom" ("On the Old and the New"). See Khomiakov, *Polnoe sobranie sochinenii,* 8 vols (Moscow, 1900-1904), III, pp. 11-29. This translation is taken from the text in I. V. Kireevskii, *Polnoe sobranie sochinenii* in 2 vols, ed. by M. Gershenzon (Moscow, 1911), I, pp. 109-20.

19. Strauss, David Friedrich (1808-74). German idealist philosopher, leader of the Young Hegelians. His work, *The Life of Jesus,* although admitting the historical reality of Christ, regarded the Gospels as myth and criticized Christian dogma.

20. Talleyrand, Charles Maurice (1754-1838). French diplomat. Kireevsky's reference is to Talleyrand's opportunism and political adaptability in the years following the French Revolution of 1789.

21. Louis Philippe (1773-1850). King of France 1830-48.

22. Isaac Syrus (died c.700). Bishop of Nineveh, who wrote extensively in Syriac on ascetic subjects. His work was subsequently translated into Greek.

23. The *Stoglavyi sobor* of 1551. A Church Council convoked by Ivan the Terrible with a view to extending state power into Church affairs.

24. *Oprichnina.* An administrative élite created by Ivan the Terrible in 1564 and used against the boyars.

25. Translated from "Po povodu broshiury g-na Loransi," in Khomiakov, *Polnoe sobranie sochinenii,* 8 vols, 5th edition (Moscow, 1907), II, pp. 51-53.

26. Translated from "Po povodu poslaniia arkhiepiskopa parizhskago," in Khomiakov, *Polnoe sobranie sochinenii,* 5th edition, II, pp. 111-13.

27. Here Khomyakov is speaking of the Orthodox Church.

28. "Unity, as understood by the Catholics, is the Church without the Christian; freedom, as understood by Protestants, is the Christian without the Church." (Khomyakov's note)

29. Written in 1860 in Germany and co-signed by leading Slavophiles (M. Pogodin, A. Koshelev, I. Belyaev, N. Elagin, Yu. Samarin, P. Bessonov, K. Aksakov, B. Bartenev, F. Chizhov, and I. Aksakov), this is an open letter written to the people of Serbia, who had gained independence after two hundred years of Turkish domination. Khomyakov's letter is full of fraternal advice to Russia's Orthodox brethren. This extract, translated from the text in A. S. Khomiakov, *Izbrannye sochineniia,* ed. N. S. Arsen'ev (New York, 1955), pp. 180-82, presents Khomyakov's advice on the social importance of Orthodoxy.

30. "Collective conscience." The Russian is *sobornaia sovest'.*

31. Translated and adapted from "Zapiska K. S. Aksakova 'o vnutrennem sostoianii

Rossii,' predstavlennaia Gosudariu Imperatoru Aleksandru II v 1855g.," in N. L. Brodskii (ed.), *Rannie slavianofily* (Moscow,1910), pp. 69-96.

32. A reference to the election of Mikhail Romanov at the end of the period known as the Time of Troubles. Prince Dmitry Pozharsky and the Nizhny-Novgorod merchant Kuzma Minin were instrumental in organizing the Russian forces which drove the Poles out of Moscow.

33. A reference to the subjugation of the principality of Novgorod by Ivan III between the years 1471 and 1489.

34. Mikhail Fedorovich: Mikhail Romanov, who ruled from 1613 to 1645.

35. Anna reigned from 1730 to 1740. Aksakov is referring to the attempt made by members of the Supreme Privy Council, created in 1726, to impose constitutional limits on the new Empress's authority. Anna accepted these limitations, which gave the Council the right to approve the sovereign's measures, but shortly after her accession she repudiated these conditions and abolished the Supreme Privy Council.

36. The *Zemskie sobory*. The first Assembly of the Land was convoked by Ivan the Terrible in 1549 to discuss reforms and the Livonian war. The Assemblies, similar to the Estates General of Western Europe, discussed particularly important issues of the time. They generally consisted of the clergy, the boyars and the serving gentry. Only in 1613, at the Assembly to proclaim Mikhail Romanov tsar, did the peasantry take part.

37. The *streltsy,* or musketeers, mutinied and marched on Moscow in the summer of 1698 while Peter the Great was abroad on his Great Embassy. The revolt was suppressed and on his return Peter conducted a bloody purge of the *streltsy* regiments.

38. Aksakov means the Pugachev revolt of 1773-75.

39. The theory of Official Nationality, proclaimed in 1833 by Sergei Uvarov, Minister of Education to Nicholas I.

PART III

1. A characteristic work of this period in Belinsky's life is *Literary Reveries* (1834), available in English translation in V. G. Belinsky, *Selected Philosophical Works* (Moscow, 1956).

2. Belinskii, *Polnoe sobranie sochinenii* (hereafter: Belinskii, *PSS*), XI, p. 282.

3. Belinskii, *PSS,* III, p. 341.

4. Berlin, "Alexander Herzen," in *Russian Thinkers,* p. 189.

5. A. I. Gertsen, *Sobranie sochinenii v tridtsati tomakh* (hereafter: Gertsen, *PSS*), IX, p.28.

6. Gertsen, *PSS,* III, p. 100.

7. Ibid.

8. Gertsen, *PSS,* XX, p. 590.

9. Ibid., p. 583.

10. Gertsen, *PSS,* VI, p. 7.

11. Alexander Herzen, *From the Other Shore & The Russian People and Socialism,* tr. Moura Budberg (Oxford, 1979).

12. See a letter to Turgenev, dated 19 December 1860, in Gertsen *PSS,* XXVII, p. 122, and a letter to his son Alexander, dated 17-19 April 1869, in *PSS, XXX, p. 87.

13. Extracts translated from Belinskii, *PSS,* III, pp. 385-419.

Wolfgang Menzel was a German journalist and political figure, whose work *German Literature* was translated into Russian in 1837-38. Belinsky's essay was provoked largely by the chapter on Goethe with its unfavorable assessment of the poet's apolitical stance. The French Revolution of 1830 saw Menzel abandon his previous liberal stance to become a reactionary figure and stern critic of those progressive writers who formed the "Young Germany" group. Belinsky's essay was written in 1839-40 when Belinsky was experiencing his reconciliation with reality under the influence of Hegelianism.

14. Johann Joachim Winckelmann. Eighteenth-century German antiquarian whose work *A History of the Art of Antiquity* was translated into Russian in 1820.

15. Omar ibn al Khattab (581-644)—second caliph, who conquered Egypt in 641 AD.

16. The reference is to Napoleon Bonaparte.

17. Kaunitz—Prince Kaunitz-Ritberg (1711-94), Austrian statesman and diplomat.

18. From Krylov's fable *The Pike and the Cat.*

19. Translated from Belinskii, *PSS,* XI and XII.

20. i. e., the idea that the individual should logically reconcile himself with historical and social reality.

21. M. N. Zagoskin (1789-1852)—conservative Russian writer, author of *Yurii Miloslavskii.*

22. *Allgemeinheit* (German)—universality.

23. Egor Fedorych—Belinsky's ironic name and patronymic for Hegel.

24. A reference to the alliance of 1835 between Russia, Austria and Prussia, which reaffirmed the conservative principles of the Holy Alliance of 1815.

25. Tiberius Gracchus (162-133 BC)—Roman statesman and champion of democracy.

26. This letter was written in Salzbrunn on 15 July 1847. Earlier that year Belinsky had written a scathing review of Nikolai Gogol's reactionary work *Selected Passages from Correspondence with Friends* for the journal *The Contemporary.* A letter from Gogol to Belinsky in June gave the critic the chance to express his indignation uninhibited by the tsarist censorship. The translation is taken, with some omissions, from Belinskii, *PSS,* X, pp. 212-20.

27. Nozdrev and Chichikov are characters in Gogol's novel *Dead Souls.* The Town Mayor is from his comedy *The Government Inspector.*

28. A reference to the Captain's wife, Vasilisa Egorovna, in Pushkin's *The Captain's Daughter.*

29. Orthodoxy, autocracy and nationality were the three tenets of the theory of Official Nationality in the reign of Nicholas I.

30. A reference to Pushkin's involuntary and demeaning proximity to the court of Nicholas I during the final years of the poet's life.

31. Gogol had indicated in the foreword to *Selected Passages* that he intended to undertake a pilgrimage to the Holy Land, which he did in fact do in 1848.

32. Shpekin is the corrupt postmaster in Gogol's *The Government Inspector.*

33. N.—probably the poet N. A. Nekrasov; An.—Annenkov.

34. Translated and adapted from Gertsen, *PSS,* III, pp.45-88.

Herzen's essay poses certain problems for the translator. In particular Herzen uses the word *nauka* ("science") to denote not only the natural sciences, but also the humanities, especially philosophy and history. The word "science" should thus be understood in the broadest sense of "knowledge" or "learning" and the term "scientist" (*uchenyi*) as "man of learning."

35. Specialized scholars (German).

36. Jean Paul—pseudonym of the German writer Johann Paul Friedrich Richter (1763-1825).

37. "I consider it necessary to state again that I am speaking solely and exclusively about the *guild-scientists,* and that the corollary of all I have said is also true: the *true* scientist will always be simply a man, and will always be respected by mankind" (Herzen's note).

38. Khlestakov—the false official in Gogol's comedy *The Inspector General* (1836).

39. Matthew, 10:39.

40. Goethe.

41. Aristotle.

42. The German word suggests something like "a manifestation of the spirit of beauty."

43. Hegel.

44. Hegel, *Philosophie des Rechts* (Herzen's note).

45. This extract is from Herzen's letter to the French historian, M. J. Michelet, first published in French in 1851 in response to the latter's unflattering views on the Russian people. The translation is from the authorized Russian text of 1858, to be found in Gertsen, *PSS,* VII, pp.332-34.

46. A reference to the westernization accomplished in the reigns of Peter the Great and Catherine the Great.

47. "To borrow the excellent phrase of one of the contributors to the journal *Il Progresso* in an article on Russia in the issue of 1 August 1851" (Herzen's note).

48. The lesson Herzen considers to have been learned in 1848 was the inadequacy of attempts to reform the European countries, and by extension Russia, without radical political and economic change, i.e., socialist revolution.

49. Herzen is describing the "seven dismal years" (*mrachnoe semiletie*), the most reactionary period of Nicholas's reign between the revolutions of 1848 and his death in 1855.

50. Translated from Gertsen, *PSS,* XI, pp.240-53.

Robert Owen (1771-1858). British socialist who believed human nature would respond positively to a progressive social environment. He established experimental colonies in Britain and America. New Lanark and New Harmony, mentioned by Herzen, were two of these. Herzen met Owen at Sevenoaks in 1852, an encounter described in Herzen's memoirs, *My Past and Thoughts,* Part 6, Chapter IX, from which this extract is taken. Interestingly, Nicholas Romanov, later Nicholas I, had visited Owen at New Lanark in 1815 and invited him to Russia!

51. François Noël Gracchus Babeuf (1760-97). Utopian communist during the French Revolution, who supported the constitution adopted by the Convention in June 1793.

52. The Federalists opposed the centralization of revolutionary authority under the Jacobins.

53. In 404 BC the people of Athens appointed thirty men to work out a new social order. These men assumed complete power and for a year ruled tyrannically.

54. A reference to the tale *Bluebeard* by the French writer Charles Perrault (1628-1703).

55. Babeuf and his comrade Augustin Alexandre Dorthès were executed on 27 May 1797.

56. Napoleon Bonaparte.

57. Field-Marshal Gerhard Leberecht von Blücher (1742-1819)—Prussian commander who joined forces with Wellington at Waterloo.

58. Marshal Emmanuel, Marquis de Grouchy (1766-1847)—Napoleonic general, whose pursuit of the Prussians at Waterloo failed to prevent Blücher's forces joining up with Wellington.

59. Baba Yaga—the witch in Russian folklore.

60. According to Catholic legend, the blood of St. Januarius, which is kept in a phial in Naples, boils on the day of this saint.

61. The slogan of the plebeian wing of the French revolutionaries.

62. An imprecise quotation from St. Matthew, 26. At this point Herzen appends the following observation:

Theologians, in general, are bolder than doctrinaires: they say plainly that were it not for the will of God not a single hair would fall from the head, yet the responsibility for every act, even every intention, they lay with man. Scientific fatalism asserts that they do not even speak of personalities, of *accidental* bearers of ideas (that is, there is no mention of our brother, the ordinary man, but as for such personalities as Alexander the Great or Peter I—our ears ring with their universal, historical vocation). The doctrinaires, you see, are like great lords: they deal with the management of history *en gros,* wholesale. But where is the boundary between the herd and the individual? When do a few grains become a heap, as my dear Athenian sophists used to ask?

It goes without saying that we have never confused predestination with the theory of probability: we are justified in using induction to speculate about the future on the basis of the past. In this induction we know what we are doing, relying on the permanence of certain laws and phenomena, but also admitting the possibility of their being infringed. We see a man of thirty and have every right to suppose that in another thirty years he will be gray or balding and will stoop a bit, etc. This does not mean that it is his destiny to go gray or bald, or to become stooped, that it is written at his birth. If he dies at thirty five he will not go gray, but will turn "to clay," as Hamlet says, or into salad.

63. The ruler of Pisa, Ugolino, was in 1288 incarcerated with his two sons and two nephews and left to die of hunger. According to legend, used by Dante in his *Divine Comedy,* Ugolino survived his children by resorting to cannibalism.

PART IV

1. An accessible account of Hegel's philosophy is to be found in Frederick Copleston, S.J., *A History of Philosophy* (London, 1961-66), Vol.VII, pt.I. On Hegel's reception in Russia see A. Walicki, *The Slavophile Controversy: History of a Conservative Utopia in Nineteenth-Century Russian Thought,* trans. Hilda Andrews-Rusiecka (Oxford, 1975), pp. 287 ff.

2. Useful accounts of the thought of these socialists are contained in G.D.H. Cole, *A History of Socialist Thought,* I (London, 1953).

3. On this disagreement see Alexander Herzen, *My Past and Thoughts: the Memoirs of Alexander Herzen,* trans. Constance Garnett, revised by Humphrey Higgins (London, 1968), II, p.586; P.V. Annenkov, *The Extraordinary Decade: Literary Memoirs,* trans. I.R. Titunik, ed. A.P. Mendel (Ann Arbor, Mich., 1968), pp. 142-43.

4. Herzen, *My Past and Thoughts,* II, p. 499.

5. These words belong to Belinsky (see Belinskii, *PSS,* XI, pp. 494, 377).

6. See Annenkov, *The Extraordinary Decade,* p. 81. We have translated Annenkov's phrase (see his *Literaturnye vospominaniia,* Moscow, 1960, p. 214) slightly differently.

7. Herzen, *My Past and Thoughts,* II, p. 491.

8. Translated from A. V. Stankevich, *T. N. Granovskii i ego perepiska,* 2nd ed., 2 vols (Moscow, 1897), II, pp. 369-70.

9. From a letter to Belinsky. Translated from Stankevich, *T. N. Granovskii i ego perepiska,* II, pp. 439-40.

10. Belinsky was known, because of his passionate moral commitments, as "furious Vissarion" (*neistovyi Vissarion*). Granovsky is likening him here to "Orlando [i.e., Roland] furioso," the hero of the epic poem of that name by the Italian poet Ariosto (1474-1533).

11. That is, Granovsky himself who was jocularly known as "shepeliavyi" (lisper).

12. Robespierre (1758-94), Jacobin leader in the French Revolution who dominated the Committee of Public Safety, the main organ of the revolutionary government during the period of terror. Robespierre himself was executed in 1794.

13. Saint-Just (1767-94) was also a leading member of the Committee of Public Safety.

14. Members of one of the political factions prominent in the French Revolution in 1791-92.

15. Mirabeau (1749-91) was a renowned orator in the National Assembly, the main governing organ in the early years of the French Revolution and an advocate of constitutional monarchy.

16. The opponents of the more moderate Girondins. The Montagnards gained the upper hand in the government in 1793-94 and formed a majority on the Committee of Public Safety.

17. The bourgeoisie.

18. From a letter to Ogarev. Translated from Stankevich, *T. N. Granovskii i ego perepiska,* II, pp. 448-49. N.

P.Ogarev (1813-77) was a lifelong friend of Herzen and himself a poet and radical thinker who espoused materialism and who in the 1860s and 1870s maintained connections with Populist revolutionaries.

19. From a series of four public lectures delivered in Moscow University in 1851 and published in 1852. Translated from "Chetyre istoricheskie kharakteristiki" in T. N. Granovskii, *Sochineniia,* 4th ed. (Moscow, 1900), pp. 241-42.

20. Tamerlaine (1336-1405) was a Turkish conqueror of Central Asia who established hiᶜ capital at Samarkand and is remembered particularly for his barbarity.

21. Alexander the Great (i.e. Alexander III of Macedonia, 356-323 BC), great conqueror and legendary hero who led his armies as far as India and laid the foundations for the Hellenistic world of territorial kingdoms.

22. Louis IX (1214-70), King of France from 1226 until his death, noted for his piety, love of peace and compassion for the poor.

23. Chancellor Bacon (i.e. Francis Bacon, 1561-1626), English lawyer, statesman and philosopher.

24. Translated from "Chetyre istoricheskie kharakteristiki" in Granovskii, *Sochineniia,* pp. 257-58.

25. The city of Arbela (modern Irbil in Iraq) was near the scene of the battle in 331 BC in which Alexander the Great defeated the Persian armies commanded by Darius III (reigned 336-330 BC), last King of the Achaemenid dynasty.

26. Cyrus II, who lived in the sixth century BC, founder of the Persian Achaemenid dynasty.

27. Parmenio (400-330 BC), greatest Macedonian general of his time.

28. Philip II of Macedonia (382-336 BC), father of Alexander the Great.

29. Aristotle (384-322 BC).

30. Translated from "Chetyre istoricheskie kharakteristiki" in Granovskii, *Sochineniia,* pp. 272-74.

31. That is, social classes, which were almost invariably termed "estates" (*sosloviia*) by Russian thinkers before the adoption of Marxism by a substantial portion of the intelligentsia in the 1890s.

32. Ruling dynasty of France from 987 to 1328.

33. Boniface VIII, pope from 1294 to 1303.

34. Jean de Joinville (c.1224-1317), French chronicler of life of Louis IX.

35. From a lecture delivered in Moscow University in 1852.

Translated from "O sovremennom sostoianii i znachenii vseobshchei istorii" in Granovskii, *Sochineniia,* pp. 28-29. Granovsky is clearly arguing the case for a view of history as a broad humanistic discipline rather than a narrow academic one.

36. German dramatist (1759-1805) whose denunciations of tyranny and injustice were enthusiastically read by Herzen, Ogarev and other Russian intellectuals in the 1830s. His work held a special appeal for Granovsky, who was always impressed by examples of moral nobility and poetic sensibility.

37. From a letter to Kavelin, January 1855.

Translated from Stankevich, *T. N.Granovskii i ego perepiska,* II, p. 453. K. D. Kavelin (1818-85) was a historian and jurist prominent in liberal circles in the 1840s and 1850s whose monograph *A Brief Survey of the Juridical Way of Life of Ancient Russia* (1847) was taken by the Westernizers of the 1840s as a definitive statement of their view of Russian historical development.

38. M. P. Pogodin (1800-75)—historian and journalist, Moscow University professor who held conservative political views and was close to the Slavophiles.

39. Translated from *P. V. Annenkov i ego druz'ia* (St. Petersburg, 1892), pp. 550-52. The extract translated here is cited, by Annenkov, with small and inconsequential changes, in his work *Zamechatel'noe desiatiletie (The Extraordinary Decade),* chapter 31.

40. These "letters" of Herzen's appear in Gertsen, *PSS,* V.

41. "I am not trying to pick a quarrel with his way of seeing things."

42. Translated from V. P. Botkin, *Sochineniia*, 3 vols (St. Petersburg, 1890-93), I, pp. 68-71.

43. Ferdinand VII of Spain changed the law of succession to enable Isabella, his daughter by Maria-Cristina, to claim the throne in preference to his brother Don Carlos. On Ferdinand's death in 1833 Maria-Cristina became regent.

44. It is tempting to compare Botkin's description of Spain, in search of her historical role, with Gogol's allusion, at the end of Part I of *Dead Souls*, to Russia's pursuit of her own destiny.

45. The Christian reconquest of Spain took place between the early twelfth and late fifteenth centuries. The final expulsion of the Moors was carried out in the early seventeenth century.

46. Granada was surrendered by the Moors in 1492.

47. Botkin's syntax falters here.

48. Botkin's translation of the Spanish is not exact; the Spanish means simply "I am better than my master."

49. From the memoirs on Gogol in Rome in the summer of 1841 in P. V. Annenkov, *Literaturnye vospominaniia*, ed. V. P. Dorofeev (Moscow, 1960), pp. 54-55. Annenkov's memoirs on Gogol were published in 1857 when the differences between the "men of the 1840s" and the young *raznochintsy* were coming to a head. Annenkov had, however, written about Italy in a similar tone long before, at the beginning of the 1840s, in his cycle *Letters from Abroad* (reprinted in *P. V. Annenkov i ego druz'ia,* especially pp. 140 ff.)

50. Translated from A. V. Druzhinin, *Sobranie sochinenii*, 8 vols (St. Petersburg, 1865-67), VII, pp. 58-61.

51. That is, Pushkin's.

52. Druzhinin has in mind Gogol's "Tale of How Ivan Ivanovich quarrelled with Ivan Nikiforovich."

53. Druzhinin is alluding to the so-called "natural school" of writers nurtured in the 1840s by Belinsky, who dealt—often in a heart-rending manner—with the poverty of the peasants and lower classes in the cities.

54. The Tatyana mentioned in this passage is the heroine of Pushkin's *Eugene Onegin*, Selifan is Chichikov's coachman in Gogol's *Dead Souls* and Akaky Akakievich the poor clerk in Gogol's story, "The Overcoat." There are also allusions in Druzhinin's celebration of Pushkin's talent to *Eugene Onegin*, Chapter VII (Stanzas 1-2), Chapter V (Stanza 21) and Chapter IV (Stanza 42) and to Pushkin's poems "The Devils" (*Besy;* 1830) and "A Winter's Evening" (*Zimnii vecher;* 1825) and to the cycle of poems he wrote to commemorate the anniversary of the opening of his school at Tsarskoe selo.

55. Translated from Druzhinin, *Sobranie sochinenii,* VII, pp. 214-15, 216-17, 226-28.

56. Druzhinin proceeds at this point to discuss particular examples of the "Olympian" poet, Homer, Shakespeare and Goethe.

57. Druzhinin is alluding to the literary criticism of Belinsky.

58. Druzhinin has in mind writers such as Eugène Sue (1804-57), author of works on the urban poor, and George Sand.

59. G. G. Gervinus (1805-71), German literary historian and politician.

60. Heinrich Heine (1797-1856), German poet and author of *On the History of Religion and Philosophy in Germany* (1834) and *The Romantic School* (1836).

61. Jules Michelet (1798-1874), French historian whose work on the French Revolution was admired by the Russian Westernizers in the 1840s.

62. The major work of Eugène Sue, published in 1842-43 and very popular among Westernizers and writers of the "natural school" in Russia in the 1840s.

63. Alphonse de Lamartine (1790-1869), French Romantic poet, statesman prominent in French political life in 1848, and historian.

PART V

1. N.G. Chernyshevskii, "Esteticheskie otnosheniia iskusstva k deistvitel'nosti" in *Polnoe sobranie sochinenii*, 15 vols. (Moscow, 1939-50). (Hereafter: Chernyshevskii, *PSS*), II, pp. 5-92; extracts from pp. 9-11, 90-92.

2. "Beskorystno"; this statement would seem to conflict with the "rational egoism" which Chernyshevsky subsequently espouses.

3. Peasant hut.

4. Chernyshevsky uses the Russian word "zaviazka" (literally a "tying" of the plot), i.e., the opposite of "razviazka" ("untying" of the plot, or denouement).

5. From the article "Bor'ba partii vo Frantsii pri Liudovike XVIII i Karle X," first published in *The Contemporary*, no.8 for 1858, and reprinted in Chernyshevskii *PSS*, V, pp. 213-91; extract from pp. 215-19.

6. The period in French history after the defeat of Napoleon when the Bourbon dynasty was restored in the person of Louis XVIII.

7. The classes, social strata (French états), not landed estates.

8. Chernyshevsky is using "Aesopian language" here, that is to say in order to steer his article past the censor he is alluding to the state of affairs in Russia by citing foreign examples of iniquity that would be readily comprehensible to his readers. If in North America (i.e., a democratic society) a radical (i.e., an extreme opponent of the regime) would be a monarchist, in China (i.e., a stagnant backward country like Russia) he would be an advocate of Westernization and in the East Indies he would oppose rigid social divisions and inequalities of the sort that were bound to persist in Russia so long as serfdom existed.

9. "Sytyi golodnogo ne razumeet"—a Russian saying.

10. From the article "Kritika filosofskikh predubezhdenii protiv obshchinnogo vladeniia," first published in *The Contemporary*, no.12 for 1858, and reprinted in Chernyshevskii, *PSS*, V, pp. 357-92; extracts from pp. 362-64, 376, 377-79, 379, 382-84.

11. The obshchina.

12. Old Russian, like the other Slavonic languages, originally had seven cases, though by Chernyshevsky's time the vocative case only survived in a few forms such as "Bozhe" (God) and "gospodi" (Lord). Chernyshevsky is referring in this passage to the Slavophiles, who venerated things Russian.

13. Chernyshevsky is probably referring to Granovsky, who spoke out against Slavophile views in the 1840s.

14. There follow numerous chemical, biological, philosophical and miscellaneous other examples, fatuous in themselves, which are intended to demonstrate the general applicability of the Hegelian dialectic.

15. Chernyshevsky's use of parentheses, in this article and others, is often intended to bring to the reader's mind mathematical procedures and thereby to create the impression that his own reasoning has the logical certainty and unassailability of arithmetical calculations.

16. Hereditary leasehold, a form of land tenure in Roman law.

17. Chernyshevsky no doubt has in mind his review of a book by the German Baron von Haxthausen (Chernyshevskii, *PSS*, IV, pp. 303-48) and his article on the Slavophiles and the commune (ibid., pp. 737-61); and he returned to the subject after the publication of his "Critique of Philosophical Prejudices...," notably in the articles "Ekonomicheskaia deiatel'nost' i zakonodatel'stvo" (ibid., V, pp. 576-626); and "Sueverie i pravila logiki" (ibid., pp. 686-710).

18. Chernyshevsky presumably has in mind the period that would have elapsed between the date when, according to the old Russian chronicles, the world was created (i.e., 5508 BC) and the date when a match incorporating phosphorous was first used (though this was probably 1831 rather than 1837 as Chernyshevsky's calculations presuppose).

19. This is one of the crucial points of the article. Chernyshevsky is saying by implication that capitalism is not a necessary phase of social development in a backward nation if other

nations have already attained to a higher phase; that is to say, Russia may progress directly to socialism without a protracted period of capitalist development since socialist ideas are already gaining currency in the West.

20. From Chernyshevskii, "Antropologicheskii printsip v filosofii," first published in *The Contemporary*, nos. 4 and 5 for 1860, and reprinted in Chernyshevskii, *PSS*, VII, pp. 222-95; extracts from pp. 240-41, 259-61, 263-64, 282-87, 288-89.

21. This sentence in Chernyshevsky's manuscript was deleted by the censor.

22. Chernyshevsky says literally: "Its convincingness is equal to the convincingness of those grounds..." The original therefore has a mathematical flavor.

23. Each number of the journal *The Contemporary*, in which Chernyshevsky's articles were published, was, like other journals of the day, a very bulky tome, which explains why Chernyshevsky refers here to a "book."

24. Deleted by the censor.

25. This is perhaps a generous translation of a sentence which is even more opaque in the original.

26. Curtius—legendary Roman hero who is said to have thrown himself into a chasm that opened up in the city's forum in 362 BC. (The seers had declared that the chasm would not close until Rome's most valuable possession was thrown into it.)

27. Empedocles—Greek philosopher of the 5th century BC who is said to have thrown himself into the volcanic crater of Mount Etna in order to convince followers of his divinity.

28. Damon was a Pythagorean philosopher famous for his friendship with Phintias (wrongly called Pythias by Chernyshevsky). Phintias, sentenced to death but reprieved, came back at the last moment to save Damon, who had provided bail for him.

29. Lucretia—legendary heroine of ancient Rome, beautiful and virtuous wife of Lucius Tarquinius Collatinus, who was raped by Sextus Tarquinius, son of the tyrannical King of Rome, and stabbed herself to death.

30. Now Sagunto, town of south-eastern Spain, which was taken by Hannibal in 219 BC after heroic resistance.

31. See Note 29 above.

32. See Note 29 above.

33. Isaac Newton (1643-1727), physicist and mathematician, formulated the theory of universal gravitation and invented infinitesimal calculus. Gottfried Wilhelm Leibnitz (1646-1716), German philosopher, writer on logic, mathematics, science, law, history, linguistics and theology.

34. Reading between the lines, the Russian reader would see here that Chernyshevsky is warning the Russian gentry not to harm national interests by defending its right to own serfs.

35. Chernyshevskii, *Chto delat'?*, in *PSS*, XI, pp. 5-336; the extracts are from "Vera Pavlovna's fourth dream," which constitutes Section XVI of Chapter IV (see pp. 275-79).

36. West Semitic goddess of fertility and reproduction.

37. Ancient Greek goddess of sexual love and beauty.

38. This section is missing from the published novel.

39. The Crystal Palace in London.

40. This is a verse from the poem "Begstvo" ("Flight," 1839) by Koltsov.

41. N. A. Dobroliubov, "Chto takoe oblomovshchina?" first published in *The Contemporary*, no. 5 for 1859, and reprinted in *Sobranie sochinenii*, 9 vols (Moscow-Leningrad, 1961-63), IV, pp. 307-43; extracts from pp. 311-14, 328-29, 330-33. The word "oblomovshchina," sometimes translated as "oblomovitis" or "oblomovism," we have left in its original form. The Russian suffix -*shchina* denotes a syndrome, the mood, qualities or characteristics associated with a particular person.

At the beginning of the article Dobrolyubov has stated his intention to write not so much about *Oblomov* as à propos of the novel. He goes on to contrast Goncharov with writers who might have tackled the subject-matter contained in *Oblomov* quite differently.

42. This is the first of a number of occasions in this extract in which Dobrolyubov uses the

word *dusha;* "being" seems in this instance a better translation than "soul" or "spirit," since Dobrolyubov, like Chernyshevsky denied the existence of an immaterial side to man.

43. A quotation from Ogarev's poem "Confession" ("Ispoved', " 1842).

44. Dobrolyubov has in mind critics such as Druzhinin (see Part IV), Botkin and Annenkov.

45. "Accusatory" (*oblichitel'nyi*) was a word used at this time to denote works that were satirical or critical of reality; "novella" translates the Russian *povest'.*

46. Other "superfluous men" in Russian literature with whom Dobrolyubov has been comparing Oblomov.

47. Hero of Lermontov's novel *A Hero of Our Time* (1840).

48. Hero of Pushkin's novel in verse *Eugene Onegin* (1823-31).

49. Eponymous hero of Turgenev's first novel, published in 1856.

50. Hero of Herzen's novel *Who is to Blame?* (1845-46).

51. One of the characters in Part II of Gogol's novel *Dead Souls* (Part I was published in 1842, Part II was never completed).

52. From an essay of 1861, written as a polemical response to N. A. Dobrolyubov's defense of utilitarian art in two articles of 1860, "Traits Characterizing the Common People" and "The Poems of Ivan Nikitin." Translation from F. M. Dostoevskii, *Polnoe sobranie sochinenii v tridtsati tomakh* (Leningrad, 1972-), XVIII, pp. 101-2.

53. Translated from F. M. Dostoevskii, *Polnoe sobranie sochinenii v tridtsati tomakh,* V, pp. 68-70.

54. From D. I. Pisarev, "Bazarov," published in *Russian Word (Russkoe slovo),* no.3 for 1862 and reprinted in *Sochineniia,* 4 vols. (Moscow, 1955-6), II, pp. 7-50; extracts from pp. 9-11, 20-21.

55. George Washington (1732-99), general, statesman and first president of the United States.

56. Garibaldi (1807-82), military leader of the Italian movements for unification and independence.

57. Copernicus (1473-1543), astronomer who propounded the theory that the planets, including the earth, move in orbits round the sun.

58. Heinrich Heine (1797-1856), German poet.

59. Herostratus, Ephesian who in 356 BC set the Temple of Artemis on fire in order, according to his own confession, to immortalize himself.

60. Pavel Kirsanov, uncle of Arkady who had befriended Bazarov while a student and brought him to stay on the family estate.

61. *Bazarovshchina:* see Note 41 above.

62. See Note 47 above.

63. See Note 49 above.

PART VI

1. N. Flerovskii (V. V. Bervi), *Polozhenie rabochego klassa v Rossii* (St. Petersburg, 1869); extracts from pp. 80-81, 191-92, 205-6, 452-53, 476-77.

2. Like other thinkers of the 1860s, Bervi uses the word "science" (*nauka*) in a broad sense, to include not merely the natural sciences but knowledge and the fruits of intellectual life in general. See also Note 34 to Part III.

3. Bervi uses the term "krest'ianskoe soslovie" (literally "peasant estate"); *soslovie* was the word normally used among Populists for "class."

4. That is, peasant.

5. See Note 3 above.

6. *Taiga* is the vast expanse of evergreen forest which covers Siberia to the south of the barren arctic tundra and to the north of the steppe.

7. Peasant hut.

8. Measurement of distance, 3500 feet (i.e., approximately two-thirds of a mile).

9. *Obrok*, a proportion of what the peasant produces, payable to the landowner; cf. *barshchina, corvée* or labor due from the peasant on the owner's land.

10. Cyrus II the Great of Persia (died c.529 BC), founder of the Achaemenid Empire.

11. *Obshchina*. It is the existence of this institution, with its socialistic practice of periodically reallocating the land at its disposal among its members according to their changing needs, that ensures Russia, in the view of Bervi and the Populists in general, of her future preeminence in the family of nations.

12. N. K. Mikhailovskii, *Chto takoe progress?* in *Sochineniia*, 6 vols (St. Petersburg, 1896-97), I, cols. 1-150. Extracts from cols. 132, 135-36.

13. P. L. Mirtov [Lavrov], *Istoricheskie pis'ma* (St. Petersburg, 1870), pp. 50-64. A second edition of the *Historical Letters* (the so-called "second edition, supplemented and corrected" and sometimes known also as the "Paris edition") was published in Geneva in 1891, and it is this edition that is reprinted in Lavrov's *Izbrannye sochineniia na sotsial'no-politicheskie temy*, 4 vols. (Moscow, 1934-35), vol. I. This second edition, however, contains much material added by Lavrov in 1872, 1881 and 1891 and cannot therefore be used to throw light on the outlook of the Populist revolutionaries of the 1870s and 1880s.

14. *Sic*. An example of Lavrov's pedantry; he means that in man's primeval phase children were not a "helpless burden" to their parents for as much as a fifth of their lives.

15. *Sic*. Though the word "organ" which Lavrov continues to use here may also have the sense of "means" or "instrument" in Russian.

16. It might have been better to say: "They assured themselves and posterity of *leisure* for the pursuit of progress. They created the possibility of progress among mankind..." But we have translated what Lavrov actually says.

17. Lavrov means *past* history here; he firmly believes that men do have some control over the present and the future; indeed a major theme, perhaps the major theme, in his writings is the obligation of the "critically thinking" individual to do all he can to change the conditions that prevail in his society in accordance with his ideal.

18. Lavrov has in mind the ascetic monastic community which developed from the 4th century in the vicinity of Egyptian Thebes; in other words he is condemning people who turn a blind eye to evil by fleeing from the real world.

19. Lavrov says here "Zlo nado zazhit'." It is impossible to preserve the full sense of this sentence in translation. The verb has no less than three meanings that are of relevance here: i) "to begin to live"; ii) "to heal" (intransitive); iii) "to work off," as of a debt. The latter meaning is the only one that is grammatically possible in the context, since *zazhit'* is used as a transitive verb with *zlo* (evil) as its direct object, but Lavrov no doubt intends the other two meanings mentioned to spring to the reader's mind as well.

20. From the third variant of the program of *Forward!* Printed in *Vpered! 1873-1877. Materialy iz arkhiva Valeriana Nikolaevicha Smirnova*, ed. Boris Sapir, 2 vols. (Dordrecht, 1970), II, pp. 152-75; extract from pp. 162-63.

21. P. L. Lavrov, "Znanie i revoliutsiia: Iz pis'ma k ***," reprinted in *Izbrannye sochineniia na sotsial'no-politicheskie temy*, II, pp. 67-89; extracts from pp. 68-70, 74-76, 76-80. The article took the form of a reply to a young revolutionary. The self-preparation which Lavrov required of the revolutionary propagandist was so extensive, however, that it was bound to act as a brake on his revolutionary activity and dampen his ardor. The article therefore invited much criticism, which Lavrov tried—though not very convincingly—to rebut in a further article entitled "A Reply to Various Criticisms" ("Otvet na raznye kritiki," ibid., pp. 89-122).

22. *Kritika*, a capacity on which Lavrov placed great emphasis in early philosophical essays and in his *Historical Letters*.

23. The expression used by Lavrov, *golodnyi tif* or literally "hunger typhus" (nowadays referred to as *sypnoi tif*), draws attention to the link between the disease and malnutrition.

24. *Barchata,* i.e., sons of lords.

25. Major rivers of the Russian heartland. The Volga region in particular was associated with peasant unrest (the great peasant rebellions in Russian history had emanated from this region), and Populists placed considerable hopes on the communities of Old Believers who had settled there and were thought to preserve a spirit of independence.

26. This attack on the disinterested scholar who does not directly apply his knowledge to the solution of social problems harks back to a long passage in the fifth *Historical Letter* and recalls, moreover, Herzen's attempts to define the relationship of knowledge to action in his *Dilettantism in Science.*

27. [M. A. Bakunin], *Gosudarstvennost' i anarkhiia: Pribavlenie A,* written in 1873, is reprinted in *Archives Bakounine,* ed. Arthur Lehning, 7 vols. to date (Leiden, 1961-), III, pp. 164-79; extracts from pp.168, 169, 170-71, 173-76, 177-78.

28. The two great peasant revolts in Russian history, led by Stenka Razin and Pugachev, took place in 1670-71 and 1773-75 respectively.

29. Chaadaev makes this point in his first "Philosophical Letter" (see Part II above).

30. The Russian village community.

31. It is difficult to improve on this sentence, which is cumbersome and opaque in the original.

32. This is a biblical reference, to Matthew 23, verse 27: "Woe unto you, scribes and Pharisees, hypocrites! for ye are like unto whited sepulchres, which indeed appear beautiful outward, but are within full of dead men's bones, and of all uncleanness."

33. The word *mir,* which we have translated here as "world," is ambiguous in Russian and may refer also—as elsewhere in Bakunin's pamphlet—to the village community. However, to the Russian serf, with his limited horizons and tied as he was to his master's land, the two concepts (world and village) were conterminous.

34. *Tsar'-batiushka,* i.e., "tsar-the little father."

35. The pretender who claimed to be the son of Ivan IV (Ivan the Terrible) and who occupied the Russian throne, with Polish backing, in 1605-6 during the Time of Troubles.

36. Bakunin has in mind a popular uprising in Novgorod in 1650.

37. Bakunin is referring to the Decembrist revolt of 1825.

38. It is worth noting that the Russian words for "state" (*gosudarstvo*) and "sovereign" (*gosudar'*) are etymologically related; the concept of the state was thus inextricably associated with the autocrat who ruled it.

39. That is, "golovy, starosty, desiatskie, starshiny."

40. The rich peasant who began to prosper after the emancipation of the serfs in 1861.

41. The Russian word *pravda,* which we have translated here as "truth," is ambiguous and may also mean "justice'—an interesting confusion.

42. Bakunin is referring to the attempt by Sergei Nechaev in 1868-69 to establish a network of revolutionary circles among the students of Moscow and St. Petersburg. The circles were broken up by the police and Nechaev himself arrested in Switzerland in 1872 and extradited. Nechaev, with whom Bakunin was himself for a while closely associated, aroused great controversy by his use of unscrupulous tactics, including the murder of a Muscovite student who belonged to his organization, and by his commendation of the Machiavellian principle that "the end justifies the means." Nechaev was tried in 1873 and imprisoned in the SS. Peter and Paul Fortress in St. Petersburg, where he died in 1882. The Populists of the 1870s vigorously dissociated themselves from Nechaev's approach to revolutionary activity though they themselves did draw inspiration from the example of those members of his circle who were brought to trial in 1871 and acquitted themselves with courage and dignity in court.

43. There follows further comment on the peaceful propagandists.

44. That is, no revision of the act of emancipation of 1861.

45. P. N. Tkachev, "Retsenziia na knigu Teodora Grizingera," first published in *The Cause (Delo),* no. 6 for 1868, and reprinted in *Izbrannye sochineniia na sotsial'no-politicheskie temy,* ed. B. P. Koz'min, 5 vols (Moscow, 1932-), I, pp. 258-73; extract from pp. 260-61.

46. Griesinger's book was on the Jesuits.

47. Zimmerman's book was also reviewed by Tkachev in *Delo,* no. 4 for 1868, and is reprinted in *Izbrannye sochineniia,* I, pp. 234-57.

48. Jan of Leiden, also known as Jan Beuckelssen, was leader of an insurrection in Münster in 1534-35.

49. Thomas Müntzer, German teacher and pastor who led the Peasants' Revolt of 1524-25. He was taken prisoner and executed when the revolt collapsed, but the revolt remained a source of inspiration for subsequent revolutionary movements.

50. Wendel Hipler (d. 1526) was one of the political leaders of the German Peasant Revolt. He tried to win the towns over to the side of the peasantry.

51. Weigand, another leading figure in the German Peasant Revolt.

52. Tkachev, "Nabat (Programma zhurnala)," first published in 1875 and reprinted in *Izbrannye sochineniia,* op. cit., III, pp. 219-31, and in *Sochineniia,* ed. B. M. Shakhmatov et al., 2 vols. (Moscow, 1975-76), II, pp. 89-102, from which the present translation has been done; extracts from pp. 89-92, 93-95, 95-96, 98-100.

53. Capitalism is taking root in Russia and is already fragmenting the peasant commune.

54. There follows a passage on the function of the revolutionary journal, after which Tkachev turns to the question as to what the short-term aim of the revolutionaries ought to be.

55. The sentence has no main clause in the original.

56. *Nepravda;* see Note 41 above.

57. There follows criticism of the strategies of Lavrov and Bakunin.

58. From G. V. Plekhanov, "Nashi raznoglasiia" in *Sochineniia,* 24 vols. (Moscow-Leningrad, 1923-27), II, pp. 91-356; extract from pp. 232-39.

59. See Note 25 to Part I.

60. The period during which Russia was subjugated by the Tartars and the princes paid tribute to the Tartar Khan (i.e., c. 1240-1380, though the process of pushing back the Tartar horde went on for almost two centuries more).

61. Ivan the Terrible lived from 1533 to 1584 and was crowned tsar in 1547.

62. Plekhanov is referring to the Time of Troubles, 1598-1613, an interregnum between the death of Fyodor, the last ruler of the Ryurik dynasty, and the accession to the throne of Mikhail, the first tsar of the Romanov dynasty.

63. The Westernization of Russia that took place in the 18th century, particularly in the reigns of Peter I (i.e., Peter the Great, sole ruler 1696-1725) and Catherine II (i.e., Catherine the Great, ruled 1762-96).

64. We have not been able to identify the source Plekhanov has in mind here.

65. An inaccurate quotation from Nekrasov's narrative poem "Red-nosed Frost" (1863), Part I, section 3.

66. This is a quotation from vol. I of Marx's *Capital,* chapter XIV, section 4. We have used, with minor adaptation, the translation done from the German original by Ben Fowkes, published by Penguin Books in association with the *New Left Review,* 1976; see p. 479.

67. Plekhanov has a footnote of his own at this point in which he quotes at length from a work by Uspensky to illustrate his contention that the growth of a monetary economy has a destructive effect on the primeval communism of the *obshchina.*

68. A critical reference to Tkachev's "Jacobin" strategy.

69. The village community.

70. Manilov is a dreamy character in Part I of Gogol's novel *Dead Souls* who never completes any of the projects on which he embarks; on the Russian suffix *-shchina* see Note 41 in Part V.

71. Latin: "If you change the name the story is about you," i.e., the aforegoing Marxist analysis of the disintegration of communes in general may be applied to the Russian *obshchina* too. The saying is taken from Horace, *Satires,* I, i, lines 69-70.

72. A popular assembly in certain medieval Russian towns such as Novgorod and Pskov.

73. Plekhanov has in mind the emergence of Moscow as the dominant principality after

the Tartars had been beaten back and the evolution of a centralized autocratic state with Moscow as its capital.

74. Prussian aristocrat who traveled in Russia in the 1840s and wrote a book (translated from the German original as *The Russian Empire: its People, Institutions and Resources*, 2 vols., London, 1856) in which he described the commune in glowing terms as a possible bulwark against the capitalism and attendant pauperization that were currently developing in western Europe in the wake of the industrial revolution.

75. The emancipation of the serfs in 1861; the statutes were signed on 19th February.

SELECTED BIBLIOGRAPHY

General

Berlin, Isaiah. *Russian Thinkers*. London, 1978.
Blum, Jerome. *Lord and Peasant in Russia from the Ninth to the Nineteenth Century*. Princeton, 1961.
Edie, J. M., J. P. Scanlan and M. B. Zeldin. *Russian Philosophy*. 3 vols., Chicago, 1965.
Florinsky, Michael T. *Russia: A History and an Interpretation*. 2 vols., New York, 1953.
Hare, Richard. *Pioneers of Russian Social Thought*. London and New York, 1951.
___ *Portraits of Russian Personalities between Reform and Revolution*. London and New York, 1959.
Kohn, Hans (ed.). *The Mind of Modern Russia: Historical and Political Thought of Russia's Great Age*. New Brunswick, N.J., 1955.
Lossky, N. O. *History of Russian Philosophy*. London, 1952.
Masaryk, Thomas Garrigue. *The Spirit of Russia: Studies in History, Literature and Philosophy*. Trans. Eden and Cedar Paul, 2 vols., London, 1919.
Mirsky, D. S. *A History of Russian Literature*. London, 1949.
Monas, Sidney. *The Third Section. Police and Society in Russia under Nicholas I*. Cambridge, Mass., 1961.
Pipes, Richard. *Russia under the Old Regime*. London, 1974.
Raeff, Marc. *Russian Intellectual History: An Anthology*. New Jersey, 1966.
Riasanovsky, Nicholas V. *A Parting of Ways: Government and the Educated Public in Russia, 1801-1855*. Oxford, 1976.
Schapiro, Leonard. *Rationalism and Nationalism in Russian Nineteenth-Century Political Thought*. New Haven, 1967
Seton-Watson, Hugh. *The Russian Empire, 1801-1917*. Oxford, 1967.
Simmons, Ernest J. (ed.). *Continuity and Change in Russian and Soviet Thought*. New York, 1967.
Utechin, S. V. *Russian Political Thought: A Concise History*. London, 1964.
Walicki, Andrzej. *A History of Russian Thought from the Enlightenment to Marxism*. Oxford, 1980.
Yarmolinsky, Avrahm. *Road to Revolution: A Century of Russian Radicalism*. London, 1957.
Zenkovsky, V. V. *A History of Russian Philosophy*. Trans. George L. Kline, 2 vols., London, 1953.

PART I

Black, J. L. *Nicholas Karamzin and Russian Society in the Nineteenth Century*. Toronto, 1975.
Clardy, J. V. *The Philosophical Ideas of Alexander Radishchev*. London, 1963.
Lang, D. M. *The First Russian Radical: Alexander Radishchev*. London, 1959.
McConnell, A. *A Russian Philosophe: Alexander Radishchev, 1749-1802*. The Hague, 1964.
Mazour, Anatole G. *The First Russian Revolution, 1825*. Stanford, 1961.
Pipes, R. *Karamzin's Memoir on Ancient and Modern Russia*. 2 vols., Cambridge, Mass., 1959.

Raeff, Marc. *The Decembrist Movement.* Englewood Cliffs, N.J., 1966.
—— *Michael Speransky: Statesman of Imperial Russia 1772-1839.* The Hague, 1957.
—— *Origins of the Russian Intelligentsia.* New York, 1966.
Reddaway, W.F. *Documents of Catherine the Great.* Cambridge, England, 1931.
Riasanovsky, Nicholas. *A Parting of Ways: Government and the Educated Public in Russia 1801-1855.* Oxford, 1976.
Rogger, Hans. *National Consciousness in Eighteenth-Century Russia.* Cambridge, Mass., 1960.
Zetlin, Mikhail. *The Decembrists.* New York, 1958.

PART II

Chmielewski, Edward. *Tribune of the Slavophiles: Konstantin Aksakov.* Gainsville, Florida, 1962.
Christoff, Peter K. *The Third Heart: Some Intellectual-Ideological Currents and Cross Currents in Russia 1800-1830.* The Hague, 1970.
—— *An Introduction to Nineteenth-Century Russian Slavophilism.*
     Vol. I : *A. S. Xomjakov.* The Hague, 1961.
     Vol. II: *I. V. Kireevskij.* The Hague, 1972.
     Vol. III: *K. S. Aksakov.* Princeton, 1982.
Gleason, Abbott. *Europe and Muscovite: Ivan Kireevsky and the Origins of Slavophilism.* Cambridge, Mass., 1972.
Koyré,Alexandre. *La Philosophie et le problème national en Russie au début du XIX siècle.* Paris, 1929.
McNally, Raymond T. *Chaadaev and His Friends.* Tallahassee, 1971.
—— *The Major Works of Peter Chaadaev.* London, 1969.
Odoevsky, V. F. *Russian Nights.* Trans. Olga Koshansky-Olienikov and R. Matlaw, New York, 1965.
Quenet, Charles. *Tchaadaev et Les Lettres philosophiques, contribution à l'étude du mouvement des idées en Russie.* Paris, 1931.
Riasanovsky, Nicholas. "Khomiakov on Sobornost" in *Continuity and Change in Russian and Soviet Thought.* Ed. E. J. Simmons, Cambridge, Mass., 1955.
—— *Nicholas I and Official Nationality in Russia 1825-1855.* Berkeley and Los Angeles, 1959.
Schapiro, Leonard. *Rationalism and Nationalism in Russian Nineteenth-Century Political Thought.* New Haven and London, 1967.
Thaden, E. C. *Conservative Nationalism in Nineteenth-Century Russia.* Seattle, 1964.
Walicki, Andrzej. *The Slavophile Controversy.* Oxford, 1975.

PART III

Acton, Edward. *Alexander Herzen and the Role of the Intellectual Revolutionary.* Cambridge, 1979.
Annenkov, P. V. *The Extraordinary Decade. Literary Memoirs.* Trans. I. R. Titunik, ed. A. P. Mendel, Ann Arbor, Mich., 1968.
Berlin, Isaiah. "Alexander Herzen," in *Russian Thinkers.* London, 1978.
—— "Herzen and Bakunin on Individual Liberty," in *Russian Thinkers.* London 1978.
—— "Vissarion Belinsky," in *Russian Thinkers.* London, 1978.
Bowman, H. E. *Vissarion Belinsky, 1811-1848: A Study in the Origins of Social Criticism in Russia.* Cambridge, Mass., 1954.
Brown, E. J. *Stankevich and His Moscow Circle.* Stanford, Calif., 1966.
Carr, E. H. *The Romantic Exiles.* London, 1968.
Hare, Richard. *Pioneers of Russian Social Thought.* Oxford, 1951.

Herzen, Alexander. *My Past and Thoughts*. Trans. Constance Garnett, revised by Humphrey Higgins, with an introduction by Isaiah Berlin, 4 vols, New York, 1968.

Lampert, Eugene. *Studies in Rebellion*. London, 1957.

Malia, Martin. *Alexander Herzen and the Birth of Russian Socialism*. Harvard, 1961.

___ "Herzen and the Peasant Commune," in E. J. Simmons (ed.), *Continuity and Change in Russian and Soviet Thought*. Cambridge, Mass., 1955.

Terras, V. *Belinskij and Russian Literary Criticism: The Heritage of Organic Aesthetics*. Madison, Wisc., 1974.

Venturi, Franco. *Roots of Revolution. A History of the Populist and Socialist Movements in Nineteenth-Century Russia*. Trans. F. Haskell, London, 1960.

PART IV

Very little has been published in English on the thinkers who are the subject of this part. See Derek Offord, *Portraits of Early Russian Liberals: A Study of the Thought of T. N. Granovsky, V. P. Botkin, P. V. Annenkov, A. V. Druzhinin and K.D. Kavelin*, Cambridge, 1985. On Granovsky see also the useful monograph by Priscilla R. Roosevelt, "Granovskii at the Lectern: a Conservative Liberal's Vision of History," in *Forschungen zur osteuropäischen Geschichte*, Berlin, 1981, XXIX, pp. 61-192; and Leonard Schapiro, *Rationalism and Nationalism in Russian Nineteenth-Century Political Thought*, New Haven, 1967, pp.73-81.

PART V

Coquart, Armand. *Dmitri Pisarev (1840-1868) et l'idéologie du nihilisme russe*. Paris, 1946.

Dowler, Wayne. *Dostoevsky, Grigor'ev and Native Soil Conservatism*, Toronto, 1982.

Frank, Joseph. "Nihilism and *Notes from the Underground,*" *Sewanee Review*, LXIX (1961), pp. 1-33.

Jones, Malcolm V. and Garth M. Terry. *New Essays on Dostoyevsky*. Cambridge, 1983.

Lampert, Eugene. *Sons against Fathers: Studies in Russian Radicalism and Revolution*. Oxford, 1965.

Leatherbarrow, W. J. *Fedor Dostoevsky*. Boston, 1981.

Offord, Derek. "Dostoyevsky and Chernyshevsky," *The Slavonic and East European Review*, LVII, no.4, 1979, pp. 509-30.

Peace, Richard. *Dostoyevsky: An Examination of the Major Novels*. Cambridge, 1971.

Pereira, N. G. O. *The Thought and Teachings of N. G. Černyševskij*. The Hague, 1975.

Venturi, Franco. *Roots of Revolution: A History of the Populist and Socialist Movements in Nineteenth-Century Russia*. Trans. F. Haskell, London, 1960.

Wellek, René. *A History of Modern Criticism, 1750-1950*. Vol. IV, London, 1966, pp. 238-65 (on Chernyshevsky, Dobrolyubov and Pisarev) and pp. 266-78 (on Grigorev, Dostoevsky and Strakhov).

___ "Social and Aesthetic Values in Russian Nineteenth-Century Literary Criticism (Belinskii, Chernyshevskii, Dobroliubov, Pisarev)," in *Continuity and Change in Russian and Soviet Thought*. Ed. E. J. Simmons, Cambridge, Mass., 1955, pp. 381-97.

Woehrlin, W. F. *Chernyshevskii: The Man and the Journalist*. Cambridge, Mass., 1971.

Zekulin, G. "Forerunner of Socialist Realism: the Novel *What to Do?* by N. G. Chernyshevsky," *The Slavonic and East European Review*, XLI, no.97, 1963, pp. 467-83.

PART VI

Baron, Samuel H. *Plekhanov: The Father of Russian Marxism*. London, 1963.

Berlin, Isaiah. *Russian Thinkers*. London, 1978 (pp. 210-37 are on Populism).

Billington, James H. *Mikhailovsky and Russian Populism.* Oxford, 1958.

Carr, E. H. *Michael Bakunin.* London, 1937.

Hardy, Deborah. *Petr Tkachev: The Critic as Jacobin.* Seattle, 1977.

Lampert, Eugene. *Studies in Rebellion.* London, 1957 (chapter 3 is on Bakunin).

Pomper,Philip. *Peter Lavrov and the Russian Revolutionary Movement.* Chicago, 1972.

Venturi, Franco. *Roots of Revolution: A History of the Populist and Socialist Movements in Nineteenth-Century Russia.* Trans. F. Haskell, London, 1960 (the definitive work on the Populist phase of the Russian revolutionary movement).

Walicki, Andrzej. *The Controversy over Capitalism: Studies in the Social Philosophy of the Russian Populists.* Oxford, 1969.

Weeks, Albert L. *The First Bolshevik: A Political Biography of Peter Tkachev.* New York, 1968 (a more tendentious study than Hardy's).

Woodcock, George. *Anarchism.* Harmondsworth, 1970 (chapter 6 is on Bakunin).

Yarmolinsky, Avrahm. *Road to Revolution: A Century of Russian Radicalism.* London, 1957.